"JIMMY HIGGINS"

Recent Titles in
Contributions in Political Science
Series Editor: Bernard K. Johnpoll

Besieged Bedfellows: Israel and the Land of Apartheid
Benjamin M. Joseph

Bureaucratic Politics and Regulatory Reform: The EPA and Emissions Trading
Brian J. Cook

Fair Housing Comes of Age
George R. Metcalf

Dimensions of Hazardous Waste Politics and Policy
Charles E. Davis and James P. Lester, editors

West Germany's Foreign Policy: The Impact of the Social Democrats
and the Greens
Diane Rosolowsky

The State and Public Bureaucracies: A Comparative Perspective
Metin Heper, editor

Revolution and Rescue in Grenada: An Account of the U.S.-Caribbean Invasion
Reynold A. Burrowes

The Merit System and Municipal Civil Service: A Fostering of Social Inequality
Frances Gottfried

White House Ethics: The History of the Politics of Conflict of Interest Regulation
Robert N. Roberts

John F. Kennedy: The Promise Revisited
Paul Harper and Joann P. Krieg, editors

The American Founding: Essays on the Formation of the Constitution
J. Jackson Barlow, Leonard W. Levy, and Ken Masugi, editors

Japan's Civil Service System
Paul S. Kim

Franklin D. Roosevelt's Rhetorical Presidency
Halford R. Ryan

"JIMMY HIGGINS"

The Mental World of the American Rank-and-File Communist, 1930–1958

AILEEN S. KRADITOR

CONTRIBUTIONS IN POLITICAL SCIENCE, NUMBER 207

GREENWOOD PRESS
New York • Westport, Connecticut • London

Library of Congress Cataloging-in-Publication Data

Kraditor, Aileen S.
   "Jimmy Higgins" : the mental world of the American rank-and-file
communist, 1930–1958 / Aileen S. Kraditor.
      p.   cm. — (Contributions in political science, ISSN 0147–1066
; no. 207)
   Bibliography: p.
   Includes index.
   ISBN 0–313–26246–2 (lib. bdg. : alk. paper)
   1. Communism—United States—1917– 2. Communist Party of the
United States of America—History. I. Title. II. Series.
HX83.K7 1988
320.5′32′0973—dc19   87–32296

British Library Cataloguing in Publication Data is available.

Library of Congress Catalog Card Number: 87–32296
ISBN: 0–313–26246–2
ISSN: 0147–1066

First published in 1988

Greenwood Press, Inc.
88 Post Road West, Westport, Connecticut 06881

Printed in the United States of America

The paper used in this book complies with the
Permanent Paper Standard issued by the National
Information Standards Organization (Z39.48–1984).

10 9 8 7 6 5 4 3 2 1

Every reasonable effort has been made to trace the owners of copyright materials used in this
book, but in some instances this has proven impossible. The publishers will be glad to
receive information leading to more complete acknowledgments in subsequent printings of
this book, and in the meantime extend their apologies for any omissions.

There is only one way of seeing one's own spectacles clearly: that is, to take them off.

Stephen Toulmin, *Foresight and Understanding*, 1961

Contents

Preface   ix

Abbreviations Used in Notes   xi

1 Introduction   1

PART 1: STRUCTURE   23

2 Jimmy Higgins   25

3 Types   41

4 The Rationale of Hate   59

5 Authority I: Leadership and Self-Image   79

6 Authority II: Theory and Scholarship   105

7 Tasks, Standards, and Self-Criticism   123

PART 2: SUBSTANCE   143

8 The Nature of Reality I: Materialism   145

9 The Nature of Reality II: Man   165

10 "The System" and Its Rulers   179

11 The People   201

12 The Soviet Union as the American Future   221

13 Soviet America and the Science of Prophecy   237

PART 3: CONCLUSION   263

14   Genus and Differentia   265

      Recommended Reading   277

      Index   279

Preface

I COMPLETED THE MANUSCRIPT for this book at the end of 1983 and first copyrighted it in March, 1984. Since then I have learned how hard it is to publish a work that deviates from the prevailing mode of interpretation of the Communist Party and, worse still, is written from a conservative standpoint. In the past four years, many books and articles have appeared that have provided valuable data, but none of these works has given me reason to make substantive changes.

The years 1984–1987 brought a benefit that more than compensated for the delay in publication: the discovery of a number of people who tried, in some cases without my knowledge, to put the manuscript on the road to publication. Some of these do not share my point of view; some who do share it and others who do not are people I have never even met. All vindicated my belief that there is no correlation between adherence to a particular worldview, on the one hand, and fairness and integrity, on the other. They all have my gratitude. In addition, I should like to thank four who helped me improve the manuscript in specific ways, although not necessarily sharing my views: Louise L. Stevenson, Paul Gottfried, David Horowitz, and Harvey Klehr. Boston University gave me a small grant to pay for the photocopying of an early draft.

My mother closely followed this project as it took shape. Over the years, she asked me questions about various themes, and I first formulated a few of them in letters to her.

I DEDICATE THIS BOOK, in loving memory, to my mother, Henrietta L. Kraditor, and my brother-in-law, Stanley B. Haber.

Abbreviations Used in Notes

CH	*Champion of Youth* and *Champion Labor Monthly*
CL	*Clarity*
COM	*The Communist*
IP	International Publishers
MM	*Masses & Mainstream* and *Mainstream*
NF	*New Foundations*
NM	*New Masses*
PA	*Political Affairs*
PO	*Party Organizer*
SP	*Spotlight*
YW	*Young Worker*

1

Introduction

SHORTLY AFTER I JOINED the Party in April, 1947, I asked an older comrade how long it would be before the revolution came to our country. He thought a moment and then said, "Oh, maybe ten years." "So soon?" I exclaimed. "Well, maybe twenty years," he replied. I thought he was still a bit optimistic, but I accepted his prediction because I assumed I had much to learn that he already knew. Yet even in 1947, when the favorable, wartime image of the Soviet Union had only recently shattered, the CPUSA had begun to shrivel. During most of my eleven years in the Party, I never knew that it was in crisis, and neither did any of my friends. We were sure the Party had a glorious future ahead of it and that its reverses were temporary. It is not hard to see that the true-believing minority of the rank and file lived in a world apart from the real one.

This book is about that separate reality. The transient members did not live in it; whether or not all the leaders and cadre did, I am not sure. The devoted, long-term rank-and-file members unquestionably lived in it. And the continuity of the Party, through all the shifts in line and leadership, was the continuity of the special mentality of those core members. The shifts in line, tactics, and leadership did not affect their enduring attitudes and feelings—toward the Soviet Union, American society, the Party, the working class, the future, toward reality itself.[1]

In fact, the continuity of those attitudes and feelings reveals what the discontinuities meant to a true believer. If, for example, Marshal Tito could change in 1948 from an innovative adapter of Marxism-Leninism to the unique conditions of Yugoslavia, to a lackey of imperialism, the question of "the national road to socialism" could not have been basic to that member's belief system. If he could suddenly, in the mid–1930s, stop believing in the united front from below and as suddenly see that the correct tactic was the popular front against fascism, it is safe to infer that neither tactic was integral to his fundamental worldview. If, in the spring of 1945, his love for Earl

Browder could turn overnight into hatred, both the love and the hatred must have had other objects than Browder.

To understand the mind of the Communist true believer we should look for what Philip Selznick calls the "latent structure" of that member's "self-perpetuating, interlocking commitments."[2] That structure was invisible to the member; he was unaware of most of the assumptions that underlay his beliefs and did not realize that other people perceived reality differently from the way he did. "Ideology" is thus not the right name for the subject of this study. The true believer's conscious beliefs rested on a set of perceptions, attitudes, and feelings, which determined how he perceived reality, what he accepted as a "fact," and what he rejected on the ground that it could not be true in the universe he lived in. "Communists," writes one of the most penetrating analysts of this mentality, "consider themselves at home primarily in the future, which for them is essentially closed rather than open. . . . In Communist eyes the future appears more real than the present." The Communist felt

himself a stranger in the present. . . . In an otherwise chaotic and inhuman present, the Party is the movement toward the future, in visible shape. A Communist does not embrace the Party on account of its policies. The opposite is true: the Party's policies change, not infrequently from black to white and again to black with dizzying speed, and the Communist will adapt himself to the shifting policies as to something that is *not* of the essence of the Party.[3]

The essence was rejection "of the entire world of order in which men find themselves."[4]

THIS BOOK will focus on "Jimmy Higgins." (The original Jimmy Higgins was a fictional character invented early in this century by Ben Hanford, a prominent member of the Socialist Party.) Comrade Jimmy was the ideal rank-and-file Communist: the anonymous, devoted comrade who sold the Party's literature, attended every meeting, performed all the humble chores that kept the organization going—and remained a rank and filer, for the Jimmy Higgins traits did not qualify a member for promotion. He differed, on the one side, from those who left the Party within a few years after joining and were never really Communists by temperament and deep conviction, and, on the other, from the cadre (influential members, who often held no official posts) and official leaders. The Comrade Jimmy in the following chapters will represent white rank and filers of both sexes and of all ages, ethnic backgrounds, and occupations (including students). (I restrict the synecdoche to whites because I cannot speculate as to whether the generalizations I make in this book applied to that very small minority of Jimmy Higginses who were black.) Of course, the Party could not succeed in getting all its members of all these sorts to think and feel exactly alike. But the use of the synecdoche is justified because, as a member approximated the Jimmy Higgins ideal, he lost some of the distinctive traits that he brought with him into the Party. The true Jimmy Higginses were a good deal more alike than were the less committed, ultimately temporary members. In fact, this sameness transcends national boundaries: memoirs by European ex-Communists contain many passages that, as I read them, "rang true" to my own recollections, suggesting that the Communist–true believer phenomenon grows out of something deeper and more universal than any doctrine or culture.

Despite this sameness, the real-life counterparts of this book's "Jimmy Higgins" were, like all people, unique individuals possessing myriad traits in unique combinations. Therefore, the reader should not expect the "Comrade Jimmy" in the following pages to "come alive," since the personification is merely a verbal convenience, shorthand for a set of traits that thousands of people shared. It is, literally, an abstraction: certain features drawn out of the flesh-and-blood reality. What the real-life possessors of Jimmy Higgins traits did not share I have ignored. Since nobody ever was or could be merely the sum total of Jimmy Higgins traits, the composite presented here cannot be expected to seem a real person.

IN HIS ANALYSIS of the "total critique of society," Gerhart Niemeyer makes the following argument:

Marx's indictment condemns not this or that concrete choice or a pattern of evil actions but the entire historical condition of human existence. His judgment, strictly speaking, is not moral at all but rather ontological: all that which has gone under the name of reality appears to Marx as a nullity. . . . Once the reality of experience has been defined in this way, the problem of discerning moral qualities of human actions vanishes. By force of the overall definition, in the present society *all* laws are unjust, *all* consciousness is false, *all* relations must be corrupt, *all* institutions appear oppressive. Marx's "unmasking" consists in the reduction of every particular aspect of society to the overall formula of falsity. . . . The ideologists' . . . denial of reality to the present society, however, forms only a part in wider circles of ontological negations—be it the annihilation of God, or the creation, or the moral order, or human nature—so that the total critique of society appears as a mere aspect of a total dissent from existence. Camus has deftly summed up the entire complex of intellectual and activist negation in the concept of "metaphysical revolution."[5]

Jimmy Higgins had undergone that metaphysical revolution. From those ontological negations he had proceeded to a series of affirmations; the result was the imaginary universe reconstructed in the following chapters.

The difficulty of reconstructing the mind of someone who lived in a radically different universe from oneself is compounded by the problem of presenting one's findings plausibly to readers. Michael Novak (who uses the term "horizons" for what I call different universes) explains why: the inhabitants of the two universes

tend to experience, understand, and judge in remarkably opposite ways, even when
confronted with the same materials. . . . At every level of discourse, each person
involved seems to experience reality in so different a way as to make direct one-to-
one arguments, even on simple matters of fact, extremely wearying. Each party sees
and perceives, imagines and judges in a way so different from the other that the
search for common ground—whether of fact, principle, or ultimate ideal—is extremely arduous. Gordon Allport once reported in his studies of psychology that
religious convictions lie at the deepest level of personality, with convictions about
political economy running a close second.

To get at the reality of the other's horizon, Novak adds, one should attend
to "the symbols, stories, and liturgies through which the human subject
experiences, imagines, and judges the world."[6] But few people can believe
that some of their own compatriots can live in different perceptual universes;
and those readers who live in Jimmy Higgins's will not recognize ostensibly
empirical statements, found in the Party literature to be quoted in this book,
as symbols, stories, and liturgies.

Some readers of this book will themselves be inhabitants of Jimmy Higgins's special universe (Communists were not its only inhabitants). Others,
who are not, will likely be unable to imagine how Comrade Jimmy could
see reality so fundamentally differently from the way they do, and hence
accuse him of hypocrisy. Having lived in his universe for many years, I
know how hard it is to communicate across that experiential chasm, in either
direction, and for inhabitants of one to concede the sincerity of the inhabitants
of the other. As Niemeyer puts it, "I personally feel that the great confrontation with political irrationality in our time has not the character of a debate
or even discussion. The prerequisite for either would be a common universe
of reason which is precisely what the ideologists have demolished."[7]

That is why this book is not a history in the conventional sense, with
respect both to the relation of the author to other historians, and to the
relation of author to subjects. Hypotheses compete and are judged *within* "a
common universe of reason," in terms of shared basic principles that stand
outside and above all the competing interpretations. (For if the community
of scholars did not share those criteria, then in terms of what even more
basic principles could they call one hypothesis true and another false?) For
most historical problems, the nature of reality is not an issue, and historians
who profess different fundamental faiths can argue over, say, the causes of
the economic take-off in nineteenth-century America, using the same criteria
of proof. But interpretations of the mentality of someone who fitted Niemeyer's description will themselves differ as fundamentally as do the two
realities. The starting-point for this volume, which is part history, part
recollection, and part rumination, is best defined by Eric Voegelin:

The conflict of Truth and Delusion . . . is not a conflict between true and false propositions. In fact, the Delusion is quite as true as the Truth, if by truth we mean an

adequate and consistent articulation of an experience. The conflict occurs between the two types of experience.

Ideology is existence in rebellion against God and man. It is the violation of the First and Tenth Commandments, if we want to use the language of Israelite order; it is the *nosos*, the disease of the spirit, if we want to use the language of Aeschylus and Plato. . . . The search for truth concerning the order of being cannot be conducted without diagnosing the modes of existence in untruth.[8]

In history, anthropology, and nonquantitative sociology, scholars must and can empathize with the people they study, no matter how foreign. It is very difficult to do so, however, unless author and subjects share(d) certain trans-cultural and suprahistorical axioms (both ontological and axiological) concerning what Voegelin calls "the order of being." Given that sharing, an anthropologist can "think into" the minds of "his tribe," and a historian can rethink the thoughts and refeel the feelings of ancient Egyptians (and a white historian, of blacks, and a male historian, of women, and so on). But a historian who confronts Jimmy Higgins, his contemporary and compatriot, may, if he does not inhabit the latter's special universe, crash against a barrier without even knowing that he is doing so. Or, if the historian inhabits Comrade Jimmy's universe, he will not know it is not the real one. In either case, the picture he paints will be incomplete or partly untrue.

Does this mean, then, that only those scholars who live in Comrade Jimmy's special universe can understand his mind and present it to the rest of us? I believe not. C. S. Lewis (arguing in a different context) explains why:

You understand sleep when you are awake, not while you are sleeping. You can see mistakes in arithmetic when your mind is working properly; while you are making them you cannot see them. You can understand the nature of drunkenness when you are sober, not when you are drunk. Good people know about both good and evil; bad people do not know about either.[9]

If Jimmy Higgins's universe was spurious, if (as Niemeyer argues) it began in the denial of reality, then no one who lives in it can understand the relation of the Party, its program, and its theory to reality.

What then of the scholar who never lived inside Jimmy Higgins's special universe? In principle, someone who never was a true believer may be able to reconstruct how Jimmy Higgins perceived and felt about the world[10]— and Lewis's argument suggests that such an observer could certainly evaluate the subject accurately. But in practice, if one may judge from the secondary literature, it is highly unlikely. No one would claim that a scholar needs to have "been there" to produce such fine works as Harvey Klehr's *Communist Cadre* and Lowell Dyson's *Red Harvest*.[11] We need more such studies. But, as I am sure the authors would agree, these books do not present the Party members' world "from within"; that was not their purpose.

Scholars who realize that reconstructions of Jimmy Higgins's mind im-
plicate the investigators' own basic philosophies may nevertheless misinterpret the subjects' beliefs and actions. It is natural, almost inevitable, for a
historian to assume that Comrade Jimmy used words the same way as the
historian and that he intended the same thing by some action as the historian
would if he performed it himself. To know what *Jimmy Higgins* meant, we
have to get inside his mind and perceive reality as he did—to undergo vicariously the "metaphysical revolution" that Camus referred to, to simulate
that "ontological judgment" and "denial of reality" that Niemeyer spoke of.
Obviously, this act of imagination is inconsistent with "scholarly neutrality,"
as Lewis implied. Such neutrality is possible, indeed obligatory, *within* a
universe of shared axioms, but if the matter at issue crosses the boundary
of that universe, choice is unavoidable. At the same time, this act of imagination demands acceptance of something that many scholarly critics of the
Communist Party cannot accept: the genuineness of Jimmy Higgins's experience with his false reality. Note that Voegelin, in the last sentence quoted
above, said, "The search for truth concerning the order of being cannot be
conducted without diagnosing the modes of existence in untruth." He speaks
of "existence in untruth," not "belief in untruth." That is why the conflict
between Truth and Delusion is not a conflict between true and false propositions, as would be, for example, an argument between two historians over
whether Hayes or Tilden really won the election of 1876. Existence in untruth
will, of course, produce false propositions, but Voegelin is referring essentially to how a person *experiences reality*.

The statements that Comrade Jimmy and his Party's theoreticians made
about reality as they perceived it were true propositions in the sense of being
true reports of the untruth that they lived in. Many such statements and
moral judgments, in the primary sources for this book, were identical to
those that could be made by someone who experienced reality as it was.
Different contexts endowed the same assertions with different meanings. For
this reason, a history based on the statements and deeds of a group of people
who fitted Voegelin's and Niemeyer's descriptions may be factually true,
fully documentable, and yet tell the reader little about how the subjects
understood their words and deeds. Furthermore, if a historian knew and
presented those "subjective" meanings, his work might still omit what is most
significant of all—that they came out of an "existence in untruth." Or, to
put the point another way: a historian who is determinedly "objective" but
unaware of the two-universes phenomenon (regardless of which universe he
lives in) is likely to treat the CP as an organization aiming to remold the
world according to Marxist-Leninist doctrine. This would be true so far as
it goes, but incomplete and misleading. More fundamentally, the Party was
an organizational expression of a world *already existing* in the minds of its
true-believing members. The "objective" historian, not realizing this, would
misinterpret the Party's failures. For if the reality had been as the true

believers perceived it—I mean fundamentally, not with respect to particular data about which anyone might err—then the Party would have fitted into that reality rather successfully. Instead, they were a group of people who, in both favorable and unfavorable circumstances, always failed to convert the majority of workers (although their theory said this conversion was inevitable) and, finally, were obliged to use force and terror, when in power, against the working class in order to make reality conform to their conception.

NIEMEYER AND VOEGELIN were describing a broader category than just Marxists or Communist Parties. The CPUSA was a species within a larger genus. Within that genus, theories and programs differ. Some such people organize themselves into parties, others into loose movements. Not all who deny reality go on to affirm that the good society exists elsewhere. Underlying the quarrels between admirers of the Soviet Union, China, and other model countries, and those who say that the good society has yet to be constructed, there is general agreement on much more basic propositions. Although some of these propositions are worded positively and others negatively, they are all aspects of the Grand Negation.

These propositions include the following: the American social order is a System; it is evil; anti-American regimes may commit abuses, but pro-American regimes commit crimes; a free-market economy distributes wealth unjustly; the profit motive is wicked; some version of socialism is progressive and on the agenda of history; human nature should be improved through social engineering; the poor are more virtuous than the rich but more easily swayed by propaganda; and it is immoral for anyone to wish to rise in the world as an individual. Many inhabitants of the real world believe in one or more of these and other such propositions, but not in all of them, not within the framework of a comprehensive ideology, by deduction from an initial Grand Negation. When they are all combined, however, each proposition forms part of the context of the others; each adds one brick, carefully fitted to the others to leave no spaces (and no windows, either), to the whole edifice of the special universe.

We can discover what was specific to the Party and what generic—that is, what the Party shared with other inhabitants of the special universe—by noting one crucial fact about the crisis caused by the Twentieth Congress of the Soviet Communist Party in 1956, when Khrushchev criticized Stalin. Many comrades, convinced that the Party was no longer the appropriate instrument for realizing their ideals, abandoned it *in order to remain faithful to their worldview.* Some went leftward, some rightward; others remained in the same location on the spectrum as the Party but rejected its authoritarianism. By far the majority of ex-members, including most of those who went rightward, remained very much to the left of the general population. Some discarded the Soviet Union as the model for American socialism and adopted another country. Others decided that no extant regime deserved the label "socialist." The Party had told its members that every outsider (except "pro-gressives" and unawakened workers) was an enemy, but most ex-members now discovered that millions of outsiders shared their most deeply held beliefs and perceptions. The ex-Communists I have just described were not the short-term members who were never true believers in the Party's specific version of the generic faith, but leaders, cadre, and Jimmy Higgins–type rank and filers who had devoted many years to the Party. Life outside the Party had been unthinkable to them. It is all the more significant, then, that when their faith clashed with continued membership they found they could, after all, leave the Party. The faith, not the Party, formed the core of their being.

JIMMY HIGGINS has not received his due in the literature on the CP. That literature comprises three overlapping categories. The majority of works focus on institutional history. They trace changes in organization, leadership, and policies; they recount activities in unions or other non-Communist mi-lieux; they analyze relationships with the Soviet Party and the Comintern or Cominform. The second category consists of intellectual and social his-tories. Some focus on the Party's doctrines; others analyze the sources and composition of its membership and/or leadership; still others, generalizing from interviews with current and/or former members, discuss the psycho-logical types found in the Party. The third category consists of memoirs and biographies. The institutional histories deal almost wholly with leaders. The intellectual and social histories do so too, or do not differentiate between the Jimmy Higginses and the other rank and filers. Most of the memoirs and biographies are by and about former leaders and other prominent people and by former spies, none of whom was a Jimmy Higgins.[12]

All secondary studies differentiate between the leaders and the rank-and-file members, and some between the leaders and the lower-level cadre and between the latter and the rank and filers. Statistical findings about the enormous turnover of rank-and-file membership are misleading in this re-spect, for that category of members included a minority—the Jimmy Hig-ginses—who stayed in the Party as their comrades were coming and going. The number of Jimmy Higginses and their ratio in the membership are impossible to estimate; but anyone who ever belonged in that category can testify to their existence and their importance to the Party.[13] Chapter two will say more on this question; at this point it is appropriate merely to explain why Jimmy Higgins's mentality warrants study.

If Comrade Jimmy had thought and felt as his leaders did, a study of their mentality would suffice. But even though the Party was authoritarian and the members obeyed the leaders, the two groups did not necessarily think of the Party and its mission in the same way. There were many things that Jimmy Higgins did not know about his leaders. For example, they insisted that the reason their policies agreed with those of the Soviet Party was that both parties guided themselves by the science of Marxism-Leninism, which was universally applicable. Moreover, Jimmy Higgins never knew of the personal rivalries and differences of opinion among the inner circles; every decision was ostensibly unanimous, the obvious application of Marxism-Leninism to the particular issue.[14] As these facts imply, the leaders regarded the rank and file as a special part of the general public, the object of propaganda. For all these and other reasons, we should not regard the members' minds as mere mirrors reflecting the leaders'. The rank and filers had their own reasons for belonging to the Party, and their reasons were not necessarily the same as the leaders'.

OF ALL the secondary works on the CP, those by Jules Monnerot, Frank S. Meyer, Philip Selznick, and Nathan Leites most closely complement the present study. But they differ from mine in scope, sources, and/or approach. Monnerot's *Sociology and Psychology of Communism* deals with a worldwide phenomenon and is not based on American CP writings. Meyer's *The Moulding of Communists* deals with cadre, not Jimmy Higgins. It is based mostly on Meyer's own experience as a leading Communist in the United States and Britain, and he cites Party literature very sparingly and only to illustrate what he already knew. Selznick's *The Organizational Weapon* analyzes how the Party shaped the core members so as to make the Party an "army," rather than analyzing how those members understood their relationship to reality. Leites's *A Study of Bolshevism* generalizes from the writings of Marx, Engels, Lenin, Stalin, and some lesser Communist authorities in several countries. All these superb books are indispensable reading for anyone who wants to understand the American Communist mentality. Their generalizations are for the most part the same as or consistent with those I arrived at by a different route. On some topics the sources caused me to dissent from explanations in those four works and to add others; on most topics, however, my findings confirmed theirs. None of them used my method: immersion in thousands of pages of CPUSA writings, interpreted with the help of my recollections as a Jimmy Higgins–type member long ago.

The reader may have noticed that none of the four books I have just mentioned is a history; each deals with aspects of the Party or Communism that did not change much during the period it covers. The same is true of the following chapters. As I indicated earlier, the successive theories, leaders, tactics, policies, and organizational forms constituted the superficies, and that which did not change constituted the inner reality of the American CP and Jimmy Higgins's mentality. But to understand that which did not change one must also understand the changeable aspects of Party life. The best histories of the Party are therefore essential background too. They provide background only, however: certain topics—for example, the rivalry between Browder and Foster for power—that are central to the Party's institutional history are irrelevant here. So far as its inner—emotional and perceptual—

life is concerned, the Party had no history. On the level of attitudes toward reality, its span of existence can be studied as a unit. The present study is, then, not a history. It would be more accurate to call it an investigation that uses historical materials and techniques, but it is also built on personal recollections and includes speculations and commentary that would not belong in a historical monograph.

Among the primary sources for this study are periodicals published by the three youth organizations (other than organizations for children) that were closely connected with the Party during the 1930–1958 period. The Young Communist League (YCL) was in effect the youth contingent of the Party and was affiliated with the youth international headquartered in Moscow. Its successors, the American Youth for Democracy (AYD) and the Labor Youth League (LYL), professed to be independent, but the Party dominated them completely.[15] None of these organizations was self-generated, as were the American and European New Lefts, the American Socialist youth organizations, and the European youth and student movements early in this century. The YCL, AYD, and LYL did not result from any spontaneous sense of grievance or common cause among groups of young Americans; they were conceived, organized, directed, and dissolved by the CP. All three contained the same three types of members as the Party: the cadre and official leaders, the true believers in the ranks, and the short-term members who were never true believers. (In the youth organizations the third type did not even call themselves Communists.) The leaders of the YCL, AYD, and LYL were all Party members and often high in the Party hierarchy. Many of them graduated to become top-level Party officials.

The youth organizations' periodicals printed Party propaganda, sometimes adapted to young people's interests. The principal publications for the purposes of this book were: the YCL's *Young Worker*, then *Champion of Youth* (later called *Champion* and then *Champion Labor Monthly*), and then *Clarity*; the AYD's *Spotlight*; and the "independent" journal for students, *New Foundations*, which in 1949, its third year of publication, hailed the founding of the LYL and became its unofficial organ. (There were other publications besides these. The YCL issued a *Review*, which one leader called "the method by which our League speaks to the masses,"[16] implying that *Clarity*, published at the same time, spoke to the more "advanced" young people.)

A second type of source material is a random sample of the books and pamphlets published by International Publishers and other Party-connected firms. Everything they printed (including some works by foreign Communists) bore the endorsement of Party leaders, and Jimmy Higgins regarded it as instructional material. Every such work not only expounded correct theory but also exemplified how the theory should be applied to all works in its field.

These works were meant for outsiders as well as for Party members, and I have relied mainly on those that were meant obviously for Jimmy Higgins's

guidance. As several scholars have pointed out, the Party printed both ex-
oteric and esoteric literature. Comrade Jimmy, of course, read the former,
mainly the *Daily* and *Sunday Worker*, but (after the mid–1930s) he knew that
much of its material was meant for the unenlightened and that it might
sometimes diverge from orthodoxy. (Illustrating the status of the *Worker* is
a conversation that Louis Budenz recalled he had had with V. J. Jerome, a
Party authority. At issue was whether an article in the paper should include
a statement that contravened the Party line on religion. Jerome said, " 'We
can use it in our agitation, or popular papers. But to put it in our propaganda,
or educational work for our comrades, would be to create illusions.' "[17]) For
this reason, the *Worker* is not an appropriate source for this study. Moreover,
it focused on short-range topics, whereas our focus will be on persisting
attitudes and feelings. When Comrade Jimmy sought clues as to how to think
about important subjects, he looked elsewhere.

He looked chiefly to the official monthly theoretical magazine, *The Communist*, renamed *Political Affairs* in January, 1945. It printed articles on every
subject—on biology, on the meaning of the latest elections, on space and
time as forms of the existence of matter, on American imperialism as the
leader of the forces of reaction, on socialism building in Romania, on the
falling rate of profit in the United States—and it published all key documents
issued by CP's throughout the world. On very rare occasions the editors
used footnotes to express uncertainty as to the correctness of views expressed
in articles; this means that articles lacking such disclaimers were authoritative.

If Comrade Jimmy was a minor functionary in his Party club or just a
very active member, he may also have read *Party Organizer*, which folded in
mid–1938.[18] During 1939, he may have read the short-lived monthly *National
Issues*. Both periodicals were official Party organs.

If interested in culture, he read the Party-controlled *New Masses* and, starting in January, 1947, *Mainstream*, which in 1948 merged with *New Masses* to
become *Masses & Mainstream*. Many non-Communists wrote for these magazines, which wanted non-Party as well as Party readers. But Comrade
Jimmy did not trust their articles, as he did those by authors who he knew
were Party members. The contributions by the non-Communists had value
to him merely as proofs of the Party's influence and for the use to which the
authors' prestige could be put. The same is true of the famous liberals who
wrote for the youth organizations' periodicals during the Party's "broader"
periods. Only the orthodox writings in those cultural journals are included
in the sources for this study.

The leaders often complained that only a minority of all members read
the Party's publications. But Jimmy Higgins was in a minority among the
rank and file, and he read much more than the less committed comrades did.
My own circle of friends, during the late 1940s and the 1950s, read at least
part of each issue of *Political Affairs* and all the new pamphlets that the Party
touted as important (such as Stalin's *On Linguistics*) and many of the full-

length books. Those who attended Party schools had required readings to study and discuss.

Certainly Comrade Jimmy did not read all the documents, covering twenty-nine years, that will be cited and quoted in the following chapters. What those documents do is to present pieces of a total picture of reality; they illustrate the ideas and attitudes that circulated within the world of the CP orally and in print; they reveal the meaning, to the members, of actions they performed that might be interpreted differently by outsiders (including historians) who lack insight into the members' minds. I shall quote copiously from these writings that Jimmy Higgins was immersed in. This will be necessary for two reasons. First, one of the chief objects of this book is to convey the cumulative impact that the literature had on his mind, and this cannot be conveyed in any other way. Second, few of the documents are quoted in the secondary literature, and none in an arrangement suitable to a systematic inquiry into the structure of reality as Comrade Jimmy conceived it. I shall use the documents as an anthropologist in the field uses the statements of his informants—to construct a comprehensive worldview. To do this, the anthropologist must learn how to empathize with his informants. But, at the same time, he must hear what they are saying "from the outside," for only thus can he hear the *un*intended meanings. My own recollections have enabled me to "turn on" that psyche and read the literature as the true believer did.[19]

Comrade Jimmy knew that those writings expressed his thoughts and feelings more clearly than he himself could. This was one reason for his faith in the Party and its authorized theoreticians. This literature answered his questions before he thought of asking them. It refuted counterarguments before he encountered them and discouraged him from reading the enemy's literature. It linked every datum with the Party's theory. It guided his thinking concerning current events, culture, scholarship, and personal problems. It proved over and over again the truth of the Party's theory and the wisdom of the Party and its leaders. He never knew that the reason these arguments seemed compelling and even self-evidently true was that they were circular. Again and again the "proof" of a certain thesis was its logical entailment by the theory's postulates, not its consistency with empirical evidence. Data were admitted, rejected, ignored, and reinterpreted to support the theory, which itself was never, ever, tested. Comrade Jimmy, however, thought the basic theory consisted of inductions from massive scholarship by Marx, Engels, Lenin, and Stalin and that "life itself" had confirmed Marxism-Leninism and Party policies. (Party members invoked "life itself" so often that Jessica Mitford entitled her spoof of Party jargon *Lifeitselfmanship*.[20]) In short, the very neatness and cogency of the arguments, achieved by the *rejection* of life itself, convinced Comrade Jimmy of their correctness.

Since my purpose is to explore Jimmy Higgins's mental universe, the huge literature on Marxism, especially that published in the past generation, is irrelevant here. For one thing, Party authorities sometimes made statements that contradicted Marxist theory, and the Party authorities were the ones who influenced Comrade Jimmy. (For example, William Z. Foster wrote on more than one occasion that the capitalists' profits were "stolen" from the workers. Marx had explicitly refuted this Proudhonist doctrine. But Foster's purpose was to arouse hatred of the capitalist "system," not to expound the Marxist economic theory.) For another thing, Jimmy Higgins would not have understood or cared about the abstruse philosophy of the Frankfurt School or other neo- or semi-Marxists. To reconstruct Jimmy Higgins's image of the world we should attend to the things *he* read, felt, believed and did.[21] Whatever the Party's line was on a particular issue at a particular time, whether dictated by Moscow or devised on "the ninth floor" (site of the American CP's national headquarters), the Party called it "Marxist-Leninist." Before and after drastic reversals of doctrine, the Party labeled its policies *the* Marxist-Leninist policies. It had to do so, because it proclaimed that everything it said and did, down to the organizing of a street-corner rally in The Bronx, was strictly entailed by the theory. And the more protean the theory was, with respect to any action the Party undertook, the more strenuously the Party insisted that the action was the only one that the theory justified.

For another reason as well, the basic theory is only tangential to the subject of this book. The Party preached "the unity of theory and practice." But practice came first in Jimmy Higgins's "development." Therefore, to analyze his mentality we should first observe the emotional predisposition that made the basic doctrines seem, to him, obviously true, as he learned them over the course of years, all the while carrying out practical tasks assigned by his leaders. His "development" was thus similar to that of the child who learns many facts in arithmetic, history, and science before he fully grasps what they mean and how they fit together. A time comes when he suddenly sees their inner logic, which he can then apply to new problems. So it was with Comrade Jimmy, who attended Party classes in basic theory, strategy and tactics, and the history of the Soviet and American CP's. He accepted tenets on faith, because authority told him they were true, and because they rationalized his feelings and attitudes. By the time he had that "aha! experience" similar to the student's, his mind had been prepared for it. The pretheoretical preparation is what made his theoretical "development" possible. It explains why doctrines that scholars and "life itself" have demolished struck him as self-evidently true.

Space limitation obliges me to omit a number of topics germane to my purpose. I made my choice by imagining the components of Jimmy Higgins's "universe" as a mosaic: I included all those "tiles" that are essential to make the picture broadly discernible and omitted those that the reader can then fill in by noting the shapes of the surrounding "tiles." The omitted topics— some are alluded to briefly, in passing—include Jimmy Higgins's ideas about the relation of theory to practice; the hideousness of American society; the

Negro and woman questions; the relation of "base" to "superstructure";
dialectics; ethics; history; democracy; art and culture; and political economy.
(Two of these are analyzed, in terms helpful to this book's purposes, by
other authors.[22]) The topics included here not only show the "shape" of those
omitted but also deal with those matters that impressed Jimmy Higgins most
deeply.

The first few of the following chapters follow more or less the same logic
as the real-life Comrade Jimmy's development, rather than the logic of Marxist-Leninist theory. Just as, over the years, he acquired discrete bits of the
theory, the reader will encounter portions of that theory before he comes to
the chapters that discuss theoretical matters more directly. The reader will,
I hope, find that by the time he has come to the latter he has found out why
Jimmy Higgins found the theory so obviously true. That is, the topical
emphases and the order in which topics are discussed were determined not
by the history or logical structure of Marxism-Leninism, or even by the
needs of the Party, but by the structure of Comrade Jimmy's mind.

After three chapters that discuss the nature of Jimmy Higgins's personality,
world, and feelings, chapters five through seven will examine his relation to
Party authority and to the Party's theory in general, and his image of the
Party and his self-image and life as a Party member. These chapters will
analyze the feelings and attitudes that had made him receptive to the arguments of the person who recruited him to the Party and, later, to the Party's
indoctrination. At this point the focus shifts from Jimmy Higgins's mind to
the Party's thinking, with emphasis on those topics that were most important
to him. This "inside" analysis is accompanied by an "outside" critique of the
distortions and manipulations of facts, by means of which the Party authorities reinforced Comrade Jimmy's allegiance. Chapters eight and nine
will discuss his notions of the nature of reality, nonhuman and human. These
chapters are in the middle of the book because their topics were central to
Jimmy Higgins's mental universe: the earlier chapters' topics prepared him
to accept the Party's theories on these matters, and the beliefs explored in
the later chapters rested on these foundations. Before long, his emotional
rejection of reality acquired an elaborate rationale, embodied in the Party's
theory of "the System"—the subject of chapter ten. He was now differen-
tiating himself sharply from "the People," and chapter eleven analyzes his
conflicting feelings about them, and the contradictory theories that reflected
his feelings. All the while, his lodestar was the Soviet Union; chapters twelve
and thirteen analyze his image of the Soviet Union and his theoretical rationale for believing he could prophesy the American future. The book ends
with some general reflections.

ALTHOUGH this book is not a history of the Party, the following key events
and trends in the Party's history between 1930 and 1958 will be referred to
or will provide contexts for the discussion.

During the 1920s, the Party was torn by factionalism. But when Stalin consolidated his power in the Soviet Union, the American CP expelled everyone who would not accept a unitary, authoritarian Party modeled closely on Stalin's. By 1930 the Party had become "bolshevized" and taken the form it retained for the rest of its effective existence, which ended with the shock following the Twentieth Congress of the Soviet Party in 1956. That shock lasted about two years, during which the Party experienced turmoil and an unprecedented freedom to question certain—though not all—of its theoretical and organizational principles. For these reasons I have chosen 1930 and 1958 as the cut-off dates of this study.

Until the mid–1930s the CP's all over the world pursued an extreme revolutionary policy predicated on the imminent overthrow of capitalism. The Party directed its main animus at socialists and others on the left who, it said, were impeding the workers' radicalization. Its policy toward unions and other popular organizations was therefore the "united front," by which it meant an appeal to the members of those organizations over the heads of their (mis)leaders. Then, in 1935, the Seventh Congress of the Communist International instructed all constituent parties to abandon this policy. The reversal actually began before the Seventh Congress, and the turnabout took several years to complete. The Party's policy was now the "popular front," that is, friendly relationships with the leaders of socialist and reformist movements, religious organizations, and unions, to counter the unexpectedly strong Nazi threat. The Party repudiated its "dual union" policy (of forming radical unions to compete with the "bourgeois" unions) and now sent its worker members into the existing unions. In 1936 it campaigned only half-heartedly against Roosevelt, whom it had earlier called a fascist. It claimed to cherish the American democratic heritage. But with the signing of the Nazi-Soviet Pact in 1939, the Party shifted leftward again. After the war began, it condemned both the Allies and the Axis powers. The former were imperialist, their democracy was spurious, and the workers of the world had no interest in the victory of either side. When Germany invaded the Soviet Union on June 22, 1941, however, the Party veered rightward; the war became a people's war and the Party's new friendliness toward the capitalist oppressors even included support of a no-strike policy for the unions.

During all these years, Earl Browder served as the Party's leader. Following the Allied leaders' conference in Teheran, he led the Party onto an even more accommodationist path: it dissolved itself in 1944 and became the Communist Political Association. Browder even foresaw cooperation between capitalists and workers for an indefinite period after the war. But in May, 1945, for reasons that had nothing to do with conditions in the United States, Moscow sent instructions to repudiate the Browder line. The instructions took the form of a letter written by Jacques Duclos, a French Party leader, denouncing Browderite revisionism. The Party reconstituted itself and shifted leftward. Browder was deposed and later expelled, and William Z. Foster finally realized his decades-long ambition to displace his rival.

The Party's fatal crisis began in 1956, with Khrushchev's "secret speech" about Stalin to the Twentieth Congress, and the rebellion in Hungary. Khrushchev admitted many of the crimes that Party members had always denounced the "bourgeois" press for inventing. The Party had been in decline since the end of the war, but Khrushchev's "revelations," coming from the source of authoritative truth, administered the *coup de grâce*.[23] The majority of members left. After the orgy of self-criticism had spent itself, however, the truest of the true believers reverted to the very same habits of thought and behavior for which they had been criticizing themselves for two years. To those who remained in the Party, de-Stalinization was just another policy shift.

Each of the earlier shifts in policy had also cost the Party many members, but in much smaller proportion to the whole membership. The vast majority of all who ever joined left within a few years; they were never true believers. The true believers, or those who were to become true believers after immersion in Party life for a few years, became deeply committed Communists for reasons far transcending any particular policy, and they therefore could take line shifts in stride. Some comrades were uneasy when the Party shifted rightward, and others when it shifted leftward. Jimmy Higgins, however, accepted the policy changes as merely tactical; he did not see them as requiring revision of his fundamental beliefs or perceptions of reality. This is why I shall play down the shifts and why I chose documents from all the periods in the 1930–1958 generation.

The temporary members, for whom particular policies and tactics and tenets were of paramount importance, joined and quit as policies, tactics, and/or tenets attracted and repelled them. Others, including true believers, sometimes quit for personal reasons. Young members matured. For others, politics moved to the periphery of their concerns as family or other interests became central. Still others experienced personality changes that were sometimes catalyzed by current events and Party-line changes. As one historian observes, "the safest generalization that can be made about American Communists is that most of them became ex-Communists." If, however, those transient members are subtracted from the whole number, many generalizations can be made about the remaining rank-and-file comrades, for whom particular theories, policies, and tactics were not the main attraction. So many of the latter left after mid–1956 that their departure transformed the Party into an insignificant sect. When the journalist Murray Kempton visited the *Daily Worker*'s office in early 1961, he found a national leader of the Party doing the work of a clerk. "The party," wrote Kempton, "has no employees left and not many more members; it is nothing but leaders. How tired they seem; how out of history." Although the Party still technically exists and has even grown somewhat since Kempton wrote those lines, it is historically proper to write of it in the past tense, as I shall in this book.[24]

* * *

The vigilance and unity of our members . . . is a unity based upon understanding and science, the science of history, founded by Karl Marx and Frederick Engels and developed, in the present era of imperialism and the rise of socialism as a world power, by Vladimir Lenin and Joseph Stalin. . . . With the deepest pride we accept the name of our most beloved teacher and guide. We are indeed Stalinists, and we hope to become ever more worthy of such a glorious name. . . . Today the name of Stalin sums up the teachings of Marx, Engels, and Lenin, represents the highest level of Marxism achieved in the unshakable foundation of a socialist society on one-sixth of the earth, symbolizes the unshakable fortress of peace and socialism in the Soviet Union, the hope and inspiration and protection of the workers and all oppressed people of the world. Truly it is a proud name, Stalinist, and we must bear it with all modesty, for it carries with it a tremendous responsibility.[25]

ANY AMERICAN CP LEADER could have written this statement—which, as it happens, was written by Earl Browder in 1938—at any time between 1930 and 1956. Those few sentences touch on most of the topics to be discussed in this book. They include the American Communist's contrasting images of the Soviet Union and the United States; the self-image of the Party member; the nature of the Party; the notion that Marxism-Leninism was a science; the Party's attitude toward Stalin and Party authority; the feelings of individual responsibility and humility and, at the same time, arrogance that the Party inculcated in its members; and much more.

NOTES

1. One thing did change: the Party's sensitivity to racism. See, e.g., William A. Nolan, *Communism versus the Negro* (Chicago: Henry Regnery Co., 1951), p. 56: "A former Negro communist told the author that Browder once reprimanded him publicly 'in language which few Southern whites would have dared to use.' " By the mid–1940s this had become unthinkable. Yet even this change did not touch the basic components of the true believer's feelings about reality.

2. Philip Selznick, *The Organizational Weapon: A Study of Bolshevik Strategy and Tactics* (New York: Free Press, 1961), p. xii.

3. Gerhart Niemeyer, *Deceitful Peace: A New Look at the Soviet Threat* (New Rochelle, NY: Arlington House, 1971), pp. 42–43. See also ibid., p. 205.

4. Gerhart Niemeyer, *Between Nothingness and Paradise* (Baton Rouge: Louisiana State University Press, 1971) p. 3; see also pp. 78–79. In addition, see Eric Voegelin, "On Debate and Existence," *Intercollegiate Review* 3 (March–April, 1967): 143–52. Of course that is not the reason I contend that the ideology under discussion is false. A belief must be tested in its own terms and by criteria independent of the motives of both the believer and the critic. In the course of this book I shall, from time to time,

have occasion to criticize various of the subjects' beliefs and also to restate my thesis as to the motives for their commitment to the Party's ideology, but these two sorts of statements should be understood as independent of each other. I believe that Gordon Leff, in *The Tyranny of Concepts*, rev. ed. (University: University of Alabama Press, 1969), p. 1, is unfair to Robert C. Tucker who, he says, commits "the genetic fallacy of arguing that Marx's own outlook was a projection of the 'urge to the Godlike.' " (Leff refers to Tucker's *Philosophy and Myth in Karl Marx*.) But Tucker's critique of Marx and his hypothesis concerning the origin of Marx's outlook are independent of each other. I happen to agree with Tucker on both points, but I also believe, as I assume Tucker does, that acceptance of either set of arguments does not entail acceptance of the other. As to the present study, immersion in the sources furnishes constant reminders of the genetic fallacy, for those Party writers repeatedly resort to it when they criticize other people's beliefs.

5. Niemeyer, *Between Nothingness and Paradise*, pp. 96–97, vii–viii.

6. Michael Novak, "The Danger of Egalityranny," *American Spectator* 15 (August, 1982): 9. I have reservations, however, about Novak's definition of the two groups as "the party of liberty" and "the party of equality." Neither my experience in the Party nor the Party documents written throughout our period supports the hypothesis that equality was such a basic value as to give the Party the label as part of the "party of equality." If it be contended that equality was the essence of those values that *were* emphasized, I reply that we should then find it mentioned often. But it was not, even when writers were depicting the far future when all the other goods had been realized. I suspect that what was true of the CP is also true of other members of "the party of equality"; that is, that their concept of equality is just a convenient slogan overlying more fundamental aims and values.

7. Niemeyer, *Between Nothingness and Paradise*, p. ix. Niemeyer and Novak—and Eric Voegelin, whom I shall quote later—and other analysts of "the total critique of society" clearly discovered this two-realities phenomenon independently—as did I. I read those works after I had formulated my own explanation of the Party mentality. It seems that many different students of this subject, starting from different places, traveling different routes, and using different materials, have all arrived at the same place.

8. Eric Voegelin, *Order and History*: Vol. 2, *The World of the Polis* (Baton Rouge: Louisiana State University Press, 1957), p. 216; and Vol. 1, *Israel and Revelation* (Baton Rouge: Louisiana State University Press, 1956), p. xiv.

9. C. S. Lewis, *Mere Christianity* (New York: Macmillan, 1960), p. 87.

10. Selznick, *Organizational Weapon*, pp. 14–16, explains how a conscientious scholar might do this.

11. Harvey E. Klehr, *Communist Cadre: The Social Background of the American Communist Party Elite* (Stanford, Calif.: Hoover Institution Press, 1978); Lowell K. Dyson, *Red Harvest: The Communist Party and American Farmers* (Lincoln: University of Nebraska Press, 1982). The same comment applies to studies of Marxism and Marxism-Leninism as bodies of ideas or even as guides to action: these do not tell us how the doctrines "worked" in the minds and feelings of true believers. The Klehr and Dyson works, and a few others, stand out from the general run of studies of the Party published in the 1970s and 1980s, most of which tend toward apologetics because their authors inhabit the special universe within which the CP was one solar system. For example, see exchange between James R. Prickett and Walter Galenson, in

Industrial Relations 13 (October, 1974): 219–43; Prickett is among those younger historians who write apologetics.

12. The following are a sample of the best books in each category. Institutional histories: Irving Howe and Lewis Coser, *The American Communist Party: A Critical History* (1957; New York: Frederick Praeger, 1962) (this also includes intellectual history); Theodore Draper, *The Roots of American Communism* (1957; New York: Viking Press, 1963); Draper, *American Communism and Soviet Russia: The Formative Period* (1960; New York: Viking Compass, 1963); David Shannon, *The Decline of American Communism* (1959; Chatham, NJ: Chatham Bookseller, 1971); Dyson, *Red Harvest*; Bert Cochran, *Labor and Communism: The Conflict That Shaped American Unions* (Princeton, N.J.: Princeton University Press, 1977). Social and intellectual histories: Nathan Glazer, *The Social Basis of American Communism* (New York: Harcourt, Brace & World, 1961); Klehr, *Communist Cadre*; Morris L. Ernst and David Loth, *Report on the American Communist* (New York: Henry Holt and Co., 1952); Daniel Aaron, *Writers on the Left* (1961; New York: Avon Books, 1965). Memoirs: Joseph R. Starobin, *American Communism in Crisis, 1943–1957* (1961; Berkeley: University of California Press, 1975) (this book could fit into the other two categories as well); Douglas Hyde, *I Believed* (New York: G. P. Putnam's Sons, 1950) (although Hyde is English, this work is full of insights relevant to American Communists); Howard Fast, *The Naked God* (New York: Frederick A. Praeger, 1957); Al Richmond, *A Long View from the Left* (1952; New York: Delta, 1975); John Gates, *The Story of an American Communist* (New York: Thomas Nelson & Sons, 1958); Elizabeth Bentley, *Out of Bondage* (New York: Devin-Adair, 1951); Peggy Dennis, *The Autobiography of an American Communist* (Westport, Conn.: Lawrence Hill & Co., Creative Arts Book Co., 1977); Harry Haywood, *Black Bolshevik: Autobiography of an Afro-American Communist* (Chicago: Liberator Press, 1978). All three of these lists could be expanded greatly; the literature is enormous.

The best institutional study—Harvey Klehr, *The Heyday of American Communism: The Depression Decade* (New York: Basic Books, 1984)—was published after I had completed the manuscript for this book. The reader who wants additional information and reliable interpretations for the pre–World War II period should consult Klehr's definitive study.

13. Statistics may be found in Klehr, *Communist Cadre*, "Introduction," which summarizes the most reliable accounts. An older source is an article by Arthur M. Schlesinger, Jr., in *Life*, July 29, 1946, reprinted in Edward E. Palmer, ed., *The Communist Problem in America* (New York: Thomas Y. Crowell, 1951), pp. 152ff. The Party periodical *Party Organizer* was full of statistics on recruiting, turnover of membership, and distribution of members among cities and states. Since future Jimmy Higginses were among the new recruits, there is no way of estimating what proportion were Jimmy Higginses from any numbers of new and old members—except that rank and filers who had been in the Party more than, say, four years were probably in that category, if they belonged to clubs that dropped inactive members. In short, the Jimmy Higgins category is defined by attitude, not solely by length of membership.

14. The Dennis and Haywood autobiographies (see n. 12), for example, must come as a revelation to the rank and filers (present or ex-) who assume that Party life was pretty much the same at both levels.

15. A fourth organization, the Young Progressives of America (1948), was student-oriented and existed mainly to support Henry Wallace's campaign for president.

Chronologically it filled the gap between the dissolution of the AYD in 1948 and the founding of the LYL in 1949.

16. Henry Winston, "Our Tasks Today," *CL* 2 (Summer, 1941): 38.

17. Louis Budenz, *This Is My Story* (New York: McGraw-Hill, 1947), p. 185.

18. On the nature of *PO*, see Philip Taft's introduction to the microfiche reprint; also "The Party Organizer," *PO* 1 (December, 1927): 2; and "Who Should Read the *Party Organizer* and Why," *PO* 4 (February, 1931): 2.

19. The source citations in the notes in the following chapters could be amplified manyfold. I cite only those documents that are quoted or paraphrased or referred to in the text and, occasionally, some of the more important others on the same points. In the case of topics thus documented by many items there were, to my knowledge, no documents contradicting those I chose as illustrations. Wherever an assertion was controverted within the Party, I included all sides. Another reason for the large number of quotations is to convey the flavor of the literature that Comrade Jimmy read every day; it was repetitious and contained in-group locutions that he absorbed and soon began to use himself. I use those locutions in my discussion for the same reason, and also to minimize the use of quotation marks. E.g., "theoretician" instead of outsiders' term "theorist," and "correct" to mean "true," "more suitable," "approved." In other ways, too, I shall sometimes formulate an idea as the Party did. The reader will, I trust, understand that I do so solely to create the "feel" of the Party member's mind at work. Several of the names signed to cited books and articles were pseudonyms, some of them of people who elsewhere were writing under their real names.

20. Originally a pamphlet published in 1956, it was reprinted as an appendix to Mitford's autobiography, *A Fine Old Conflict* (New York: Alfred A. Knopf, 1977).

21. For the same reason, the many excellent critical studies of Marxist theory have only tangential relevance here, although they are essential for other purposes. Those works include: H. B. Acton, *The Illusion of the Epoch: Marxism-Leninism as a Philosophical Creed* (1955; Boston: Routledge & Kegan Paul, 1972); Leff, *Tyranny of Concepts*; Robert Tucker, *Philosophy and Myth in Karl Marx* (Cambridge, Eng.: Cambridge University Press, 1961); M. M. Bober, *Karl Marx's Interpretation of History*, 2nd ed., rev. (Cambridge, Mass.: Harvard University Press, 1950); Adam B. Ulam, *The Unfinished Revolution: An Essay on the Sources of Influence of Marxism and Communism* (New York: Vintage, 1960); R. N. Carew Hunt, *Marxism Past and Present* (New York: Macmillan, 1955); and J. L. Talmon, *Political Messianism: The Romantic Phase* (London: Secker & Warburg, 1960). Although these books often do show how the true believer perceived reality and how he construed the Party's theory, they do not draw these generalizations from the literature that the true believer read. That their deductions from the canonical writings and other data overlap my *in*ductions from Party writings (read as the true believer read them) is all the more significant, especially in view of the fact that I formulated the latter before I read many of the former.

22. On art and culture, see Aaron, *Writers on the Left*. On the Negro question, see two books by Wilson Record: *Race and Radicalism: The NAACP and the Communist Party in Conflict* (Ithaca, N.Y.: Cornell University Press, 1964), and *The Negro and the Communist Party* (1951; New York: Atheneum, 1971). A third topic, the unity of theory and practice, deserves a chapter, for it played an important role in Jimmy Higgins's thinking. Owing to space limitations, I shall merely offer a comment that applies both to the Party and to its theory everywhere else. It is ironic but not

remarkable that Marxism, a theory that makes the unity of theory and practice basic, survives on the sole condition that theory and practice (other than the practice of scholarship) not be allowed to influence each other. Wherever Marxists have attained the power to act on their beliefs, the theory has either been redefined beyond recognition or become a set of incantations that nobody believes in; where the theory has flourished, the custodians have invariably been without power to reshape reality in accordance with it. One might conclude, then, that this fact both refutes Marxism and confirms the mutual dependence of theory and practice; that is, that one of the theory's tenets refutes that part of the theory which depends on practice for its verification.

23. Howe and Coser, *American Communist Party*, p. 491.

24. Murray Kempton, *America Comes of Middle Age* (Boston: Little, Brown, 1963), pp. 24–25; Klehr, *Communist Cadre*, pp. 83, 14. The shriveling and aging of the membership were evidently accompanied by a decline in the intellectual acumen of its top leaders. The quality had never been high, but during the Party's most successful years its uppermost echelons would not likely have boasted of a general secretary who could write as Gus Hall did in 1970:

As the molecules in steel becomes agitated it results in a red hot metal. Through this process the steel becomes tempered and purified. As the metal heats up bubbles appear on the surface, and in short order many of them disappear. Social and political movements in a sense develop in similar ways. When the social molecules become agitated it results in mass upheavals, the waves of radicalization. Class contradictions and relations sharpen up. This propels the revolutionary process. It results in new levels of mass class and socialist consciousness. There is a speedy growth of movements and organizations. They also become tempered and purified in the struggle. Such is the path of revolutionary development. . . . When concepts based on unreality are bounced back by reality it results in frustration. . . . Thus when the concepts based on unreality meet the reality of class struggle they bounce back. . . . The relationships between the objective processes and the tactics of struggle are not simple. It is an intricate process. . . . Working-class consciousness leads to concepts of class unity. It leads to rejecting tactics that lead to disunity. Petty-bourgeois radicalism does not see the concept of class or mass struggles. From this it follows that it does not see the need for class unity. It reflects the individualism of its class nature.

(Gus Hall, "Crisis of Petty-Bourgeois Radicalism," *PA* 49 [October, 1970]: 3–10. Paragraphing has been ignored.) The same issue of *PA* pays tribute to Hall's "great talents as a leader of the working class and the American people" in the course of whose struggles "he gained preeminence as a Marxist-Leninist and achieved the standing of one of the foremost leaders of the Communist movement, not only in this country but on a world scale." ("Happy Birthday, Gus!" ibid., p. 1.) This is as good a sign as any of the catastrophe that had hit the Party.

On the significance of the 1930 and 1956–1958 cut-off dates, see Draper, *American Communism and Soviet Russia*, Chapter 18, and Shannon, *Decline of American Communism*, pp. 292–371.

25. Earl Browder, *The Democratic Front* (New York: Workers Library, 1938), p. 84.

PART 1
Structure

2

Jimmy Higgins

THREE CERTAINTIES—that socialism was good, that socialism was coming inevitably all over the world, and that the Soviet Union was the model socialist society—were inseparable in Jimmy Higgins's mind. The moral judgment, the prediction of the future, and the supposedly empirical observation constituted one thought. The psychological significance of the Twentieth Congress lies in its forcing some devoted rank and filers to realize that these were really three independent propositions, requiring different sorts of supporting evidence or reasoning. A very few dropped the first, a few more the second, and still more the third. The few who stayed in the Party continued to combine the three propositions in one mental image expressible in three ways. During the unprecedentedly free debate following the Twentieth Congress, Party writers reiterated that the Party was reexamining its fundamental beliefs, but in the very same paragraphs they showed which assumptions they could not reexamine—these three propositions among them—even as they criticized certain specific deeds and tenets in the Soviet Union and the CPUSA. These fundamental constituents of their thinking defined the boundaries beyond which critical thought could not go—not because of conscious taboos or fear, but simply because of inability to think in any other way, or to understand people who could.

John Gates's article "Time for a Change" (published in the November, 1958, issue of *Political Affairs*) has come to symbolize the Party's fatal crisis. Gates rejected "sectarianism" and the various means by which the comrades had alienated their potential allies. What is most significant about his argument in the present context, however, is how much of the Party's ideology this spokesman for the "right wing" did *not* question, even on his way out of the Party. He continued to refer to "our scientific socialist ideology," Browder's "mistaken concepts of progressive capitalism and postwar national unity," the inevitable rise in the standard of living in socialist countries and decline in capitalist countries, "the main enemy, monopoly," and so on. A little over a year later, William Z. Foster set forth, for the guidance of the faithful remnant, the "seven basic Marxist-Leninist principles": the Party's socialist perspective; proletarian internationalism; democratic centralism; the Party's duty to struggle against American exceptionalism while taking account of national characteristics; the united front; vanguard role; and self-criticism.[1] To Foster, the disagreements between him and Gates were basic; to Gates, they concerned important means, but not ends. They were both right, for both inhabited the same reality, Foster a smaller circle within it. But from the standpoint of the "first" reality, their differences were minuscule. Just as the basic attitudes remained constant over the generations, so, too, they transcended factional disputes at any given moment.

UNAWARE that it was "the entire historical condition of human existence" he was condemning, the true-believing Party member embodied all evil in an existing social order, called it "the capitalist system," and epitomized it in the United States. To prove that the evil need not exist, he embodied all good in another existing social order, called it socialism, and epitomized it in the Soviet Union. We shall examine Jimmy Higgins's image of the latter in chapter twelve. Here we should pause to notice a curious fact: when he characterized one of these countries, he asserted what most people perceived as true, or partly true, of the other. When Jimmy Higgins looked at the United States he saw a unitary System, regimentation, slavery of the workers, a drive to conquer the world, a meaningless electoral system, oppression of subject nationalities, and lack of free speech and thought. When he looked at the Soviet Union, he saw fraternity among all peoples, pacific intentions toward other countries, individual freedom, rising productivity in industry and agriculture, voluntary support for the regime among almost all its citizens, respect for other countries' sovereignty, and reward for merit.

How could Jimmy Higgins, looking at facts, describe them so mistakenly? One easy answer, preferred by anti-Communists, is that he did not: the Party consisted largely of neurotic and/or power-hungry people who knew the facts as well as others did. The easy answer preferred by people on the Left is that rank-and-file Communists were idealists who merely erred about certain facts, mostly concerning the Soviet Union. But the easy answers in this case are deductive, not empirical; they assume that all emotionally normal people perceive reality the same way. As to the first one, we have no reason to believe that the incidence of neurosis was greater in the Party than outside it or, to concede as much as possible to that hypothesis, that emotional disturbance was sufficiently prevalent to justify generalizations about the whole organization. As to the second, the true-believing Communists held too tenaciously to their false perceptions to allow us to explain them on the basis of mere error. As Charles Horner points out, "Facts are believed when a framework exists that will allow for their acceptance."[2] If Niemeyer and Voegelin are right, the true believers suffered from *spiritual* disorder: what Voegelin has called "disorder of the soul." Since this contention crosses the boundary between the two universes, it cannot be proven or disproven by the usual scholarly criteria. I believe, however, that it enables us to make sense of many otherwise inexplicable aspects of the primary sources, including my own recollections.

Reflection on those recollections and on Party literature has led me to hypothesize a three-level structure of the mind of the true believer. The foundation level was described in chapter one: a condemnation of all reality. How this moral judgment originated in individuals is a question I leave to psychologists and theologians. The second level translated this condemnation into ostensibly factual propositions. It consisted in the focusing of the hostility on identifiable targets: in general the System, in specific on "the capitalist class" and other "enemies of the people." It was on this level that the switching of perceptions concerning the United States and the Soviet Union, summarized above, occurred; that is, what the true believers perceived as "facts" were what the Grand Negation required to be facts. Resting on the universe of "facts" thus perceived was the third level: specific moral judgments consistent with the "facts."

It is over that third level that I disagree with some anti-Communist commentators—those who insist that Jimmy Higgins knowingly defended the Gulag, the deliberate starvation of millions of peasants in the 1930s, and the other crimes committed by the Soviet regime. On the contrary, when Jimmy Higgins looked at the Soviet Union, he did not see what others saw. With some exceptions, he did not defend what others abhorred or abhor what others praised. He evaluated what he saw as would anyone who saw as he did. For example, if you look at a certain population center and see a home for rescued victims of oppression, you will call it good. If you see a concentration camp, you will call it evil. If you see a means of segregating enemies of a good society and rehabilitating or punishing them, you will call it a sad necessity. The value-sign follows the perception. Inhabitants of the two universes, in short, differ widely about facts and only partly about values. Since this question is the basic interpretative problem created by the two-universes phenomenon, it warrants extended discussion.

Most observers, including anti-Communists, agree that the typical recruit to the Party acted out of idealism. They disagree over whether he could remain a member for many years without becoming cynical and corrupt. I shall argue not only that Comrade Jimmy—never a leader—retained his idealism, but that the Party could not have functioned if he had not. My principal argument will concern the connection between the ideals professed by socialist theories on the one hand, and Jimmy Higgins's motives on the other. Primary sources, supplemented by firsthand recollections, have convinced me that Comrade Jimmy believed fervently in the ideals of peace, brotherhood, justice, the ending of poverty, the ending of discrimination against minorities, and social solidarity, and that he equated them with socialism, believed that the Soviet Union implemented them, and thought he could help create the good society in this country by being an active member of the CP. He dreamed of a society that acted out values that virtually everyone believed in (though he derived them from history, not God). Some anti-Communist writers seem to think that if they imputed good faith to the ordinary Communist, they would be palliating Soviet atrocities. In my view, Jimmy Higgins's sincerity makes that hideous reality more hideous.

Consider two reviews of Vivian Gornick's book *The Romance of American Communism*, which is based on interviews with ex-Communists. One reviewer exclaims:

What all Miss Gornick's subjects have in common . . . is quite simply how *nice* they are. . . . How, one begins to wonder, with all these shrewd, tender, feisty, and gallant souls in its ranks, did the American Communist party manage to rack up a record for duplicity and servility to Moscow unsurpassed in the rest of the Communist world?

In my opinion, this rhetorical question is not only a real question but also *the* starting point for the discovery of what is most important about this subject. Another reviewer writes:

Even before its first implementation, Marxism was effectively criticized and exposed; after its Russian embodiment, endless testimonies have been provided to prove that Marxism creates slavery and hell. But the American Communists chose freely and deliberately *not* to listen to that evidence and to do everything they could to inflict communism on America.[3]

Other critics of the Party impute that record to stupidity or neurosis. All such explanations imply that the authors and readers are basically different from Jimmy Higgins. But if we exclude our own nice, intelligent, honest, and healthy selves from the category of potential victims of ideological self-delusion, we are showing as great a lack of self-awareness as those Communists did. I agree with the following complaint by Gornick:

For thirty years now people have been writing about the Communists with an oppressive distance between themselves and their subjects, a distance that often masquerades as objectivity but in fact conveys only an emotional and intellectual atmosphere of "otherness"—as though something not quite recognizable, something vaguely nonhuman was being described. This distance sets those being described (i.e., the Communists) apart from those doing the describing in such a manner as to imply that the observers would never have been guilty of what the observed are guilty of: as though *they* were infantile while *we* are mature; as though *we* would have known better. . . . In short, as though the Communists were made of other, weaker . . . stuff, and what was in them is not in us. . . . Ironically, this dissociativeness cultivated by the intellectual anti-Communists is the very crime for which the Party itself is hated and reviled.[4]

If we reflect upon the Nazi Holocaust, which image of the Nazi would horrify us more: that of a beast different in kind from ourselves, or of a man acting out the worst possibilities of our own human nature? Is not the dehumanization of the Nazi a temptation to smugness? We react to a bear's killing of a person differently from the way we react to a murder by a neighbor we had known as an ordinary man. If we refuse to acknowledge self-contradictoriness and complexity in the doer of evil, what are we saying about ourselves? The Communist did just that, and in him we can easily see that by denying his common humanity with the "enemies of the people" he was dehumanizing himself, just *because* he never questioned his own motives. His environmental-determinist theory bolstered his complacency: he could credit fortunate external influences for his escape from the ideological conditioning that had victimized "the masses." The believer in free will who refuses to admit his own vulnerability to self-delusion is even more smug, for he cannot say, "I'm good because circumstances have made me so"; he must say, "I have freely chosen to be better than the man whom I'm condemning." He should instead (as the quotation from C. S. Lewis in chapter one implied), be able to look at any evildoer and say, "He reveals something that is, right now, within me." Yet writers who know the truth about communism and refuse to admit their common humanity with Jimmy Higgins—"*I* couldn't possibly be like *him*!"—also insist that he was *just* like themselves: "No one could really believe those things," so he must have been lying.

The process of ideological self-delusion takes place below the level of consciousness where "free and deliberate choice" occurs. In Jimmy Higgins's case it was helped by the rigid censorship of reading that comrades imposed on themselves. To say this is not to exculpate Comrade Jimmy but to specify what his sin was: the moral complacency—producing lack of curiosity about the consequences of his beliefs and acts, and weak resistance to the lure of wishful thinking—that put the guns into the hands of the actual killers. Arthur Koestler, Will Herberg, Frank Meyer, and other well-known ex-Communists (other than ex-spies), and thousands of ex–Jimmy Higginses who did not write books, did not become moral and intelligent only when they defected. Nor did they necessarily shed their character flaws in that act. Even those who felt they had undergone a sort of rebirth recognized the continuity of their former and current selves. Those who have never been ideologically self-brainwashed will never comprehend the nature of ideology until they understand how millions of intelligent and generally decent people—including themselves—can fall prey to it.

Even some who have returned from that other reality cannot understand this. Defectors have always tended to doubt the good faith of those who defected after they themselves did. If Jones saw the light after the purges of the mid–1930s, then the evils of Stalinism must have been obvious to everyone from then on. Smith, who did not wake up till the Nazi-Soviet Pact of 1939, can understand how well-meaning people could misinterpret the purges as he had, but of course no one after 1939 could be blind to the truth. Brown, who was shaken into reality by the Duclos letter in 1945, is certain that that was the first event that no one could misconstrue. And so on. To understand that the rank-and-file Communist who remained in the Party after their own awakening was as sincerely idealistic as they were, Jones, Smith, and Brown would have to grasp that the purges, the Pact, and the Duclos letter were the precipitants, not the causes, of their new ability to see things as they were. Many memoirs suggest that the process had been going on in the back of the mind for some time, and that it had consisted chiefly in the lessening of the need to wear distorting lenses.

Ex-Communists Bella Dodd and Douglas Hyde—an American and a Briton respectively—have told of many comrades who, year after year, accepted poverty and great risk to serve genuine ideals that they identified with communism. The literature describing individual members is full of confirmations of this generalization.[5] In the 1950s I knew many such people—elderly garment workers, middle-aged machinists, housewives, students—people who did not steal, commit adultery, or cheat on exams, at least no oftener than their neighbors and classmates did. They loved their families, helped people in trouble, wept over news of suffering—and would have staked their lives on the "facts" that Soviet citizens were free, that there were no slave laborers in Siberia, that anti-Semitism had been wiped out in all the socialist countries, and that the defendants in the Moscow trials had been fascist traitors. Only the uncomprehending would protest; "But the evidence was available in abundance! Did these people think that all those refugees from communist tyranny were *lying*?"[6] Of course they did. In people possessed by an ideology, the need for what the ideology offers is so strong that it determines what they accept as evidence. Facts and logic can never make them change their fundamental worldview so long as the need for it remains as the organizing principle of their personalities.

Once Jimmy Higgins had made his initial commitment to the Party's worldview, he knew a priori that anti-Communist exposés were lies. That is, rather than pondering each challenge to his faith as it came along, he made *one* basic decision, and every other judgment followed inexorably for the rest of his Party life: the falsity of the Enemy's "facts" and arguments, the self-evident truth of Party doctrine, the goodness of the Soviet Union. As several Party writers reiterated, socialism did more than make democracy possible: it guaranteed it (until the Twentieth Congress, at any rate). Therefore, investigation of particular events was a waste of time. Comrade Jimmy could no more ponder the truth claims of reports of the Gulag than he could those of a neighbor who said he had been inside a flying saucer. His answer was not "they aren't true" but "they *can't* be true—in the nature of things"— that is, in the nature of the universe he lived in.

The Party's ideology offered its own "facts," which Comrade Jimmy knew were facts because they fitted into the universe as he perceived it. What must be grasped if anything else about him is to be understood is that his image of the Soviet Union originated in his initial condemnation of the reality around him. In a book published a few years ago—*Political Pilgrims: Travels of Western Intellectuals to the Soviet Union, China, and Cuba*—Paul Hollander confirmed what I had discovered earlier from personal experience. Hollander's subjects were liberals and fellow travelers, and if they could misperceive the Soviet Union, Jimmy Higgins could too, here at home where his "information" came mostly from Party publications and Russian movies. His "Soviet Union" was not constructed from news items, even false ones. It was a land first created by his imagining the opposites of all the bad things he "saw" in the United States and only then filled out with "empirical evidence" furnished by Soviet and Party propaganda. Some such perceptions were, by coincidence, accurate—most notably that of racial discrimination. Others were false—for example, the perception of total power wielded in all sectors of American society by reactionary capitalists.

The way Comrade Jimmy combined all these perceptions reflected his predisposition to reject the American social order and his need to construct a coherent theoretical system. These two determinants of his thinking induced him to ascribe all evils to the System in the United States and then to impute all their opposites to the Soviet Union. American racism became Soviet fraternity among all peoples. American imperialism became Soviet peacefulness and the impossibility of war between socialist countries. The American worker's wage slavery became the Soviet worker's participation in the dictatorship of the proletariat. The fake rivalry between the Democratic and Republican parties became the true democracy implemented by the one party in the Soviet Union. The American worker's freedom to strike really meant he was forced to strike, whereas the Soviet worker never had to strike because he helped run his factory. American factories' speedup became socialist emulation. This list could be extended indefinitely, and each Communist could emphasize a different element in it, depending on what he hated most fiercely in his own society. If his neighbor was a religious hypocrite or his grocer cheated him or a teenager mugged him, he blamed the System that corrupted morals and discouraged cooperativeness. Such things did not happen in the Soviet Union, or, if they occasionally did, they were residues of capitalism.

Changes in Party line could not touch this way of thinking. So long as he needed to wear distorting lenses, only an earthquake, with its epicenter in Moscow, could crack them. This is why Khrushchev's speech in 1956, coming from Utopia itself, not only decimated the ranks of the Party but also helps us understand Comrade Jimmy's commitment before 1956.

Just *because* Comrade Jimmy genuinely believed in the Party's professed ideals, he could not justify atrocities. The Party's leaders, who knew more of the truth about the Soviet Union but who said that Communism would act out most of the conventional values, were tacitly admitting the strength of those values among the rank and file. Jimmy Higgins did adjust the traditional values somewhat (for example, he gave more emphasis to "equality of result" and denigrated self-reliance). But he was wholly unlike Ivanov in Koestler's *Darkness at Noon* (or O'Brien in Orwell's *Nineteen Eighty-Four*), who, starting from one basic postulate, justified every atrocity with airtight logic and total amorality. Koestler shows that if one rejected any of the means, no matter how distant they might be from the syllogism's end/starting point, one must, to be consistent, reject the whole syllogism, but that anyone who accepted the end/starting point of Marxism-Leninism as good and true could not consistently reject any means. Comrade Jimmy did not reason in that manner. This does not contradict the earlier statement that he was attracted by the logical coherence of Marxism-Leninism, that he needed to believe that all reality could be comprehended—in both senses of the word—in one theory. Although his syllogism was identical to Ivanov's in logical form, it differed in substance. Ivanov and his real-life counterparts solved the problem of relating fact and value by eliminating values from all parts of the theory except the ultimate aim of Communism. Comrade Jimmy could not shed his moral heritage so easily. So he reconciled fact and value, and satisfied his need for a coherent theory, by inventing the facts: a Soviet Union that realized the traditional values and an American System that trampled upon them. In short, just because he could not relinquish his moral values, he had to distort the facts.

What made *Darkness at Noon* so shattering to some Communists on their way out of their special universe (when they finally could bring themselves to read it) was its airtight logic. This fact requires an amendment to my remark that Jimmy Higgins's syllogism was the same as Ivanov's in logical form: Comrade Jimmy never followed his axioms to their last corollaries. In this respect his cognitive error did have moral implications. Deep down, he may have suspected where the syllogism led. I have known several true believers who partly freed themselves from the ideology but then shrank from the consequences of taking the next step. Great courage in facing hecklers, hostile neighbors and colleagues, and estranged relatives seems to be compatible with moral cowardice in the presence of an inner adversary. The struggle with oneself is so painful that, as Bella Dodd found out, "it takes time to 'unbecome' a Communist." Apparently realizing how hard it would be to convey her experience to others, she tried two different metaphors: "Now, like some Rip Van Winkle, I was awakening from a long sleep," and, a few pages later, "it was as if I had been ill for a long time and had awakened refreshed after the fever had gone."[7] These statements are obviously not about ex-cynics or reformed criminals; they are about idealists who were a little better than what they had believed in.

It is perfectly possible for a person to both love *Humanity* and manipulate *people* as means. This is the crux of my argument with the writers quoted earlier: forgetting Dostoyevski's Grand Inquisitor, they deny the possibility of this mixture. Those who sympathize with the Party think the good intentions rule out the manipulation; those hostile toward the Party think the manipulation proves the absence of the good intentions. But ex–Jimmy Higginses who have returned from their special universe know that these attitudes worked synergistically. Those ordinary, decent Communists who acted out the conventional virtues also met secretly in Party caucuses before union meetings to plan how to steer the debates and votes; they lied about the Party membership of comrades who held union offices; they carefully orchestrated conversations with potential recruits so as to lead them to the correct conclusions; they joined nonradical organizations and pretended to agree with their aims, so as to transform them into Party fronts. To someone who respects the integrity of the immediate reality and the self-justification of virtue in daily life, these acts look cynical. But for the Communist the meaning of the union meeting and of the potential recruit lay not in what they were but in what they were to become. The farther they diverged from the ideal, and the higher the ideal, the more acceptable became those tactical lies that were needed to close the gap. Although Comrade Jimmy never rationalized atrocities, he did justify lesser sins in order to realize utopia within history.

Yet even the lesser sins sometimes caused struggles between Comrade Jimmy's "bourgeois" and "Bolshevik" consciences (especially if he belonged to Type II as analyzed in the next chapter). When the Communist conscience won, he felt all the more virtuous for having sacrificed a spontaneous impulse toward bourgeois honesty to the higher honesty. When he refused a quarter to a beggar, so as not to reinforce bourgeois social relations, he felt virtuous just because he was aware of a twinge of misapplied conscience. He had discovered in himself a vestige of the enemy's ideology and triumphed over it. Since the Party had trained him to assume that everything "linked up," he loathed the very thought that anything could be "good in itself," whether it was generosity, candor toward his fellow union members, art for art's sake, learning for the sheer enjoyment of learning, or virtue as its own reward. Reality was hierarchical; everything, including himself, served something higher.

This was true of beliefs as well as of morality. For example, when Comrade Jimmy nimbly accepted a drastic shift in his Party's line, he did so because the ideal so far transcended any tactical line as to make it relatively painless to drop one and adopt the next. I say "relatively" because the bit of soul searching that always took place assured him of his devotion. He had hesitated because he had "failed to understand" the merely tactical nature of the old line, and by suppressing his doubts he proved his growth in commitment and "mastery of Marxism-Leninism." This is the mental process that produced those periodic orgies of "self-criticism," when comrade after comrade arose in meetings to castigate themselves for "white chauvinism" (or whatever the current sin was) and felt purged and purified—while well aware of the admiration of their less courageous or conscience-stricken comrades. The ensuing feeling of comradeship was genuine—among the rank and file, at any rate—as other types of collectives have understood.[8]

That warm feeling came from the satisfaction of the comrade's need to know he was serving a Cause that transcended his selfish interests. Everything he did was for the Cause of Humanity. Those adjustments of conventional morality were eased by the intraparty ethics, which demanded that he make *himself* a mere means to the Party's ends. A young Communist of working-class origin could see a parallel between his parents' self-sacrifice for his sake and his own, more noble, self-sacrifice for the sake of his brothers the world over. But "self-sacrifice" is a misleading term. To him it was self-realization. What he "struggled to root out" was a bourgeois pseudo-self. Many Communists gave up promising careers to work in factories; they accepted ostracism; they devoted their leisure time to routine Party work; many gave their lives in the Spanish Civil War. So, when Comrade Jimmy "used" his unenlightened neighbors, he was doing no more to them than he was doing to himself. The difference was one of "level of development": he did it consciously and voluntarily, as they would in the future. In the meantime, he defined self-interest differently from the way they did. He felt superior to them, because they lived inside an ideological box; his home was the whole universe. He understood the past and the future too, his neighbors saw only the present, the daily job, their families and friends. What meaning could their lives possibly have, inside that box? And how could anyone call his living outside it a sacrifice? Or so he thought. In fact, he was the one who lived in a box. The more his philosophy encompassed everything, the more he shrank reality to the compass of his own (and his leaders') mind and character. Ex–Jimmy Higginses are always surprised at how much bigger the world is than they had thought.

THE RELATION of ends to means in the CP is, then, more complicated than most outsiders realize. The Party leaders could use Jimmy Higgins as the means to their own power only because he thought the Party's future power was the means to noble ends. Though he saw himself as a means to the goal of the Party's power, he saw the Party as (among other things) the means to the goal of socialism, and socialism the means to the goal of racial equality, abolition of poverty, and other things he considered both good and realizable. It is because of this reversal of ends and means that the leaders could use the devoted rank and filer as means to their own, power, ends.

Jimmy Higgins knew that the world of the Party consisted of a series of concentric circles. The leaders (from the national down to the section level) and cadre comprised the first circle. The club officers and long-term core members, including himself, comprised the second. The third circle consisted of the transient members, and beyond them were the nonmember sympathizers. Comrade Jimmy willingly subordinated himself to the members of the inner circle because he assumed that their motives, their arrangement of means and ends, were the same as his own. He never knew the most important facts of all, concerning his relationship to Party authorities.

Some facts he knew, but not their implications. Consider the Party's use of the term "masses." "Masses" did not necessarily call to mind large numbers; it meant primarily the unenlightened who must be led, often despite their will, although they had the right instincts. Yet the leaders regarded the Party's own rank and file as "masses." Jimmy Higgins, reading articles in the official magazines that expressed this thought, doubtless assumed they referred to the "less developed" comrades. But there are many indications that his leaders included him in that category.[9]

Much misunderstanding of the status and mentality of Jimmy Higgins has resulted from the customary division of the Party into only two concentric circles, the leaders and cadre in the inner, and all rank and filers in the outer.[10] It is easy to see the leaders' cynicism—although I believe their writings contain inadvertent proof that some of them lived within the special universe, too—and the naïve, temporary rank and filers' idealism. Anti-Communists usually impute the leaders' cynicism to the true believers among the rank and file, and sympathetic writers usually impute the rank and file's idealism to the leaders. Both imputations ignore the circle that mediated between the outer and inner circles and shared traits of both. If Jimmy Higgins's circle had not existed, the leaders could not have wielded influence over the outermost members or the thousands of sympathizers. The second circle welcomed the discipline that the third balked at. It also combined two traits found among sympathizers: those who wanted to act in behalf of "progressive" ideals but disdained theory, and intellectuals who accepted the theory but disdained activism. Jimmy Higgins knew that theory and practice must be united.[11] He thus was able to urge activism on the intellectuals, preach true theory to the merely instinctual progressives, and give a principled aura to the leaders' power-oriented tactics. He was the most genuinely committed Communist of all and, by the same token, the most deluded.

Arthur Koestler put it succinctly: "we were not fishermen, as we thought, but bait dangling from a hook." Jimmy Higgins could no more rise to leadership than a fly can become a fisherman. The more he combined absolute belief in the theory with the proselytizer's activism, the more he insured that he would remain a rank and filer for his entire Party life. He was useful to the leaders only because he assumed that they were as idealistic as he and defined ends and means as he did. Howard Fast explains that, if the rank and filers

are people of conscience, tenderness and integrity, as they often are, they will never be able to make the hotly contested climb toward power above; for the crown is not to the bold, the inventive, the imaginative or the humane. Quite to the contrary; the test is dogma, the criterion orthodoxy, and the way through unbending rigidity. The requirements include a good nose for the wind, skill at tactical infighting, patience enough to wait out and side with the winner in any inner dispute, a thick skin, a divorcement from the deep needs of people and an unbending devotion to what is called "the Party line."

Jimmy Higgins was indispensable to the leaders *because* he was not like them *and* thought *they* were like *him*, only better. It would, says Jules Monnerot,

be an error of method to ignore the motives of the pure. *For the motives of the pure are the justifications of the rest.* . . . To understand a movement it is indispensable to understand the psychology of its sincere believers, for in a sense the whole thing depends on them.

Douglas Hyde, reflecting upon his own experience, concludes that "the most evil thing in communism is that it claims some of the best and molds their minds and twists their consciences so that they can be used for the worst."[12] Those anti-Communist reviewers whom I quoted earlier should be disturbed by Vivian Gornick's book not because its depictions of idealistic Communists are false, but because they are true.

"The romance of American Communism" was, then, not wholly a lie. I knew many people like Gornick's respondents. I also knew many just like those relatives she describes in her autobiographical discussion—fervent, dogmatic, argumentative, generous, hard-working, oppression-hating inhabitants of an imaginary reality. Communism *was* a romance to them. That is its horror. And that is why I think certain reviewers have missed the point— as did Gornick herself, a radical who thinks the CP betrayed the radical cause. But anti-Communists who agree with John Roche, that Gornick's is "a quite silly book,"[13] will not grasp the full meaning of what Monnerot and Hyde are trying to tell us. *The Romance of American Communism*, if read right, tells us something about universal human nature.

To sum up, Jimmy Higgins created a Soviet Union to represent his ideal society and defined American society in terms that approximated the truth about the Soviet Union. He was a total rebel who believed in most of the traditional values. Hating the authority and power he thought he saw in what was, in reality, an exceptionally free and fluid society, he subordinated himself to authority in an extremely hierarchical organization and glorified a totalitarian regime. He felt humble and self-critical and at the same time behaved arrogantly toward the unenlightened. He projected his own mind's contents onto the world yet contemned a self-centered life. He needed to comprehend and control, by thought, the whole universe (or at least know that his leaders did); yet he accepted every shift in line that was forced by his Party's wrong predictions and analyses in the past. He was spiritually blind, seeing reality as wholly material, and therefore located his ultimate ideals within history and defined "idealism" and "materialism" in ways that were exactly the opposite from most of his compatriots'.[14]

He stayed in the Party for many years because it gave him what he wanted. That is why the Party writings that will be sampled in the following chapters are reliable guides in our reconstruction of his special reality. Since the world as he saw it was the projection of his own mind, when we construct that world from the Party's writings with the aid of empathy we are seeing external reality as he saw it. We can then retroject it back inside his head and see how the theories and concepts dressed up his feelings, needs, and attitudes in "objective" costume. The result will be a picture of Comrade Jimmy's mind more accurate than he himself could have painted it, for self-delusion was an integral part of his own mind. The fact that a wholly "inside" depiction would omit the Gulag shows the limitation of the "inside" approach. The absence of this knowledge from his mind reveals something other than ignorance of the same sort as an ordinary person's ignorance of how his car's engine works. The repeated denial of a mountain of widely published facts reveals not a gap where knowledge should have been, but a pattern of perception that had filled in that space in advance with counterfacts. Thus the Gulag is relevant to a reconstruction of Jimmy Higgins's mind, which therefore cannot be accurately depicted wholly from within. He could not have believed in most of the traditional values and at the same time have understood the true nature of the Soviet Union. He served his leaders' real aims precisely because he did not know them. The synthesis of those opposites—of the leaders' power quest and Jimmy Higgins's ideals—was the Party's theory. That is why neither the anti-Communists who emphasize the power aspects of Marxist-Leninist theory, nor the sympathizers who emphasize the lofty ideals, can understand Jimmy Higgins; both underestimate the importance and functions of the theory as a theory.

The current relevance of the imaginary world explored here is not to the Party, which barely exists today, but to a permanent part of human nature: the capacity for wishful thinking, for constructing a special universe and assuming that everyone lives in it, for perceiving facts so distortedly as to look at evil and see good, and at oppression and see freedom—and vice versa. If Niemeyer, Voegelin, and Novak are right, those ex-Communists who fought their way back to the real universe—Koestler, Meyer, Herberg, and others—were a microcosm of civilization in struggle against its destroyers.

NOTES

1. William Z. Foster, "The Party Crisis and the Way Out, Part II," *PA* 37 (January, 1958): 61–65. See also Joseph Clark, "Venture in Theory," *MM* 9 (October, 1956): 57: "We live at a time when Marxists are re-studying all questions from the beginning," but then, four sentences later, he alludes to "the need for a creative

development of socialism on scientific, democratic and American foundations"—thus unconsciously revealing where "the beginning" of reexamination was located.

2. Charles Horner, "The Facts about Terrorism," *Commentary* 69 (June 1980): 45.

3. Vivian Gornick, *The Romance of American Communism* (New York: Basic Books, 1977); Marion Magid, "Tender Comrades," *Commentary* 65 (February, 1978): 78 (this review, however, contains several keen insights); anon., "Gornick's Machinations," *Chronicles of Culture* 2 (March/April, 1978): 23. Cf. John Diggins's admirable review, "Love Story," *National Review*, April 28, 1978, pp. 534, 536–37.

4. Gornick, *Romance*, pp. 18, 20.

5. Bella V. Dodd, *School of Darkness* (New York: P. J. Kenedy & Sons, 1954), passim, e.g., p. 71; Douglas Hyde, *I Believed* (New York: G. P. Putnam's Sons, 1950), pp. 81–84. See also, e.g., Jessica Mitford, *A Fine Old Conflict* (New York: Alfred A. Knopf, 1977), p. 170; Morris L. Ernst and David Loth, *Report on the American Communist* (New York: Henry Holt, 1952), passim.

6. In asking the question that way I am echoing D. Keith Mano, who asks (in *National Review*, April 16, 1982, pp. 440): "Did she think, for God's sake, that Solzhenitsyn was *lying*?" The "she" is Susan Sontag, who had just publicly denounced Communism before a hissing audience of her fellow radicals. Mano, insisting she must have known the truth all along, thus means his question to be rhetorical. Yet Sontag's choice of a public meeting of radicals to drop her bombshell, doubtless knowing what the reaction would be, is evidence to me that she *had* thought Solzhenitsyn a liar. Besides, it is a safe bet that not one in twenty American radicals has read *The Gulag Archipelago*. Ideology and curiosity are deadly enemies. Very few Jimmy Higginses in the period we are dealing with read exposés of Soviet reality; Party writers read them and interpreted them for the rank and file. As to non- and even anti-Communist radicals, just as Party members deplore "Stalinism" as an aberration of Soviet socialism, so others on the Left can easily find Soviet socialism (before and after Stalin as well as during his reign) an aberration of "true" socialism, no matter how conclusively Solzhenitsyn and others prove otherwise. Many acknowledged the inconvenient fact of the Cambodian holocaust only after they found a way to blame the United States for it. Those who contend that "true" socialism has never yet existed stand on safer (for polemical purposes only) ground: even though every regime that has put economic and political power in the same hands has undermined freedom; even though there is a strong correlation between the proportionate size of the private sphere, on the one hand, and freedom and economic development, on the other; even though government planning has never worked as intended; even though countries with command economies that have been forced to make reforms have invariably reformed in the direction of capitalism—they insist that "true" socialism will work and safeguard freedom, some day. What has all this to do with evidence?

7. Dodd, *School of Darkness*, pp. 228, 240, 245.

8. See, e.g., Maren Lockwood Carden, *Oneida: Utopian Community to Modern Corporation* (1969; New York: Harper Torchbooks, 1971), pp. 71–77.

9. As a careful reading of documents such as the following will show: T. Gusev, "The End of Capitalist Stabilization and the Basic Tasks of the British and American Sections of the C. I.," *COM* 12 (January, 1933): 45; F. Brown, "The Party Building and Daily Worker Drives," *PO* 10 (March-April, 1937): 15; Jack Stachel, "Recruit

the Masses!" *PO* 10 (October, 1937): 4; John Williamson, "A Program for Developing Communist Cadres," *PA* 24 (April, 1945): 365.

10. Historians who deal with the subject statistically are especially vulnerable to this misconception, for "the rank and file" as a whole do statistically fit the pattern of transience, inactivity, and weak commitment. "The leaders and cadre," on the other side, do statistically fit the definition of "the professional revolutionaries," who were available to be sent to remote cities to work in factories where Party agitation was needed, to attend the Lenin School in Moscow, to abandon family and friends to undertake secret assignments, and so on. Jimmy Higgins was not available for these tasks; but neither was he inactive, transient, or weakly committed. Similarly, with respect to time of joining the Party: the statistics show an increase in recruiting during the Great Depression, and most of the recruits were reacting to the depression and did not remain in the Party for long. But the aggregate numbers do not distinguish those who would have joined even if there had been no depression—the future Jimmy Higginses.

11. On the importance of theory, a personal recollection may be helpful. I recall a moral tale that was popular among the comrades (I do not recall its provenance): During the Bolshevik Revolution a peasant soldier was assigned to guard a small bridge and let no one pass. Someone asked him, "But why must you let no one cross?" He replied, "There is the capitalist class and the working class, and no one crosses the bridge." The story supposedly depicted the incorruptible loyalty of the illiterate peasant who knew the one basic truth on which all else rested. When I first heard it, I said nothing, but I did not like its implications. It seemed to me that this young man had memorized a formula that he did not understand. And if that one basic truth was enough to insure his devotion and make him the object of admiration of Communists the world over, then why were *we* reading dozens of books and pamphlets, attending the Jefferson School, and working so hard to master the science of Marxism-Leninism? It is hard to believe that other comrades I knew did not have the same reaction, but none of us ever mentioned it to each other, even among trusted friends. Fear of being thought a heretic was not the reason, for close friends discussed problematic issues (mutual suspicion among friends was not so prevalent as some memoirists have said). I can give only my own reasons. I think I sensed that our faith was not grounded in theory but rested, as did that Soviet soldier's, on attitudes and feelings. Exegeses of theory could change, the Party line could swing wildly, but we kept on guarding the bridge because the one basic truth never changed. This was, however, unconscious; consciously the theory seemed all-important; we insisted that the "science" shaped our perceptions of reality. What this means is that Jimmy Higgins's commitment cannot be understood by a study of any particular doctrine or the Party line at any particular time. But some theory there had to be, to sustain that illusion. This suggests how the theory should be approached. One would not argue that, because a neurotic's symptoms are not the real problem, they should be ignored. The symptoms help both to repress and to express the underlying problem, and one must understand *them* if one is to understand *it*. Similarly, an understanding of Jimmy Higgins (emotionally healthy or not) entails an understanding of the picture his intellect painted of reality, as well as feelings and attitudes that made the picture plausible to him. This is why many years elapsed before I grasped both that Soviet militiaman's resemblance to me and why I could not admire him as I was supposed to.

12. Arthur Koestler, in Richard Crossman, ed., *The God That Failed* (1950; New York: Bantam Books, 1965), p. 38; Howard Fast, *The Naked God: The Writer and the Communist Party* (New York: Frederick A. Praeger, 1957), p. 87 (Fast probably exaggerates somewhat, and his book in general should be used with caution); Jules Monnerot, *Sociology and Psychology of Communism* (Boston: Beacon Press, 1953), p. 255; Hyde, *I Believed*, p. 303. On the concentric-circles structure and the gulf between leaders and rank and filers, see Ernst and Loth, *Report*, pp. 22, 125, 181, 184; Nathan Leites, *A Study of Bolshevism* (New York: Free Press, 1953), pp. 291, 368 (Leites uses the metaphor of an island in the midst of a hostile ocean to depict the Party's self-image in relation to outsiders, but he also distinguishes between circles within the Party); and esp. Philip Selznick, *The Organizational Weapon* (New York: Free Press, 160), pp. 84–85. A somewhat similar image appears in Alain Besançon, *The Rise of the Gulag* (New York: Continuum, 1981), p. 234.

13. John P. Roche, "A Word Edgewise," *National Review*, January 22, 1982, p. 69.

14. The reader may be wondering whether these generalizations apply also to the French and Italian CPs, which have enjoyed grass-roots support that the CPUSA never had. The appeal of Communism in different countries must be explained in historical and cultural terms, so far as the "third circle" of members is concerned. One generalization that is true of those millions of European CP members, however, is that few of them have ever wanted what CP-ruled regimes deliver. The appeal of the Party is, in most cases, the positive appeal of some ideal, originating in the negative appeal of an escape from some present situation. A great intensification of these appeals marks the difference between a CP true believer and a fellow traveler or "democratic socialist," and between the latter and a statist liberal. But the fact that none of them wanted the society that the postrevolutionary regimes create is proven by the fact that those regimes have kept their power only by abolishing democracy, including democracy within the ranks of their former supporters. The obvious question—why did the Twentieth Congress not have quite as great an impact on other Western CPs as on the CPUSA?—is among those I cannot deal with here. Hints of answers may be found in, among others, Hadley Cantril, *The Politics of Despair* (New York: Basic Books, 1958); Gabriel Almond and others, *The Appeals of Communism* (Princeton, N.J.: Princeton University Press, 1954); Jeane Kirkpatrick, ed., *The Strategy of Deception* (1963; New York: Noonday Press, 1964), esp. Chapter 3.

3

Types

If any one generalization emerges clearly from the study of men and women who have joined the Communist party in the United States during the last 30 years it is the fact that despite the twistings and turnings of the party line, communism always has appealed to the same kind of people. The recruits of the 1950's in temperament and background are very much like the recruits of the 1920's.

So WROTE Morris L. Ernst and David Loth in 1952, after interviewing "several hundred men and women who have been in and out of the Communist party."[1] Although the method of the present study is different from theirs, its results are consistent with that generalization—except that we should speak not of "kind" but of "kinds." Most attempts to explain the appeals of Communism recognize both a variety of personality types and a degree of overlap between Jimmy Higgins and non-Communist Americans in that respect.[2] What were the main types? My own answer to the question comes out of my experience first as a Party member and then as a college teacher who knew many radical students and professors. It avoids one difficulty of reconciliation with other observers' explanations in that it excludes the Party's leaders, who may have included other types. My hypothesis recognizes, on the one hand, that some people were more vulnerable than others to the Party's appeal and, on the other, that the Party was not the only arena in which those people's special needs could find satisfaction.

As a college teacher in the 1960s and 1970s, I encountered three sorts of radical students often enough to realize that they were indeed "types." I shall describe one actual individual who epitomized each in exceptionally pure form. None belonged to the CP, but before the late 1950s they all might have.

I. Miss A seemed driven by hostility. The general targets of her hatred were "the System" and "the capitalist class." Her specific targets were the university administration and her professors, most of whom were well to the left of center and bent over backward to prove their progressiveness. She adopted a stiff courtesy when speaking to nonbelievers, but she seemed to consider the obligation to do this as just one more grievance against the System. Even as she spoke of love for the People and of the future society of peace, brotherhood, and equality, it was not love but zealotry that shone in her eyes. She was active in a campus radical club and was always quick to volunteer to circulate leaflets and petitions and to walk on picket lines. An excellent student, she spoke often in class, usually to offer ingenious refutations of her professors' opinions and point out flaws in the reading material.[3] When Oscar Wilde said that socialism would fail because it took too many evenings, he perhaps underestimated the disproportionate influence that radicals like Miss A could exert. Their energy is boundless; they revel in the incessant meetings and activities; their weeks seem to have fourteen evenings each.

II.   Mr. B felt genuine love for the People and pity for their sufferings. He was generous and kindly toward everyone, including "reactionaries." During one of our chats, he told me that he and nine friends were planning to open a cooperative book store and send the proceeds to liberation movements overseas, keeping only enough to pay their minimal living expenses. He hoped to go to Nicaragua to help the revolution then in progress. When he discovered that I disagreed with most of his beliefs, he did not conclude that I was a wicked person. In fact, we had a most amiable debate. He was a naïve idealist who assumed that most people were as selfless as he.

III.   Miss C was a radical only because she had never come across an alternative way of thinking since entering college. Not an ideologue by temperament, lacking Miss A's zealotry and Mr. B's otherworldliness, she had acquired her beliefs by unconscious contagion from her friends, professors, and assigned readings. One day in my office, when we were discussing current events, I mentioned certain facts and theories that were common knowledge outside radical circles. This straight-A student had never heard of any of them. With the excitement of discovery she asked for more; over and over she asked: "Why haven't I ever heard of these things?" Except for "red-diaper babies," this Type III is mostly a post–1970 product of the liberal arts departments of academia, in which radical beliefs and attitudes are equated with common sense, and their opposites are unworthy of consideration.

Radicals of all three types can be found off campus, too. Type III includes some birthright radicals, the children of radical parents who provide them with a milieu like that of the campus in recent years. A Type III radical who does not change into a Type I or Type II is merely a follower of his more highly motivated associates, and I shall therefore say nothing more about him—except to say that as a Party member he tended to be less active and less single-minded than his comrades of the other types.

Most of the books, pamphlets, and articles produced by Party writers during the period covered by this study are dull tracts that reveal nothing about their authors: they discuss tactics; report on campaigns undertaken; analyze national, international, or local issues; and so on. When we survey those writings that bear the stamp of their authors' personalities, we discover a significant pattern: Type I shows up far more often than Type II. This may be due to the fact that Type I's feelings were aroused most by the thought of the oppressors, and Type II's by the thought of the victims; furious exposés of the doings of evil people best suited the needs of agitation and propaganda. Another pattern is probably less trustworthy: ex-Communist memoirists depict themselves most often as Type II's. Sometimes we can tell which authors had experienced a genuine (and rare) change in personality, and which ones, consciously or unconsciously, falsely painted themselves as duped idealists. Elizabeth Bentley, who had been a courier for espionage agents, was clearly Type III, with a bit of Type II mixed in. It was an accident that the first person she became attached to who could put her mild idealism to use was a Communist, and a spy at that. If he had been a reformer or a Trotskyist, she would doubtless have followed him onto that path—and lost that faith as readily as she lost her Communist faith when her lover died. In the case of Bella Dodd (see next chapter), inadvertent evidence in her autobiography shows her to have been Type II. Yet even Dodd says that she had, during her Party years, felt hate and rage. Most likely she imbibed them from her Party associates. The memoirs of novelist Howard Fast suggest a Type I personality both before and after his defection.[4] The traits of Types I and II did not, then, wholly exclude each other. Miss A and Mr. B were, as I said, exceptionally pure types. Moreover, intense emotion cannot be sustained all day, every day. For most of the time, both the predominantly Type I and the predominantly Type II comrades went about their Party business in a matter-of-fact way, indistinguishable in this respect from each other or anyone else. The emotional fuel was, however, ready to be ignited on appropriate occasions.

The difference between the hater and the lover of humanity was not the difference between cynicism and sincerity; they were both sincere. Both believed they loved the People and therefore hated the People's oppressors, but Type I's love for humanity was spurious. Both sincerely believed that Party theory had been proven true by experience and logic and that it fitted their own feelings and intuitions. But Type I was mistaken about his own feelings, just as Type II was mistaken about the theory. The hater projected his generalized hostility onto external "enemies"; the lover of humanity identified his altruism with a theory that, he thought, increased his ability to do good. Type I "loved" on the intellectual level to ratify the hatred he felt; Type II "hated" on the intellectual level because he thought that hatred was the corollary of the love he genuinely felt. In each case a feeling lay deepest in the personality; the feeling shaped the perceptions of reality; and the perceptions found an intellectual rationalization in a theory. Like all people, these students, and the Jimmy Higginses of both Types, harbored a variety of feelings, in varying proportions. Whereas custom, tradition, and religion are all designed to weaken feelings that are dangerous to others and to ourselves, the Party provided a haven for people whose morally disapproved tendencies dominated.

The Party needed both Type I and Type II, and within the Party they needed each other. Unlike other haters, such as certain sorts of criminals or misanthropists, a Type I comrade had a theory that justified his hostility on the ground of empirical facts about the "capitalist System." The presence of his Type II comrades assured him that *his* hatred for the Enemy was only the counterpart of *their* love for the People, which he could then believe he felt too. A Type II Communist differed from an ordinary lover of humanity (who expressed his love in his home, church, charitable institution, or reform movement), in that the Party gave him a systematic theory, expounded mostly by his Type I comrades, and an assurance that the good society was surely coming soon. Both felt the need to live for Humanity, with a capital H, that is, humanity as it could be and as it would be in the future. But whereas one Type devoted himself to this mission out of love for real people, whose best potentialities were supposedly suppressed by evil institutions, the other Type did so because it exempted him from the duty to love people in the present.

According to some analysts, the Party's leaders were motivated mainly by a thirst for power. They manipulated all Types of rank and filers, but it was Type I who shared the leaders' power drive. Type I therefore mediated between the leaders and Type II, who were the most unwitting tools of others' intentions, just as Type II mediated between the Party and the outside world. Our analysis therefore should focus on Type I.

INSIGHTS can sometimes be obtained from analysis of extreme cases. The mass suicides (and murders) in Jonestown, Guyana, in November, 1978, can throw light on the problem we are dealing with here. The members of the People's Temple were motivated by something deeper than a desire for brotherhood and community when they moved to a clearing in the jungle. That something was the rejection of American society—a motive that reveals the link between them and most other radicals. The latter too, although believing they are struggling for a better world, are first of all impelled by rejection of all that is.

As long ago as 1901, a leader of the Socialist Party warned his comrades against immersing themselves in the movement so wholly as to lose their perspective. He had known some comrades who had believed that the revolution was imminent and who, when disappointed, lost all reason for living and killed themselves. Others turned to terrorism. "Their eagerness, their enthusiasm," he explained, "carried them beyond the bounds of reason. . . . Let us," he pleaded, "not sever ourselves from our brothers in the economic movement" (the unions). Of course, Thomas J. Morgan, who uttered these admonitions, was a committed socialist and could not have known what later historians can find evidence of in abundance: that those who retain their deviant ideology longest are those who do sever themselves from the outside world. Those who followed Morgan's advice usually left the movement after a while. But sometimes reality breaks through even to those who remain in the closed society of the movement, and when that happens, so do the suicides of members who are unable to accept what they see they must accept.

The Guyana horror differs only in degree from those private tragedies, which include the suicides of several well-known young radicals in the early 1970s. The difference reflects the differing degrees to which the victims had cut themselves off from society. The followers of Jim Jones were physically at the end of the world, surrounded by sea and jungle; their geographical isolation and their ideological isolation reinforced each other. But it would be a mistake to overlook their resemblance to the self-destructive young radicals who took their lives either in solitary despair or, as Jones said, as a protest against an inhuman world—which amounts to the same thing. A person can isolate himself from reality without ever leaving his hometown. All he need do is join a movement that calls the rest of society deviant, associate mainly with other members, read mostly movement literature, and withdraw from some of the other roles and institutions that each claim a small part of people's allegiance. Acceptance of conventional roles and allegiances gives a person a place to stand, a way of keeping his balance, if he should become disillusioned in any one role or institution. The person who deposits his whole personality in and gives all his loyalty to one ideology, one role, one institution comes to identify it with the very meaning of his life.[5] Even if he is outwardly a member of society, the movement's ideology preinterprets all current events and personal problems for him. To outsiders, such people may appear like others, but in their own minds they are living in a clearing in the jungle.

This attitude, by the way, sheds light on the Party's obedience to directives from Moscow. No one forced Jimmy Higgins to obey those dictates, and other parties and organizations on the far Left did not obey them. A comrade who did not want to could switch to another organization, and many did; others, who found no sect or party satisfactory, founded their own. Idealization of and allegiance to the Soviet Union were therefore not basic attributes of either the Type I or Type II personality, though they were requirements of the CP versions of those Types. The Party's subservience to Moscow was thus that particular radical organization's way of living in its own clearing in the jungle and at the same time keeping a reassuring connection with the outside world.

According to Philip Selznick, the person who has lost his allegiance to his traditional culture and ties and has joined the Party

> becomes susceptible to extreme types of behavior, called for in the name of abstractions which have little to do with his daily life and which he has had no opportunity to test and reshape. Alienated from other objects of deference and devotion, the individual may focus all of his deference strivings on the new symbols; but since this is ultimately unsatisfactory, tension is not alleviated and an ever new expenditure of emotional energy is required. At the same time, the individual's stake in his new attachments is very great in the absence of other sources of satisfaction. All of this results in a measure of need which permits extensive manipulation.[6]

Jimmy Higgins did not despair. He was certain he could clear the entire jungle that was American society; the Soviet Union symbolized the inevitable triumph of his efforts. Hatred for reality plus pessimism may evoke thoughts of suicide; hatred for reality plus optimism, especially within the Party community, engenders zeal. Yet Comrade Jimmy's optimism depended on his isolation in his mental clearing in the jungle. The only threat to his equanimity was reality, for the reality he rejected and the "reality" he denounced were two different realities. The spurious "reality" that he thought he perceived and that he was working to alter was a "reality" he needed to believe in.[7] His isolation was self-imposed, independently of the anti-Communist propaganda and persecution that also fostered it.

Scores of articles, in the Party periodicals written for active members, complained of the comrades' reluctance to associate with fellow workers and urged them to "root the Party in the shops."[8] Whether the Party could have "rooted" itself in non-Party milieux if the members had obeyed these exhortations is a separate question (the answer, I think, is No). But such articles would not have appeared so often if even half the members had acted out their own doctrines.

The Party's closed environment reinforced the members' parochialism. One document that illustrates this style of thinking is the book *Trotskyism: Counter-Revolution in Disguise*, by M. J. Olgin, a major CP theoretician during the 1930s. The book's ostensible purpose was to prove the wickedness of Trotskyites and to mobilize hatred against them. Yet a large portion of the work deals with highly technical, theoretical matters, discussed in a scholastic manner incomprehensible and boring to anyone not immersed in Party ideology. Nevertheless, Olgin obviously assumed that everyone interested in world affairs would find the tract interesting and enlightening. He began by insulting any reader who was not already convinced:

> Before we proceed we must say a word about the method applied here in discussing Trotskyism. The question is treated from the point of view of Marxism-Leninism. It is assumed that Leninism has proved itself correct both as the theory and as the

practice of revolution. It is therefore taken for granted that opposition to Leninism is incorrect.

Now, we are fully aware of the fact that many a reader may disagree with the Leninist point of view. He may be opposed to the proletarian revolution, to the dictatorship of the proletariat, to the socialist system. Such a reader may find solace in Trotsky's attacks upon Leninism. But then he must admit that he seeks in Trotsky not a confirmation but a repudiation of the Leninist solution of the social problem. With a man of this kind, who draws from the muddy stream of Trotsky's denunciations convenient arguments against Socialism and against the Communists of his country, we have no argument on these pages. The only thing a person of this stripe is requested to do is to acknowledge that he uses the Trotsky ammunition *against* everything that Marx, Engels and Lenin stood for and against everything Stalin, together with the Communist International, stand for today.[9]

Olgin may have proved to his own satisfaction that anyone who did not believe in Leninism was ipso facto of the Trotskyite "stripe," seeking "ammunition" and needing "solace" and so on. But by failing to recognize that the overwhelming majority of the readers he wanted to persuade had no such motivations, he guaranteed that his book would be read only by other Olgins. He obviously was unaware that he wrote it just to vent his venom. Having immersed himself in intra-Party affairs for decades, he had apparently become unfamiliar with the way outsiders thought. Thus, the spleen-venting motive and the psychological isolation reinforced each other.

As Ignazio Silone put it, belonging to the Party meant "living like a foreigner in my own country."[10] In terms of the typology offered above, we may conjecture that Type I members sought this atmosphere and Type II members accepted it. At least some of those who lived like foreigners in their own country joined the Party largely because they wanted to live that way. They told themselves, however, that they had in effect been expelled from their society. Their hostility toward others thus became a virtue; their isolation, proof of their purity. Their conviction that capitalism dehumanized people was, for those comrades, a rationalization for their own felt separation from outsiders, owing to fear or hostility.[11]

The Party's theory reconciled the will to isolation with the duty to "root" the Party among the people. The comrades had to feel that they could mingle with the people because they possessed an antidote to the ideological poison pervading their society. The theory thus had a double purpose: not only to guide the struggle for socialism but also to exert intellectual control over the comrades' spontaneous feelings and attitudes. This need meshed perfectly with another: Type I members' need to feel they had intellectual control over all reality. Irving Howe and Lewis Coser contend that

a considerable proportion of the Stalinist militants harbored feelings of powerlessness and personal inadequacy which they tried to overcome by identifying with authorities who seemed potentially invincible and immediately omniscient. . . . This . . . sense of

insignificance from which they suffered was accompanied by a free-floating aggres-
siveness and *ressentiment*.

The antidote was identification with two kinds of power: "the physical power
of the Soviet Union" and "the power of systematized intellectual reassurance." Douglas Hyde, an English ex-Communist, was alluding to the same
mind-set when he remarked that "the Communist has a vested interest in
disaster." That world "interest" should be interpreted in two ways at once,
to mean both the emotional engagement and the "systematized intellectual
reassurance" that "interested" him because it enabled him to handle the
feelings. William Z. Foster, for example, shows both sorts of "interest" in a
speech delivered in early 1941, when the Party's attitude toward the war
was "a plague on both their houses."
"The reactionary Polish Government," he wrote,

has been shattered; fascist Italy is already practically defeated; the reactionary French,
Dutch and Belgian empires have been split and overrun; and the British empire is
fighting with its back to the wall. Germany and the United States still seem to be
very strong and vigorous, but these two powers also are rotten at the heart, both
economically and politically.

Meanwhile, "the Soviet Union, standing intelligently aside from the war, is
rapidly increasing in strength," while the workers all over the world, including in the United States, are losing their illusions and are becoming
ready to overthrow capitalism. Foster was obviously hoping for worldwide
holocaust in which the Allies and the Axis would destroy each other, leaving
the Soviet Union to pick up the pieces. As Hyde puts it: "Economic crisis,
social upheaval, defeat in war, or a victory which leaves a nation bled white
even though victorious—these are the preconditions of communism. It would
be less than human and, indeed, idiotic, for the Communist, in his heart of
hearts, not to long for them."[12]
  There was nothing heretical in Foster's theory of the nature of the war.
But when it did become "incorrect" a few months later, with Germany's
invasion of the Soviet Union, the ease with which he and his comrades turned
about-face shows that the authentic portion of the passage quoted was the
vision beneath the theory. They were "interested" in the theory because it
was a theory and not just because of what it said. *Some* theory must direct
every aspect of reality, including the members' feelings, as completely as the
Party was to direct the whole society after the revolution.
  Another Party leader, Betty Gannett, almost admitted the real motive for
intellectual certainty, in a polemic against John Lewis, an English Marxist
philosopher, in the July, 1948, issue of *Political Affairs*. She thought he had
allowed too active a role to the knower in the subject-object transaction.
Gannett homed in on the kill:

According to Lewis, we would have to say, "as far as I know" the society in which we live is capitalism; "as far as I know" its main contradiction is between the social character of production and private appropriation; "as far as I know" it is creating the conditions for its replacement by socialism. But these are only *my* conclusions, as a result of *my* particular relationship to capitalism, under the unique conditions of *my* knowing at this moment. And since we know that the capitalists and the many capitalist apologists would not agree, what we would have, to follow Lewis, is differing points of view but not objective knowledge. We would not have knowledge corresponding to objective reality, to absolute truth, about the nature and the laws of capitalist development. We would therefore be devoid of the firm, scientific knowledge that could serve the working class as a powerful instrument in its struggle, that could infuse the working class with confidence in the truth and ultimate victory of its cause.[13]

When Lewis read this, he probably noticed the glaring non sequitur; the objective, scientific nature of our knowledge is independent of how certainly we feel it to be true, for one who questions the objectivity of his knowledge is not thereby making his mind "devoid" of it. Gannett had unwittingly revealed that the feeling of certainty was the most important thing to her. The astonishing fury of her attack—one must read the entire article to savor this—suggests panic at the thought that her beliefs might not be absolutely true. Nowhere did she argue this point with evidence from what the Party was forever calling "life itself"; the authorities she cited were all Marxists, and her method was logical deduction from a few postulates—that is, the only method that yields absolute certainty. Lewis had, she complained, given "a totally one-sided emphasis to the difficulty of knowing things in their changes and relations." Evidently, then, she not only knew things in their changes and relations but also knew it was easy to know them, even for nonscholars such as Gannett and the rank and filers among her readers.

Party writers would not have had to preach year after year that "Marxism is not a dogma but a guide to action" if, in reality, the members had been willing and able to treat Marxism as a guide to action rather than as a dogma. Yet once more, in 1956, in response to the worst crisis that the Party had ever undergone, Eugene Dennis intoned, "our job is not to study Marxism in the abstract or as a catechism, but to study the problems and developments *in our own country* by means of the living, dialectical method of Marxism," and that "we need to develop a method of theoretical-political work where we examine continuously and more concretely the actual facts in each given situation"—as though the same admonition had not appeared in Party publications and been taught in Party classes for a generation.[14] Even the crisis following Khrushchev's speech about Stalin and then the Hungarian uprising, which evoked the most self-critical, agonizing reappraisals in the history of the Party, had no effect on the remnant who remained in the Party after the uproar had run its course. They reverted to the same way of thinking as before—as any scanning of their literature in the years since 1958 will show.

All the evidence in the world, proving that that way of thinking was wrong and harmful to the Party's prospects, could not prevail over the need for absolute certainty that a doctrine that preaches absolute control over reality is absolutely correct.

We can get an inkling of the threat thus exorcised, in a movie review in the *Young Worker* of October 9, 1930: The Marx Brothers' *Animal Crackers*, wrote the reviewer, proves that "things are coming to a breaking point. In so-called 'normal times' you couldn't have a picture quite as nutty as this one," and he went on to give a Marxist-Leninist analysis of "the antics of Groucho, Harpo, Chico and Zeppo Marx. . . . You laugh and laugh at their almost inconceivably funny stunts—and then wonder what you're laughing at. . . . It's worth while seeing, fellow-worker, if only to realize, by contrast, how incomparably better a 'Potemkin' or a 'End of St. Petersburg' is." In plain English, this said: "I'm ashamed that I laughed while watching *Animal Crackers*, and I must find a Marxist-Leninist analysis of the movie to excuse my enjoyment. Nevertheless, since all movies must be judged on a single scale, and since *Potemkin* and *End of St. Petersburg* are Soviet movies, they must be better than *Animal Crackers*." Deep down, he knew he enjoyed the latter more, but spontaneous fun and sheer foolery did not fit into his ideology. His Communist conscience forced him to justify his enjoyment. It told him, "if you don't, you may find yourself enjoying a piece of capitalist propaganda some time in the future!" Indeed, the threat was real. If, for example, one even sympathized with the attitude of tolerant skepticism, one might end up in the swamp of liberalism, as John Gates implied in his recollection of a debate he had had with James Wechsler, then editor of the New York *Post*. Wechsler had

said that one thing which he objected to most strenuously about communists was that we were so certain and cocksure about everything that we never entertained any doubts. I responded by saying that doubt was the hallmark of liberals and led to paralysis of action, while communists made up their mind and acted.[15]

Harry K. Wells (one of the Party's two chief philosophers) summed up the grievance and threat in a comment on a long quotation from John Dewey's *Experience and Nature*. Wells italicized all the sentences in which Dewey expressed the difficulty of obtaining certain and abiding knowledge of the world. Then he added:

Such is the sum and substance of Dewey's philosophy. The only thing that man can be sure of is that the world is "hazardous," "perilous," "uncertain," "full of risk," "invisible," "unseen," "ominous," "unpredictable," "precarious," "uncannily unstable," "dangerous," "inconstant," "irregular," "irrational," "fearful," "awful," "unknown forces," "untouched," "ungrasped." . . . Thus would Dewey reduce man to ignorance and perpetuate slavery.[16]

The same non sequitur appears here as appeared in Gannett's remarks: Dewey would reduce man to ignorance and perpetuate slavery not by denying man knowledge but by denying him the *certainty* that he had absolute knowledge. Marxism-Leninism, we are to infer, depicted a world describable by the opposites of all those quoted words, which clearly were far more important to Wells—and to Gannett—than any particular contents of its doctrines.

Fear of chaos within engendered a hankering for absolute control over the external world as well as over the mind's contents. The affection for totalitarian controls will be explored in a later chapter, and it will suffice here merely to suggest this attitude. Olgin's polemic against Trotskyism contains an unusually frank self-portrayal, although it was not meant as such. Trotsky, he wrote, envisaged several political parties in the United States just after the socialist revolution.

There must be several parties with equal rights, *i.e.*, with no special privileges for any. Whom will those parties represent?

If the Communist Party represents the workers, then obviously the other parties must represent the rich farmers, the poor farmers, the middle bourgeoisie, the petty bourgeoisie, perhaps the intellectuals. How will those parties function? Naturally, by struggle. . . . Splendid. A Soviet very much resembling a bourgeois parliament. Several parties represented in it *with equal rights*. Each party fighting the others. Several parties making a coalition to defeat the dangerous common rival. Why not a coalition of all the other parties against the party of the workers? . . . The population will have its choice of parties, groups, programs. No special discipline is needed for any party; no monolithic unity for the Communist Party. . . . A majority of votes in the legislative chamber will decide the policy to follow. . . . Should there be a majority of votes against collectivization [of agriculture], this will then be the "will of the people." Each party and group will have its own press, "for Soviet America will not imitate the monopoly of the press by the heads of Soviet Russia's bureaucracy."

Trotsky's model, added Olgin, assumed "no necessity for the workers to . . . be organized in a powerful fighting political organization with discipline of an almost military strictness and with unity of will and action which insures quick and effective striking possibilities." Rather, Trotsky envisaged "a heterogeneous mass of humanity divided, owing allegiance to various parties and party splinters and defending their 'interests, groups and ideas.' How unity can be achieved under those conditions, remains a secret of Trotsky's."[17]

Olgin's sarcasm sent a message to Jimmy Higgins: that he must consider the opposites of Trotsky's propositions too self-evident to need defending. Among the truths not needing demonstration were the following: a majority of the votes of elected representatives did not have the right to reject collectivization; each party represented a separate class; a dissenting press was harmful to workers' interests; and total agreement by all proletarians on all important issues was inevitable once the Party was leading them. As to that last, Olgin's remarks are ambiguous because the Party itself always was. Theory said that opinions reflected a class's interest. Disagreements among workers were due to the influence of bourgeois ideology, but under Party tutelage all would learn their class interest and would henceforth agree on all important matters. The repression of dissenters in the Soviet Union therefore had to be due to the strength of surviving enemies of socialism. Yet if the workers chose socialism by a vast majority, as Party theory predicted, how dangerous could the remaining enemies be? Nevertheless, when the Hungarian workers rebelled in 1956, Herbert Aptheker's explanation, in *The Truth about Hungary*, would have had the approval of Olgin (then deceased): Aptheker reiterated, on page after page after page, that almost all Hungarian workers supported socialism and welcomed the Soviet tanks.

TWICE, BEFORE AND DURING World War II, circumstances forced the Party to venture from its clearing in the American jungle. If we use the model of American Communist mentality offered here, the results are predictable. The Party shifted from "left" to "right" in 1935, then back again when Stalin signed his Pact with Hitler in 1939, then back to cooperation with the American bourgeoisie after the Germans invaded the Soviet Union, and finally "left" again in the spring of 1945. One might expect the Type I comrades to have felt uncomfortable with the first and third shifts and the Type II comrades to have felt uncomfortable with the second and fourth. The leaders, it is true, accomplished each reversal "without so much as a blush of embarrassment."[18] Some leaders of the abandoned lines did have qualms, but they restricted their arguments to their own circles. Many rank and filers, however, blushed in public. Some voted against the new policy with their feet—in the Party there was no other way than to withdraw—and some wrote letters to the Party press. Statistics published in official Party magazines show that each shift in line caused losses of members who preferred the line just abandoned, and recruitment of people who no doubt preferred the new one. But the hard core of rank and filers, those who clung grimly to the policy pendulum, preferred the "left" lines. During the "right" periods, they faithfully followed orders, although the tone of their periodicals suffered from the loss of revolutionary élan. This occurred mainly, however, during the second of those periods, when Browderite "revisionism," as Foster charged, gutted Marxism-Leninism; before the war began the Party line remained well within the boundaries of orthodoxy.

As one historian observes, *National Issues* (published during 1939, before the Pact) "strongly resembled the liberal *New Republic* and *Nation* of the time not only in format but in editorial stance as well,"[19] but not, it should be added, in liveliness and sense of genuine conviction. We find articles on "Planes and Plain Talk," "Notes on Government Spending," and "Congress and the Small Business Man." The same thing happened after the Soviet Union entered the war. Before then, *Clarity*, the YCL's magazine, had been lively and polemical; the writers' feelings were engaged by Roosevelt-the-warmonger and the predatory imperialists. All of that was crushed by the German tanks heading eastward in June, 1941, but the reluctance of the editors and writers is shown by the gradualness of the change. By the summer of 1942 it was complete. Now we find "Notes on Apprenticeship for War Production," "Mobilize Youth for Victory Crop," "Labor Sports in the United Automobile Workers Union," "Organizing Home Front War Service," and "Farm Youth Fights for Victory." Very few articles dealt with the YCL and its mission. By the middle of 1942, *Clarity* had clearly lost its *raison d'être*. The YCL had become a sort of auxiliary of the War Production Board, so there was no longer any reason for young radicals to prefer the YCL and *Clarity* to any of several other youth organizations and periodicals. By spring, 1943, the magazine had run out of things to say, and it folded.[20]

The core members' fidelity to the Party in that period proves the near-total authority of the leadership.[21] It is all the more remarkable, therefore, that dissent broke through on occasion. *New Masses* published a letter in its issue of June 12, 1945, that voiced what must have been widespread discomfort during the just-ended reign of Browder. The magazine had received the letter before publication of the Duclos letter (the signal from abroad to reconstitute the Party and get back on the far-left track). This reader complained that the magazine had become "something between a church magazine and an OWI release."[22] But as a leading theoretician insisted in the same journal a few months later, "the Party's inner core remained uncorrupted" during the Browder period. An English ex-Communist agreed, though he would have used a different value judgment: "Most of the leaders and the rank and file were . . . only too glad to get back to the class war again after years of what had seemed to many of them, curiously un-Marxist co-operation and deplorably positive policies." Jessica Mitford recalled "much rejoicing in the ranks" when the Duclos letter signaled that the Party should be reconstituted. "Many comrades had had deep reservations about the Browder policies."[23]

As the ex-Communists quoted above testify, it was "sectarianism" combined with Type I feelings that came more naturally to most core members. The inadvertent evidences for this are the most convincing. One such is a letter to the editor of the *Young Worker* (April 14, 1936). "E. A. M." first quoted young nonmembers at YCL dances as complaining that the comrades preferred to dance with one another and treated outsiders as though they did not exist. One outsider had said, "I never saw a gang more wrapped up in themselves. And did you ever notice—they're always too busy going somewhere to stop to talk." E. A. M. then asked:

how many times have you heard our League comrades say, boastingly perhaps, that they have at least one meeting every night? They say they don't have time for the friends they had before they joined Y.C.L.—and truthfully they don't.

"Why don't you write a letter to the Young Worker about this?" I asked one girl who was in the League two years ago. . . . Maybe they don't see it as you see it."

"Oh-h-h, don't be silly!" came the answer. "Of course they know it. They've talked about it time and time again. They fought sectarianism when I was in the League—and the Young Worker is always full of the same kind of talk. And it just remains talk. They talk about not remaining sectarian—and then they turn around and do just what they say they shouldn't do."

. . . There's more truth in the statement of these people than I care to admit. I've seen YCL members in New York and Chicago and other cities—and it's the same all over. We talk about getting out of our narrow circle. We take in new members—and in a short time they become like us in that they remain in the little circle—or else . . . they drop out altogether. . . .

We won't win the workers if we remain in our circles (they're fun, I admit) instead of getting out among young people. And we shouldn't do this in a mechanical fashion. Some of our League members do go out and mix with large groups and become known as "regular fellows," but how many don't? And how many of the "regular fellows" who are in these clubs, etc., in the first place and come to us do we lose?

Perhaps the most revealing statement in this document is that the "sectarian" behavior was "fun." Even one who complained eloquently about it and knew it conflicted with the ostensible mission of the organization felt more natural with it. Most of the members who left when the Party rejected Browderism had never temperamentally been Communists and had joined only recently, during the revisionist period.

The Party's subservience to Moscow doubtless saved it from having to confront its fatal dilemma: Fosterism was certainly more congenial to the devout rank and filers, the stable core who gave the Party what vitality it had; yet Browderism was more conducive to mass recruiting. Like all radical organizations, the CP was impaled on the horns of the dilemma of purity versus popularity, although it needed to be both pure and popular.[24] From the Marxist-Leninist standpoint, Foster was right and Browder was wrong, even in terms of the altruism of the Type II members. Their genuine love for humanity did not necessarily engender a preference for the sort of attitude displayed by *Clarity* during the war, and by Browder when he advocated postwar class-collaborationism. In doing so he betrayed the Party's very reason for being, its basic theory, and its appeal to its own core members.

Yet some members welcomed Browderism, which gave them the right to be patriotic and feel themselves in the main stream of American life. Maurice Isserman describes David Lester, a minor functionary in Rochester, New York, who showed "naive delight in rubbing shoulders with a part of the city's social elite. . . . The role of a steeled Bolshevik agitator, immune to and scornful of conventional symbols of respectability, offered its own satisfactions, but many Communists shared Lester's craving for the acceptability that the Teheran policies seemed to offer."[25] These facts give no indication whether Lester was Type I or Type II. In fact, a Type I, carrying a large chip on his shoulder and daring the bourgeoisie to knock it off, might secretly feel attracted to what he hated. It is not surprising that when Moscow gave the signal for a certain degree of friendliness toward the American ruling class, the Party went too far—as far rightward as the Fosterites sometimes went leftward. With each swing of the pendulum, self-contradictory feelings were suppressed and other self-contradictory feelings were afforded outlets, in the same members. There was no simple solution. Members wanted the benefits of isolated superiority and the ego-boosting hostility of the enemy, but without having to pay the penalty of small size and lack of influence. And they wanted great size and influence without having to pay the penalty of ideological fuzziness, free debate, and loose organization. And worst of all, many wanted the Party to remain small in size, although they would have denied this vehemently. The only way to get the good and avoid the bad was to take power. Before that happy day arrived, the members had to continue to live in an intolerable situation, and so, regardless of what they told themselves and each other, one of the Party's principal functions was to provide rationalizations for their feelings.

NOTES

1. Morris L. Ernst and David Loth, *Report on the American Communist* (New York: Henry Holt and Company, 1952), pp. 220, 1.

2. See esp. Gabriel A. Almond and others, *The Appeals of Communism* (Princeton, N.J.: Princeton University Press, 1954), passim; Irving Howe and Lewis Coser, *The American Communist Party* (1957; New York: Frederick A. Praeger, 1962), Chapter 11. For attempts at categorization of Communists, see, e. g., Ernst and Loth, *Report*, passim; Arthur Koestler, *Arrow in the Blue* (New York: Macmillan, 1961), p. 272; K. A. Jelenski, "The Literature of Disenchantment," *Survey*, No. 41 (April, 1962), pp. 109–19.

3. " 'Blind' passion has eyes for some things and clairvoyance sees others; but in his clairvoyant hatred the victim of passion notices things that would escape him if he were only clairvoyant without being impassioned as well. And from this point of view ideology may be defined as a mixture of pathological blindness and pathological sharpsightedness. The critical faculty is suspended in certain directions but intensified in others." Jules Monnerot, *Sociology and Psychology of Communism* (Boston: Beacon Press, 1953), p. 139.

4. Elizabeth Bentley, *Out of Bondage* (New York: Devin-Adair, 1951); Bella V. Dodd, *School of Darkness* (New York: P. J. Kenedy & Sons, 1954), p. 224; Howard Fast, *The Naked God* (New York: Frederick A. Praeger, 1957). A clearly Type I was Harry Haywood, whose candor in depicting himself is balanced by his unreliability in recounting facts. See his *Black Bolshevik* (Chicago: Liberator Press, 1978).

5. In *The Gulag Archipelago*, vols. 1–2 (New York: Harper & Row, 1973), p. 414, Aleksandr Solzhenitsyn explains why the defendants in the Moscow Trials confessed to deeds they had not committed: "Bukharin (like all the rest of them) did not have his own *individual point of view*. They didn't have their own genuine ideology of opposition, on the strength of which they could step aside and on which they could

take their stand." See also Robert A. Nisbet, *The Quest for Community* (New York: Oxford University Press, 1953, 1971), pp. 34–37 and passim.

6. Philip Selznick, *The Organizational Weapon* (New York: Free Press, 1960), pp. 289–90. See also Granville Hicks, *Where We Came Out* (New York: Viking, 1954), p. 47.

7. See Robert Conquest, "The Role of the Intellectual," *Encounter* 51 (August, 1978): 40–42, esp. middle paragraph on p. 42, for insights relevant to the theme of this section.

8. In addition to many articles entitled "Rooting the Party in the Shops" or having similar titles, there was also a regular section, containing several articles, with that umbrella heading, in most of the issues of *PO* in mid–1932. See also, e.g., Earl Browder, "Approaching the Factories as Insiders and Not as Outsiders," *PO* 5 (May-June, 1932): 4; Howard Rushmore, "As I See Things," *YW*, November 19, 1935, p. 7; "Experience in Keeping New Members, " *PO* 3 (May, 1930): 13; Browder, "Rooting the Party in Basic Industries," *PO* 6 (August-September, 1933): 5; Max Bedacht, "Work in Mass Organizations," ibid., pp. 77–78; "J. L.," "Fluctuation and Methods of Stopping It," *PO* 6 (December, 1933): 14; Central Org. Commission, "Where Shall We Place Responsibility for Our Weaknesses?" *PO* 7 (October, 1934): 18–21; Browder, "Building the Party and The Daily Worker," *PO* 10 (August, 1937): 1–5; C. A. Hathaway, "On the Use of 'Transmission Belts' in Our Struggle for the Masses," *COM* 10 (May, 1931): 409–23; "The Tasks of the Communist Party U.S.A.: Resolution for the Central Committee Plenum," *COM* 11 (April, 1932): 310–24; "The Winning of the Working Class Youth Is the Task of the Entire Party," *COM* 13 (May, 1934): 477. Similar examples could be cited for the 1940s and the 1950s.

9. M. J. Olgin, *Trotskyism: Counter-Revolution in Disguise* (New York: Workers Library, 1935), p. 23.

10. Ignazio Silone, in Richard Crossman, ed., *The God That Failed* (1949; New York: Bantam Books, 1965), p. 88.

11. See the interesting comments in Vivian Gornick, *The Romance of American Communism* (New York: Basic Books, 1977), pp. 176–78: one of Gornick's informants comments there on how the Party, which taught that capitalism dehumanizes people, dehumanized its own members and made them unable to empathize with one another. (My interpretation of this passage differs from Gornick's.) Frank Meyer, in *The Moulding of Communists: The Training of the Communist Cadre* (New York: Harcourt, Brace, 1961), p. 130, refers to "this narrowing of the area of awareness of men as men, . . . this progressive depreciation of the value of personality." The usual challenge to this sort of hypothesis is: "But what about those who accepted the theory simply because it made sense to them?" Answer: Types I, II, and III would all have claimed this; they all accepted the Party's theory because it seemed true. The question I am asking is why it seemed true. My point is not that the theory is disconfirmed at every point at which it meets reality, though I believe this is so. The reason for pushing the question back to "*Why* did it seem to make sense?" is that the people I am discussing knew it was true before they ever held it up to the relevant evidence and, when they did, never let facts interfere with their faith. The question here is not what they believed (true or untrue) but how they believed.

12. Howe and Coser, *American Communist Party*, pp. 519–20, 31; Douglas Hyde, *I Believed* (New York: G. P. Putnam's Sons, 1950), p. 31; *The Path of Browder and Foster* (New York: Workers Library, March, 1941), pp. 9–10.

13. Betty Gannett, "Marxism and Idealism: A Rejoinder," *PA* 27 (July, 1948): 633–34. Paragraphing has been ignored.

14. Eugene Dennis, "For a Mass Party of Socialism," *PA* 35 (June, 1956): 3. For other such admonitions, see, e.g., A. Landy, "Some Observations on How to Study the 'History of the Communist Party of the Soviet Union (Bolsheviks),' " *COM* 18 (May, 1939): 467: "Marxism-Leninism can be studied as a science only if it is studied as a guide to action and not as a dogma"; Robert Minor, "Continued Political Struggle against Hitler by Military Means," *CL* 2 (Summer, 1941): 11: "Our political science has never been a dogma, but has always been a guide to action"; Harry Haywood, "Further on Race, Nation and the Concept 'Negro,' " *PA* 31 (October, 1952): 48: " 'Marxism,' says Lenin, 'is not a dogma but a guide to action' "; William Z. Foster, *History of the Communist Party of the United States* (New York: IP, 1952), p. 151: "as every Communist theoretician *has pointed out time and again*, Marxism-Leninism is not a dogma, but a guide to action" (emphasis added). Other such statements can be found throughout the Party's lifetime. Sometimes the writers quoted Lenin directly; see V. I. Lenin, *The Tasks of the Proletariat in Our Revolution* (New York: IP, 1932), p. 38, where he attributes the statement to "Marx and Engels"; more often the writers did not cite an authority or quoted Stalin, in *History of the Communist Party of the Soviet Union (Bolsheviks)* (New York: IP, 1939), p. 356, where it has a paragraph to itself and cites no earlier authorities.

15. John Gates, *The Story of an American Communist* (New York: Thomas Nelson & Sons, 1958), p. 128.

16. Harry K. Wells, *Pragmatism: Philosophy of Imperialism* (New York: IP, 1954), pp. 182–83.

17. Olgin, *Trotskyism*, pp. 78–81.

18. John P. Diggins, *The American Left in the Twentieth Century* (New York: Harcourt Brace Jovanovich, 1973), p. 129; Diggins is referring to the first of those reversals.

19. Harvey A. Levenstein, introduction to reprint of *National Issues* (Westport, Conn.: Greenwood Press, 1970), p. [1]. It is questionable, however, whether "liberal" is the right label for *The Nation* of those years. See quotations and commentary in William L. O'Neill, *A Better World: The Great Schism: Stalinism and the American Intellectuals* (New York: Simon and Schuster, 1982), passim.

20. Maurice H. Isserman, in "Peat Bog Soldiers: The American Communist Party during the Second World War, 1939–1945" (Ph.D. dissertation, University of Rochester, 1979), p. 384, makes comments similar to mine on the YCL and *Clarity*. See also most issues of *Spotlight*, published during the war; it contained articles by famous entertainers, congressmen, and other public figures; articles on many nonpolitical subjects; a poem about sadness in springtime by a young Communist who has since become an eminent historian; a piece by Duke Ellington entitled "Swing Is My Beat"; and so on. *Spotlight* did not, however, lose its Marxist perspective, as *Clarity* did.

21. Isserman, "Peat Bog Soldiers," p. xiii, n. 6. Isserman notes that some young historians like "to write a party history from the bottom up" and he is right when he disagrees with one of them who calls the leaders' control over the rank and filers "fairly limited." Chapter five below will discuss the extent and limits of that control.

22. Philip Pollack, letter, *NM*, June 12, 1945; see other letters as well, on pp. 17, 22; and in other issues in the same period. Most letter writers sided either with

Browder or with Foster; a few tried to reconcile the two positions. Some were quite perceptive; see esp. one from "M. J. F." in the issue of August 7, 1945, p. 22.

23. A. B. Magil, "Scientist of Socialism," *NM*, January 22, 1946, p. 9; Hyde, *I Believed*, p. 270; Jessica Mitford, *A Fine Old Conflict* (New York: Alfred A. Knopf, 1977), p. 65. See also William A. Nolan, *Communism versus the Negro* (Chicago: Henry Regnery Co., 1951), pp. 154–55: after quoting a particularly class-collaborationist statement by Browder, he notes, "Many of the rank and file, however, lacked the flexibility of the party leadership. If it had not been for the fact that the war was going their way, factionalism would have become a serious problem." Another way of saying that is: the rank and filers were more principled Marxist-Leninists than were the current leaders.

24. See Aileen S. Kraditor, *The Radical Persuasion, 1890–1917* (Baton Rouge: Louisiana State University Press, 1981), pp. 24–33, for discussion of this dilemma (and others) as encountered by the Socialist Labor Party, the Socialist Party, and the Industrial Workers of the World before World War I.

25. Isserman, "Peat Bog Soldiers," p. 425.

4

The Rationale of Hate

BELLA DODD, a very naive, second-level leader in the Party's New York State organization, became disillusioned and wanted to join the Catholic Church. Yet, like others in the same position, she could not bring herself to make the break. The Party made the decision for her: it brought her up on charges that were mere pretexts, for her real offense was doubt. At her "trial," she recalls, she encountered cold hatred, and suddenly

the futility of my life overcame me. For twenty years I had worked with this Party, and now at the end I found myself with only a few shabby men and women, inconsequential Party functionaries, drained of all mercy, with no humanity in their eyes, with no good will of the kind that works justice. Had they been armed I know they would have pulled the trigger against me.

Dodd admits that she had earlier resembled her judges: describing her change of heart, she writes, "I had to drain the hate and frenzy from my system."[1] Those feelings were so common in the Party that an effort to reconstruct Jimmy Higgins's mentality must confront a number of problems relating to them.

The first problem is whether the hatred, so abundant in Party polemics, expressed the writers' true feelings or was merely a pedagogical device. Frank Meyer, once a leader in the American and British Parties, observed that

the developed Communist is, on the whole, remarkably free of aggressive attitudes towards the symbols against which the Party mobilizes the masses (including its own neophyte members). Indignation, moral or otherwise, towards hostile symbols is almost entirely confined to agitational occasions, when the use of rhetoric perhaps stirs up a certain amount of fervor in the speaker himself. . . . In fact, if a developing Communist gives vent to such emotions he will be—reasonably gently—rebuked: "What do you expect from the class enemy?" The question is put in a matter-of-fact, conversational tone. Energy is not to be frittered away on emotionalities.[2]

Some of the heated rhetoric in the printed literature was certainly contrived for agitational purposes. But I do not believe all of it was. For one thing, Dodd's testimony as to her own "hate and frenzy" is matched by that of many other ex-Communists. For another thing, I recall my own and my friends' reactions to news that such-and-such a person had been expelled. It did not matter what his offense had been, and we rarely asked. But we felt hatred, or at least visceral revulsion, if we happened to see him. And the mere labeling of someone as a Trotskyite or "renegade" was enough to evoke hatred toward him. Third, the venom in some of the printed polemics is simply too self-discrediting to have been contrived. It suggests that the writers had scoured the language for the most lethal epithets they could find, to express feelings that they could not suppress if they wanted to. Finally, we have the evidence of Communist Parties in power, that is, those that have had the guns and no inhibitions about using them. True, the mass killings in the Soviet Union, even the Cambodian holocaust, were due in part to coldly rational decisions about what must be done if the Party was to consolidate its power and be free to implement its leaders' policies. But most people who are capable of justifying such acts on those grounds cannot commit them unless they first hate the victims.

One qualification is necessary: not all American comrades who hated Trotskyites, renegades, expellees, Browder (after May, 1945), and other "enemies" would have killed them if given the chance. Dodd was partly wrong: if supplied with guns, at least some of her judges would suddenly have discovered that their hatred was not quite as lethal as they had thought. A spark of the same ingrained, traditional ethic, which Dodd had unknowingly cherished in a corner of her mind, certainly survived, albeit more dimly, even in some Type I members.

It may not be necessary for present purposes to decide whether the documents to be surveyed below expressed genuine hatred or whether they were mere pedagogical or agitational tools. In either case they produced the same effect on the rank and filer, and not just the neophyte. If Type I, he received the message that the Party endorsed his hatred and showed him its proper targets; if Type II, that his love for the people required him to hate the people's enemies. The documents to be quoted below are more vitriolic than most Party writings. Any picture of all Party gatherings as orgies of hatred, with members taking turns raging against enemies, would be false. But neither are these quotations atypical in the sense that they expressed a deviant current within the Party.

IMMEDIATELY UPON JOINING the Party, the new member was urged to read all the Party's publications regularly. This literature had three crucial functions. The first two are self-evident: to promulgate correct theory, both basic and issue-oriented, and to direct activities. The third function was to guide the members' feelings. In these writings, expressions of love for the masses

are rare, and they do not ring true. The objects of most of the expressions
of love were Lenin, Stalin, the Soviet Union, and the American Party leaders.
Expressions of hatred appear more often. These invariably purported to be
performing the first function—of promulgating correct theory, by linking
the target of hatred with American imperialism's drive to war and fascism.
They sent Jimmy Higgins three other messages too, however: (1) you must
not investigate the target's arguments; (2) you cannot love the Party, the
people, and the Soviet Union unless you hate this particular target; and (3)
all the targets, eminent and obscure, helped American imperialism's drive
to war and fascism. That third message provided the theoretical justification
for the first two—and successfully, inasmuch as it drew its emotional charge
from Jimmy Higgins's hostility toward American reality in general.

Here is how a writer in the *Young Worker* saw his country in 1931:

My country
Land of dreams and dollar bills,
Land of booze and whiskey stills,
Land of golf, and crap[s] and cards,
Land of talkies and movie-stars.
Land of stocks and bonds and notes,
Land of Packard, Ford, rum-boats. . . .
Land of rack[e]teer and gang,
Land where Sacco-Vanzetti hang,
Land of Hoover, Fish, Capone,
Land with Morgan on the throne,
Land of "credit," "Buy Now," "Save"!
Land of everything you crave. . . .
Land of congress, hoboes, bums,
Land where workers get the crumbs. . . .
Land of mortgages and rent,
Land of banking four per cent. . . .
Land of millions and starvation,
Land of the breadlines' daily ration,
Land of layoffs, five and tens,
Land of Mooney in the pens,
Land of Hearst and poisoned news,
Land of ragtime, jazz and blues,
Land of grafting A. F. of L.,
Land where everyone tries to sell,
Land where the worker is the boss' slave,
Yes, land where the Red Flag will some day wave,
    'Tis of thee we sing![3]

Some of the details in this parody became obsolete, but the hatred of American society it expressed could always find new targets. It accurately reflected
Jimmy Higgins's feelings at any moment during the Party's lifetime, for it

expressed a basic element in Party doctrine: that all evils were due to the System.

Eighteen years later the world capitalist system, according to Herbert Aptheker, was still "so putrid . . . that it no longer dares permit the people to live at all." Four years after that, the same writer, reviewing Cleveland Amory's *Last Resorts*, a description of the rich, said that "these are the rulers as depicted by a court-scribe. They have the morals of goats, the learning of gorillas and the ethics of—well, of what they are: racist, war-inciting, enemies of humanity, rotten to the core, parasitic, merciless—and doomed." Perhaps so, but there was nothing in the review that showed them to be the rulers or war-inciting. But Jimmy Higgins would not have noticed this omission, for he, like Aptheker, rejoiced at finding a target for his hatred of the System and supplied the causal connection himself. Two years later, in a diatribe against the government's policy of sending spies into the Party, Aptheker explained that

behind it all [is] a policy of fascism and war; behind it all the State apparatus, the courts, the prosecutors, the police, the politicians, the whole gamut of ultra-respectability with malice aforethought using venomous creatures and filthy means to whip up an anti-Communist hysteria, an anti-Soviet hysteria—a paralysis of mind and nerve, the better to put over the destruction of the Bill of Rights and the launching of atomic war.

The central means—the Big Lie of Hitler. And then, jail the Communists, smash the organized labor movement, discredit the New Deal traditions, identify dissent with treason and finally—Heil!

William Z. Foster's version went as follows:

It is nauseating to listen to self-righteous big capitalists and their mouthpieces hypocritically blathering about their "moral leadership of the world." Goebbels . . . was a novice compared with the war propagandists of the United States. . . . American imperialism, which is the organization of the most ruthless gang of fascist-minded capitalists on earth, is insolently pictured by its orators and pen-pushers as the champion of democracy, the defender of world peace, the moral guardian of mankind.

Other hatred-evoking words in the vicinity of this passage are: cynical, sinister, duplicity, cold-blooded, monstrous, brazen, hypocritical, barefaced, slanderous, ridiculous, blatant, bloated, parasitic, and madly.[4]

In addition to the System and its chief beneficiaries, the Party had a long list of more specific targets. One favorite was Sidney Hook. If this philosopher and anti-Communist socialist had not existed, the Party would have had to invent him, for he provided its writers with their second (after Trotskyites) most welcome opportunity to vent their venom. Thoroughly familiar with the Marxist canon, he was the most formidable antagonist among all anti-Communist polemicists. In 1952 Herbert Aptheker accused Hook of having said nothing about Communists that had not been said by Hitler, Mussolini, Franco, Al Capone, "and other statesmen." A lie uttered by Hitler in 1932 remained a lie when uttered by Hook twenty years later; "it is the same Big Lie, fabricated and spread for the same reason—to prepare the way for fascism and world war."[5] The association of a nonfascist and non-Nazi with Franco, Hitler, and Mussolini was a common rhetorical device in Party literature after the rise of Hitler.[6] Needless to say, when congressional investigators asked hostile witnesses about their Communist associates, all Party writers denounced the imputation of guilt by association. If someone had confronted Party writers with this contradiction between profession and practice, they would have replied that Hook, Trotskyites, and other enemies of the people were not just ideological associates of Hitler, Mussolini, and the rest but were in fact profascists (recall Aptheker's statement that Hook's "reason" for spreading the Big Lie was to prepare the way for fascism and war). As many Party writers explained, all anti-Communists belonged to the same "camp," worked for one end, dividing the labor a dozen ways.

The most dangerous of all were the Trotskyites (never "Trotskyists"; "ites" was a pejorative suffix). Since procapitalist propaganda no longer impressed the workers, the capitalists had to hire seemingly anticapitalist purveyors of profascist, prowar, anti-Soviet propaganda within the ranks of working-class organizations. Intellectually, this theory made sense, given Party postulates. Yet the seething hatred in the polemics against Trotskyites—"that putrid clique" that the Communist movement had "vomited forth"—suggests something more than rational conviction. Every show trial in the Soviet Union sent the American Party into paroxysms of fury. All the periodicals savored every detail of the secret connections of the Soviet defendants with American Trotskyites. One such article ended on a near-hysterical note:

As for those who plotted the crippling of Soviet industry and Soviet farming and planned to have the only workers['] country ruled by the lords of money again—to them DEATH!
THIS SHOULD BE THE MESSAGE OF EVERY YOUNG WORKER TO OUR ENEMY CLASS, THE BOSSES OF THE WORLD, AND WE MUST BUILD OUR WEAPONS OF STRUGGLE, ABOVE ALL THE YOUNG COMMUNIST LEAGUE AND THE YOUNG WORKER!

Sometimes the emotion was strong enough to produce heretical rhetoric:

Every friend of the Soviet Union, every decent human being, will bless the Soviet authorities for their vigilance and energy in discovering in time the conspiracy and checking it. Every friend of human decency, let alone anti-fascists, Socialists, trade unionists, will give a sigh of relief at learning that the conspirators, excepting their "master mind," Trotsky, were safely disposed of and were unable to carry through their murderous plans. . . . They did succeed in assassinating Kirov. . . . But this time they did not succeed. And blessed be the power of the Soviet people that brought this about.[7]

These two "blessings" were bestowed in a period when the American CP was publicly denouncing religion. The writer's materialist lexicon apparently lacked the words to express his joy at the liquidation of the defendants, a joy so soaring as to suggest vicarious participation in "pulling the trigger."

The 1938 trials evoked another diatribe; a writer in the April issue of *The Communist* instructed his comrades, workers, and other progressives to equate incorrect thinking with fascist plotting:

Behind the mask of those so-called "ideologies" which are proved to be in the interests of the people's enemies, in the interests of reaction, fascism and war—behind the mask of these "ideologies" will be found spies and provocateurs that parade in public as representatives of certain "ideologies." Such will be found today everywhere in the labor movement and in all the other movements fighting for democracy and peace. . . . Among these paid agents there is usually a coordinated division of work: some do only espionage, wrecking and diversion; others do "propaganda," "ideological" work; and others do both. . . .

This does not mean of course that *everyone* making such propaganda for the fascist aggressors is necessarily a paid agent of their intelligence services. Not necessarily. There may be volunteers. . . . Personal intent makes no difference; it is the result that counts. . . .

Behind all propaganda favorable to fascist aggression one way or the other, behind all "ideologies" which militate against the camp of democracy and peace and thus promote the interests of the camp of fascism and war, behind all these there is the conscious manipulating hand of the fascist powers and their collaborators operating through a host of spies and provocateurs within the labor and progressive movements, operating under various guises and by various methods, including espionage, wrecking, terrorism, diversion, propaganda and "ideology."

The Moscow Trials were evidently a godsend to certain people who needed a rationale for a pre-existing, colossal hatred of their rivals on the Left. "We must," cried *Party Organizer* in February, 1937,

be more vigilant everywhere since the Trotskyites are subtle in their propaganda. . . . We must prevent workers' libraries and bookshops from becoming a medium through which they spread their poisonous propaganda. Clean out the libraries and throw out Trotskyite literature. It is our task to develop mass indignation not only against the assassins and wreckers in the Soviet Union, but their followers in the United States. . . .

Among the longer tracts on Trotskyism was the earlier-discussed 160-page book by Moissaye J. Olgin, entitled *Trotskyism: Counter-Revolution in Disguise.* This book was a lesson in slippery-slope logic. Olgin's starting postulate was Trotsky's denial that socialism could exist in one country. Therefore, what the Soviet Union had was not socialism. Therefore, Trotsky wished to destroy the Soviet Union. Therefore, he wished to kill Stalin and the other leaders. Trotsky, wrote Olgin,

has a dream now. To see the Soviet Union wrecked, to see the Bolshevik Party destroyed, to see the leaders of Bolshevism assassinated, to see the world Communist movement crushed, to see the Communist International wiped off the earth,—how that would gladden his heart! How he gloats over this vision! Of course, he does not say so outright. He cannot expose himself before the world. It is his accursed task to win recruits to counter-revolution by means of radical phrases. He is a master phrase-counterfeiter. But it is to make his dream come true that he directs all his actions.

In this he is a brother-in-arms to Matthew Woll and Randolph Hearst. . . . Birds of a feather.

Elsewhere throughout the book Olgin named other American brothers-in-arms to foreign Trotskyites. His method was always the same: first he denounced Trotsky for hating the land of socialism; then he asserted that American Trotskyites shared that hatred; and finally he named certain other Americans who also hated everything the Soviet Union stood for. For example:

This small band of disgruntled petty-bourgeois individuals [American Trotskyites] has one aim—to discredit revolutionary theory and revolutionary practice. . . . These people have nothing but hatred—hatred for the living revolutionary movement of the masses, hatred for an organized Bolshevik Party that heads the revolutionary movement, hatred for democratic centralism which guarantees a maximum of force with a maximum of initiative from below in a Bolshevik Party, hatred for the prototype of Bolshevism—the Communist Party of the U.S.S.R., hatred for the leaders of that Party, and hatred for the Communist International.

In the name of "Communism" they speak the same language as Hamilton Fish, Matthew Woll, William Randolph Hearst, and Abraham Cahan.

That hatred leads by inexorable logic "to the decision of some inflamed follower to kill the leaders of the revolution." Many other people, named elsewhere in the book, are also filled with hatred; Olgin seemed unable to envision any non-Communist otherwise than as consumed with hatred for Communists. The capitalist world in general, he wrote, was "full of malice and venom, hates and fears." Of course, the more hatred for the Party that a Party writer perceived in his targets, the more hatred he was duty-bound to feel toward them. Or would it be more accurate to say that the more hatred he felt toward them, the more he perceived them as hating the Party (in contradistinction to merely opposing and fighting it)? The rank-and-file reader was supposed to see only cool rationality in Olgin's characterization of the Fourth (Trotskyite) International as this hodge-podge of reformist and Trotskyite degenerates, this pack of disgruntled intellectuals aching to be mass leaders, this medley of sentiments, wishes, opinions, programs, "plans" all eaten through with hypocrisy, all covering up reformism with high-sounding "revolutionary" and "Marxist" phrases, all intended to convey something different from what the principal figures actually believe—this concoction which is only besmirching the name Communist, is advanced as that international body which is destined to win away the workers of the world from the Communist International.

Party members did see such screeds as objective statements of fact—this I can testify to by firsthand experience. The readers' feeling toward expellees was, supposedly, a rational response to "objective" enemies. In other words, the Communist reacted to these documents differently from the way an outsider would have who did not share that feeling, much less rationalize it by theory.[8]

That Trotskyism was merely the occasion for expression of a general hatred is proven by the presence of the latter before the Stalin-Trotsky split: the *Young Worker* during the 1920s, for example, viciously attacked a host of other enemies, including clergymen, and rejoiced at the death of Woodrow Wilson. Almost anyone could serve as target. The Catholic author of a novel reviewed in the *New Masses* was an

isolated young neurotic hugging his miseries and raveling his maladjustments in the monotonous twilight of the disintegrating Church, [who] panders to the hatreds and vices of a ruling minority which has glutted itself with the chattels of a material world while postulating at the same time the ecstasy of merging with a non-material Absolute. The Church whistles in the dark and hopes to be heard by the fascist barbarians, who are sufficiently "civilized" to recognize the advantage of having a worthy ally in lifting the swag.

Two prominent writers during the 1930s were "the slimy J. Donald Adams" and "the still slimier Malcolm Muggeridge," and the grand old man of the Socialist Party was "the slimy American Socialist, Morris Hillquit." The anti-Stalinist Left magazine *The New Leader* was "that sty of Republicans, Trotskyites and Social-Democrats."[9] And so on.

These personal characterizations illustrate the Party's habit of equating a person with his beliefs and "objective role." This is why the Party's scholars had the right to include ad hominem insults whenever they refuted the works of adversary scholars (the eminent historian Allan Nevins wrote "undoubtedly with one eye on his bankbook," and Sidney Hook was asked "Do they pay that well, Professor?") and why critics of union leaders had the right to attack them personally (David Livingston was a "foul-mouthed renegade" and the A. F. of L. leaders were invariably "corrupt").[10] It also explains what some outsiders have found inexplicable: the vilification of Browder in May, 1945, by people who had worshiped him in April. Surely John Gates could have proved his orthodoxy without writing that "Browder's latest writings and diatribes" were "degenerate . . . outpourings of filth . . . which pour out of Browder like pus from gangrene."[11]

One purpose of this equation of a target with his objective role was to make the rank and filer afraid not to adopt a new line or not to believe in one of the Party's tenets. Consider, for example, the Party's switch on the question of universal military training (called "UMT"). The Party favored UMT during the war but denounced it after the cold war began. In 1944, one George Zuckerman wrote a letter to *Spotlight* arguing against the AYD's endorsement of UMT. His letter was brief, reasonable, and unvituperative— in every respect unlike the reply by Robert Thompson, then the co-chairman of the AYD. Thompson first attacked Zuckerman's pacifism and his argument that military training fostered indifference to killing. Then he said that Zuckerman's argument "serves fascism whether it is consciously intended to do so or not," evidently considering it possible that Zuckerman consciously intended to do so. Then came the "theoretical" rationale:

We differ with the pacifists in that we do not "tolerate" the military training which is enabling young Americans to help save this world from becoming a fascist hell. *We glory in that military training.* . . . Universal conscription for youth for a minimum of military training as a permanent feature of American life was publicly proposed by George Washington as early as 1783. . . . Jefferson championed obligatory military training. . . . President Lincoln fought for and applied a system of universal conscription in the Civil War. . . . The brightest chapter in our tradition of universal conscription is the thoroughly democratic Selective Service Act now in operation. . . . [American youth] are going to see that this war stays won. . . . May God help those who think and plan otherwise.

If poor Zuckerman needed any more convincing, the editor of *Spotlight* clinched the argument by placing him in unsavory company: "In the dark corners of America where treason lurks voices are being raised against the establishment of postwar universal compulsory military training." But of course it was Jimmy Higgins, not Zuckerman, at whom this message was aimed. By the spring of 1952 the United States had resumed being an imperialist threat, and now the Party's youth periodical intoned, "The designs of the Truman administration for war, their immorality, their utter disregard for the wishes of the American people, their willingness to sacrifice a whole nation for the sake of profits was clearly shown in their latest proposal, a bill calling for universal military training."[12] Gone were the invocations of Washington, Jefferson, and Lincoln. But not gone was the resort to loaded, ad hominem epithets signaling to the readers: Direct your animus this way, not that way.

The reason the UMT issue illustrates how irrelevant any particular issue was to the hatred is that, both before and after 1946, non-Communists' arguments on both sides involved a variety of motives and philosophical principles. During the war some advocates of UMT were anti-Soviet and some were pro-Soviet; some opponents of UMT were pacifists and some were not. And after the start of the cold war the pacifists, who of course remained opposed to UMT, were not necessarily anti-Soviet or anti-American. But in both periods the Party polemicized indiscriminately against everyone on the "wrong" side. It rationalized its animosity by means of the theory of "objective historical role," which enabled it to homogenize all people who disagreed with the current line. On this issue, as on all others, it assumed that everyone perceived the facts exactly as it did. Only rarely did Party writers impute honest error to someone who disagreed. Their flipflop on the UMT issue, then, strengthens the hunch that the person who equates error with sin is emotionally unable to tolerate disagreement, and that when he adds a moral dimension to the disagreement he is rationalizing a hostility that he cannot help feeling.

Howe and Coser tell of an episode in a San Francisco union local in 1938, which illustrates this point. The Communist leaders had been ousted by a rank-and-file progressive group, and when Molly Goldberg, one of the latter, criticized Harry Bridges, a Communist "took the floor to say—the sentence should be engraved as a classical contribution toward the understanding of Communist psychology—that he now appreciated the Moscow trials: 'In Russia traitors like Goldberg are lined up against a wall and shot.' "[13] It is hard to believe that that person, as an individual, could have evoked such lethal hatred (any more than Bella Dodd could); she was merely a symbol for a "category"—left-wing non-Communists. Party theory here transformed hatred, which "bourgeois" culture regarded as a vice, into a virtue.

The chief significance of the writings sampled above is that they transmuted emotion into theory and then theory back into emotion. It is true that when the developed Communist asked the developing comrade "what would you expect from the class enemy?" he was saying that the Communist must expect atrocious behavior of the class enemies (capitalists, Trotskyites, expellees, and so on). If he exploded in anger, he was showing surprise, and this meant he had not mastered the theory that predicted the behavior. Nevertheless, hatred sometimes boiled over, whether spontaneously or by design. The theory, in short, played a dual role: it rationalized and channeled the hatred, but by the same means *it gave the member permission to hate*. The developed rank and filer, or even the novice of Type I, did not see emotion in many of the documents that impress outsiders as being filled with it. What he saw were statements of fact. Hate meeting its own expression may not recognize itself as such; and in the Party it was easily disguised as theoretical understanding meeting correct theory.

That theory took a back seat to feeling is shown in the Party's most common accusations of all: that such-and-such a person was a fascist and that the American capitalist class wanted fascism. Communists were the world's most fastidious sticklers for correct terminology. Their Party had a "scientific" definition of fascism, furnished by Georgi Dimitroff: "the open terrorist dictatorship of the most reactionary, most chauvinistic and most imperialist elements of finance capital. . . . Fascism is the power of finance capital itself," not an inevitable stage in the evolution of capitalism but a policy that that portion of the capitalist class adopts when the bourgeoisie can no longer "maintain its dictatorship over the masses by the old methods of bourgeois democracy and parliamentarianism," owing to the radicalization of the proletariat and poor farmers. Fascism therefore results not from the strength but from the weakness of the bourgeoisie.[14] American Party literature contained countless complaints about the Party's weakness and admissions that the workers were still enthralled by bourgeois ideology; in Dimitroff's terms, then, the rulers had no need for fascism. Yet the literature often called the American capitalist class as a whole, and its agents, fascist. "Fascist" thus served as an all-purpose epithet, that is, an expression of hatred rather than a scientific designation. People labeled fascists included Charles de Gaulle, William Randolph Hearst, a justice of the New York State Supreme Court, Governor Eugene Talmadge of Georgia, Elinor Wylie, the Daughters of the American Revolution, the American Legion, local patriots who prevented Mike Gold from delivering a speech, Bernarr McFadden, a number of unnamed American trade-union leaders, the Veterans of Foreign Wars, and Grover Whalen (a New York City official).[15]

The emotional, rather than scientific, source of these characterizations can be inferred from passages such as that in the *Young Worker* of May, 1930, which called Grover Whalen "one of the Fascist chiefs who with the American Legion is on a crusade against the 'Reds' in New York City. The workers will know how to deal with Mr. Whalen when the time comes." And, it added on March 27, 1934, "only with the aim of deceiving and disarming the workers, social-democracy denies the fasciszation of bourgeois-democracy, making a distinction in principle between the democratic countries and the countries of the fascist dictatorship." Dimitroff was careful to make that very distinction a year later, and the Party widened it still more during World War II. Although we may be sure that the writer of that passage went along with the line, his own spontaneous hatred for American society was more accurately expressed in his homogenization of all nonsocialist countries.

The same observation pertains to the comrades' feelings about people. One of the Party's chief philosophers, for instance, admitted that John Dewey was not a fascist but said his theories led logically, step by step, to a justification of a "religion-centered theocratic society, which revival at this time would be a fitting ideology for a fascist corporate state."[16] This was the same logic by which Olgin had proved that Trotsky wanted to assassinate Stalin, and by which Bella Dodd's judges had viewed her as an enemy of mankind. Up to the moment of her trial, she had done nothing whatever to harm the Party. Why then did they hate her so much?

PHILIP SELZNICK suggests an answer: the need for symbolic targets of hatred, as a means of fostering loyalty to the Party. Furthermore, since the Party was an army locked in mortal combat with the enemy of all humanity, to leave it was to desert the battlefield.[17] Both these hypotheses are supported by the sources, but they pose a chicken-and-egg question: did the Party impute world-historic significance to itself, to its every act and pronouncement, to the lowliest comrade's most trivial thought and action, in order to justify its equally great hostility toward enemies? Or did it foster such enormous hostility because of the enormity of the enemy and the world-historic significance of its own role? Probably both generalizations are true, but the documents give priority to the first.

Both processes came into play in a situation described by Selznick: "party work in his place of employment offers the individual the opportunity to invest an often routine and emotionally unrewarding job with a moral significance. His job takes on a new meaning, that of the struggle for power, adding new and often welcome responsibilities and status."[18] This helps us to understand a Type I person, with general hostility needing a focus, and working for a fairminded employer. The Party linked that employer to a hated bourgeoisie, and the Communist employee to the bourgeoisie's destined destroyer. "The bourgeoisie" was too abstract to focus the hostility. By perceiving his relationship to his boss as an encounter between two world-historic forces, the Party member could channel the hostility in the boss's direction with a clear conscience and at the same time find the daily routine in the shop meaningful. Of course, his coworkers were mystified by that hostility toward an unoffending boss, but the same theory attributed their lack of hatred to false consciousness.

All movements of ideological zealots use propaganda to incite their followers to action and to hostility toward their adversaries. The more significance they impute to their cause, the more dangerous to humanity they believe the opposition is. Sometimes hatred results, but I have encountered the same tone, the same intensity of hatred, only in the writings of National Socialist, racist (black as well as white), anti-Semitic, and anti-Catholic movements. In all five of those "causes," members' feelings are engaged more by what they oppose than by what they favor. Was that true of the Communists? It would seem not; their literature abounds in visions of the good future society in the United States and in idyllic descriptions of the Soviet Union, to a far greater degree than the corresponding positive element appears in the writings of any of those other movements. There is, perhaps, a way to explain the difference: The others rejected basic American values, whereas Communists professed to be the heirs and destined realizers of those values. This is why Type II radicals—whose main motivation was expressed in the positive elements in the Party's ideology—could be Communists. But it is also why Type I comrades could find in the Party permission to hate.

That permission came from the highest authority. The series of Soviet show trials furnished the model. They even furnished some of the American Communists' most common locutions. Yehoshua A. Gilboa's study of *The Black Years of Soviet Jewry, 1939–1953*, for example, quotes some of them. Before the defendants in the Doctors' Plot trial had even been convicted, a *Pravda* editorial denounced them under the title "Foul Spies and Murderers," and it said that "the bosses of the U.S.A. and their British junior partners" were "feverishly preparing for a new world war." The editorial also contained epithets such as "despised degenerates," "rotten degenerates," and "loathsome vermin."[19] "Feverishly" and "frenzied" were very common American CP descriptions of capitalists—as in "feverishly planning war" and "frenzied drive toward war and fascism." Both the vocabulary and the intensity of the emotion it expressed were justified by the Party's foreign mentors.

This was only logical, since in the American Communist's mind the Soviet traitors and home-grown enemies were interchangeable. The crimes of the former helped to rationalize his hatred for the latter; and the crimes of the latter reinforced his belief in the guilt of the former. Together the two sorts of enemies formed the troops of a single, worldwide conspiracy, the general staff of which was the American ruling class. The American CP therefore was uniquely privileged: it was the only CP in the world that lived and worked within the enemy's home camp. This fact gave world-historic significance to every American Communist, every individual enemy, and every act committed by either of them. Clearly, one of the most attractive features of the Soviet Union was that the Communists there had the power to liquidate the enemies. I refer to something more than mere vengefulness, the wish to settle scores, although that was certainly present. The more glorious the Soviet Union was, the more evil its enemies had to be. So the idealization of the Soviet Union (to be discussed in a later chapter) nourished Jimmy Higgins's tendency to regard himself as both very important and surrounded by plotting enemies. The wish to settle personal scores could be disguised *and* justified by the image of the Soviet Union that required the Soviet Party to liquidate its own enemies. In Jimmy Higgins's mind, the enemies abroad and at home merged, and so did the existing Soviet Party and the future American Party.

The proper naming of the target was the spell that released the arrow of hate. When an ordinary person hates his boss, his hatred is as specific as the act that elicited it. The Party member hated his boss for being "the boss"; that the boss happened to be a certain individual was an unimportant accident of circumstances, and in fact the comrade might have agreed that that man was a decent person who treated his employees well. The Communist who hated William Randolph Hearst may never have seen a Hearst newspaper; the name "Hearst" was a shorthand expression for "propagandist for reaction." The average Communist never read a word written by Arthur Koestler, but he was conditioned to seethe with hatred at the mention of the name and could never bring himself to glance at *Darkness at Noon*. It was certainly not Koestler or any particular writing of his that raised the Communist's gorge. "Arthur Koestler" was a purgative that brought up a quantity of general venom. The same is true of the terms "Trotskyite," "renegade," "Social Democrat," "Schachtmanite," "Cannonite," "fascist," and so on.[20]

Party writers needed only to attach one of those labels to a certain person's name, and though that person had been a friend, a comrade, even a spouse, the rank and filer's feelings toward him or her were changed forever. Most people can like, even love, others who disagree with them; the ideological zealot cannot. With him, doctrine intervenes in his encounter with another person and tells him how to feel. A change in belief can make him drop his positive feelings in an instant and be flooded with hatred. But if comradeship, admiration, love, friendship can change in a flash to hatred, what was the nature of the original feeling? It must have been based largely on ideas; that is, not only enemies but friends too were deindividualized, defined as members of categories.[21] Permission to hate is the other side of permission to love. But beneath both feelings, and beneath the ideas and theories, lay an animus seeking targets.

An incident related by one of Vivian Gornick's informants illustrates this point in reverse. This man was distributing Party leaflets one cold night on the Lower East Side of New York. "All I had on," he recalled, "was a thin jacket." An old, poorly dressed woman came up out of the subway and, seeing him, cursed him in Yiddish and continued on her way. But then she turned back and, taking her scarf from her neck, said, " 'Bubbela, . . . what are you doing, dressed like that on a night like this? You'll get pneumonia.' And she wound the scarf around my neck."[22] That old woman was taking pity on a fellow human being, knowing he was a Communist. She had the capacity to see the person separately from his beliefs. No Communist would have given her scarf to a shivering Trotskyite handing out leaflets on a winter night.

In the ideological style of thinking, people and actions lost their individuality; they were defined by the labels they wore. For example, a theoretical error, if committed by a fellow-traveling liberal, usually elicited a friendly criticism,[23] but if committed by an anti-Soviet liberal, the same error became evidence of his depravity. If a black murdered a white person, he was protesting against oppression, but if a white murdered a black, he was manifesting the degeneracy of our culture. The murder was never just murder; it had no moral significance in itself. Nothing was what it seemed to be; everything was a sign of something else, which the science of Marxism-Leninism revealed to the adept. Consequently, in an unfamiliar situation the rank and filer did not react to data on their own terms; he first found out how to categorize them and only then felt free to interpret them. He was responding not to the data themselves but to the familiar categories, which switched on the correct responses. Thus, what appear to be intellectual judgments were actually moral judgments. What appear to be cognitive categories were really moral-emotional categories, which came in pairs: We versus Them, the People (and the Party as their vanguard) versus the Enemy; the Good versus the Bad; the Future versus the Past.

The hatred displayed in the sources is thus inextricably linked with doctrinal totalism. The Party's totalistic ideology covered every aspect of life, thought, and feeling. It gave meaning to every act however trivial. The believer felt uncomfortable if he did or thought or felt anything that he could not connect to the ideology. He could identify an enemy by a trivial word or deed, because it was necessarily an element in the totality. There were no neutrals, no middle ground. Lenin himself said so: there were only proletarian and bourgeois ideologies; there was no third kind.

Totalism in theory implied total responsibility shouldered by each rank and filer. Party writings repeatedly told Jimmy Higgins that everything he did contributed to or impeded the struggle for socialism and that momentous consequences hung on his carrying out his "tasks." It told him: You, the rank and filer, will determine the whole course of history. No matter how humble your task, it is an integral part of the total movement of humanity toward the glorious future, and if you fail in your task, you will set humanity back in its struggle.

All the themes we have been discussing—the world-historic significance of trivial acts, the total responsibility shouldered by each individual Communist, totalism in ideology, permission to hate disguised as cold rationality as well as by love for the people, verbal triggers of hatred, and the deindividualization of human beings—are discernible in a remark by V. J. Jerome in the October, 1937, issue of *The Communist*:

It is from Marx we inherit the quality of fierce partisanship rising from objective historic[al] analysis; his writings live today not as disembodied, cold philosophy, but, because of their intensive scientific objectivity, bright with the fires of hatred for the oppressors, which is but the other aspect of love for the working class and its vanguard.

Someone who believed all these propositions could find no stopping place between mild dislike and murderous hatred, if the object was labeled "enemy." There was no Party tenet, cognitive or ethical, that Bella Dodd could have invoked that would have condemned her ex-comrades' killing her if they had the power and desire to do so. Lenin himself had said that Communists disapproved of terrorism and assassination only on grounds of expediency, not of ethics. "Those orgies of venom" that according to Howe and Coser "seemed a necessity of . . . [Mike Gold's] soul"[24] were not a necessity for all the members' souls and were not obligatory, but they were permissible, for Party theory gave such people permission to hate. To such members as the one who threatened Grover Whalen with retribution "when the time comes" and the other who wished Molly Goldberg shot, the Party said, in effect: Their blood will not be on your hands; your hate for them is really love for the people and their vanguard; it will all be scientific and impersonal; the Party ratifies your hatred now and will be your proxy in acting it out when the time comes.

Permission to hate was implied not only by the Party's doctrinal totalism but also by its institutional totalism. All other organizations claimed only parts of their members' loyalties, leaving other parts to be claimed by family, neighborhood, church or synagogue, fraternal organizations, unions, and other institutions. For its members, however, the Party superseded them all, individually and combined. When it did so, it also replaced the other institutions' moral guidelines with its own. For the Party member, therefore, doctrinal authority, institutional authority, and moral authority were concentrated in one place as they were for no other Americans except members of celibate religious orders.

We should link these facts to the previously mentioned belief in the world-historic significance of the Party: Bella Dodd's ex-comrades saw themselves and her as rivals in shaping the course of history. Whatever the personal springs of their hatred of her, their theory justified it. They were not a handful of unimportant people meeting in a dingy hall in Manhattan; they were representatives, respectively, of the salvation and of the damnation of the human race. The slippery-slope logic that Olgin used—to pass from Trotsky's denial that socialism was possible in one country, to the inevitability of Trotskyites' assassination plots against Stalin, and his own (Olgin's) perception of hatred everywhere around him—the same logic condemned Bella Dodd for merely doubting.

NOTES

1. Bella V. Dodd, *School of Darkness* (New York: P. J. Kenedy & Sons, 1954), pp. 218–19, 224. A significant detail of this passage may be overlooked: When Dodd suddenly saw those people as a bunch of shabby nonentities rather than as representatives of a world-historic movement, she was showing that she had lost a crucial ingredient of the true believer's mentality. She now saw reality plain, instead of through an ideological haze.

2. Frank S. Meyer, *The Moulding of Communists* (New York: Harcourt, Brace, 1961), pp. 73–74.

3. Sam Pevzner, "My Country 'Tis of Thee," *YW*, November 23, 1931, p. 5. The patriotic songs such as *Ballad for Americans*, *This Land Is Your Land*, and so on, that the Party favored after World War II were more subtle than Pevzner's parody; they expressed love for the land and the common people and a faith that the people would one day repossess their country from the exploiters and corrupters.

4. Herbert Aptheker, "Hustlers for War," *MM* 2 (May, 1949): 27; Aptheker, "The Filthy Rich" (first published in 1953), in his *History and Reality* (New York: Cameron Associates, 1955), p. 112; Aptheker, "The Informer System and Justice," ibid., p. 248; William Z. Foster, *The Twilight of World Capitalism* (New York: IP,

1949), pp. 39–41. On p. 37 Foster likens "American imperialism" to "a monstrous, all-consuming spider."

5. Aptheker, *History and Reality*, pp. 91–92. This is one of the mildest passages in the chapter, all of which (see pp. 89–103) was devoted to Hook. A few sample quotations here would not convey the sustained tone of snarling sarcasm and ad hominem viciousness on page after page. Among the many other attacks on Hook are: Aptheker, "Hustlers for War," pp. 22–25; Don Merit, "Sidney Hook: McCarran Stooge," *NF* 6 (January-February, 1952): 12–13; Max Young, "Sharpen the Fight for the Central Slogan of the World Communist Party—Soviet Power!" *COM* 14 (January, 1935): 51–52; L. Rudas (a professor of philosophy at the Institute of Red Professors in Moscow), "The Meaning of Sidney Hook," *COM* 14 (April, 1935): 326–49; V. J. Jerome, "A Year of 'Jewish Life,' " *COM* 17 (September, 1938): 854. Hints as to the reason for this venom can be found in Robert W. Iversen, *The Communists and the Schools* (New York: Harcourt, Brace, 1959), pp. 196–97.

6. E.g., see Aptheker, *History and Reality*, pp. 58, 224, 239; Herbert Aptheker, *Laureates of Imperialism: Big Business Re-Writes American History* (New York: Masses & Mainstream, 1954), pp. 88–89; Herbert Aptheker, *The Truth about Hungary* (New York: Mainstream Publishers, 1957), p. 105; Earl Browder, *Social and National Security* (New York: Workers Library, 1938), p. 39; Robert Minor, "Workers' Education and the War against Hitler," *COM* 20 (November, 1941): 974–75. The equations here are of Hitler, Pareto, and Mosca with Walter Lippmann; Goebbels with President Truman; Goebbels with Whittaker Chambers; Mussolini and Hitler with Senator Pat McCarran and William Randolph Hearst; Mussolini and Hitler with Dwight Macdonald, Raymond English, William Barrett, Reinhold Niebuhr, Peter Viereck, Will Herberg, and Bishop Fulton J. Sheen; Mussolini, Hitler, Franco, and Goebbels with David Sarnoff; Hitler, Mussolini, and "the Mikado" with Norman Thomas; and Hitler with Trotskyites and Lovestoneites.

7. Mac Weiss, "We Are for a Principled United Front," *YW*, September 25, 1934, p. 6; "Death Penalty Demanded!" *YW*, November 27, 1930, p. 4; "Review of the Month," *COM* 15 (September, 1936): 813 (paragraphing has been ignored).

8. M. J. Olgin, *Trotskyism: Counter-Revolution in Disguise* (New York: Workers Library, 1935), pp. 22, 135, 24, 142–43, and passim. For interesting comments on this mentality, see Stanley Rothman and S. Robert Lichter, *Roots of Radicalism: Jews, Christians, and the New Left* (New York: Oxford University Press, 1982), p. 153.

9. Peter Martin, review of Erik v. Kuhnelt-Leddihn, *The Gates of Hell*, in *NM*, May 1, 1934, p. 25; Joseph Freeman, "Critics in Mufti," *NM*, June 5, 1934, p. 21; "Socialists in 1917 Helped Bosses Drag Young Workers into World War," *YW*, July 28, 1930, p. 4; Aptheker, "Hustlers for War," p. 23.

10. Bernice Rose and Jack Haywood, "Historians against Labor: Poison in Our Texts," *NF* 5 (Fall, 1951): 12; Aptheker, *History and Reality*, pp. 90–91; Alex H. Kendrick and Jerome Golden, "Lessons of the Struggle against Opportunism in District 65," *PA* 32 (June, 1953): 26; and various places scattered throughout the literature, esp. by Foster, on "corrupt" A. F. of L. leaders.

11. John Gates, *On Guard against Browderism[,] Titoism[,] Trotskyism* (New York: New Century, 1951), pp. 5, 10. Gates resumed cordial relations with Browder after he himself left the Party.

12. *SP* 2 (February, 1944): 28–29 (note, by the way, Thompson's highly unscientific invocation of the name of God, another obvious instance of the use of religious termi-

nology to express extreme hostility); "From the Editor" (Claudia Jones), *SP* 2 (April, 1944): 2; Jack Cohen, "UMT: The People Win a Round," *NF* 5 (Spring, 1952): 6.

13. Irving Howe and Lewis Coser, *The American Communist Party: A Critical History* (1957; New York: Frederick A. Praeger, 1962), p. 384.

14. Georgi Dimitroff, *United Front against Fascism* (New York: New Century, 1935), pp. 7, 6. Fascists differed from social-fascists. Socialists were called social-fascists during the early 1930s when the Party was in one of its far-left swings. Illustrations of this label can be found in every issue of every Party publication during that period. Unlike "fascist," "social-fascist" was used precisely and "scientifically."

15. See, e.g., among many documents: William Z. Foster, *History of the Communist Party of the United States* (New York: IP, 1952), p. 464; Mike Gold, *Change the World!* (New York, IP, 1936), pp. 38, 125, 150, 185, 192, 201, 229, 247; A. B. Magil, "Earl Browder, People's Teacher," *NM*, August 5, 1941, p. 6; "The Work of Our Trade Union Fractions," *PO* 3 (June-July, 1930): 22; "Fascists on May Day," *YW*, May 1, 1930, p. 2; "Chief Cossack Whalen," ibid., p. 4. See also Elizabeth Gurley Flynn's calling fascist *Modern Woman: The Lost Sex*, by Ferdinand Lundberg and Marynia F. Farnham, in *PA* 26 (March, 1947): 218, and (April, 1947): 376–81 (in both locations Flynn misspells Farnham's name, in different ways). In the latter place, a review of the book, Flynn calls it "487 pages of chicanery" and other dreadful things, in vituperative, even hysterical, language. "It is hateful and contemptuous of women, snarling and mean in tone, downright lewd in language. It has the ugly face of fascism. Hitler is its logical forerunner." And so on.

16. Harry K. Wells, *Pragmatism: Philosophy of Imperialism* (New York: IP, 1954), p. 178.

17. Philip Selznick, *The Organizational Weapon* (New York: Free Press, 1960), pp. 45, 29.

18. Ibid., p. 48.

19. Yehoshua A. Gilboa, *The Black Years of Soviet Jewry, 1939–1953* (Boston: Little, Brown, 1971), pp. 294–96.

20. A related point is illustrated by William Z. Foster, *American Trade Unionism* (New York: IP, 1947), p. 297: "the trade unions should be especially keen to checkmate those elements, such as Lewisites, Trotskyites, Coughlinites, Thomasites, etc."; and p. 302: "the Hoovers, Lindberghs, Hearsts, Byrds, Reynoldses, Dieses, Pattersons, Hoffmans, Howards, Kaltenborns, Peglers, Coughlins, Smiths, Norman Thomases and John L. Lewises, etc." were "fifth-column and near–fifth column elements." The *ites*es and plural forms sent the message that these people were merely representatives of categories.

21. See Meyer, *Moulding of Communists*, pp. 129–30.

22. Vivian Gornick, *The Romance of American Communism* (New York: Basic Books, 1977), pp. 122–23.

23. Usually, not always. The theoretical labels could rationalize purely personal antagonism even within the Party. For example, Dodd describes Benjamin Davis's viciousness toward other leaders who disagreed with him; all he had to do was call them white chauvinists or, if black, Uncle Toms. See Dodd, *School of Darkness*, pp. 180–86, 189.

24. V. I. Lenin, *"Left-Wing" Communism, An Infantile Disorder* (New York: IP, 1940), p. 18; Howe and Coser, *American Communist Party*, p. 400. For interesting

comments on the general theme of this chapter, see Igor Shafarevich, *The Socialist Phenomenon* (New York: Harper & Row, 1980), p.185; and Alain Besançon, *The Rise of the Gulag: Intellectual Origins of Leninism* (New York: Continuum, 1981), pp. 211, 217, 234.

5

Authority I:
Leadership and Self-Image

A NEW MEMBER of any organization is bound to feel diffident and to accept on faith things he does not understand. "Soon," he tells himself, "I'll be an insider, and I'll know." The Party recruit might have added: "In time I'll understand something here that I've never come up against in any other secular organization I've belonged to: the strange etiquette, the extreme deference that my fellow club members accord to visiting higher-ups, some of whom don't even hold office but are called 'cadres.' " Before long, he realized that the deference reflected the Party's structure and that those who would not defer soon became ex-members. To trace Jimmy Higgins's growing commitment to the Party, we should examine those aspects of its structure and writings that most impressed him at first and guided his adjustment to it. They can all be grouped under the general heading of "authority." In this chapter we shall examine the structural aspects of this authority and how they both reflected and shaped Party members' self-image; in the next chapter we shall examine the authority of the Party's doctrine.

To be temperamentally suited to stay in the Party meant, among other things, to be predisposed to accept what Frank Meyer calls "a state of tutelage"; even the cadre, he says, had the feeling of being in that state, throughout their years in the Party.[1] A large proportion of Party members were young people to whom the Party offered a way-station on the road to adulthood. Having rebelled against their parents' authority, they were not quite ready to stand on their own. The enormous turnover of membership each year can be accounted for in part by their growing up; just as Daddy had shrunk to human size earlier, so did the Party's leaders later. For other members, the state of tutelage lasted much longer. Bella Dodd recalled that her blind faith in the leaders and the Soviet Union was the last spell to be broken as she detached herself emotionally from the Party.[2] For the lifelong members, the state of tutelage never ended.

Long before the member grasped the meaning of the deference to authority, he was bombarded by evidences of it. The Party deliberately fostered dependence on authority. Almost every issue of *Party Organizer* featured a quotation from a Communist authority on its cover. M. J. Olgin gave detailed instructions in *New Masses* on how to read certain Soviet books and how to think about them. Whenever William Z. Foster published a book, one of the periodicals published a "study outline" subdivided by topics and subtopics and questions and answers. The most blatant sign of the "tutelage" status was the incredible glorification of leaders. The Party had its own versions of George Washington and the cherry tree and of Abraham Lincoln walking miles through the snow to return the penny. This genre must be quoted at length to convey its cumulative impact on the true believer.

First, however, it should be observed that Marx and Engels did not receive such extreme adulation. True, their image showed no warts, but neither did it show a halo. I recall a large portrait of Marx in the office of a teacher in the Jefferson School; under the frame was the label "Founder of the Firm." No comrade would have treated Stalin with such levity. In most nations and churches, the degree of hero-worship matches the length of time the hero has been dead; in the Communist world the reverse was true. Lenin evoked more intense feeling than Marx, and Stalin more than Lenin. The idol had to be alive or recently alive—that is, a "father" or "grandfather"—to receive the adoration illustrated in the following documents.

Paeans to Stalin appeared throughout the period of his rulership; the following are typical.

In 1935 Stalin was

the fighter who, together with Lenin, steered the October revolution, . . . [t]he great strategist of the civil war, whose plan of military action, quickly and decisively executed, brought about the decisive victory on a front of several hundred miles in South Russia over the White forces of General Denikin, . . . [t]he author of the Five-Year Plan, a momentous undertaking on an unheard-of scale, setting one hundred and sixty million people to work on the task of remaking one-sixth of the earth's surface according to a certain social design, . . . [t]he fearless leader who always fights ideological battles against opportunism, who detects hidden opportunism no matter how cleverly disguised, who in the very early stages of the Trotsky opposition predicted with astounding clarity that it is to become the "rallying point of non-proletarian elements which are trying to disintegrate the dictatorship of the proletariat," . . . [t]he builder of the life of minority nationalities in the U.S.S.R., the man who worked out the practical problems of the Leninist solution of the national problem and has directed the building of Socialism in a manner to create a rich, colorful, many-sided cultural life among one hundred nationalities differing in economic development, language, history, customs, tradition, but united in common work for a beautiful future, . . . [t]he world leader whose every advice to every Party of the Comintern on every problem is correct, clear, balanced, and points the way to new, more decisive class battles.[3]

Each of the ellided passages in this document denounces Trotsky. Here as elsewhere the worship of Stalin matched the vilification of the current anti-Stalin.

In 1937 Browder wrote that the Party's "practical work must be more illuminated by the theory of Marx, Engels, Lenin and Stalin—those greatest educators of the people known to history, the leaders of the realization of socialism."[4] This grouping of the four Authorities is typical; Marx and Engels appear most frequently in the company of their two main apostles. In fact, one gets the impression that Marx and Engels received their status from their association with Lenin and Stalin rather than vice versa.[5]

In 1940 a writer in *Clarity* needed capital letters to express his feeling:

EVERY ONE OF COMRADE STALIN'S UTTERANCES IS A MIGHTY SEARCHLIGHT LIGHTING UP THE PATH OF THE REVOLUTIONARY YOUTH MOVEMENT, AND FILLS THE HEARTS OF THE YOUTH WITH FAITH IN THE VICTORY OF THE WORKING CLASS. . . . The young workers and toilers of the capitalist countries who are groaning under the yoke of capitalism look with great love and hope to Comrade Stalin, the leader of the world proletariat and the great continuer of the cause of Marx, Engels and Lenin. They see and know that the people of the Soviet Union, whose happy life is for them a bright beacon, are indebted to the Bolshevik Party and its great leader, Comrade Stalin, for the flourishing of their youth and their happiness. Stalin rears the young generation like a careful, experienced gardener.[6]

In 1941, Stalin, "genius of socialist construction," was "this greatest man of our era. . . . With every passing hour the titanic figure of this magnificent leader becomes more inextricably bound up with the very destiny of world humanity." He was also "the greatest scientist of all."[7]

In 1943, he represented

the historic interpenetration and synthesis of the individual and the progressive society, of the "accidental" and the necessary. The greatness of Stalin is not only an individual, private greatness, it is the greatness of Soviet society, of the people who built that powerful bulwark of the democratic world. Stalin is the true forward-looking son of his epoch—the epoch of man's struggle for a higher democracy. Basing himself on the economic and political realities; rooted in the people, especially the working class and its Party; and guided by Leninist theory, the individually gifted and socially endowed fighter for freedom, Joseph Dzhugashvili, became Joseph Stalin.[8]

In 1949 Alexander Bittelman proclaimed that "what Stalin means to the world is what the Great October Revolution means to the world." More controversial were two other statements:

Stalin will be honored by the Jewish masses in the United States—for his historic contributions to the solution of the national question in general and of the Jewish question in particular, for his leadership in the fight against anti-Semitism, for outlawing anti-Semitism, for full equality of rights for the Jewish masses, for his world leadership in the fight against fascism, for his leadership in the defeat and military destruction of Nazi-fascism in the last war;

and

Stalin's greatness and genius stand out so clearly and beautifully that progressive humanity has no difficulty in recognizing them.... To live with Stalin in one age, to fight with him in one cause, to work under the inspiring guidance of his teachings is something to be deeply proud of and thankful for, to cherish.

Another article in the same issue of *Political Affairs* quoted from a Soviet-published biography of Stalin:

his work is extraordinary for its variety, his energy truly amazing. The range of questions which engage his attention is immense, embracing complex problems of Marxist-Leninist theory and school textbooks; problems of Soviet foreign policy and the municipal affairs of Moscow, the proletarian capital; the development of the Great Northern Sea Route and the reclamation of the Colchian marshes; the advancement of Soviet literature and art and the editing of the model rules for collective farms; and, lastly, the solution of most intricate theoretical and practical problems in the science of warfare.

Everybody is familiar with the cogent and invincible force of Stalin's logic, the crystal clarity of his mind, his iron will, his devotion to the party, his ardent faith in the people, and love for the people. Everybody is familiar with his modesty, his simplicity of manner, his consideration for people, and his merciless severity toward enemies of the people.[9]

The April, 1953, issue of *Political Affairs* published tributes by leading American Communists to the fallen leader. To Elizabeth Gurley Flynn he was "the best loved man on earth of our time.... No tyrant, no dictator, would be so loved by the people." To Betty Gannett, he was "the beloved leader of working humanity."[10] And an ad listing Stalin's works on the back cover of that issue exhorted the reader to "Read, Study, Discuss The Great *Life-Giving* Teachings of Joseph Stalin" (italics added).

All this showed not simply Stalin-worship, but a mode of thinking, for most of the American CP leaders were also eulogized at one time or another— on their birthdays or when they published major books, went on trial, went to prison, or died.[11] Naturally, the top leaders received the greatest adulation. To Joseph North, Foster was

the Communist man, prevision of tomorrow's generation of American. His Odyssey as class-conscious worker, labor leader, strike organizer, to leading Communist—the foremost theoretician of Marxism-Leninism in this country as well as the greatest strategist and tactician our working class has produced—is a twentieth century American classic. A latter-day Dreiser will tell this epic. Foster is an eager student of various fields of science, particularly genetics. The question of environment and heredity occupied him through the years. He possesses a wide grasp of the question.

He was also, said North, preeminent in the field of medicine. He allocated his time wisely to his various tasks, was prompt in arriving at appointments, and was unfailingly helpful.

Associates and others who have written books—on a wide variety of subjects—have solicited his criticism, his advice, and he has never been too busy to read their manuscripts and offer his views. Be it a book on the Negro question, on trade-unions and strike strategy, on literature and criticism, on atomic energy, economics, or a novel, Foster's door is open.[12]

As to Browder, James W. Ford wrote in 1941 that he

symbolizes all that is fine, honest and progressive in the working class of our country. To him belongs the honor of having consolidated the Communist Party of the United States, the Party of the working class, champion of the Negro people, of all the toilers of our country, the best representative of the true national interests of the American people. This historic contribution . . . accords to Browder the place of foremost American in the present era.

He was "the outstanding Marxist-Leninist in the Western Hemisphere," and to celebrate his fiftieth birthday Communists would work "to bring the brilliant teachings of Browder to a vast number of Americans."

Earl Browder is the best friend in America of the people of China because of his profound Leninist understanding of their struggle for national freedom. For many years Earl Browder worked with the people of China and helped them organize the struggle against the imperialist powers intent on dismembering China. . . . He has a complete understanding of the struggles of the Negro peoples, their achievements, their aspirations and the great contribution they are making and will increasingly make to the liberation of all the toilers in America. . . . The persecution of Browder and the Communist Party is a blow at the rights of the Negro people. Its aim is the paralyzing of the struggle for the liberation of the Negro people.

Robert Minor even dared to compare Browder with Lenin: "I recall . . . that one of the terms applied by the Bolshevik Party to Comrade Lenin was *Nash Uchityel*—'Our Teacher.' . . . Earl Browder [is] the teacher of our Party."[13]

To get the "feel" of Jimmy Higgins's special world, the reader should imagine many, many such passages pervading Party literature. They were not so much statements about Jimmy Higgins's heroes, to be read in the same way as his compatriots might read eulogies of outstanding Americans, as they were expressions of an integral part of his own mind. This exaltation of the top leaders set the tone for the relationship of members to leaders at all levels and affected all Party thinking and behavior.

The quoted passages illustrate how leader-worship was intermingled with several other themes: Party-worship, flattery of the masses, identification of the Party with the masses, the omnicompetence of Marxism-Leninism, and the providing of models for the rank and file to emulate. We shall discuss each of these themes in its own terms in its appropriate place. What should be noticed at this point is that leader-worship, and the authority principle in general, simplified the leaders' task of securing rank-and-file assent to any doctrine or policy they promulgated. For, despite their claims, it was not the correctness of the doctrines and policies that justified their authority but their authority that made the doctrines and policies correct.

The Party's authority principle resembled that of an army at the front: even when an officer's orders are wrong, the army would lose more than it gained if each soldier exercised his private judgment as to which to obey. The Party was an army in combat: the shock troops in the class war. (Robert Minor wrote: "Lenin repeats several times the following words that are classics in Marxian literature: 'War is the continuation of politics by other . . . means' "[14]—thus making it likely that the young people to whom he was speaking would, if they ever came across the original, assume that Clausewitz had plagiarized from Marx.) Just as an army court-martials soldiers for disobeying even bad orders, the Party expelled members for "anti-leadership tendencies" regardless of the particular issues over which they disagreed with their superiors. On this as on all other disciplinary questions, Jimmy Higgins acquiesced voluntarily, on solid doctrinal grounds. On one sector of a battlefield (Comrade Jimmy's particular shop or neighborhood or organization), even a lieutenant cannot see the entire field. Only the general staff knows how a soldier's assignment fits into the over-all battle plan.

In the American Communist "army" the highest rank was the equivalent, perhaps, of colonel. The generals resided in Moscow, and the American officers seem to have shared the rank and file's sincere belief in the supreme general's perfection. Only this can explain the American leaders' automatic use of the word "revelations" when they referred to Khrushchev's account of Stalin's crimes. Party writers had been reading—and denouncing—the American news media's accounts of those crimes long before Khrushchev made his 1956 speech, but they could no more credit allegations from the enemy's press than an army officer can credit propaganda from the other side of the battlefield.

So, for example, Foster referred to "the sweeping revelations of the Stalin cult of the individual"; Benjamin Davis, to "Stalin revelations"; and Dorothy Healey, to "Khrushchev's revelations on Stalin." On one page of an editorial in *Political Affairs* we read of "the impact of the Khrushchev revelations," "these revelations," and "the shocking disclosures." The closest any of the writers came to admitting that the enemy press had been right all along was in Howard Selsam's statement that "suddenly came the revelations of the Twentieth Party Congress of the Soviet Union—revelations which, amidst enormous socialist progress, confirmed many of the worst charges of its enemies and misgivings of its friends."[15] To which the obvious response is: Then why call them revelations?

The inadvertent confessions of parochialism took other forms as well. The editors of *Mainstream*, in the March, 1957, issue, criticized Howard Fast, who had said that the Party had been compromised by events beyond its control; they asked: "How compromised? By matters of which its members could not know." Could not, or would not? The events had been daily news for two decades. Or consider Herbert Aptheker's assertion, in his book *The Truth about Hungary*, that "the terrible revelations of coerced confessions in the lands of Socialism, which have come with such shattering impact, naturally cast extreme doubt on all court proceedings there."[16] This implied that everyone was surprised. Yet in passages just before and just after this remark, Aptheker denounced those whose belief system had enabled them to accept the facts that now stunned the Communists. In his book, an apologia for the crushing of the Hungarian uprising, Aptheker was still presenting the image of the Soviet Union that had made the facts "revelations" to him.

The Party press had featured many refutations of scholarly exposés of Stalinism and of refugees' accounts; the Party writers therefore knew the contents of the "revelations" long before 1956. It seems, then, that they were using the word "revelations" in its religious, rather than journalistic, sense. Consider Eugene Dennis's plea that "the facts disclosed about the errors [N.B.] of Stalin in regard to the absence of collective leadership are, of course, new to us."[17] This was a literal lie but a deeper truth: the facts were not new; their meaning was. Truth was not what fitted reality; it was what the hierophants uttered. The source of a doctrine, news item, or any other statement carried more weight than the content of it; the feeling about the source preceded and determined the true believer's reaction. When the Party's writers unanimously refrained from admitting that they could have got a more accurate picture of Stalin's regime from the "bourgeois" press than from their own, they were not just omitting an embarrassing fact but making a positive statement: that those other publications *remained* evil purveyors of lies. The Party writers hated them as intensely after 1956 as before, for the news media's real sin was hostility toward the Soviet Union.

After the furor following Khrushchev's speech died down, the Party took the position that "well, nobody's perfect," but only in words; in practice the Soviet Union and its top leaders remained infallible. In this the Communists differed from other radicals who may admire the Soviet Union, China, Cuba, Vietnam, or some other socialist country, as convenience dictates. What made the Soviet Union the permanent image of all good, for the CP, was the hierarchy of authority, the "state of tutelage."

In the earliest years the Party and the YCL frankly admitted receiving "directives" from the Comintern and the Young Communist International.[18] By the late 1930s, however, such candor had become imprudent, and in an article published in March, 1939, Browder denied that the Party had ever received orders from Moscow. He quoted a statement he had made in 1938, that if the Party received " 'any such orders it would throw them into the wastebasket.' " He now added:

As an important confirmation of this fact, . . . let me cite the words of Joseph Stalin, spoken in *1927* in reply to a question put by the delegation of American trade unionists (non-Communists) who were visiting the Soviet Union. Stalin said:

> "The assertion that the American Communists work under 'orders from Moscow' is absolutely untrue. There are no Communists in the world who would agree to work 'under orders' from outside against their own convictions and will and contrary to the requirements of the situation. Even if there were such Communists they would not be worth a cent."

Browder added that Stalin had said that the Parties *consulted* the International, and why not? The American Federation of Labor consulted international labor organizations. "This quotation," concluded Browder, "confirms that my statement" of 1938 represented a longstanding position.[19] In short, he proved his independence of Moscow authority by invoking Moscow authority—and quite logically, for who would *not* want to obey him whose every utterance was a mighty searchlight lighting up the path and so on? The point, however, is that Browder did not even realize that he was refuting his own contention by the means he used to prove it.

People who joined the Party after Browder made his disclaimer did not read the old issues of the Party publications that contained "directives" from abroad. The new line—that all Communist Parties agreed on every question only because the science of Marxism-Leninism applied to all countries—made perfect sense to them. Jimmy Higgins knew that disagreement with Moscow was unthinkable. He also knew that the most important doctrines and policies did not change unless word came from abroad (with rare exceptions identified by Party crises). Yet he tried hard to convince himself that the conferences among the world's Communist Parties were no more rubber stamps for the Soviet Party than the democratically elected Soviet parliament was for the Politburo. To the degree that Comrade Jimmy convinced himself of this, he enhanced the authority of his own leaders over him, for he thought they had helped to work out the line and therefore understood it better than he did. It was enough that the line was correct, whether it originated in directives, advice, or simply authoritative pronouncements followed voluntarily.

Authoritative pronouncements appeared in the Party's writings as often after the Party announced its autonomy as they had before.[20] For example, when the *History of the Communist Party of the Soviet Union (Bolsheviks)* came out, the leaders of the American, French, British, German, and Italian CPs passed a resolution (adopted August 10, 1939) declaring that the appearance of this book

is one of the greatest events in the life of the Communist world movement and of the international labor movement, in the struggle of the working people of all countries for emancipation. Written with the immediate participation of Comrade Stalin and authorized by the Central Committee of the C.P.S.U.(B.), the *History* occupies an extraordinary place among the classic works of Marxism-Leninism,

and the statement then explained why. The book thus became an instant classic, the New Testament to Marx and Engels' Old Testament.[21]

Most of the evidences of unquestioned authority were less direct, however: for example, Herbert Aptheker invoked Stalin's wisdom and authority ten times in a ten-page article on "The 'New Conservatives' " in *Masses & Mainstream* (April, 1953), and an editorialist in *New Foundations* (Summer, 1945), writing on white chauvinism, used Stalin's definition of a nation without attribution or quotation marks, as one might incorporate phrases from the Bible or Shakespeare because they have passed into common discourse.

The extent of the Party's autonomy was best revealed during crises. When the Duclos letter (transmitting, through the French Party, Moscow's disapproval of Browderism) became public in the spring of 1945, but before its implications had become fully clear, the editors of *New Masses* were unable to ignore it. They therefore worded their comments very carefully so as to avoid what only later might turn out to be incorrect. But it was Khrushchev's bombshell in 1956 that did most to destroy all pretense of autonomy. A hitherto respected comrade, William Mandel, rashly wrote an article in *Masses & Mainstream* very early in the episode, arguing that "one cannot wait for the Soviet Party to offer answers" to questions concerning one-man rule. In their reply, the editors called him "Mr.," an unmistakable signal to those who knew the code. "We do not," they wrote,

ask Mr. Mandel to provide the answers for which he cannot wait. We do, however, urge him to pause a few moments for the answers which are apparently on their way from the people who are in the best, if not only, position to give them: the present leadership of the Communist Party of the Soviet Union.

They deplored the "haste which threatens to cloud Mr. Mandel's *apparent* friendliness toward the Soviet Union and its leadership." (Emphasis added.) Mandel's sin, then, was simply to form an opinion before instructions had arrived; this was enough to cast doubt on his loyalty. Unwilling to admit this, the Party used the pretext of ignorance. In the next issue of the same magazine, Charles Humboldt wrote:

Every answer, even the best possible or most plausible, which we may give to questions concerning what happened in the Soviet Union, Hungary, or wherever else, is vitiated by its being based on utterly insufficient knowledge. Therefore, even the most earnest and hard-thought-out reasoning on these matters must have a taint of presumption just as the most impatient questioner must have a touch of the dilettante no matter how earnest the query and how well-meant the answer.[22]

But insufficient knowledge had never stopped a CP writer from pronouncing authoritatively on any subject, provided he had received what the American Party was now waiting for: the word from the Source. Lest it be thought that the editors of *Masses & Mainstream* hesitated only because they were not top leaders of the Party, it should be noted that the leaders themselves reacted in the same way. In the April, 1956, issue of the Party's official monthly, General Secretary Eugene Dennis trod very cautiously. Our ability to judge the past errors and present reassessment, he said, "is greatly limited by the absence of first-hand knowledge or contact." In plain English: we are waiting for instructions.

Nevertheless, some younger historians have recently revived the old question: How subservient to Moscow was the American CP? The answer depends on how the question is worded. Did Moscow determine every policy? Of course not; it had more important matters to attend to. But did the American CP ever knowingly say or do anything contrary to Moscow's wishes? No. The word *knowingly* is key, and Browder's deviation is proof. His error was to take literally certain *Realpolitik* pronouncements endorsed by Stalin at the Teheran conference. Browder, like a good scholastic, reasoned these forecasts of postwar cooperation to the ultimate absurdity (from the Bolshevik standpoint) of class-collaborationism and "progressive capitalism." Many members grumbled quietly but went along. What is most interesting in the present context is that the period of their grumbling was the period of the most extravagant Browder-worship.

It may not be coincidental that the period of the Moscow Trials and of the worst oppression in the Soviet Union was the period in which Stalin-worship reached its peak. We can discern the psychological process at work, in four eye-witness reports of the Trials in 1936, written by Joshua Kunitz, a prominent member of the Party's literary circle. (Here I should remind the reader that we are reading the documents as Jimmy Higgins may have, knowing nothing about the author.) In the second article (in *New Masses*, October 27, 1936), Kunitz's writing style betrayed ambivalence and worry. Perhaps he found it hard to convince himself that the defendants really had degenerated from good Bolsheviks to traitors, and that their confessions were genuine. His analysis of their degeneration proved how dangerous it was to criticize the Party even with the best of intentions. These men, he wrote, had started out honest and well-meaning in their criticisms of the leadership. But, cut off from the masses and flattered by enemies of the Party, they had drifted farther and farther into conscious opposition. Then, "to justify themselves in their own eyes and the eyes of the revolutionary world, they tend more and more to ignore the virtues and achievements of the party and dwell on its real and imaginary faults and failures," till finally they see only the bad things. "Before they know it, and while they still speak and think of themselves as revolutionists, they become out and out counter-revolutionists—so much more dangerous, because of their former service and revolutionary associations." In retrospect, he concluded, we can see how flawed their characters were long before their outright treason. Kunitz did not say so, but he was obviously sending a message to his comrades at home (and maybe himself), about well-meaning criticism and the slippery slope leading from it. Faithful comrades could be incipient renegades without even knowing it themselves. The present reader should notice that Kunitz used the present tense in the passage just quoted; he was discoursing on a process that could happen with anyone at any time.

Many members left the American CP after the Trials, and many others overcame their doubts only after anguished arguments with themselves. Maybe this is why Stalin-worship became most extravagant, even hysterical, during the Trials: the prospect of release from the "state of tutelage" frightened them. An American CP totally on its own was not what the true believer wanted to belong to. So, when he told his "contacts" that the Party's policies coincided with Moscow's only because both parties guided themselves by the same science, he was not being quite frank—with himself. One part of his mind believed this formula, but another recognized and wanted the "state of tutelage."

THE NOT-QUITE-FRANK ADMISSION of the "state of tutelage" suggests that we should not push the analogy of the Party with an army too far. The Party resembled two other institutions: community and family. Like the latter two but unlike the army, the Party identified the office with its occupant. The army teaches the recruit to salute the uniform, not the person wearing it. Although Party leaders could be demoted or become traitors overnight, the respect they received during their tenure always belonged to them personally. Moreover, as Meyer emphasizes, some highly authoritative Party members held no formal office.[23] The fact that authority was a personal and not formal function eliminated any rational restraint upon the members' reverence. The authority relationships in normal communities and families are more a matter of emotion than of ideology. The Party thus competed for its members' loyalty not only with institutions defined by functions or beliefs but also with the real community and real family—a fact that the comrades may have had trouble admitting.

One way to make this point without seeming to was to report a news item from the Soviet Union. Mike Gold wrote an essay on "Soviet Children" in which he described several exemplary youngsters, all of whom showed that the new children the October revolution *has given birth to* . . . grow up in a world as remote from the life their parents led as the first cultivator of the soil was from the primitive animal existence men followed in the dawn of the earth. They are socialist children; they are the generation brought up and schooled in teachings of Leninism; *Socialism is their great mother*. (Emphases added.)

In case any of his American readers missed the point, Gold then recounted a "struggle" between a farm woman and her son. Eleven-year-old Kolya wrote a letter to a newspaper telling of how his mother yelled at and beat him and calling such treatment a holdover from czarist society. The woman retorted that, since Kolya was her fifth child, she ought to know by now how to bring up children. The people on the collective farm discussed the matter in a meeting; the only remarks that Gold quoted were critical of the mother, who said nothing. Two months later the newspaper published a letter from her saying she had stopped beating Kolya and that he had become a good boy. Gold ended his article thus: "And so the children give birth to different mothers; the new remakes the old."[24]

Gold's essay originally appeared in a publication that American comrades read. Many of them were under twenty-one, and many of those were rebels against nonradical and/or middle-class parents. But even for the Communist children of good Communists, the parents' authority must be conditional, legitimized by the correctness of their beliefs. The political institution, not the family, engaged their strongest emotions—or rather, the Cause that they identified with the political institution, the Party. In the member's mind, then, the parents had become surrogates of the state vis-à-vis their children, if they lived in CP-ruled countries; in the United States the Party played that role. The Party, in fact, prefigured the socialist society to come. The presumed authority relationships between state and citizens in the Soviet Union were duplicated, to the extent possible, by the authority relationships between the Party and its members in the United States.

The single most important fact about authority in both places was its all-encompassing nature. One ex-member recalled the Party's "soul-absorbing authority": "More and more, our entire lives became enmeshed in the party to the point where every judgment on every question ranging from high politics to family matters issued from this source." He recalled that many years before, he and another young street-corner speaker "were more concerned with the reaction of the comrades to our behavior than that of the 'masses.' "[25]

This relationship to authority does not, however, imply passivity. In fact, members often had to struggle to achieve proper subordination. Some had to fight their shyness when assigned to sell *The Worker* door-to-door; some invented excuses to get out of difficult assignments. When the Party won such inner struggles, its victory was that of the comrades' own Communist conscience against their "bourgeois tendencies" or against what the New Left would call "hangups." In short, the committed member actively participated in his own subordination to authority, and the harder the struggle, the more precious the prize—and the more central to his whole life.[26]

All this made dependence on other institutions and people unnecessary, for no matter what question a member had, what problem—intellectual, emotional, professional—the Party was competent to deal with it. The Party resembled a suburb that has all sorts of shops and services, so that the resident need never go to the city. Nor did the comrades want to go elsewhere; the documents furnish abundant evidence that they resisted the leaders' incessant commands to mingle with non-Party workers and neighbors. Year after year the periodicals urged the rank and file to "turn to the masses" and "root the Party in the shops and neighborhoods," but to no avail. Some writers occasionally ridiculed the in-group jargon that seemed to come so naturally because it proved the user adept in mysteries closed to outsiders. Old members sometimes behaved cliquishly toward recruits.[27] There were, in short, many ways of building fences between Us and Them—Them meaning not just the enemy but also the workers among whom the Party must agitate to justify its existence.

Understandably, then, the exhortations and criticisms had no effect; what the Party called "sectarian" behavior came naturally. When John Gates wrote his memoirs shortly after he left the Party, he recalled that Robert Thompson had attacked a less doctrinaire comrade for harboring "Hamlet-like doubts about the future of the party." Gates commented that "perhaps we would have been better off if Thompson had had just a few doubts about the correctness of his policies."[28] I disagree. If authoritarians and dogmatists such as Thompson had not dominated the Party, it would, I believe, have disintegrated sooner than it did. The core of committed rank and filers needed and wanted authoritarianism—doctrinal and structural. Their need coincided with the Party's need to keep the ranks in line and manipulable. In other words, there are two contradictions here: first, the Party's mission to go to the "masses" versus its own centripetal tendencies, and second, the members' duty to proselytize and recruit versus their wish to belong to a privileged elite that gave their lives meaning.

The Party reinforced the very behavior it criticized. It prohibited members from consorting with far-left but non-Communist radicals and expellees, even if those people were old friends or relatives. It induced members to feel that life outside the Party was inconceivable, that expulsion meant exile into outer darkness. In theory, one should be able to work out in the cold world while living psychologically within the warm community of the Party. But in practice this proved possible only for the few who became "cadre," "professional Bolsheviks." Others who were forced to venture outside—such as young men who fought in the Spanish Civil War or later in World War II— often found that outer darkness not so dark after all and did not rejoin the Party upon their return. The average rank and filer did not go through this experience. All he knew was that the Party gave him a mission in life, answered his questions, had a theory that enabled him to feel in control of the universe, at least potentially, or vicariously through his leaders. He felt grateful to them, identified with them, tried to emulate them.

When a citizen of the least hierarchical and most mobile, tolerant, and permissive country in the world voluntarily joins the most hierarchical, intolerant, and disciplined organization available, either he has made a mistake or he wants to belong to just such an organization. Those who mistook the nature of the Party left within a few years. The explanation for Jimmy Higgins's remaining was explored in earlier chapters; we should now fill out the picture by surveying the Party's self-image, which he accepted. For we can understand better the nature of his need by examining his image of that which satisfied it.

* * *

The Communist Party is the organized theory, embodied in growing tens of hundreds of thousands of men and women preserving and transmitting the experience and wisdom of past generations, enriching it by the experience of the present, transmitting it to the broadest masses, providing thereby the illumination, the guidance, the leadership, which will organize victory for the masses in their age-old struggle against the forces of darkness and reaction.[29]

ACCORDING TO THIS STATEMENT by Browder—which Foster too could have made, after Browder's expulsion—the organization that Jimmy Higgins decided to remain in was the Marxist-Leninist Word made flesh. It alone inherited and enriched every good tradition—thus appealing to Comrade Jimmy's ingrained respect for tradition as well as to his rejection of it. It identified itself with the struggling masses, but it also distinguished itself from them by virtue of its superior insight. And it prophesied a bright future. These claims constituted the Party's self-image. We shall here examine the first two, leaving the last two for later chapters.

The Party's leaders repeatedly urged their followers to feel confident of victory. But since rank-and-file members must be humble and self-critical, the primary objects of their trust must be the Party and its mission; they could feel *self*-confident only insofar as they identified themselves with the Party. This logic can be observed in Foster's assertion that

Marxism-Leninism . . . produces a rational, powerful, well-balanced optimism and a fighting spirit for socialism. . . . There is no pessimism among Communists. . . . Communist parties . . . have in their ranks almost none of the drunkards, dope addicts, criminals, sexual perverts, and the various other social nondescripts that infest the capitalist world.[30]

The causal chain, then, began with Marxism-Leninism (the Word) and proceeded through the Party (its incarnation) to the optimistic and healthy individual, Jimmy Higgins, who knew that Foster was talking about him and his comrades.

The fundamental basis for the Party's optimism was its possession of Marxism-*Leninism*; in the imperialist era the only Marxism was the form that Lenin had given it, with further improvements by Stalin. As one theoretician noted in 1946:

"The Marxian doctrine is omnipotent," wrote Lenin, "because it is true." A disarmingly simple statement. And yet it embraces ages of philosophic contention and social struggle. Of what other doctrine can it be said, not that it is brilliant or original or streaked with valid insights but that it is *true*? True not only today, but for the whole of human history—true because it is derived from and corresponds to the actual process of social evolution.

Added another: Leninism "is becoming the banner and rallying ground of all that is honest, creative and humane in mankind."[31]

The second link in the causal chain, the Party that embodied the truth, need not be large to warrant its members' supreme confidence, for the truth of Marxism-Leninism "is the source of its strength—a truth that makes even a numerically small American Communist Party the legatee of an invincible power." Since only the CP was truly Leninist, it was "not 'a' but 'the' vanguard party." The future would vindicate it, for it "represents the unity of the present and the future, the link between the class struggles of today and the socialist goal." It was "a unique group" that represented "honest thought and culture" and "the search for beauty" and "the creative power of the masses." "The Communist Party is *the* party of the working class. . . . The Communist Party is not only *the* Party of the working class, but also *the* party representing the true interests of the nation." It "is the guardian of devotion to truth and reality."[32]

All these statements, and countless others like them, reiterated a principal tenet: the uniqueness of the Party. Leninism was *the* banner, the CP was *the* vanguard, *the* link between past and future, and so on. Every thought was stated in either/or terms; the world was divided into two "camps," with all good and light on one side and all evil and darkness on the other. (After the Party embarked on its crusade against "white chauvinism," however, it outlawed the light-darkness metaphor.) This either/or way of thinking helped the leaders transform the recruit into a true believer. Because the Party was unique, he must not compare it to any other group. They thereby denied him any external criterion by which to judge its deference to authority, its glorification of leaders, or its rigorous discipline.

Accordingly, Jimmy Higgins must not misinterpret the word "party." True, the CP demanded the rights enjoyed by other political parties; it entered election campaigns; it objected on constitutional grounds when outsiders denied that it was a bona fide party. To have its cake and eat it too, it explained that it was a special type of party. Said Foster: "To cope with the tasks of the American class struggle the working class needs what Lenin called a party of a new type. This party, as Stalin explains it, must be a party able to 'see farther than the working class; it must lead the proletariat and not follow in the tail of the spontaneous movement. . . . The Party is the political leader of the working class.' " As a writer in *New Foundations* put it, "the Communist Party is not a political party in the ordinary partisan sense of the term that it aims merely to win votes and elect candidates to office. Its program and activities have the aim of bettering both the immediate and the long-range welfare of the entire people," and therefore its members worked within other parties, including (at the time this article appeared) the Progressive Party.[33]

Convincing though these theories were, the writers supplemented them with appeals to Jimmy Higgins's pride. Among the documents in this genre is the "Convention Notebook" that Joseph North kept while attending the founding convention of the Communist Political Association in 1944. He prefaced it with an italicized message to Hank Forbes, a comrade who had died at Anzio a few weeks earlier:

You will never die, Hank, never, so long as the things you died for live on: and they lived and burned bright in the convention of your comrades. How can I tell you what happened there? It would require volumes. For what happened there is the synthesis of what is happening throughout the country, throughout the world today. . . . The world issues were clear at the convention, etched luminously by the light of Marxism. You know what I mean. The convention reflected the deep-felt aspirations of America's people, Hank, of men like yourself whether Communist, Democrat, or Republican. America will come to realize that soon, I'm certain. You, Hank, a boy of the sidewalks of New York, as Manhattan as Al Smith or Walt Whitman, would have been inspired by the proceedings as we all were; inspired by the men and women who spoke your ideas, who talked United States. Browder and Foster and Minor and Gurley Flynn and Mother Bloor and Jim Ford and Ben Davis and Pete Cacchione. Yes, and by the many new names from all over America we do not know so well as yet. Your heart would have beat proudly if you had heard that little woman from Chelsea tell how they work in the neighborhoods; in the wards and in the precincts. Down to rock bottom. You would have felt, as all of us did, that America's Marxists had come a long way, had not only studied the books but studied the people, were part of them as you were part of them, Hank. . . . [34]

North's sentimental folksiness was not a temporary product of Browderite revisionism, for versions of it are sprinkled throughout the literature in all periods. Whether or not those who wrote in this mode believed what they wrote, these documents told Jimmy Higgins how to feel about his Party.

Other writers sent the same messages in less gushy form. One compared ex-Communist witnesses against the Party to Judas. He did not explicitly liken the Party to Jesus, but the thought may have occurred to the readers.

On a more mundane level, Browder proclaimed that the American CP represented "the American tradition of democracy, of government of, by and for the people"; that is, it was the legitimate heir of the best traditions handed down by illustrious Americans of past generations. Foster wrote that the Party continued and carried forward everything that was sound in the works of such American thinkers as Benjamin Franklin, Jefferson, Frederick Douglass, Lincoln, Lewis Henry Morgan, Thomas A. Edison, and Theodore Dreiser.[35] Some writers made the point negatively; for example: "To destroy human beings by the millions, as is the plan of the atomic warriors, it is necessary to breed a contempt for humanity as a value in itself. [Whittaker] Chambers is providing a platform for intellectual war on Paine, Thoreau, Douglass, Whitman, Mark Twain, Dreiser." In fact, Communists had helped to create this heritage; typical claims were that "the influence of Communists was a factor in persuading Lincoln to proclaim Emancipation, as in many other vital matters affecting the conduct of the [Civil] War," and that the Party was "the inheritor and continuer and developer of the very flesh and blood and spirit of the true past of the great Negro people."[36]

So many heritage-claiming statements appeared in Party writings that the members probably saw nothing new in Browder's announcement in 1934, repeated in 1935: "We Communists claim the revolutionary traditions of Americanism. We are the only ones who continue those traditions and apply them to the problems of today. *We are the Americans and Communism is the Americanism of the twentieth century.*" Outsiders who have repeatedly quoted this italicized sentence are evidently unaware that there were dozens of similar statements in Party writings. (I refer to the essential claim; Browder was forced later to explain away certain flaws in his formulation.)[37]

The third link in the chain, after Marxism-Leninism and the Party, was the individual members. How gratified Jimmy Higgins must have felt to read such descriptions of himself as the following: "The Communists, as Stalin said in his last speech, have been and always will be *'in the struggle for the radiant future for the peoples.'* " And that in the critical circumstances of late 1945 "the people . . . need loyal, courageous and honest leadership, men and women who combine clarity of vision with the qualities of firmness in principle and flexibility in tactics," in short, Communists. And that "the American Communists are the leaders of the working people of their country, of all democratically-minded Americans[, . . .] the staunchest opponents of Jim Crow, segregation and terrorization of the Negro people. *They are in the forefront of the fight for peace.*" Herbert Aptheker as usual alternated his praise of Communists with attacks on their traducers:

Always and everywhere the reactionaries who despise life and have played the role of leeches turn to violence; it is never the revolutionaries who first resort to violence for they cherish life and exist to ennoble it. . . .

We who understand the indivisibility of true freedom, the essential identity of

interest of all the common peoples of the world and the immortality of these people—
we possess an unquenchable confidence. We know that neither slander nor illegality
nor torture nor crematoria—should they build ovens for ten times the millions already
burned—will keep the working men and women of this earth from their inheritance
of peace and dignity. . . .

Militant, organized mass struggle to be waged by a united and aroused people
against the onslaught of reaction, for the winning of immediate demands, for democracy, for the realization of socialism, of the human epoch of history—this is the
road to world emancipation. It is because the Communists know this road that they
have earned the hatred of Thiers and Bismarck, of Hitler and Hirohito, of Mussolini
and Franco, of Churchill and Dulles. This hatred is a crown of glory. Its existence
certifies the veracity of Marxism-Leninism.[38]

The reader may have noticed in these excerpts a chronic ambiguity concerning the relationship between the Party and the people. Was its influence
on them a present fact or a future certainty? The Party's possession of the
truth diminished the significance of its small size; yet it had to claim that
millions of Americans already accepted its leadership. At the same time, to
induce psychological cohesion and discipline among the members, the Party
had to depict itself as a small, elite guerrilla army surrounded by all-powerful
enemies. In his *History of the Communist Party of the United States*, Foster
expressed both sides of this ambiguity within a few pages. During the trial
of the top leaders in 1949, he wrote on page 512, "the small Communist
Party was pictured as a 'clear and present danger' to American imperialism,"
which, he implied, it could not possibly have been. Yet on page 506 he had
boasted that it was just that: the capitalists attacked the Party so as to "break
down working class opposition to their drive for imperialist mastery of the
world. For these rulers understand very well, even if many workers and
their friends do not, that the Communist Party is indeed the vanguard of
the working class, the true party of the people." The rulers have learned this
from the many struggles led by the Party. For example, wrote two reviewers
of Foster's book, unemployment insurance was a "concession" wrung from
the capitalists by the struggle of the unemployed, "and it was the Communists
who made this gain possible."[39] The capitalists knew that the Party was their
main enemy. Indeed, if it was not, then why (from the standpoint of Party
thinking) did the enemy put the leaders on trial and thus attempt to behead
the working class? In our effort to reconstruct Jimmy Higgins's thinking we
have to search for some belief or mode of thinking that permitted Foster and
then the publishers and then Jimmy Higgins, as he read the book—and heard
the same pair of arguments elsewhere—to overlook this glaring contradiction.
For there is no doubt that he overlooked it; as a member I never noticed it
and never heard anyone else point it out even in private conversation among
trusted friends.

Each half of that contradiction is, of course, easy to explain. On the one
hand, the Party's small size buttressed the contention that the enemy needed

a scapegoat to direct the workers' attention away from the real cause of their suffering; that is, the accusations against the Party were obviously false. On the other hand, every activist movement tends to think its influence is much greater than it really is. The movement is central to the lives and thoughts of its members, who find it impossible to realize that most people are indifferent to it.[40] But within what framework of thought can these two beliefs be reconciled? The key to the answer, I think, is a mental quirk that has been remarked upon[41]: Communists' tendency to conflate the present and the future, to look at someone or something and see only what he or it was destined to become. When the trial of the leaders in 1949 made it tactically wise to argue that the Party was too small to be a clear and present danger, then the present dominated. But most often the longsighted perception came naturally.

Because the prediction-as-statement-of-present-fact was better propaganda as well as more compatible with the members' self-image and good for their morale, Party writers bombarded Jimmy Higgins with recitations of his Party's enormous influence. He could hardly fail to see that these claims did not apply to him and his club. But he accepted them as descriptions of a large enough proportion of his comrades elsewhere to make them true of the Party as a whole, and in so doing he acknowledged his own shortcomings. The zealous member's mental image of the Party gave him an unremitting incentive to live up to it. Critics who emphasize that the Party served its members' needs are right, but the members thought of the relationship in the opposite way. They felt they had to deserve to belong to the Party and to serve *its* needs and thus the needs of the oppressed.

THE PICTURE of the Party drawn so far will have struck the reader as belonging to a bygone era. Many of its professed ideals—including admiration for order, discipline, and self-sacrifice—and the institutions that fostered them were weakening or losing their religious sanctions in the society at large. The Party appealed to certain people's nostalgia for the old ways, a nostalgia expressed in ideology. Browder spoke for them when he said that "an individual, group, party or class, which is guided by any theory except Marxism-Leninism, finds its theory breaking up and failing in the moment of crisis and change," especially now (1938) when "all the old landmarks are drifting, breaking up, disappearing."[42] This function of Marxism-Leninism gave the new member a powerful incentive to accept the truth of the theory and the intellectual authority of its official expounders, long before he knew much about the theory itself. As we shall see in the next chapter, the Party went to great lengths to strengthen this predisposition.

NOTES

1. Frank S. Meyer, *The Moulding of Communists* (New York: Harcourt, Brace, 1961), p. 143.

2. Bella V. Dodd, *School of Darkness* (New York: P. J. Kenedy & Sons, 1954), p. 139. Dodd's adding "the Soviet Union" is important; some members distinguished between the Cause and the leaders: Fred Beal, for example, saw the leaders' flaws clearly but tolerated them out of devotion to the Cause. See his autobiography, *Proletarian Journey* (New York: Hillman-Curl, 1937), p. 158. But Beal was exceptional in that he associated with the leaders; Jimmy Higgins did not.

3. M. J. Olgin, *Trotskyism* (New York: Workers Library, 1935), pp. 148–49.

4. Earl Browder, "Building the Party and The Daily Worker," *PO* 10 (August, 1937): 5.

5. See, e.g., the wording in the second paragraph of Earl Browder, "The Study of Lenin's Teachings," *PA* 24 (January, 1945): 3. An exception is Browder's calling Marx and Engels "the two most cultured men of history"; see Earl Browder, *Communism and Culture* (New York: Workers Library, 1941), p. 5. An example of Stalin's paramountcy is in Howard Selsam, *Socialism and Ethics* (New York: IP, 1943), p. 166: Engels's theory of the state, though "generally true," was "incompletely worked out and inadequate," according to Stalin, whose amendments Selsam accepts without question—not, it should be noted, in the spirit of the scholar who accepts new developments in his field but in the spirit of the religious who has taken a vow of obedience.

6. N. Slutsker, "Lenin, Stalin and the Communist Youth Movement," *CL* 1 (April–May, 1940): 70, 72; see also passim. As to the statement about Stalin's every utterance, cf. Frank Cestare, "Earl Browder—Molder of Character," *CL* 3 (Spring, 1942): 36–37: the Nazis teach youth "that their 'Fuehrer' can do no wrong."

7. Donald MacKenzie Lester, "Stalin—Genius of Socialist Construction," *COM* 20 (March, 1941): 257, 258 (see also passim; the article consists largely of explanations that "Stalin showed" this and "Stalin taught" that); William Auer, "Soviet Culture in the Fight against Fascism," *COM* 20 (November, 1941): 996.

8. V. J. Jerome, "The Individual in History," *NM*, May 18, 1943, p. 19.

9. Alexander Bittelman, "Stalin: On His Seventieth Birthday," *PA* 28 (December, 1949): 2, 1; "Stalin: The Lenin of Today," ibid., pp. 14, 15.

10. Elizabeth Gurley Flynn, "He Loved the People," *PA* 32 (April, 1953): 43, 46; Betty Gannett, "Stalin: Architect of Socialism," ibid., p. 55; see also other articles in the same issue. This habit was so ingrained that it sometimes went to comical lengths. A Soviet article reprinted in *PA* included the statement: "The adoption by the U.S.A. of the Declaration of Independence was, as G. M. Malenkov emphasizes, an act of historic progress." ("On the Study of the Modern History of Capitalist Countries," *PA* 34 [January, 1955]: 58.) How did the writer choose which authority to cite in support of this truism? (Malenkov was at that time the temporary occupant of Stalin's recently vacated office.) Why did he think his readers would need any authority at all to believe it? Where did Malenkov acquire his expertise in American history? How did Marxist experts in that field receive this dictum?

11. See, e.g., Michael Gold, "William L. Patterson: Militant Leader," *MM* 4 (February, 1951): 34–43: Richard O. Boyer, "Elizabeth Gurley Flynn: An Epic of American Labor," *MM* 5 (May, 1952): 5–20; Sender Garlin, "Publisher on Trial: The Lifework of Alexander Trachtenberg," *MM* 5 (October, 1952): 17–27; Herbert Aptheker, "Ideas on Trial: The Intellectual Leadership of V. J. Jerome," *MM* 5 (March, 1952): 1–11. Compare such eulogies with even the most admiring eulogies of non-Communists in the "bourgeois" press.

12. Joseph North, "Bill Foster: An American Epic," *MM* 4 (March, 1951): 10, 17, 19. The occasion of this article was Foster's seventieth birthday, and other articles in the same issue pay tribute to him. They include a poem by Meridel Le Sueur.

13. James W. Ford, "Earl Browder—Leader of the Oppressed," *COM* 20 (June, 1941): 529, 535, 530, 531, 535; Robert Minor, "Workers' Education and the War against Hitler," *COM* 20 (November, 1941): 972, 973.

14. Robert Minor, "Continued Political Struggle against Hitler by Military Means" (a speech to a YCL meeting), *CL* 2 (Summer, 1941): 15. This claim of other people's statements for Marxists was not unique; in addition to Clausewitz's aphorism (in several places), Terence's dictum that nothing human was alien to him was also claimed for Marx. See Mike Gold, *Change the World!* (New York: IP, 1936), p. 71.

15. William Z. Foster, "Draper's 'Roots of American Communism,' " *PA* 36 (May, 1957): 37; Benjamin Davis, "The Challenge of the New Era," *PA* 35 (December, 1956): 17; Dorothy R. Healey, "On the Status of the Party," *PA* 37 (March, 1958): 48; "The Communist Party Convention" (editorial), *PA* 36 (April, 1957): 3; Howard Selsam, "Do Ends Justify Means?" *MM* 9 (September, 1956): 2, 17. See also, e.g., William Z. Foster, "The Party Crisis and the Way Out: Part I," *PA* 36 (December, 1957): 56, 60; Charles Humboldt, "On Politics and Culture," *MM* 9 (May, 1956): 8, 9, 12; William Z. Foster, "Communication Concerning Edward Kardelj's Article," *MM* 10 (February, 1957): 50; The Editors, "A Comment," *MM* 10 (March, 1957): 40; "More Comments on Howard Fast," *MM* 10 (April, 1957) (consisting of "comments" by five authors): Herbert Aptheker on pp. 42, 43, Phillip Bonosky on p. 48, and Louis Harap on p. 55. A poignant document was a letter in *PA* 37 (February, 1958): 62, signed "A Youth Struggling to Be a Marxist-Leninist." He describes the confusion among his classmates at the Jefferson School after the Twentieth Congress, but adds that "though we were shocked at some of the things revealed, no one became dispirited." The genuineness of this surprise is inadvertently shown later when he describes himself and his classmates as "We young people, who had all come to our Marxist-Leninist views out of *experience*, study and *life itself*" (italics added). He kept his illusions, for the letter ends by affirming the validity of the very ideology that had caused him to be shocked by facts that were common knowledge.

16. Herbert Aptheker, *The Truth about Hungary* (New York: Mainstream Publishers, 1957), p. 117.

17. Eugene Dennis, "Questions and Answers on the XXth Congress, CPSU," *PA* 35 (April, 1956): 24. Here is how he excused the Party's ignorance: the Soviet Union has always, he said, been attacked by capitalist forces, including

the whole network of calumniators, vilifiers and slanderers whose unremitting hostility to the Soviet Union was hostility to Socialism and to working-class rule under any conditions. Our attitude has been similar to that when confronted against unions and workers in the course of a strike [the fuzzy syntax is Dennis's]. We support the workers and their organizations and are not deterred by the fact that some secondary errors on their part have been used as a pretext for denouncing the strike by those who are against all unions and against the workers generally.

Later he added that the government's restrictions on passports, which prevented comrades from getting firsthand information, had also hindered the acquisition of knowledge about the Soviet Union (this was, of course, a lie, since the restrictions were in force for only a short time and not at all during the 1930s, and since Communists frequently traveled abroad under assumed names). (See ibid., pp. 25–26.)

18. See, e.g., "Comintern Documents: Directives of the Politsecretariat of the ECCI to the Communist Party of the USA . . . ," *COM* 10 (May, 1931): 402; C. A. Hathaway, "On the Use of 'Transmission Belts' in Our Struggle for the Masses," ibid., p. 412; "On Ninth Plenum of the Y.C.I.[:] Resolution on the Report of Comrade Chemodanov," and "Our Guide to Action! Every Young Communist Must Study and Apply the Ninth Plenum Decisions," both on p. 5 of *YW*, April 1, 1933; Slutsker, "Lenin, Stalin and the Communist Youth Movement," p. 73 (a reference to "These Stalinist Directives"); "Resolution of the Twelfth Plenum of the E.C.C.I.," *PO* 6 (August-September, 1933): [1]. As one historian has pointed out, a report by the House Un-American Activities Committee in 1947 needed eight pages to list just the titles of the directives from Moscow to the American CP, and in another report the texts of these documents covered more than 300 pages. See William A. Nolan, *Communism Versus the Negro* (Chicago: Henry Regnery Company, 1951), p. 15 and nn. 78 and 79 on p. 210. This, incidentally, may be one of the many reasons for the Party's vilification of the Committee: It insured that no rank and filer would ever read the Committee's publications—after the Party press itself had stopped publishing directives and started claiming that it received none.

19. Earl Browder, "America and the Communist International," *COM* 18 (March, 1939): 211. For similar disclaimers, see, e.g., Bruce Minton and John Stuart, *The Fat Years and the Lean* (New York: IP, 1940), p. 254 (explaining the Party's replacement of the Trade Union Educational League by the Trade Union Unity League, as owing to lessons learned by experience, with no mention of the Comintern policy shift); and Herbert Aptheker, *History and Reality* (New York: Cameron Associates, 1955), pp. 144–45 (the accusation that the CP is part of a movement with its headquarters abroad is McCarthyism and fascism).

20. Those that appeared before the disclaimers included a violently anti-Zionist document: "On the Communist Approach to Zionism," *COM* 15 (July, 1936): 666–70. This was a reply to a memo from the Jewish Bureau of the Pittsburgh District of the Party about recent events in Palestine. It was prefaced thus: *"Below, we present a statement by the Jewish Bureau of the Central Committee, giving the correct approach to the problem.*—EDITORS." The reason for the assured tone is made clear on the first page of the document itself: "The Communist position on Palestine was outlined at the Seventh Congress of the Comintern by Comrade Hadyar, who stated. . . . " The article is signed by J. Sultan, *"for the Jewish Bureau of the Central Committee, C.P.U.S.A."* It should be remembered that a disproportionate percentage of the Party's members were Jews who, of course, had to accept the line set forth here.

21. "On the Distribution and Study of the 'History of the C.P.S.U.(B.)' and the Propagation of Marxism-Leninism in the World Communist Movement," *COM* 19 (January, 1940): 73–84. In any disagreement between Marx and Stalin, Stalin prevailed automatically. The *History of the CPSU* was read by rank-and-file members far more than were the writings of Marx and Engels. College students read the latter, but all serious members read the former and the pamphlets that comprised the Little Lenin Library (which included works by Stalin) and used and quoted them constantly. As to my calling the *History of the CPSU* the Communists' New Testament, cf. Eric Voegelin, *The New Science of Politics* (Chicago: University of Chicago Press, 1952), p. 140: "In the Communist movement . . . the works of Karl Marx have become the koran of the faithful, supplemented by the patristic literature of Leninism-Stalinism." (On Voegelin's p. 139 he explains why he calls Marx's works a koran.)

22. The Editors, "The Communists Take Stock," *NM*, June 12, 1945, p. 17; William Mandel, "A Communication: Democracy and the Left," and editors' statement, *MM* 9 (April, 1956): 57–62, quotations at pp. 57 and 62; Charles Humboldt, "Second Thoughts on Politics and Culture," *MM* 9 (May, 1956): 8.

23. Meyer, *Moulding of Communists*, p. 13.

24. Mike Gold, *Change the World!*, pp. 162–65. Most of the essays comprising this volume originally appeared in the *Daily Worker*; a few, in the *New Masses*.

25. George Charney, *A Long Journey* (Chicago: Quadrangle Books, 1968), pp. 33, 32.

26. The strength of the motive could enable a member to work wonders. Frank Meyer, in *Moulding of Communists*, pp. 82–84, tells of a drunkard who without stopping his drinking lost the traits of the alcoholic, and of a homosexual who, faced with the threat of expulsion, "transformed his life," married, and led a normal life thereafter.

27. On this last point, see, e.g., Browder, "Building the Party and The Daily Worker," p. 3.

28. John Gates, *The Story of an American Communist* (New York: Thomas Nelson & Sons, 1958), p. 186.

29. Browder, *Communism and Culture*, p. 16.

30. William Z. Foster, *The Twilight of World Capitalism* (New York: IP, 1949), p. 101.

31. Alexander Bittelman, "Where Is the 'Monthly Review' Going?" *PA* 30 (May, 1951): 37; A. B. Magil, "Scientist of Socialism," *NM*, January 22, 1946, p. 9 (see also Browder, *Communism and Culture*, p. 41, on the same point, among other documents); Alexander Bittelman, "Lenin's Teachings and the Liberation of Humanity," *PA* 31 (January, 1952): 11.

32. Magil, "Scientist of Socialism," p. 9; William Z. Foster, "The Party Crisis and the Way Out, Part II," *PA* 37 (January, 1958): 63; James E. Jackson, "A Reply to Comrade Healey," *PA* 37 (April, 1958): 33; Browder, *Communism and Culture*, pp. 20, 23; William Z. Foster, *History of the Communist Party of the United States* (New York: IP, 1952), p. 564; Sidney Finkelstein, "Soviet Culture: A Reply to Slander," *MM* 3 (January, 1950): 54.

33. Foster, *History of the CPUS*, p. 260; David Biron, "Communists and The Progressive Party," *NF* 2 (Fall, 1948): 32. On this theme the basic texts that conscientious members relied on most were Stalin's *Foundations of Leninism*, Chap. 8, and scattered passages in the *History of the CPSU*; both works quoted copiously from Lenin.

34. Joseph North, "From a Convention Notebook," *NM*, June 6, 1944, p. 3.

35. Milton Howard, "The Holy War on Reason," *MM* 5 (July, 1952): 1–2; Browder, *Communism and Culture*, p. 23; Foster, *History of the CPUS*, p. 15. An English Communist claimed for his Party the heritage of Shakespeare, to whom "there would have appeared nothing outrageous in the Marxian view of life." Coming closer to the present, he added that "for the greatest part of the eighteenth century a materialist view of life would have been accepted without question by many of the greatest British writers." Ralph Fox, *The Novel and the People* (New York: IP, 1945), p. 22; see passim for similar claims to the heritage of other British writers. Another English comrade recalled that his Party claimed John Ball, Wat Tyler, Cromwell, Milton, Bunyan, Shakespeare, among others. Douglas Hyde, *I Believed* (New York: G. P. Putnam's Sons, 1950), p. 175. A Soviet speaker to a YCI congress claimed for the young Communist's heritage Copernicus, Newton, da Vinci, Edison, Darwin, Pas-

teur, Cervantes, Shakespeare, Goethe, Heine, Schiller, Balzac, Stendhal, and others. See "Time, Forward! Excerpts from a Forthcoming Pamphlet on Youth in the Soviet Union, by Chemodanov, Based on His Report to the Y.C.I. Congress," *YW*, February 1, 1936, p. 9.

36. Howard, "Holy War," p. 13 (the inclusion of Theodore Dreiser in these lists may puzzle the reader unless he knows that Dreiser was a fellow traveler and then a Party member, joining in 1946, thereby earning a place in the pantheon; even an embarrassingly public exhibition of his anti-Semitism in the 1930s elicited only a slap on the wrist); John Howard Lawson, *Film in the Battle of Ideas* (New York: Masses & Mainstream, 1953), p. 49; Samuel Robinson, "The Negro People Speak," *PA* 31 (February, 1952): 63.

37. Earl Browder, "Who Are the Americans?" *YW*, July 2, 1934, p. 9; Earl Browder, eighth article in series entitled "What Is Communism?" *NM*, June 25, 1935, p. 14 (paragraphing has been ignored). Browder criticized the formulation and clarified his intention, in "Concerning American Revolutionary Traditions," *COM* 17 (December, 1938): 1079–82. He did not go far enough, according to Howard Jennings, in "Revisionism in American History," *PA* 25 (August, 1946): 742–47. But while denouncing Browder's false view, Jennings did not repudiate the heritage-claiming theme; on the contrary, his essay (pp. 742–62) amplified and elaborated on it in greater detail than Browder had done.

38. Herbert Aptheker, *Laureates of Imperialism: Big Business Re-Writes American History* (New York: Masses & Mainstream, 1954), p. 93; "Present Situation and the Next Tasks: Resolution of the National Convention of the Communist Party, U.S.A., Adopted July 28, 1945," *PA* 24 (September, 1945): 827; "Free the Eleven," *NF* 3 (Fall, 1949): 3; Herbert Aptheker, "Communism and Chaos," *MM* 1 (September, 1948): 28–29.

39. George Blake and Herbert Aptheker, " 'Flesh and Bone of the Working Class . . .'—On Foster's 'History of the Communist Party,' " *PA* 31 (September, 1952): 50.

40. *PA* continued to provide monthly evidence of this after the close of our period. For example, in 1971 a leader of the Philadelphia branch of the Young Workers Liberation League, the Party's youth organization at the time, denounced the Young Socialist Alliance, an affiliate of the Socialist Workers Party. The YSA was, he wrote, the chief obstacle to black-white unity within the peace movement. Moreover, it hindered "the building of the people's front, with the working class at its center, which is the only basis for defeating fascism"; and "by retarding the struggle against racism the SWP-YSA aids the ruling class in its efforts to retard the Black liberation struggle"; and so on. See Tony Monteiro, "Trotskyism: Racist Voice in the Left," *PA* 50 (July, 1971): 40, 49. The outsider reading this would of course ask: How many supporters of "the peace movement" or of "the Black liberation struggle" ever heard of either the YSA or the YWLL? Could either grouplet have achieved, for good or ill, what Monteiro imputed to it?

41. See chapter one, n. 3, and the text passage to which it refers, above.

42. Browder, *Communism and Culture*, p. 14. Cf. Robert A. Nisbet, "The Twilight of Authority," *Public Interest*, Number 15 (Spring, 1969), p. 4: "The human mind cannot support moral chaos for very long. As more and more of the traditional authorities seem to come crashing down, or to be sapped and subverted, it begins to seek the security of organized power. The ordinary dependence on order becomes

transformed into a relentless demand for order." See also the rest of the essay (pp. 3–9). According to a leading Party theoretician, "Marxism is able to shape order out of the turmoil of new developments in science as in social life, which appear so chaotic to the bourgeois mind"—and to the Communist mind, though he did not add this. See N[emmy] Sparks, "Marxism and Science," *PA* 26 (December, 1948): 1114.

6

Authority II:
Theory and Scholarship

ACCORDING TO THE PARTY, its enemies controlled the mass media; they were
the professors of the student comrades; their ideas were in the air. The leaders
therefore had to take countermeasures to ensure that the rank and filers
remained certain that the Party was always right.[1] Because it took years for
a recruit to learn all the doctrines, the leaders had to teach him at the outset
to reject the intellectual *authority* of outsiders at the same time as it taught
him to reject their *doctrines*; the discrediting of each entailed the discrediting
of the other.

The crucial lessons can be expressed as a syllogism—and they should be,
because it was logical deduction and not evidence of achievement that endowed the leaders with intellectual authority. First premise: Marxism was
both the body of doctrines and the method that must guide all intellectual
work; any idea inconsistent with Marxism was untrue and unscientific, and
every element in another belief system that was consistent with Marxism
was really Marxist. Second premise: the leaders of the Party were by definition the best Marxists in the country, and the leaders of the Soviet Union
were the best Marxists in the world (having led the first successful socialist
revolution). Conclusion: the Party's leaders and theoreticians were qualified
ex officio to speak authoritatively on all subjects, including scholarly disciplines, and the bourgeois specialists in those fields were not. The second
clause in the conclusion was not just a negative form of the first, for if Marxism
was all-embracing, no non-Marxist could really understand his own field.
Marxists and non-Marxists could not be equally authoritative; there was only
one correct way to think about any subject. And the Party leaders and
theoreticians decided what was Marxist.

AMERICAN COMMUNISTS, including Ph.D.'s, did not find it incredible that
Stalin could pass judgment on history, economics, biology, linguistics, political theory, military science, philosophy, music, literature, and psychology
by applying the few basic principles that Marx, Engels, and Lenin had

worked out. If Stalin could do it, so could (up to a point) Foster, who also had no university training. One did not need a scholar's knowledge of any subject to understand the essential truths about it. Jimmy Higgins knew the Party's theory was true, even before he knew much about it. To most working-class comrades, faith in the correctness of the theory, and in its authoritative expositors, was probably sufficient. But a disproportionate part of the membership consisted of students, intellectuals, and professionals, who were interested in the contents of the Party's theory, that is, in the topics it dealt with; and they were more exposed to the enemy's theories. The Party had to take greater care to insure their orthodoxy. Professionals and intellectuals were considered unreliable by nature.[2] The thoroughly dependable Ph.D.'s—such as Herbert Aptheker, Philip Foner, Harry K. Wells, Howard Selsam, and Samuel Sillen—were few and had only tenuous connections with the scholarly communities. Others, who had close connections with their professional colleagues, had to be guided and occasionally corrected. The college students, who comprised a very large proportion of the coming generation of Party members and most of the future leaders, must learn how to resist the influence of their bourgeois professors and textbook authors. They must learn the correct approaches to the subjects they studied, and they must feel absolute confidence that the Party's theory had all the answers.

For those members the Party went to great lengths to demonstrate both the omnicompetence of its theory and the importance of that theory to them as individual Communists. It sponsored the Workers School and later the Jefferson School of Social Science, both in New York, and similar schools elsewhere. The Party's youth organizations after World War II focused on college students, and their periodicals published bibliographies in various disciplines,[3] to give student comrades enough supplementary reading to help them judge the material they encountered in class. The same magazines published syllabuses for group and individual study in various fields as well as in Marxist theory. The Party's official magazine printed course syllabuses and guides for the study of Foster's historical works and Stalin's latest contributions to theory. The Party held classes in Marxism, strategy and tactics, the Soviet Union, and the relationship of the Party to American history and society. There were classes for new members[4] and more advanced courses for future leaders and current leaders marked for promotion. Attendance was as much a duty as any other assignment.

The theory's omnicompetence did not necessarily provide a tempting short-cut for lazy students who would rather memorize a few simple dogmas than put in long hours of study. No doubt some felt attracted to it for that reason, but Party writers told the college students to take their academic studies seriously, and most did.[5] They must master not only Marxism-Leninism but also the subject matter of their college courses. An editorial in *New Foundations* told them to study hard, attend every class, and get good grades.

We have to be good students, . . . both to qualify for later jobs and to cut away the overgrown forest of misleading theories which obscure the real nature of our world. . . . We must provide the tool-arsenal which will help to level the towering falsehoods built up by servants of the property-owners to insure their exploiting position. We must see every fact of history and political economy, every concept of philosophy, art, and science which lays bare the true character of reality, as added ammunition to the arsenal which we will bring to the side of the workers. . . . We have the vital obligation to explode the myths that claim capitalism and democracy are synonymous, that despair of changing human nature, that see our society's evils as incurable—the sophisticated falsehoods promoted in our classes to train us as supporters of the reactionary *status quo*. We must seek within the writings of Marxist-Leninists the guides through the mass of confusing theories and data propounded in our books to discover the kernel of rational truth which may increase our understanding of reality.[6]

A writer in another of the youth periodicals quoted Lenin himself: " 'The task now is *to master science, to hammer out new forces of Bolshevik specialists in all branches of knowledge, to learn, learn and learn in the most stubborn fashion. What we need now is an influx of revolutionary youth into the field of science.'* " Similar exhortations pertaining to particular fields are scattered in Party literature, for example, Philip Foner's that "a major task confronting American Marxists today is that of rescuing labor historiography from two schools of writing which have gravely retarded the working class."[7]

All this was time-consuming labor, and the obligation was assumed mostly by students who carried regular course loads (which meant more courses, much more reading and writing, and higher standards of grading than is the case nowadays), often held part-time or full-time jobs, attended at least one and sometimes two or three Party meetings a week, were active in one or more campus organizations, and still had time for normal social activities. In addition, they wrote, mimeographed, and distributed leaflets; provided personnel for picket lines and demonstrations off campus; and attended Party and front-organization "rallies." (With respect to energy level, discipline, and diligence, these young Communists differed greatly from New Leftists.) Nonstudents must study, too, though the Party had less success with its exhortations to adults. In the issue of March, 1930, *Party Organizer* offered them advice on "Organizing Study Groups." These were small, voluntary classes, separate from official Party schools. Instruction #7 said: "The study groups should avail themselves of all American institutions which in any way can aid them with material in their work, such as libraries, museums, scientific institutions, etc., but never take any guidance or advice from such sources."

The command to master all knowledge must seem a tall order to non-Marxists, especially to academics who have learned that competence in one part of one field requires a lifetime of application and that each field of knowledge has principles and methods peculiar to it. The Party taught its members that these obstacles to omniscience applied only to the superficies; the basic principles and truths in every field were knowable to all accomplished Marxists, and only to them.[8] Whereas the professors and textbooks had the facts, the student comrades knew their meaning—or could get it by reading Marxist literature. At the start of a semester, conscientious young comrades looked up the Marxist works relevant to each of their courses and felt confident after reading critiques of assigned readings.

The new Party member must grasp that Marxism-Leninism was a unified *system* of thought. Just as all reality was interrelated, so was the science that comprehended it mentally. This claim enhanced the practical authority of the leaders over the rank and file, for an unbreakable thread connected the correct theory of the origin of life and the correct interpretation of primitive society to the inevitable leadership of the best Marxists—Earl Browder or William Z. Foster, as the case might be—and of the approved Party scholars. Because all things were interrelated, Party authorities repeatedly exhorted members to "link up" the workers' struggles for economic gains or union recognition, and students' struggles to get a good education, and other practical interests, with the truth about the Soviet Union, capitalism's responsibility for their problems, and so on. Bourgeois ideology also allegedly linked up everything, although it tried to obscure the connections. So, for example, a Communist should not be surprised to learn that a historian who misinterpreted the Reconstruction period of American history was also hostile toward the Soviet Union. "*All* official and liberal science *defends* wage slavery in one way or another. . . . To expect science to be impartial is as silly and naive as to expect impartiality from employers on the question as to whether the workers' wages should be increased by decreasing the profits of capital." This "link-up" of theory and real life meant that, since the capitalist *System* was doomed, so was its scholarly component. In capitalist societies, scholarship had reached its farthest point and would not progress in the future. Even the physical sciences, of all disciplines the least dependent on ideology, were degenerating into "mysticism."[9]

The Party had specialists—members and fellow travelers—in a variety of fields, who wrote books and articles and provided others with facts and bibliographies. (In addition to those mentioned elsewhere, these included Bernhard J. Stern in sociology, and Annette T. Rubinstein in literature. In science, the experts included J. D. Bernal and J. B. S. Haldane, both Englishmen, and various Soviet writers.) Their writings and credentials proved to Jimmy Higgins that Marxist scholarship deserved to be taken seriously by the academic community; that Marxist-Leninist generalizations were compatible with the most rigorous scholarship and in fact helped a scholar in his work; and that when Foster and other nonscholars ventured onto scholarly terrain, they drew upon the findings of credentialed specialists. As a group the Party scholars wielded enormous influence over the members, who had to look to them as guides to the application of Marxism to particular subject matters.

In the field of history, for example, the omnicompetence of Marxism-Leninism meant that

virtually all of the contemporary advances in American historiography are being made by scholars of the Left—William Z. Foster, Herbert Aptheker, Philip S. Foner, Harry Haywood, John Howard Lawson, James S. Allen and others. Indeed, if you take away these names and also those of the Negro people's historians—Dr. Du Bois, the disciples of Carter G. Woodson, etc.—what is there left worth mentioning?[10]

The scholarly credentials of Foster and Haywood were leadership positions in the CP; Lawson was a film writer; the historical works of Allen (pseudonym) were all published by Party-connected publishers. The author doubtless would have attributed the modest standing of all these men in the historical profession to the ideological corruption of those academics whose names were not worth mentioning. The student comrade, naturally, realized that these latter included his professors and the authors of the books they assigned.

The inclusion of nonhistorians on the list of those responsible for "virtually all of the contemporary advances in American historiography" implied that the only credential needed was mastery of Marxism-Leninism. This entailed more than theoretical achievement; other essentials were devotion to the interests of the working class and participation in its struggles.[11] The result was a hierarchy of authoritativeness that would have seemed odd to any outsider: nonhistorians, nonphysicists, nonphilosophers, and nonsociologists in the Party leadership spoke more authoritatively on all those fields than the Party's own specialists who had Ph.D.'s. In fact, Foster's endorsement of a historical work by a history Ph.D. carried more weight than the latter's endorsement of a historical work by Foster. But the oddness went even further: Foster and, earlier, Browder were ex officio authorities in *all* fields.

AT THE PINNACLE of the hierarchy of scholarly authority stood Marx, Engels, Lenin, and Stalin, and, just below them, Soviet scholars. We have already encountered this use of the Founders' writings, and we shall meet it again in later chapters; a few examples will suffice here.

When Stalin's essays on linguistics were published as a pamphlet in English,[12] every American Party branch was instructed to have an "educational" on it. The members, having read the pamphlet at home, were to discuss it and reach full acceptance and understanding. I recall that at the end of that discussion in my club, the leader asked if anyone still had any problems with Stalin's theses. One person did. The leader told him and one of the more "advanced" comrades to go into another room and talk the problem out. Meanwhile, the club went on to the next item on the agenda. Doubters invariably ended up in full agreement.

Soviet scholars stood just below Stalin on the ladder of living authority. Party and youth-organization periodicals occasionally published essays by them, and some of these were quite technical. For example, *The Communist*, which every Party member was supposed to read, published a four-part article that had appeared originally in a Soviet publication, on a very abstruse subject, in the issues of April, May, June, and July, 1941. It is hard to believe that the editors (Browder was officially the editor) thought that the readers would understand the technical parts of "Space and Time—Forms of the Existence of Matter," or that the editors understood them themselves. Evidently the hidden message was conveyed by the fact of publication. The work contains locutions and comments that suggest it was originally written to impress laymen. Its obvious purpose was to use the authority of the latest physics and mathematics to confirm what Marx, Engels, and Lenin had written. For the American Communist reading it, it also enhanced the authority of the American CP leaders whose decision it was to reprint the work for his enlightenment.[13]

The next level of authority in scholarship comprised the chairmen of the various countries' CPs. A particularly revealing evidence of Browder's intellectual authority is in a negative review by a nonhistorian, in *Clarity* (Winter, 1942), of Carl Van Doren's *Secret History of the American Revolution*. "Writing at the time of the Moscow treason trials," wrote the reviewer, "Earl Browder had given historians a lead to follow in studying the secret history of fifth column activity against the American cause. In his pamphlet *Traitors in American History*" Browder had described the Conway Cabal of 1777 and shown its similarity to the plot headed "by Tukhachevsky in the Soviet Union." Party writers often claimed that a Marxist-Leninist's understanding of the past helped him to understand the present; here, the reader learned that his Marxist-Leninist understanding of the present helped him to understand the past. That was why Browder, as the leader of the present struggle, could grasp the meaning of the American Revolution better than Van Doren did, and why the reviewer did not question his own qualification to decide who was the better historian.

Foster's enormous scholarly output covers the entire history of the Western Hemisphere. His history of the American CP begins in 1793 and does not get to the Party's founding until chapter twelve. He was also the ostensible author of a comprehensive history of American blacks, and an *Outline Political History of the Americas*. These three tomes were published in 1952, 1954, and 1951, respectively, and each comprised more than 560 pages exclusive of endnotes. And he wrote a history of the three Internationals (published in 1955 and containing 580 pages) and autobiographies, analyses of labor history and strategy, and many articles and pamphlets on other subjects. The books on American history contain many comments on other fields, justified by and demonstrating the "linking-up" principle. In the *History of the Communist Party of the United States*, for example, we learn that "during the Coolidge boom of the 1920's . . . James-Dewey pragmatism, the hard-boiled philosophy which says that whatever the capitalists are and do is right, flourished and spread in bourgeois circles" (p. 317). And, "The apostles of confusion and social reaction . . . have imported the putrid theories of Sartre, Heidegger, Kierkegaard and other devotees of cosmopolitanism, fascism, demoralization, and death. The capitalist-minded scientists are engaged in the reactionary and impossible task of harmonizing science with religion" (p. 535). We have no reason to believe that Foster had read James, Dewey, Sartre, Heidegger, or Kierkegaard, or that, if he had read the last three, he would have understood them. Rank and filers studying philosophy nevertheless took their cue from such comments—and there are others on other disciplines elsewhere in Foster's writings. Foster had to be right, because all bourgeois culture and scholarship were permeated by bourgeois ideology (with certain exceptions that Stalin explained in *On Linguistics*), which masters of Marxism-Leninism alone could discern. As Foster put it:

Under capitalism science is a slave to the class interests of the bourgeoisie. Thus biology justifies the mad class struggle and war; economics puts an unqualified blessing upon wage slavery; history proves that capitalism is society perfected; psychology explains away poverty on the basis of inferior beings, etc. Capitalist science is also a veritable fortress of metaphysical concepts of every kind. But Socialism strikes all these fetters from science. . . . Marxian dialectical materialism destroys the metaphysics that paralyzes bourgeois science.[14]

Underlying all aspects of this intellectual crisis of bourgeois society was its economic crisis: "The general crisis of capitalism is a highly complex matter, involving every phase of economics, politics, and the many other aspects of the capitalist system. Perhaps one can best explain the significance of this crisis by describing some of its major manifestations"—which Foster then proceeded to do. Jimmy Higgins had to infer that Foster knew all the complications omitted from the ensuing account. But how, one might have asked Comrade Jimmy, do you know that Foster knows? Answer: "Because he's chairman of the Party, and he wouldn't be if he didn't know."

It appears, however, that the submissive attitude was not quite universal, and the exceptions, such as the following episode, doubtless reinforced Foster's suspicion of petty-bourgeois comrades. *The Communist* of September, 1938, published an article by Foster on professionals in the Party. In response, a professionals' branch in the Midwest sent a letter to the editor, which appeared in the December issue. The writers explained that they had discussed Foster's article and that it had helped them correct certain errors in their thinking. But most of the physicians in the club balked at Foster's assertion that the medical doctrines of the American Medical Association (AMA) were reactionary. They thought a layman was unqualified to judge. The other members replied that Comrade Foster had undoubtedly sought advice from experts for that part of his essay and that "a man can tell a good egg from a bad one without being able to lay one." The club then discussed how the AMA had retarded the development of medical science and was subservient to business interests. But they wished the article had been worded "less bluntly." The letter was signed "Comradely yours, Medical director of professional branch." The tone throughout was humble and respectful; the writers had obviously chosen each word with extreme care.

Foster began his reply with a comment on the denial of a layman's right to judge the field of medicine:

Such a point of view cannot be accepted by Marxists. It is a remnant of the guildism characteristic of bourgeois professionals: the tendency to conceive of their profession as a sort of mystery quite beyond the understanding of all outsiders. It is in this narrow craft and caste spirit that we find engineers arguing that only trained engineers can know the real course of industry; artists contending that only artists are really qualified to explain art, etc. Such people try to make intellectual monopolies of their occupations, to build Chinese walls of incomprehensibility around them.

But Marxists do not recognize such unscalable technical barriers. One need not be an expert in the details of a profession in order to understand its general tendency, although, of course, the more detailed knowledge one has the better. If this were not true, then it would have been impossible for Marxian theoreticians, especially Engels and Lenin, to make their scientific analysis of the wide field of science, art and letters.

We cannot know whether any of the doctors, in his secret thoughts, doubted that that last invocation of the authority of Engels and Lenin clinched the matter, or whether he entertained the heretical thought that Engels might have been as unequipped to speak as authoritatively on anthropology and chemistry, and Lenin on physics and epistemology, as Foster was on medicine. *The Communist* published nothing more on the matter.[15]

Fourteen years later another comrade offered a mild—and *very* respectful— criticism of the portions on Indian history in Foster's *Outline Political History of the Americas*. Foster replied to him as he had to the doctors. About the current academic work on Indians, he wrote that "some of the . . . stuff is of real value"—he mentioned "Radin," omitting the first name (Paul) of this eminent anthropologist, thus implying casual familiarity with the literature— "but for the most part it suffers from the usual shallowness and class bias of bourgeois historians." Only Communist scholars, he added, could write the true story of the Indians. "Obviously, this letter is no place to outline all the problems and tasks that confront the Marxist historian of the Indian peoples; but at least a few of these may be indicated. They include:. . . . " And there follow five pages of small-print, extremely detailed history, which must have been provided by a specialist in the field.[16]

On the next rung down on the ladder of intellectual authority were the Party's theoreticians. Some held Ph.D.'s, and others were intellectual commissars, most notably V. J. Jerome, who often played the role of watchdog of ideological purity. This function was especially necessary because many comrades read certain magazines that the Party influenced but did not control, or Party journals that might err owing to the parochial concerns of their writers. In the former category was *Science and Society*; in the latter, *Jewish Life*. In a two-part article in *The Communist* (December, 1937, and January, 1938), for example, Jerome reviewed the first year of publication of *Science and Society* and in the first installment excoriated Marxist intellectuals who did not accept every tenet of Marxism as interpreted by the Party. They were (if sincere) dilettantes at best. He criticized one essay by philosopher V. J. McGill on logical positivism, and he wrote equally patronizingly about an essay by mathematician Dirk Struik on mathematics. In the second installment, Jerome attacked an essay on literary criticism by William Phillips and Philip Rahv, published before they were "exposed as Trotskyites." In the critiques of other articles, Jerome showed himself to be conversant with Keynes's economics, the underdevelopment of Puerto Rico, Italian agriculture, the Supreme Court's decisions on civil rights, literary theory, Honoré Daumier, Henry Adams, and literary opposition to Utilitarianism in early-nineteenth-century England. In each critique Jerome offered suggestions for improvement: in general, the writers should be less abstract and conciliatory toward anti-Communist academics, write more polemically, and participate in the struggle against Trotskyism. Finally, he complained that the first volume of *Science and Society* had included no articles on the Soviet Union and its achievements. Jerome's tone throughout, where it was not vituperative, was condescending. He closed the survey by saying that the journal had begun auspiciously and gave reason to hope it would fulfill its purposes.[17]

Generalists such as Jerome could write authoritatively on all subjects because they could deduce particular theories from the overall theory of Marxism-Leninism. Specialists in the various fields might provide supporting material, as well as proof to outsiders that the Party fostered research and could match bourgeois scholars datum for datum. The writings of Party economists Victor Perlo and Anna Rochester were as full of statistics and other facts as those of bourgeois economists. The historical works of Aptheker and Foner cited primary sources as copiously as those of bourgeois historians. Jimmy Higgins received the impression that the authors had confronted all the evidence and arguments in the works they were refuting.[18] But these Party works resembled conventional scholarship only superficially. Since the "conclusions" followed deductively from Marxist-Leninist theory, none of the authors ever tested the correctness of the master theories. The "linking-up" principle required each specialist to incorporate in his writings facts and generalizations in fields concerning which he knew nothing but what his comrades had written (and occasional statements by bourgeois scholars accepted by Party scholars). And those comrades, specialists in their own fields, had relied on material furnished by the specialists who in turn relied on *them*. The philosophers got their history and economics from the Party's own historians and economists; the latter got their philosophy from the Party's philosophers; and so on. The scholarly interchange was circular, and the scholars were intellectually insulated from external challenges.

On a still lower rung of the ladder of intellectual authority were those with no real claim to academic expertise but whose names evoked respect on other grounds. One such authority was the screenwriter John Howard Lawson, whose book *Film in the Battle for Ideas* was published by *Masses & Mainstream* in 1953. In his comments on the film *The Red Badge of Courage* Lawson revealed the essence of the abolitionist movement, the Reconstruction era, capitalism in the Gilded Age, the Homestead and Coeur d'Alene strikes, the panic of 1893, and the Populist movement (see pp. 31, 33). Whether Lawson's solutions of controverted historical problems were true is less significant than the absolute confidence with which he offered them. Like the credentialed scholars and the other Party polymaths, he relied on authority and deduction from basic theory. And, like them, he in effect offered Comrade Jimmy a model for the latter's own approach to scholarly issues.

Because Party scholarship was dependent on authority, deductive in method, and largely self-contained, it was relatively static. Academic scholarship meanwhile kept benefiting from new findings and freewheeling controversy. Non-Marxist criticisms of Party scholarship were disposed of with ad hominem allusions to the critics' bad faith or, if they were "progressives," to their inadequate understanding. As a result, Party scholars often relied on outdated theories. The consensus in academia was automatically suspect; no member of the CPUSA could accept it unless the top authorities told him to. The Party thus paid for the permanent and comforting authority of Marxism-Leninism by falling farther and farther behind "bourgeois" scholarship. Of course it did not see the relationship in this way, for Marxism-Leninism had one feature that no other worldview had: it both transcended and informed all the disciplines from the most general propositions to the most trivial statements of fact.[19] Therefore, all assertions in Party scholarship that touched on more than one discipline were circular, so far as the testing of their correctness was concerned. The sole test was consistency with other assertions that in turn were tested by their consistency with those that were tested by their consistency with *them*. So long as the whole assortment of assertions fitted together, each must be correct. It is not surprising, then, that Party anthropological ideas leaned heavily on Engels's *The Origin of the Family, Private Property, and the State* (1884) and Morgan's *Ancient Society* (1877).[20] Or that Herbert Aptheker kept repeating that certain turn-of-the-century racist historians of Reconstruction typified academic scholarship in that field, long after this had stopped being true. The Party scholars' loyalty as scholars was not to their professional guilds but to the Party. Those two loci of intellectual loyalty differed profoundly in their very nature, for the usual specialized knowledge and standards of achievement in the professional communities were irrelevant to a Party in which the top authorities were generalists.[21]

Reciprocal validation of scholarly assertions, combined with isolation from academia, had another consequence: gross misstatements of fact went uncorrected. Aptheker, for example, wrote that the philosophy of "a professor at Cambridge University, Mr. Michael Oakeshott, . . . postulates not only no world but also no values." It would be uncharitable to infer that Aptheker knew his readers would probably not check the statement against what the distinguished British conservative had written; let us surmise that he had misunderstood Oakeshott. But any academic journal would have rejected—and not because of ideological bias—a manuscript containing this evidence of ignorance of its subject. Or, if the article had managed to get published, readers would have written letters to the editor citing quotations from Oakeshott and wondering what had happened to the editors' standards. Foster's *The Negro People in American History* contains dozens of elementary factual errors. One of them deals with the Dred Scott case. The decision, he wrote, made it possible for slaves to "be legally bought and sold in New York and Boston." Foster would have learned differently if he had read the primary sources or any secondary account. A non-Party publisher would have sent the manuscript to an outside reader who would have caught the error; but Foster's book was issued by International Publishers.[22]

As JIMMY HIGGINS, when still a new member, absorbed the Party's attitude toward scholarship, he received strong encouragement from the extremely polemical tone used in references to enemy intellectuals. There was, in addition, a sort of Index of forbidden books and authors. Sidney Hook, Arthur Koestler, and other anti-Communist intellectuals were invariably depicted as monsters. Former Communists have admitted that many years had to pass, after they had consciously rejected the Party and its way of thinking, before they could bring themselves to read those men's works. The Party's glorification of Pavlov,[23] it seems, had more than one justification: the very mention of the names of the writers on the Index activated a conditioned reflex of revulsion that reason alone could not overcome.

These automatisms—the hatred for people whose works the member never read, and the taken-for-granted framework for all beliefs—coexisted with an extreme self-consciousness (different from self-awareness). One gets the feeling, from reading the lower-level writers, that they were constantly spying on themselves, vigilantly choosing just the correct words and staying well within the boundaries of approved ideas. Their meticulousness had its counterpart in the Party's rejection of "spontaneity" in tactics (Lenin and Stalin were the authorities for this abhorrence of any action not guided by theory), as well as its horror of the very idea of an economy running itself without a central planning agency, or of a spiritual realm that did not obey the laws of cause and effect. This theoretical prejudice suggests a divided personality that was constantly looking over its own shoulder from behind, ready to pounce on any inadvertent slip into randomness. Some Party writings, in fact, convey the impression that beneath all the usual grievances against capitalism lay a visceral revulsion against a planless life, a fear of the unexpected. Some comrades seem to have dreaded the prospect of taking each day as it came and accepting things for their own sakes or rejecting them out of sheer personal taste. The horror of such a life must have been far more than a matter of theory. The Party's merging of operational and theoretical authority protected members against this threat.

Some people who feel thus threatened find their comfort in compulsions to punctuality, others in arranging the pencils on their desks so that they all point in the same direction. Others become ideologues of system. Not all rank-and-file Party members possessed this trait, of course; the Communist commitment had several sources and satisfied a variety of needs. But the Party appealed to people who had this trait; it made them feel comfortable and safe. Unlike the nonideological compulsive, this type of person devoted his life to bringing the blessings of system to all. Granted, religious people also have have an image of what they should be and watch themselves so as to spot their lapses and nurture their virtues. The difference is that the religious person's vigilance is rewarded by greater self-awareness and hence humility; the Communist's, by successful projection of his personal traits onto external things and hence arrogance.[24]

The Party helped fend off the threat also by disguising the nature of its authority: its writers reiterated that Communists always thought for themselves, that they never took any assertion on faith but individually applied dispassionate, scientific logic to every intellectual problem.[25] The student comrades thought of themselves this way. Their bourgeois classmates learned what the professors taught and stopped there; the Communists had the further task of linking Marxist-Leninist theory with everything they were taught. My recollection is that they were on the whole brighter than the average student, and they certainly read much more. They formed Marxist study groups on campus and discussed arcane questions endlessly. A few wrote articles in the Party's youth periodicals, and these were often carefully thought out.

But their intellectual sharpness had an unfortunate consequence: it reinforced their natural tendency to patronize the great thinkers of the past. Their theoreticians provided them with models and justifications. Party writings on philosophy, for example, dismissed the theories of Plato, Kant, and other geniuses as reflections of the interests of the ruling classes of their societies.[26] The student thereby learned to approach past thinkers not as possible teachers but as moments in the intellectual history of class society. He must learn not *from* them but *about* them. To admit the former possibility would have been to open the comfortably closed, preinterpreted, wholly controlled universe to the unpredictable. (For, paradoxically, timeless truths about human nature consist with unpredictable outcomes of free choice, and the Marxist theory of a changing human nature consists with scientific predictability.) This attitude toward the great thinkers of the past must have been especially congenial also to the young members. A tendency to condescend toward past philosophers is—as every professor knows—virtually a defining trait of bright seventeen- to twenty-two year-olds. No youngsters patronize the great athletes, inventors, generals, or physicists of the past, but any sophomore in Philosophy 101 can refute Aristotle. The common explanation—that the youngster imagines himself standing at the pinnacle of knowledge—will not do, for the same student, standing at the pinnacle of knowledge of physics and the other sciences, respects earlier scientists who knew less than he does. It is a question of subject matter. In the same category as philosophy belong macroeconomic theory, religion, political and social theory, history, and psychology—fields that deal with man and interpret his nature. The bright nonradical student who, after taking an introductory course, can refute all past philosophers is evincing a modern attitude toward the humanities that differs from the Party's merely in degree.

The student Party members pushed this attitude much further, owing to the mutual reinforcement of certain personal traits and Party doctrine. Not coincidentally, their favorite game was chess, which requires great concentration, analytical ability, and a good memory, but needs no understanding of the depths of human nature or confrontation with the ultimate questions. They played scholarship the way they played chess. They pushed concepts and facts around the universe of matter-in-motion, according to the laws of dialectical and historical materialism, and never lost sight of the pattern in which even a lowly pawn, across the board from the main action, played an essential part. And their delight when they discovered a new combination was not the "aha! experience" of the scientist but the relief felt by the obsessive seeker after connections who cannot bear loose ends and at the same time wants only to win. These young comrades defined learning in terms of fitting the data furnished by "bourgeois" scholars into the Marxist framework. They never noticed the large questions that the Party literature begged, that its "conclusions" flowed from carefully selected data, its shallow depiction of man, and the breezy arrogance with which the Party theoreticians disposed of Plato, Aristotle, Kant, all theologians, and most other geniuses of Western civilization, including even poor Hegel, who did not know he was standing on his head.

Deep down, these students were really not much interested in the fundamental questions raised by all those thinkers, or in the past. They, and the other Jimmy Higginses, focused their minds more on the present and the future, and specifically on their "tasks" as members of the Party destined to lead the revolution.

NOTES

1. See A. Rossi, *A Communist Party in Action: An Account of the Organization and Operations in France* (New Haven, Conn.: Yale University Press, 1949), pp. 205–6.

2. For Foster's attitude toward middle-class radicals and intellectuals, see, e.g., his *History of the Communist Party of the United States* (New York: IP, 1952), pp. 99–106, 119–21, 427. See also M. J. Olgin's characterization of petty-bourgeois intellectuals, in his *Trotskyism* (New York: Workers Library, 1935), Chap. 2. Another example is Samuel Sillen (a Ph.D. in English), "The Irrationals," *NM*, October 29, 1940, pp. 20–22. According to Morris Ernst and David Loth, *Report on the American Communist* (New York: Henry Holt & Company, 1952), p. 4, the Party members they surveyed worked mostly in jobs and professions that "call[ed] for no manual dexterity." "In the medical profession, they are more likely to be diagnosticians and psychiatrists than surgeons. They tend more toward the law or teaching than to engineering or architecture. They hold clerical jobs in industry rather than work at machines." And so on.

3. *New Foundations* published many such bibliographies. E.g.: "Marxism and Philosophy," 1 (Fall, 1947): 90–96, contained over 300 titles, including difficult works, some in Russian and other foreign languages, and afterward "Notes on the Use of This Bibliography," which included insistence on assimilation, not rote learning, of those items labeled "Basic Works." The last such Note is: "All other works must be analyzed critically; they are not all completely authoritative." Then there is "Marxism and Political Economy," 1 (Spring, 1948): 168–74; this bibliography of about 175 items included a section on "Keynes and Keynesism." Later issues had bibliographies on the arts, education, the Soviet Union, Negro history, the American working class. These lists were clearly the products of long hours of hard work, and genuine knowledge of the fields.

4. See, e.g., curriculum in *PO* 9 (December, 1936): 24–30; one of the questions the teacher was to ask was: "When did classes of society come into existence?"

5. See the interesting comments by Al Richmond, in his autobiography *A Long View from the Left* (New York: Delta, 1972), pp. 123–25.

6. "Just to Learn Is Not Enough," *NF* 2 (Fall, 1948): 4, 6. See also Frank Cestare, "Earl Browder—Molder of Character," *CL* 3 (Spring, 1942): 33; V. I. Lenin, *The Young Generation* (New York: IP, 1940), pp. 30, 32–34; and comment by Granville Hicks, *Where We Came Out* (New York: Viking, 1954), p. 38.

7. Carl Ross, "Lenin and Stalin—The Leaders of Youth," *CL* 1 (Fall, 1940): 61; Philip Foner, "Labor's Story: Myth and Reality," *NM*, August 26, 1947, p. 3. (Foner has followed his own advice ever since, having published more than fifty books, two of which have been proven, in print, to contain wholesale plagiarism. See exchange between James O. Morris and Foner in *Labor History* 12 [Winter, 1971], and book review by Thomas Dublin in *Labor History* 19 [Fall, 1978].)

8. E.g., Joshua Strauss, book review, *PA* 25 (August, 1946): 765: "That is not to say that anthropologists and archaeologists have not added a great deal to our knowledge of primitive institutions. They have learned much, but about surface phenomena." On the same logic, the Party conferred the title "scientist" on anyone it admired. Aptheker referred to "scientists of social change such as the two giants of the last and the present centuries—Frederick Douglass and Paul Robeson." ("The

Negro Scientist and Inventor," *MM*, February, 1951, reprinted in Aptheker's pamphlet *Toward Negro Freedom* [New York: New Century, 1956], p. 145.) If Douglass and Robeson were scientists, anyone could be, including Jimmy Higgins, and real scientific credentials were meaningless.

9. Herbert Aptheker, *The American Civil War* (New York: IP, 1961), p. 5; space-filler in *PA* 28 (February, 1949): 92, quoting Lenin's *Marx-Engels-Marxism*. For an excellent illustration of the linking-up of science with politics, by both Marxists and anti-Marxists, see Hyman Lumer (a biology Ph.D.), "The Achievements of Marxism-Leninism in the Field of Genetics," *PA* 29 (July, 1950): 32–54. On the decay of science, see, e.g., Philip M. Tilden, "Lenin's 'Materialism and Empirio-Criticism' and the Crisis in Physics Today," *PA* 32 (October, 1953): 50–51, 54, 59–60; Hal Jorling, "Science," *YW*, September 17, 1935, p. 8. For a criticism of the linking-up principle, see Sidney Hook, *Reason, Social Myths and Democracy* (New York: John Day, 1940), Chap. 10.

10. Samuel Robinson, "The Negro People Speak," review of Aptheker's *A Documentary History of the Negro People in the United States*, in *PA* 31 (February, 1952): 63. See also Herbert Aptheker, *History and Reality* (New York: Cameron Associates, 1955), p. 218; and Aptheker, *The Truth about Hungary* (New York: Mainstream Publishers, 1957), p. 11; in both places he calls W. E. B. Du Bois the "dean of American scholars." Du Bois earned a place among distinguished American scholars, but he was hardly "the dean" of them all. In Aptheker, "Historians Ask New Questions," *MM* 9 (January, 1956): 11, Du Bois is "the dean of American historical scholars." See also Aptheker, "Cold-War Liars and New Historians," *PA* 50 (August, 1971): 90, and Aptheker, "The American Historical Profession," *PA* 51 (January, 1972): 52; those two pages contain identical passages in which Du Bois is characterized as "the most distinguished and creative historian then [the late 1930s] living in the United States" and "the dean of real American scholarship." As to Haywood, his "scholarly" achievement was his book *Negro Liberation* (New York: IP, 1948). His autobiography, *Black Bolshevik* (Chicago: Liberator Press, 1978), reveals a scantily furnished mind; Haywood drops names of scholars freely as though he were familiar with the literature, but most of them are misspelled and misused. As to the other pretensions of Party scholars, see, e.g., Harry K. Wells, " 'Philosophy in Revolution,' " *PA* 36 (July, 1957): 35, in which Wells says that Selsam's book *Philosophy in Revolution* is "the best book of any 'school' by an American philosopher, to appear in the last two decades." And Robert Thompson, in his review of Foster's *Outline Political History of the Americas*, in *PA* 30 (February, 1951): 93, wrote: "It has fallen on the shoulders of the foremost Marxist of our Party, Comrade Foster, boldly to invade territory which the bourgeois historians cannot tread."

11. See, e.g., Aptheker's catalog of Foster's qualifications, in "On Foster's 'History of the Three Internationals,' " *PA* 34 (May, 1955): 3–4.

12. John Gates characterizes these essays in typical fashion in his pamphlet *On Guard against Browderism*[,] *Titoism*[,] *Trotskyism* (New York: New Century, 1951), pp. 6, 7.

13. Another article about which the same comments might be made was M. Alpatov, "On the Transition from the Ancient World to the Middle Ages," reprinted from a Soviet historical journal in *PA* 31 (July, 1952): 45–59. All the footnote citations are to works by Marx, Engels, Lenin, and Stalin. It begins, "The comments of J. V. Stalin concerning the revolution of the slaves mark a new stage in the development

of the Marxist-Leninist science of society. For the first time in the history of science the question of the revolutionary transition from the ancient slave social relations to feudalism in Western Europe was comprehensively answered." Stalin's comments were in a speech to the All-Union Congress of Collective Farm Shock-Workers and in a report to the Seventeenth Congress of the Soviet CP. (This is linking-up with a vengeance.) See also M. Kammari and F. Konstantinoff, "Science and Superstructure," *PA* 32 (February, 1953): 51–65; all the footnote references are to works by Marx, Engels, Lenin, and Stalin.

14. William Z. Foster, *Toward Soviet America* (New York: Coward-McCann, 1932), pp. 111–12. This book was repudiated some years after it appeared. One reason, probably, was the title; that slogan was dropped in 1936. The book also contained some undiplomatic language about religion that conflicted with later Party policy. The basic doctrines and attitudes, however, remained unaltered throughout the Party's lifetime, and the book's very frankness makes it valuable in the present study.

15. Engels on anthropology: see esp. *The Origin of the Family, Private Property and the State* (New York: IP, 1942). Engels on chemistry: *Dialectics of Nature* (New York: IP, 1940); this book contains physics and other science too, as well as an anthropological essay, "The Part Played by Labour in the Transition from Ape to Man," which was also available as a pamphlet. Lenin on physics and epistemology: "Materialism and Empirio-Criticism," pp. 87–409 of V. I. Lenin, *Selected Works*, Vol. 11 (New York: IP, 1943). In addition, many pamphlets published in English by the Foreign Languages Publishing House, Moscow, were available to Jimmy Higgins. One such (my copy has a penciled-in price of 15¢) was S. I. Vavilov, *Lenin and Philosophical Problems of Modern Physics*, 1953. See also William Z. Foster, "Elements of a People's Cultural Policy," *NM*, April 23, 1946, pp. 6–9, which contains erudite allusions to many societies in all periods and their forms and social structures, giving the reader the impression that Foster was fully qualified to draw the conclusions in the article. In "Soviet Stress on History Writing," *PA* 33 (December, 1954): 56, Foster said "there is nothing so complicated that it cannot be said in a form that the workers and their political allies can readily understand," and that bourgeois historians had for too long been free to distort history and thus "poison the minds of the people." Cf. Nemmy Sparks, "English or Algebra?" *PA* 35 (March, 1957): 64 (written during the thaw following the Twentieth Congress): "Marxist writing, in its handling of the most technical theoretical questions, cannot expect to be always comprehensible to all, any more than can any other science." Sparks was criticizing his comrades' penchant for writing jargon. But the problem was a real one: Foster had to be right, if he and other self-professed polymaths were to wield intellectual authority; but Sparks had to be right, if Marxism was to enjoy the scientific status that made Party members superior to everyone else.

16. "On a Marxist History of the North American Indians: A Reader's Letter and a Reply from William Z. Foster," *PA* 31 (May, 1952): 52–60.

17. See also V. J. Jerome, "Unmasking an American Revisionist of Marxism," *COM* 12 (January, 1933): 50–82, on all aspects of philosophy (the revisionist here was Sidney Hook). Jerome reviewed the first year of publication of *Jewish Life*, in *COM* 17 (September, 1938), in the same way as he had discussed *Science and Society*.

18. Comrade Jimmy did not notice the gap between the documentary evidence and statistics, on the one hand, and the ideologically colored "conclusions," on the other. A typical example of what he overlooked is in Herbert Aptheker's pamphlet

The Labor Movement in the South during Slavery (New York: IP, n.d.), which is full of facts, dates, and names, and lists an impressive array of works in fifty-five footnotes for twenty pages of text, but is also full of non sequiturs and overgeneralizations from the data and statements that had nothing to do with the data that ostensibly supported them. Sometimes Party scholars identified genuine topics that had been neglected or needed reexamination. But the way they treated such topics is a different story. See, e.g., Aptheker's *Negro Slave Revolts in the United States, 1526–1860* (New York: IP, 1939), a sixty-nine-page pamphlet, and his book *American Negro Slave Revolts* (New York: Columbia University Press, 1943), which has been criticized by several scholars for an assortment of flaws, all traceable to his ideological apriorism.

19. See Frank S. Meyer, *The Moulding of Communists* (New York: Harcourt, Brace, 1961), p. 52.

20. On rare occasions the Founders were corrected. See, e.g., J. B. S. Haldane's footnotes to a republication of Engels's "The Role of Labor in the Transition from Ape to Man," in *CL* 2 (Summer, 1941): 82–94. Haldane was exceptional in being both a distinguished scholar and a devoted Communist—and therefore relatively invulnerable to criticism by Party commissars. But even someone of his stature would not have got away with a correction of Lenin or Stalin.

21. Party scholars have caught up with academia in recent years. As the latter has moved leftward, non-Communist scholars have accorded Party-member colleagues more respect (and teaching posts and access to publishing facilities). The Party scholars' allegiance is still primarily to the Party, but their interpretations of particular subject matters are no longer so far from the main stream. Their basic intellectual framework and postulates remain what they were, but they have broadened the subject area they deal with.

22. Aptheker, *History and Reality*, p. 32; Foster, *The Negro People in American History* (New York: IP, 1954), p. 174 (see also p. 178).

23. But cf. Ralph Doyster's critical review of Harry K. Wells's recently published *Ivan P. Pavlov: Toward a Scientific Psychology and Psychiatry*, in *MM* 10 (March, 1957): 55–59. Though published by International, Wells's book evidently went too far toward mechanical cause-effect explanations. The review is, in fact, devastating and insightful. According to Raymond A. Bauer, *The New Man in Soviet Psychology* (Cambridge, Mass.: Harvard University Press, 1952), passim, Soviet psychologists had long since abandoned simple conditioned-reflex theory for one that gave scope to free will and thus individuals' responsibility for their behavior.

24. See, in general, Jules Monnerot, *Sociology and Psychology of Communism* (Boston: Beacon Press, 1953), pp. 129–31.

25. See, e.g., Herbert Aptheker, "The Question of Academic Freedom," *PA* 35 (May, 1956): 50. For a comment on this question as it concerned French intellectuals, see Rossi, *A Communist Party in Action*, pp. 226–28. As to my word "dispassionate," it did not mean nonpartisan; partisanship on the side of the working class was a scientific necessity.

26. See, e.g., Howard Selsam, *Socialism and Ethics* (New York: IP, 1943), and Harry K. Wells, *Pragmatism: Philosophy of Imperialism* (New York: IP, 1954), both passim. One of many models for this sort of thinking was Harry Martel, "Some Aspects of Materialism and Consciousness," *The Benjamin Rush Bulletin*, No. 2 (May, 1949): 7: a reference to "the scholasticism of concepts which made the philosophies

of Berkeley and Hume possible and detrimental to the development of science." Their epistemological theories, said Martel, "could arise only because of a divorce of theory and practice." The student comrade reading this article knew he escaped this limitation, because he understood and acted out the unity of theory and practice.

7

Tasks, Standards, and Self-Criticism

ACCORDING TO PARTY THEORY, the "objective" prerequisites for the socialist revolution in the United States had existed since the 1890s, when the era of imperialism, the highest stage of capitalism, began. The Party's "task" was to create the "subjective" prerequisites, that is, to convert the majority of workers and small farmers, and some petty-bourgeois allies. No matter how dreadfully the workers and small farmers suffered, they could not discover socialist truth by themselves. Jimmy Higgins's Party life consisted largely in his carrying out an unending series of "tasks," all of which served the Party's overall "task" of educating and leading the masses.

Observers of the CP who have written about its fondness for certain terms—"concrete," "life itself," "scientific," "correct," and others—should put "task" at the top of the list. It was chiefly by means of the "tasks" concept that the Party linked the objective and subjective conditions for socialism, and that Comrade Jimmy related himself to objective reality. He could hardly have helped doing so; the literature he read constantly was saturated with "tasks." Here are some examples of how Party writers used the term.

"The central mass task of the Party," wrote Clarence Hathaway in 1932, "is the task of seriously preparing and organizing the immediate struggles of the workers against the bourgeois offensive with the particular objective of drawing the workers quickly into the broadest mass struggles against the danger of war and for the defense of the Soviet Union." In 1934 the national leaders told members to "ask the questions: 'How much of our concrete tasks have we carried out? Why have we failed to carry out certain tasks? Who is responsible for not carrying out these tasks?' . . . We must make every Party member, from the members of the Central Committee down to the newest member in the units, feel individual responsibility for carrying out these tasks." In 1941 a leading theoretician wrote, "our task" is "to activize millions of housewives. . . . Our task is to convince them that their place is in a greater arena than just the four walls of their kitchens. . . . Naturally that task requires that we approach the women *in the home*." He then quoted Browder who had said, "our task [is] to win the majority," who include women, and that since the female relatives of unionists were not yet a source of strength to the unions, *precisely there is the problem which sets the main task of our work among women.*" In 1949, according to Frederick V. Field (the Party's chief authority on Asia): "It is our task, as American Communists, to help mobilize the forces of labor and all anti-imperialists in our country, to deal such further blows at Wall Street, that the Chinese New Democracy may consolidate its victories and move firmly and powerfully on the road to Socialism." Finally, another randomly chosen document will illustrate how the youth periodicals used the term: "the fight for the youth is becoming now [1931] exceptionally grave, hence, the task of winning the majority of the toiling youth becomes the chief and decisive task of the YCL. This task is organically linked up with the problem of winning the majority of the working class to the side of Communism."[1] Thousands of examples of "tasks," in titles and texts, may be found by random scanning of Party literature.

Every segment of the Party and of its youth organizations had its tasks—for example, to build this or that union or organization, to publicize some new book by Browder or Foster or Stalin, to increase the circulation of the *Worker*, to raise specified quotas of money in the frequent fund drives. Jimmy Higgins received his individual tasks at club meetings. Club leaders "checked up" on his fulfillment of his tasks. Section leaders "checked up" on the clubs' work. Higher-level leaders "checked up" on the work of the sections. The Moscow authorities often commented on the American CP's fulfillment of its tasks. Each level above the section had a "control commission" to supervise the checking up and to assign "control tasks" to delinquent members, who were on probation while they were carrying out their control tasks. In short, Party members interpreted the "tasks" concept strictly and literally.

They did so not only because performance was monitored, but also because Party theory said that all the tasks were fulfillable. These documents did more than inspire and exhort; they implicitly, and sometimes explicitly, predicted success, *if* Comrade Jimmy carried out his tasks. This meant that if the predicted results did not occur, he had not carried out his tasks correctly. Party members became so accustomed to these prophecies of victory that many who left the Party continued to believe them. Memoirs of ex-Communists abound with speculations about how much more effective the Party would have been if not for this or that "error." They usually blamed the leaders. The leaders almost always—except when Moscow blamed them—blamed the rank and file. So did Jimmy Higgins.

To understand why he blamed himself, we must note the role of "tasks" in the Party's theory of history. Marx had said that, within constraints imposed by technology and class structure, man makes his own history—implying that the course of history might have been somewhat different from its actual course. Whole classes, said the Party, had their tasks—implying that fulfillment was not foreordained. The early bourgeoisie had the task of smashing feudal class relations so as to develop the productive forces, and the working class now had the task of smashing bourgeois class relations and the bourgeois state.

The fact that the word "tasks" came naturally to the writers' minds, when they were discussing both the course of history and Jimmy Higgins's handing out leaflets at a factory gate, implies that History itself, speaking through the leaders, had assigned him his tasks. The rest was up to him. "It is not written anywhere that the workers must accept the Party leadership," wrote one leader; we must prove our right to lead them. "We are the bearers of American culture and civilization," intoned Browder, "and we must use every hour to qualify ourselves for that noble and historic role." Georgi Dimitroff went even further: "we Communists bear responsibility for the fate of the working class, of the labor movement, responsibility for the fate of our own nation, for the fate of all toiling humanity." But the reward will be as great as the responsibility: "To us, the workers, . . . belongs the world. . . . The present rulers of the capitalist world are but *temporary rulers*."[2]

Comrade Jimmy's responsibility was all the greater in view of the bright prospects for success. In 1933, "Communists need only to exert even slight efforts and the leadership [of masses of American workers] will fall into their hands." A year later, the Central Committee announced that "the central task of the Party" was to lead the workers "in the general class battles for the overthrow of the capitalist dictatorship and the setting up of a Soviet government." Since conditions were so favorable, that outcome must have been within sight—in April, 1934. In July, 1935, prospects looked even better:

Developments are moving our way. Larger masses than ever before are drawn into political discussion and struggles in which the central question . . . is the question of power, of form of government. And we will have from now on much greater possibilities to present to the masses and to win larger numbers of them to our . . . answer . . . : Soviet Power, a Soviet America, a Soviet Constitution, a government of Workers and Farmers.

Two years later, Foster spoke directly and ominously to Comrade Jimmy: "the objective situation is highly favorable to the growth of the Party and . . . if our Party is not growing faster the cause is to be found elsewhere than in the objective situation." "The winning of the young generation in America," wrote a YCL leader, "is not a very difficult task once the Party understands its importance."[3]

Since understanding was the key,

only he can lay claim to the title of Marxist in the U.S. who knows not only the general writings of Marxism but the history of his own land, and who tries to apply these writings to the solutions of the problems of America. This also means that the student must study American economic, social, and political history, the trade union movement, the Socialist and Communist movements, the Negro question, not only in the works of the founders of Marxism, but also in the writings of the early American Socialists and Communists and present-day Marxists, a list of which works is available through International Publishers and New Century Publishers. It is necessary to know well the history of the struggle for Socialism in our land. Moreover, it is essential to study the works of bourgeois writers—of course critically.

These tasks apparently would leave plenty of time for study of more specific subjects: "we set as the task of all leading bodies of our Party to more consciously assimilate and master the lessons of Comrade Stalin's leadership, so gloriously exemplified in the Communist Party of the Soviet Union and its world historic achievement of building the socialist society."[4]

Not just the leaders, but Jimmy Higgins too, had to master those lessons. He must also know how to apply what he learned: "Let every one of us master the democratic program and the slogans that express it, in order to become master-agitators among the people." "A Communist, to fulfill his role as an advanced worker," said *The Communist* in 1932,

must be able to impart to the workers . . . the significance of these struggles, the lessons to be learned from them, and a wider comprehension of the historical role of the working class. He must be able to make these struggles successful, not only from the point of view of winning this or that demand—which, of course, is of first importance—but also from the point of view that the workers engaged in these struggles emerge from them with a keener political understanding. This is a task for every Communist.

The graduate of a Party training school, summarizing what she had learned, concluded that "when our comrades understand more fully the role and tasks of our Party, . . . we will be able to leap ahead in the organization of the unorganized, in the building of the Farmer-Labor Party, in becoming a real mass party of the revolutionary American working people."[5] From which it obviously followed that if those things did not happen, the comrades had not fully understood the role of the Party and their own tasks. Another version of this incredibly onerous task was Browder's statement that "every member must assume the task of leading and educating at least one worker outside the Party; he shall consider himself a real Bolshevik only when fifty to a hundred workers regularly look to him for guidance and leadership in the problems of the class struggle." Moreover, these tasks were unremitting. The "Thesis on Agitation" promulgated by the International in 1922 had said that every Communist

must consider himself an agitator among the masses. This can always take place wherever and whenever workers shall gather—in the workshop, in the trade unions, at mass meetings, in workers' clubs, in sport clubs, musical societies, tenants' and consumers' organizations, in people's houses, in workers' restaurants, on the trains, in the villages, etc., and even in the homes of the workers (house-to-house agitation).

An American CP leader quoted that Thesis in 1935 and complained that Party members were still falling short.[6]

Many articles, especially in *Party Organizer*, spelled out instructions in minute detail—for example, a sample speech for outdoor orators to use on Lenin's birthday; the order in which comrades should raise topics in public meetings; the slogans they must chant on picket lines; the questions a teacher of a new-members' class should ask, and the syllabi he should use, with topics, subtopics, and sub-subtopics. In club meetings and from the Party press, Jimmy Higgins learned what arguments to use in conversations with his "contacts" and the order in which he should broach them. One might conclude, then, that he could feel he had done his duty if he merely obeyed all these instructions. On the contrary, the very literature that went to great lengths to dampen Jimmy Higgins's initiative contained innumerable complaints that he did not show enough of it.[7]

One criterion for leadership, said Browder (paraphrasing Dimitroff), was "ability to make decisions, to find the correct course independently, to take responsibility and initiative." To students in the CP's national training school, he defined "Bolshevik methods of work" in terms he must have thought helpful to Comrade Jimmy, too, for his address was published in *The Communist*: you must be so well grounded in Party theory and methods of work "that you can give the correct answer alone among great masses, engaged in the struggle—and not only give the correct answer, but know how to make that answer the answer that the masses will demand."[8] It is hard to believe that the leaders really meant this. They themselves often did not know the correct answers before receiving word from Moscow. In theory, the Party line was always the one and only application of the science of Marxism-Leninism to a particular situation, and any developed Communist should have been able to work it out for himself. In practice, however, initiative could mean deviation, and deviation meant public criticism, or, in serious cases, the assignment of control tasks or expulsion. The Party's lines on specific American issues sometimes reflected events in Moscow and the thinking of men who knew little about the United States. Yet the Party theoreticians never failed to prove that these lines were the only correct and obvious ones, which any developed comrade should have arrived at on his own.

It was even "the duty and task of Marxists to enrich the theory with new experiences of the class struggle and to develop the theory further and to advance it," said Alexander Bittelman. But (as Bittelman himself found out the hard way some years later) woe to anyone who took this dictum literally.[9] The Party's line on "the Negro question," worked out in Moscow, is a good example. One specialist in this field, violently attacking his comrades for defining it solely as a race question, added: "The fact that no one questioned the correctness of this formula was itself indicative of the passivity and general lack of clarity in the Party in the field of Negro work." A good Communist should not have needed the Fourth Congress of the Central Committee of the Communist International to tell him that "to consider this question as a 'race' question is to underestimate the intrinsic revolutionary strength of the Negro liberation movement, to fail to understand its basis in the final analysis as the struggle of the Negro masses upon the Black Belt for national independence, i.e., for self-determination."[10] Yet nothing in "a good Communist's" experience could have enabled him to "develop the theory" in this direction.

In short, Jimmy Higgins was constantly aware that he was earning a grade from teachers far away, and that therefore his own day-to-day experience could never furnish him with reliable guides or criteria by which he might evaluate his own work. His initiative was about as great as that of the ladies' auxiliary of a local Rotary Club to decide whether to serve cake or pie at the annual picnic.

Yet the leaders had to insist that Jimmy Higgins show initiative, for, as Max Bedacht (a top-level leader) admitted, "a Party that depends for its initiative only on the top is not in close contact with these issues." The leaders learn only of the big issues

exploding in the country here and there. But these issues that the individual worker feels, his treatment in the shop, his wages, the conditions of work in general—those issues do not always automatically create such high waves that they reach in their details the leading committees of the Party.[11]

Bedacht's meaning could not have been clearer if he had said, "if things don't work out as we wish, don't blame us, the leaders." His statements of fact were, of course, true. What he omitted was another fact: that Jimmy Higgins had no part in determining the large policies. Although the leaders invited all members to join the Party-wide discussions on "draft resolutions" before conventions, Comrade Jimmy contributed nothing to the final versions. The leaders, admittedly out of touch with the people who must be converted by the millions, decided policy and assigned Jimmy Higgins his tasks.

It took a crisis for the Party to glimpse this contradiction. In late 1945, following the publication of the Duclos letter and the demotion of Browder, John Williamson complained that the Party's work was too often directed

from the top. Too many top-directives are issued. We organize at the top Citizens Committees in support of our Party candidates. The radio talks are prepared from the top. Most of the leaflets and other election material are similarly prepared from the top, as are most of the meetings planned. What happens to the Party Clubs? They are required primarily to respond to these directives, supply manpower and do the leg work. . . . The result is that our Clubs do not function politically as a force in the community; they are not creative in their activity. . . . While we might decide otherwise in a resolution, in practice we relapse back to this old habit of reducing our Clubs to bodies that merely carry out directives from above. . . . The main help needed by our Clubs is of a political character to assist them in finding their way to the masses, to help them display initiative and leadership in the mass struggles.[12]

   This self-critical mood did not last long. For a few years, Browder served as a convenient scapegoat.[13] But after 1945, as well as before, the leaders wrote the same complaints about the members' lack of initiative and imposed the same sanctions on those who showed it. They published the same predictions of inevitable victory, provided Jimmy Higgins performed his tasks with understanding and initiative, and they expressed even more confidence now that the Browder incubus had been removed. Foster lectured the members about the wonderful prospects for success and Jimmy Higgins's responsibility—in both senses of the word: duty and blame. "The year 1947," he announced,

must bring about a radical strengthening of the Communist Party. This is made imperative by the dangerous political situation in our country, and by the heavy new responsibilities which this puts upon our Party.... Not only must our Party this year achieve the goal of a membership of 100,000 it has set for itself, but, no less important, it must also drastically improve the quality and quantity of all its work. It must develop more political initiative, greater flexibility, in working with its allies, more intense membership activation, and a higher Communist morale generally.... There is far too much passivity among the membership, too much hesitancy in displaying proper Communist initiative in mass work.... Moreover, largely as a reaction against Browder's opportunism, we now also have certain "Left"-sectarian tendencies that have to be resolutely combatted. Never more than at the present moment ... was it necessary to be keenly alert to the need to fight simultaneously both dangers—Right-opportunism and "Left"-sectarianism.... A drastic end must be put to remnants of the passivity and sluggishness that crept into our Party, particularly during the last years of the Browder regime.[14]

Many members surely preferred passivity and sluggishness to walking the tightrope between "Right-opportunism" and " 'Left'-sectarianism." It was so easy to fall off, especially since definitions could change without notice.

   But Jimmy Higgins did not react in that way. Each time the Party failed to realize some goal, how could he not blame himself, knowing as he did that his leaders were masters of the science of Marxism-Leninism, that correct action had already brought victory in the Soviet Union, and that objective conditions were ripe? His leaders had not so much *imposed* tasks *on* him, as *entrusted* them *to* him. So he took to heart the documents that complained of the rank and file's negligence, of the Party's failure to grow, of the tiny circulation of the Party press even among members, of the failure of fund drives to reach their quotas, and of the huge proportion of members who dropped out every year and the consequent enormous turnover of membership (this was called "fluctuation").[15]

   A particularly accusatory version of the conditions-are-ripe thesis was the assertion that the workers were "ahead" of the Party, engaging in struggles without Party leadership. The sole roadblock on the road to power was the workers' lack of theoretical clarity; therefore the more ready and militant they were, the more any failure must be due to shortcomings of those Communists in daily contact with them. "Whether the toiling masses of America will go upon the path of determined class struggle," said Browder, "whether they will take the road toward the revolutionary way out of the crisis of capitalism, or whether they will be turned into the channels of social-fascism or fascism—this question will be decided by the work of the Communist Party"[16]—not, it should be noted, by the workers themselves, or the capitalists, or the non-Communist union leaders. The outsider may marvel at the incongruity between the grandiose yet assured goals and the candid admissions of the Party's ineffectiveness; but Comrade Jimmy did not notice the contradiction.

The top leaders may have known they were setting unrealistic goals, in the immediate sense at any rate. Whether intentionally or not, by imposing impossible tasks on Jimmy Higgins and then blaming him for the failures, they enhanced their own authority over him. If he had carried out his tasks correctly over a long period and experienced the immediate successes that had been predicted, and then if the predicted long-range consequences did not ensue, he might have questioned the theory and leadership. But the failure of the short-range successes to occur made the leaders and theory invulnerable. Whatever the leaders' motives, then, success must always be both assured and beyond reach.

To ACCEPT a series of tasks, knowing that one's worth will be judged by one's performance—this choice in shaping one's life recalls a theme common in fairy tales: the young prince who goes forth to kill a dragon or fetch a jewel from the end of the earth, and thus prove his manhood. Another version comes to us from the literature of chivalry: the knight who accepts a series of tests to prove himself worthy of his lady's love. She is someone else's wife and so forever out of reach. (One such lady, in Zoë Oldenbourg's novel *The Cornerstone*, imposes seven "trials" on her knight.) Tasking and testing are also ingredients in religious disciplines around the world. Clearly, this theme reflects a permanent need in the human psyche, which, if not satisfied in a person's ordinary milieu, will seek satisfaction elsewhere. The Party appealed irresistibly to certain people precisely because it placed heavy demands on them.

Jimmy Higgins's duty to strive toward Marxist-Leninist perfection through performance of his tasks produced a Communist conscience that required him to act out most of the traditional virtues as well as a few modern ones: loyalty, humility, dependability, punctuality, diligence, admiration of achievers, self-discipline, service, self-sacrifice, altruism, future-orientedness, postponement of gratification, faith in a transcendent ideal. The institutions that the Party hated most (only, however, during its "left" periods) were not those that disparaged these traits but those that fostered them in the service of different goals.

This aspect of Party life seems to have appealed most to the young members, who were least likely to see the yawning chasm between their leaders' profession and their practice. Young people's idealism and yearning for service, their habit of submitting to adult authority, and their naive confusion of words with reality—all these characteristics of youth enabled the Party to put the conventional virtues to its own use.

In many articles throughout its lifetime the *Young Worker* vilified the Boy Scouts. Not surprisingly, some of the YCL's own lectures to youth sounded like Boy Scout homilies. A top YCL leader in 1940, for example, declared:

a Communist strives to act always in an exemplary manner of "clean living"; in the face of persecution or terror a Communist never weakens, or betrays the confidence of his class or his organization but remains courageous and firm; a Communist always carries on a relentless struggle against the enemies of the working class.... Lenin and Stalin taught further that the education in the spirit of the working class necessarily means embuing youth with loyalty to the vanguard party of that class, the Communist Party, and with faith and confidence in the land in which the working class is successfully building Socialism, the Soviet Union.

Another author proclaimed that "in the unremitting struggle against the class enemy one must learn to overcome difficulties and dangers to develop revolutionary fortitude and endurance, a Bolshevik will, firmness and tenacity." The future belongs to the workers, but it "can only be conquered by difficult and self-sacrificing struggle," devotion, and service. "Always and everywhere by personal heroic action set an example to the youth of their country!" An expert on the Soviet Union exhorted American Communist youth to emulate their Soviet brothers and sisters, who "compete with one another for the chance to do the hardest tasks."[17]

The unexpressed ground for the hostility toward the Boy Scouts and other organizations that taught morality is best revealed in a speech by Browder to the YCL convention in 1939. This address, wrote the editor of *Clarity* in 1942, gave the organization "that slogan which best expresses its guiding thought: 'Character Building and Education in the Spirit of Socialism.' " "By character building," said Browder,

is meant the accumulation of consistent and sustained habits of life and work, which best fit the individual into society, and equip him to sustain and improve society, making him a strong and reliable individual within the collective life.... It means establishing, as habits of life, those attitudes and relationships from which will best grow up strong and healthy social organizations from the smallest to the most general and all-embracing. It means the systematic combatting and elimination of the destructive influences of a disintegrating capitalist system upon the individual, the family, and society. Education that goes to accomplish these things must *be*, in the first place, character building.

Another author claimed for Browder the heritage of George Washington, Thomas Paine, and Poor Richard's maxims, although his teaching was "different in one respect, that it is based upon the sound principles of Marxism-Leninism."[18]

The phrase "character building," which the YCL used very often during the war, went out of style among young Communists when it did among other Americans. Emphases and terminology changed from time to time, as the Party shifted between left and right lines and circumstances altered. But the catalog of specific traits that added up to the ideal Bolshevik remained constant, and they were the same for adult Jimmy Higginses as for the teenage members of the youth organizations. The leader—first Browder, then Foster, and always Stalin—personified the traits that Comrade Jimmy must cultivate, and the living models did so in exactly the same sense as a teacher personifies the traits that schoolchildren must acquire. According to Monnerot, the Soviet Party was "the parent party" of the CPs in other countries, and the latter "came more and more to resemble under-age children subjected to a strict and vigilant guardian." Thus, the worldwide Communist movement was one great school system.[19]

The image of the ideal Bolshevik appears repeatedly in the literature, in the positive form of tributes to outstanding comrades—the sort of encomia that outsiders save for postmortem eulogies—and in the negative form of criticisms of errant comrades. Sometimes the documents claimed to be describing the typical Communist. Sometimes they exhorted the members to develop the various traits. Others described the "new man" already existing in Soviet society. What needs repeating is that most of the traits preached to Jimmy Higgins in all these forms were good by anybody's definition and that the Party could not have put them to its own uses if they had not appealed to genuine needs and good impulses.

As usual, Stalin provided the basic texts. One favorite was a passage in his address to the graduates of the Red Army Academy in 1935: "Remember, comrades, that only those cadres are any good who do not fear difficulties, who do not hide from difficulties, but who, on the contrary, go out to meet difficulties, in order to overcome them and eliminate them. It is only in combating difficulties that real cadres are forged." Another often-quoted dictum of Stalin's went as follows:

We Communists are people of a special mold. We are made of special material. We are those who comprise the army of the great proletarian strategist, the army of Comrade Lenin. There is nothing higher than the honor of belonging to this army. . . . It is not given to all to be members of such a Party. It is not given to all to withstand the stress and storm that accompanies membership in such a Party. . . . In departing from us, Comrade Lenin bequeathed to us the duty of holding aloft and guarding the purity of the great title of member of the Party. We vow to you, Comrade Lenin, that we will fulfil[l] your bequest with honor.[20]

The best and most successful Party branches, said Browder, were involved in their communities, knew what their neighbors were thinking and how to answer their questions, worked modestly and energetically in all organizations, became known as militant and constructive influences, circulated Party literature among outsiders, organized their work and involved all comrades in it, combined strong leadership with rank-and-file initiative, made branch meetings interesting and lively, and encouraged members to study on their own to improve their ability to be useful to the Party and community. Unfortunately, he added, most branches did not fit this description. Nevertheless, in another place Browder depicted his Party as exemplifying these virtues: "The Communist Party is the most conscious, the most active, the most loyal, the most courageous, the most disciplined army in the struggle for democracy and peace, and through democracy, to socialism."[21]

The virtues explicitly named over and over in Party literature included modesty; ability and willingness to learn from the masses; heroism; steadfastness; devotion to the interests of the people; singlemindedness; readiness to sacrifice; dauntlessness; patriotism; reliability; outspokenness; honesty in personal dealings with allies and opponents; energy; resoluteness; cooperativeness; comradeliness; integrity; self-criticalness; principledness; understanding of the use of flexible tactics; courage; feeling for people; and ability to understand, lead, encourage, build confidence in, and discuss issues with the people. Moreover, Communists were psychologically healthy: "though neurosis is not merely a deformation of ideology, ideology is a potent shield against neurosis, at least what passes for neurosis among individuals socially disoriented." Finally, contrary to the slanders disseminated against the Party, "the Communists are staunch upholders of the family. We consider sexual immorality, looseness and aberrations as the harmful product of bad social organization."[22]

Jimmy Higgins believed in all those values and regarded the Party as the true heir of mankind's moral traditions. This fact may help to explain his resistance to the truth about the Soviet Union. Since the Party satisfied his need for discipline, self-sacrifice, and connection with something higher than himself, and his need to link his moral code with effective action in the world, he could hardly entertain the possibility that the other parts of its ideology were false. The Party had integrated all the elements in his personality in the service of noble values; how then could its belief system as a whole be wrong? This may also help to explain why the "left" swings of the policy pendulum were more congenial to him than the "right" ones. His very being as a Communist was bound up in his refusal to "adjust" to the corrupt society outside the Party. By the same token he was under constant pressure to "adjust" to the surrogate society called the Communist Party. The principal method used to effect this adjustment was the practice of criticism and self-criticism.

THE PARTY forced each comrade to be self-conscious all the time, constantly on the watch for ideological errors and for selfish motives. It gave him a picture of himself as he wanted to be, the perfect Bolshevik. This was the case even with the more easy-going who accepted their shortcomings; when they acknowledged their faults and did not "struggle" against them as a good Bolshevik should, they reinforced the ideal for themselves and for their comrades. The mental image of the perfect Bolshevik was what the ideal of the godly man must have been to the Puritan: an ever-present taskmaster and critic, even for the less zealous. Comrade Jimmy accepted criticism in the same spirit as that Puritan did: as criticism from his own better self. He knew that outsiders laughed at this custom, and he scorned them for their egotism.

Unlike Puritan and other religious theories, however, Party theory denied that human nature was forever divided, that the thirst for virtue warred eternally against the appetite for sin. Evil originated, rather, in bad institutions, and its manifestations within the individual were foreign to his nature. The Party's practice of criticism and self-criticism thus had a different rationale from that of the public confession practiced by Protestant sects. The religious person had to acknowledge sinfulness as his own. The Communist had to impute it to the evil social order: he had not yet succeeded in extirpating its influence upon him. "It is not I who am selfish or cowardly or uncomradely; it is the capitalist system using me, and I have been allowing it to do so." Murray Kempton has observed that "the Communists offer one precious boon: they take away the sense of sin." It is true that they abolished God and the duty to obey His laws. But they retained the inner voice commanding obedience to a moral law higher than themselves, and the sense of guilt when aware of their transgressions. In fact, they induced a far stronger sense of "sin" than most Americans of their generation felt. This was, paradoxically, one of the sources of the Party's appeal to certain people, for it offered them moral discipline and objective standards that, for one reason or another, they did not find in acceptable form in the religious communities. Unlike religious people, however, they did not have the comfort of believing that their tendency to sin was ineradicable. The Party taught that people were naturally good, or naturally neither good nor evil, and that evil infections could be cured rather easily, by theoretical clarity and criticism and self-criticism. Every comrade could grasp the theory; this was implied in the many writings by nonscholars on abstruse subjects. Every comrade could and should engage in criticism and self-criticism. In short, Jimmy Higgins had no excuse for not being an exemplary Bolshevik.

The first rule of the ritual of criticism and self-criticism,[23] then, was "Don't be personal." A comrade must never attack his critics' motives. Those critics could attack *his* motives, but they were not thereby being personal, for bad motives as well as bad thoughts were caused by bourgeois ideology. Being personal could take the form of "going easy on" the errant member out of friendship or compassion, or of venting personal animosity under cover of criticism of error. (Both these incorrect approaches were, however, common.) The second rule was that both criticism and self-criticism had to expose the entire chain of implications of the error. A failure to show up at the appointed time to distribute leaflets, or a theoretical deviation, was like a pebble dropped into a pond and causing ever-widening ripples; even a trivial error postponed the revolution and increased the danger of imperialist war. Third, in all criticisms the current Party line constituted the law on which the indictment was based. A member must never defend his action by criticizing the line. Fourth, although in theory a rank and filer could criticize even the national chairman, in practice the higher-level comrades criticized the lower- , and comrades on the same level criticized each other; Jimmy Higgins did not criticize a high-level leader. Fifth, the process did not end until the culprit had transformed the criticism into a self-criticism. He must criticize himself at least as severely as his critics had criticized him; by disclosing additional sins or evidence, he proved his sincerity. If necessary, the discussion continued through the night or took weeks of daily sessions. He could not end the process by saying, "Well, I'll think it over."

Needless to say, these rules operated only within the Party. Negative comments from outsiders were attacks, not criticisms. When the independent socialist magazine *Monthly Review* suggested, in 1949, that the worldwide cause of socialism would benefit from frank discussion of the Soviet Union's shortcomings, the Party counterattacked. This seemingly helpful assertion, wrote Alexander Bittelman, could open the door to spurious "criticisms" from

reactionary Social Democratic leaders, and the fascist crews of Trotskyites and Ti-toites. . . . It is impossible any more for an honest and informed socialist not to know that the innocent-looking proposition of the so-called principle or right to discuss "shortcomings as well as accomplishments" of the Soviet Union links up directly with Wall Street's warmongering incitements "to criticize Russia." . . . As to real and honest criticism of shortcomings, who can do it better, who in fact *is* doing it better, than the peoples, and their leaders, of the Soviet Union itself? Was it a secret to the editors of the *Monthly Review* that criticism and self-criticism is systematically practised and cultivated in all fields of Soviet life from top to bottom and bottom to top?[24]

(An American Communist, however, would never say that a Russian must not criticize the American CP on the ground that no one could "do it better" and was "doing it better" than the American Communists themselves.)

The Party's periodicals published several actual self-criticisms to show members how to do it better. When the Ohio State Board of the Party engaged in a series of self-critical discussions and then summarized them in an article, the editors of *Political Affairs* thought it should "be made available to the entire Party membership." The same magazine also reprinted from a Soviet publication the *mea culpa* of Eugene Varga, the Soviet economist who had erred in economic theory. Varga wrote that when a scholar resists criticisms, he inevitably goes from one mistake to another and ends up in the swamp of reformism.[25]

In addition to presenting how-to models, the periodicals allow us to follow the process from error to criticism to self-criticism to absolution. The following episode in particular is worth a close look, because in tone and content it typifies many others, including episodes involving obscure comrades and never recorded in print.

In the Fall, 1948, issue of *New Foundations*, Jack Kroner, a member of the magazine's board, published an essay on William Faulkner. Unfortunately for Kroner, the Party was about to begin its four-year-long self-critical frenzy over "white chauvinism." Comrades soon began picking over one another's written and oral statements for hints of deviation. In the issue for Spring, 1949, the magazine summarized the letters it had received criticizing Kroner's essay. The editors agreed with the letter writers "that Kroner's failure in any way to expose and combat the chauvinism inherent in Faulkner's works constitutes an acceptance of chauvinism which is entirely inconsistent with a Marxist approach." This was unfair; Kroner's article was typical Marxist-Leninist literary criticism, and his real sins were some errors in terminology and his failure to be vituperative. The editors' statement almost admits this:

Any article dealing with a writer like Faulkner, a subtle apologist for the Southern slaveocracy, must polemicise against his false representations of the Negro people and his numerous distortions of the history of the South.... Kroner's failure to combat Faulkner's chauvinist ideology produces the same result as if he himself had expressed chauvinistic beliefs and indicates that he himself has accepted them. His use of such words as "half-caste" and "half-breed," further, indicates what may be only charitably termed an unconscious acceptance of Faulkner's racist concepts.

This criticism, the statement concluded, is vitally important because the Negro people are among "the most powerful and decisive allies of the working class." The imperialists try to divide the working class from its allies by telling white workers that they are superior to Negroes and to colonial people abroad. Therefore, *"Any concession to white chauvinism today is a concession to imperialism and fascism"* and must be exposed and fought.

We recognize that we must be severely criticized as a group for our failure to recognize, until it was brought to our attention, the chauvinistic content of this article; that we did not stems from the existence of chauvinistic tendencies which we must learn to destroy. Because the struggle against chauvinism is key to the whole fight against imperialism, the board has agreed to censure the white members for their lack of sensitivity and their failure to react to the chauvinism in the Faulkner article before it was published. Their past and future work on this question is being placed on review. Certain goals have been established which must be reached in the struggle to overcome their manifestations of chauvinism. Further, the board agrees that for two reasons, Kroner should be suspended from the board: first, because the board cannot have as a member anyone who has expressed openly chauvinistic attitudes until he has shown that he has overcome them; and, second, because the members feel that he should devote his full attention to his own further struggle to overcome these attitudes.

Kroner's "Reply to Criticism" appeared in the issue for Summer, 1949. He fully accepted the charges, among them "that I not only failed to polemicize against his [Faulkner's] ideas, but I fell into the pitfall which inevitably attends such an approach; I unconsciously adopted some of his conceptions." Faulkner, explained Kroner, writes only about "the grim side of life. His world is sick and chaotic. It is nonetheless a real part of the bourgeois world." The Marxist critic must also point out that those who enjoy reading Faulkner are expressing not health but sickness. "He appeals to that in us which is utterly sick and bourgeois. . . . The glory of the coming day of men's lives is yet to be sung. When that day comes men will no longer live in a nightmarish world, and will cease to enjoy its literary counterparts." After criticizing some of his critics for not being harsh enough, Kroner reported the results of his self-examination:

Since the criticism of my article I have done a great deal of research on the Negro question. I have found that my ignorance of the conditions of the Negro nation, their needs and desires, was amazing. . . . I can well understand, now, that my tacit acceptance of chauvinist concepts was a "concession to imperialism and fascism." Appearing in a Marxist journal, this kind of thinking could do nothing but alienate the Negro allies of the progressive movement and further confuse the thinking, and hence, the activities of white progressives. Thus the presentation of fuzzy and chauvinist notions could serve only to weaken what must now be a powerful and victorious struggle. It is a struggle for life itself. . . . I want to publicly express my appreciation to my fellow editors of the New Foundations board and those who brought the issue to our attention. I have learned a great deal from the discussions which have taken place. The criticism opened up a vast field of knowledge for me; it has enhanced my understanding of literature immensely.

Kroner's reply closed with a general lesson to all good Communists: "For those to whom criticism connotes a destruction of their 'individual liberty' I hold no quarter. We can grow only through mutual knowledge and advice. . . . Criticism is intended to improve and is the highest indication of *camaraderie*. . . . For us criticism is a sign of maturity, mutuality, not antagonism." At the end of this document the following statement appears, signaling the close of the episode: "*Because, as indicated by this article, Kroner has shown a willingness and ability to struggle against white chauvinism, he has been reinstated on the editorial board.* —EDITORS."

It will be noted that Kroner's comrades judged his self-criticism successful primarily because it had brought his thinking and vocabulary into conformity with the Party's theory on the Negro question. That theory (that Negroes were a nation and the Black Belt was therefore entitled to self-determination) had not emerged from anyone's experience in the outside world, much less from the beliefs of blacks. Yet although the theory hindered recruiting among blacks, the Party did not drop it until permission arrived from its foreign mentors. The failures caused by the theory were, of course, blamed on the members' failure to put it into practice.[26] In any other organization the leaders and members would eventually have questioned the theory. But, as was mentioned earlier, in the CP the failures of predicted short-range successes to occur actually enhanced the authority of the theory and the leaders, by making Jimmy Higgins self-critical and ever more diligent in carrying out his tasks. But those failures only enhanced the leaders' authority; they did not create it. Jimmy Higgins accepted his place in the Party because he believed in the Party's mission: to abolish an American reality that he loathed.

THE AMERICAN REALITY that Jimmy Higgins loathed and dedicated his life to destroying was, however, the product of his own mind, part of the special universe that he lived in. The next two chapters will discuss some of the main characteristics of that universe.

NOTES

1. C. Hathaway, "The Election Campaign and the Struggle against Sectarianism," *PO* 5 (May–June, 1932): 6; "The Eighth National Convention of the C.P.U.S.A.," *PO* 7 (February, 1934): 1; A. Landy, "Two Questions on the Status of Women under Capitalism," *COM* 20 (September, 1941): 824–25; Frederick V. Field, "The Meaning of the Chinese Revolutionary Victory," *PA* 28 (January, 1949): 74; "YCI Letter to Sixth National Convention," *YW*, August 3, 1931, p. 4. (YCI stood for Young Communist International, with which the American YCL was affiliated.) The Party's youth organizations used Stalin's *The Tasks of Youth* and Lenin's *The Young Generation* as outlines of their assignments and role. These pamphlets, published by International in 1940, were volumes 27 and 26 of the Little Lenin Library (a set of pamphlets that formed the core of Jimmy Higgins's personal library). The essays in both pamphlets were available in English before 1940. In the Lenin, "task(s)" appears ten times on pp. 34–35. For another very important assignment of world-historic tasks to the Communist youth, see N. Slutsker, "Lenin, Stalin, and the Communist Youth Movement," *CL* 1 (April–May, 1940): 69–74.

2. W. W. Weinstone, "Plenum Material: Keynote of the Fourteenth Plenum," *PO* 5 (March–April, 1932): 3; Earl Browder, *The Democratic Front* (New York: IP, 1947), p. 68; Georgi Dimitroff, *United Front against Fascism* (New York: New Century, 1947), p. 144. See also "Where Should We Place Responsibility for Our Weaknesses?" "by Central Org. Commission," *PO* 7 (November, 1934): 17–21.

3. T. Gusev, "The End of Capitalist Stabilization and the Basic Tasks of the British and American Sections of the C.I.," *COM* 12 (January, 1933): 39; Draft Resolution of the Central Committee, quoted in F. Brown, "The Key to Our Central Problem—The Winning of the Majority of the Working Class," *COM* 13 (April, 1934): 363; Alex Bittelman, "The Supreme Court, the New Deal and the Class Struggle," *COM* 14 (July, 1935): 595; William Z. Foster, "Political Leadership and Party Building," *COM* 16 (July, 1937): 646; Gil Green, "Party Must Help Y.C.L. Win Youth for Class Battles," *PO* 6 (November, 1933): 24. See also Nathan Leites, *A Study of Bolshevism* (New York: Free Press, 1950), pp. 91–92, for Stalin's insistence that objective conditions could not be blamed for failures, and Leites's comments. One particularly significant document was "Prepare for Power!"—an editorial in *YW*, January 30, 1934, p. 4; on p. 1 of that issue we learn that in the recent fund drive the Party had raised $175 of its goal of $1,000! Many issues of *PO* contain this sort of evidence of the gap between fancy and fact, and of the writers' blindness to its existence.

4. William Weinstone, "Independent Self-Study of Marxism," *PA* 26 (November, 1947): 1046; Browder, *Democratic Front*, p. 86. See also *YW*, March 10, 1936, p. 5: Gil Green says that at the recent national conference the YCL proposed that every club establish a circulating library, so that young people who could not afford to buy books could read. The article's context makes it clear that he had Marxist literature in mind.

5. Browder, *Democratic Front*, pp. 86, 45; "Marxist Study Courses," *COM* 11 (May, 1932): 479; Elizabeth Austin, "What the District Training School Taught Me," *PO* 10 (May, 1937): 39.

6. Excerpt from Earl Browder, *Democracy or Fascism*, in *PO* 9 (October, 1936): 9; Alex Bittelman, "For Effective Mass Agitation—To Reach Millions," *PO* 8 (March, 1935): 29.

7. According to A. Rossi, the same was true of the French CP. See his *A Communist Party in Action: An Account of the Organization and Operations in France* (New Haven, Conn.: Yale University Press, 1949), pp. 198–99.

8. Browder, *Democratic Front*, p. 66; Earl Browder, "Mastering Bolshevik Methods of Work," *COM* 17 (June, 1938): 503. The latter theme is echoed in John Williamson, "A Program for Developing Communist Cadres," *PA* 24 (April, 1945): 367, parag. 2.

9. Alexander Bittelman, "Lenin's Teachings and the Liberation of Humanity," *PA* 31 (January, 1952): 9. Bittelman was expelled in 1959 for revisionism. See Joseph R. Starobin, *American Communism in Crisis, 1943–1957* (Berkeley: University of California Press, 1972, 1975), pp. 243, n. 14, for a succinct account of the incident.

10. Harry Haywood, "Against Bourgeois-Liberal Distortions of Leninism on the Negro Question," *COM* 9 (August, 1930): 694; see rest of article for fascinating amplifications of this assertion.

11. "Work in Mass Organizations: From Speech of Max Bedacht, Member Polburo C.P.U.S.A.," *PO* 6 (August–September, 1933): 77–78. A similar statement is in Earl Browder, "Building the Party and The Daily Worker," *PO* 10 (August, 1937): 1–2. See also "From Resolution of 17th Plenum, C.C., C.P.U.S.A.," *PO* 6 (November, 1933): 1; "Excerpts from Earl Browder's Speech to Seventeenth C.C. Plenum," ibid., p. 2; and "Editorial," ibid., p. 3; and other articles in the same issue, all of which

demand initiative from Jimmy Higgins and blame him for the Party's failure to prosper.

12. John Williamson, "New Organizational Problems of the Communist Party," *PA* 24 (December, 1945): 1112. But earlier complaints along the same line were occasionally heard; see, e.g., "Fluctuation and Methods of Stopping It," *PO* 6 (December, 1933): 14; John Adams, "The Inner Life of Our Party and Its Work among the Foreign-Born Workers," *COM* 13 (April, 1934): 369–73.

13. See, e.g., William Z. Foster, "On the Expulsion of Browder," *PA* 25 (April, 1946): 348, last paragraph.

14. William Z. Foster, "For a Stronger, More Active Communist Party!" *PA* 26 (February, 1947): 152–53. "Left" was almost always put in quotation marks to show that those who pretended to be to the left of the CP were really to its right.

15. See virtually every issue of *PO* for such complaints and for supporting statistics. Typical of the many devastating criticisms is "Control Tasks on Building the Party and the Circulation of Our Press," *PO* 10 (March–April, 1937): 1–9.

16. "From Comrade Browder's Report," *PO* 6 (August–September, 1933): 5.

17. Carl Ross, "Lenin and Stalin—The Leaders of Youth," *CL* 1 (Fall, 1940): 57–58; Anon., "The Communist Youth—Fearless and Invincible," ibid., pp. 63–69; Jessica Smith, "Where Dreams Come True," *CH* [1] (June, 1936): 10.

18. See "The Celebration of Our Twentieth Anniversary," *CL* 3 (Spring, 1942): 3, 5–6 (Browder quotation at p. 5); Frank Cestare, "Earl Browder—Molder of Character," ibid., pp. 30, 34–35, 39.

19. Jules Monnerot, *Sociology and Psychology of Communism* (Boston: Beacon Press, 1953), p. 92. This was sometimes true almost literally. See Jennie Morris, "Y.C.L. Reconstruction," *YW*, March 24, 1936, p. 8. A YCL club undertook study projects reminiscent of the public schools' "project method" popular at that time. But whereas schoolchildren did "an Eskimo project" that included material on history, geography, nutrition, art, and so on, these YCLers had a science group that studied "food adulteration, fake advertising on the many items we use in our daily life, exposing the fraud which the bosses pull on the consuming public." Another difference was that the Communists could not look forward to graduation day; they never graduated.

20. Among many quotations of these passages, see, e.g., cover of *PO* 8 (June, 1935): Slutsker, "Lenin, Stalin and the Communist Youth Movement," p. 73; and space-filler, *COM* 18 (January, 1939): 56. The second Stalin quotation was often shortened to include only the first three or four sentences.

21. Earl Browder, *Social and National Security* (New York: Workers Library, 1938), pp. 29–30; Browder, *Democratic Front*, p. 94.

22. A sample of documents in which these virtues are preached, or presented as descriptions of fact, or included in eulogies of model Communists, are: "To Our Leader, Our Teacher, Our Friend—Earl Browder," *CL* 2 (Summer, 1941): 4; Robert Minor, "Continued Political Struggle against Hitler by Military Means," ibid., p. 10; John Gates, "For the Military Defeat of Hitler," ibid., p. 67; Max Weiss, "The Twentieth Anniversary of the Young Communist League," *CL* 3 (Spring, 1942): 14; Frank Cestare, "War Service Through the Young Communist League," *CL* 3 (Summer, 1942): 3; William Z. Foster, *American Trade Unionism* (New York: IP, 1947), p. 358; William Z. Foster, *The Twilight of World Capitalism* (New York: IP, 1949), pp. 102–5; A. B. Magil, "Earl Browder, People's Teacher," *NM*, August 5, 1941, p. 6; Austin, "What the District Training School Taught Me," p. 38; Williamson,

"Program for Developing Communist Cadres," pp. 362–63, 367; "Present Situation and the Next Tasks: Resolution of the National Convention of the Communist Party, U.S.A., Adopted July 28, 1945," *PA* 24 (September, 1945): 828; Gus Hall, "The Importance of Communist Cadres," *PA* 31 (January, 1952): 41; John Swift, "On Stalin's Method," *PA* 32 (April, 1953): 74. The last two quotations are from Milton Howard, "Materialism and Psychoanalysis," *MM* 5 (November, 1952): 26, and Browder, *Democratic Front*, p. 54. On the essential role of ideal models, to evoke emotions that mere ideas cannot, see Monnerot, *Sociology and Psychology of Communism*, pp. 159–60. For more on the Party's image of the ideal Communist, see Frank S. Meyer, *The Moulding of Communists* (New York: Harcourt, Brace, 1961), pp. 11–12, 16–17, 77, 122. That the Party used a double standard in applying these principles is too well known to require documentation here. It considered Jimmy Higgins courageous only if he acted bravely in the service of the Party's goals; what outsiders considered sins were not always sins if their commission did not harm the Party; and so on down the list.

23. The ensuing "rules" are not stated in the sources. I have formulated them by generalizing from the evidence and my own recollections. An excellent discussion is in Meyer, *Moulding of Communists*, pp. 120–21, 152–53. Maurice H. Isserman, "Peat Bog Soldiers: The American Communist Party during the Second World War, 1939–1945," Ph.D. dissertation, University of Rochester, 1979, p. 208, mentions the "ritualistic quality" of criticism and self-criticism.

24. Alexander Bittelman, "Where Is the 'Monthly Review' Going?" *PA* 30 (May, 1951): 34–35.

25. "Self-Criticism and the Struggle for Collective Leadership," *PA* 30 (June, 1951): 31–39; Eugene Varga, "Against Reformist Tendencies in Works on Imperialism," *PA* 28 (December, 1949): 74–86. Other typical self-criticisms include James S. Allen, "A Comment on State Capitalism and Socialism," *PA* 27 (May, 1948): 426–39, and an unnamed YCLer's statement in *YW*, March 27, 1934, p. 11. As usual, however, the basic texts on criticism and self-criticism came from the Soviet Union. One passage quoted repeatedly appeared in the *History of the Communist Party of the Soviet Union (Bolsheviks)* (New York: IP, 1939), p. 361; see, e.g., John Williamson, "The Reconstitution of the Communist Party," *PA* 24 (September, 1945): 811 (Williamson's own remarks on criticism and self-criticism and the quote from the Soviet work). See also Joseph Stalin, "Criticism and Self-Criticism," and editor's prefatory remarks, *PA* 23 (March 1954): 9–15. China provided authoritative texts too, before its split with the Soviet Union; see Wu Ch'iang, "On Problems of Self-Criticism," *PA* 31 (August, 1952): 53–64.

26. On the source of the theory on the Negro question, its harmfulness to the Party, and the relief felt when permission arrived to drop it, see William A. Nolan, *Communism versus the Negro* (Chicago: Henry Regnery, 1951), passim. For a wholly different view, by a comrade who had helped to formulate the theory while in Moscow and who defended it after his expulsion from the Party, see Harry Haywood, *Black Bolshevik* (Chicago: Liberator Press, 1978), passim. Cf. Herbert Aptheker, *History and Reality* (New York: Cameron Associates, 1955), p. 98: in a lengthy diatribe entitled "Communism and Truth: A Reply to Sidney Hook," reprinted from *MM*, Aptheker says, "The Kremlin has never ordered anyone to believe anything about the Negro people," and Hook's "idea that from this position [that Negroes constitute a nation] one arrives at a Jim Crow state reflects not only your colossal ignorance of this whole question, but also the crassest white chauvinism."

PART 2
Substance

8

The Nature of Reality I: Materialism

THE UNIVERSE consisted of eternal matter eternally in motion.[1] If any member of the American CP had an experience intimating that Something Else existed, he either explained it away or left the Party. A theist who joined because he agreed with its economic doctrines or particular policies encountered hostility to his faith and probably did not remain a member for long. A "developed" Communist knew that Party doctrines on all subjects comprised a single system of thought that "reflected" an equally integrated reality; its cause-effect relationships left no room for miracles. Matter, moving according to the "laws of dialectics," produced ever higher "integrations," from the physical to the biological to the level at which matter became conscious of itself: the mind of man.

As in our examination of other subjects of Party thinking, here too we shall omit expositions of the theories themselves, except where the context requires them, and focus instead on reconstructing the mind-set of Jimmy Higgins.

IN ITS FIRST DECADE, the Party considered religion a major adversary and attacked it ferociously. *The Young Worker* seemed obsessed by it, featuring articles and cartoons about "religious dope peddlers" and capitalists' encouraging wage slaves to hope for "pie in the sky" instead of demanding more pie on earth. One article ended with "DOWN WITH RELIGION, THE TOOL OF THE BOSSES!!!" Another described the Young Workers League's campaign against "religious dope." A news item, headlined "Jewish Jingoist Press Raves at Y.W.L. Trial Against Heavenly Dope," told of the League's "trial" of a member in New York "who had participated in religious ceremonies."[2]

In the early 1930s the tone began to moderate. Some comrades now wondered whether the Party's new efforts to win friends among religious people meant that it was abandoning its struggle against religion. "On the contrary," Browder assured them in 1935:

it is only now that we are seriously beginning this struggle where it really counts—
that is, among the religious masses themselves. The very means of taking the antireligious struggle among the religious masses, is what has disquieted our questioners.
That is only another sign of the old disease of sectarianism from which American
revolutionaries have so long suffered.

It is true that the Communist Party is participating in united-front movements in
which religious organizations are taking an ever more active part and, to some degree
even, including churches. This is not compromise on our part. Our united front is
on burning social issues. . . . The Communists, estimating religion as "the opiate of
the people" and combatting it untiringly, do so on the basis of our program of complete
and unconditional religious freedom.

A YCL leader showed that the new line was merely tactical when he wrote
in *Clarity*: "Are we to pin the blame [for the depression] on the likes and
dislikes of a temper[a]mental God and thus escape the real answer[?] Some
people may, but we do not."[3] Less than a year later the same magazine
published an article entitled "Has the Church Failed?" and identified its
author in the subtitle as "An Assistant Pastor" who "Examines Religion
Frankly and Finds It Lacking in Many Respects But Sees Some Hopeful
Signs." The fate of organized religion, he argued, depended on whether it
aligned itself with progressive social forces. Two issues later, *Clarity* published a letter from an Oregon woman urging the magazine to "keep up the
good work. I hope you and your contributors realize," she added, "that God
is . . . on our side. He is always in the midst of every fight for social justice
or social improvement; and with His help we cannot fail."[4] Jimmy Higgins,
however, understood that the new line was directed at outsiders. Not for a
moment did he wonder whether God was with the Party.

Once truth and tactics had thus been placed in separate compartments,
the Party's statements became less honest than those quoted above. The more
the Party attracted respectable clerical allies, the more its propaganda sep-
arated the basic philosophical from the economic, political, and social parts
of its creed. It even went so far as to suggest that materialism was something
a member could take or leave as he chose. In a speech delivered in 1939
Browder announced that "an increasing number of Party members are active
communicants of the various churches, finding in the Party program and
activities, as distinct from its background and base of Marxian philosophy,
what they themselves describe as 'the nearest we can find to applied Christianity.' " Only the Party's program could realize the "communistic traditions
and ethical teachings" of most religious. We do recognize, he remarked, the
philosophical conflict between the churches and the Party, but we insist that
it be kept in its proper place. It is "a conflict of ideas, which does not
necessarily, and should not, result in a *conflict between persons who agree upon
the immediate program* while disagreeing upon the intellectual path by which
they reached that common point."[5]

Yet, even as these conciliatory statements were being published, other documents were expressing the members' real attitudes. In 1932 a writer in *Party Organizer* had criticized the comrades' tendency to show contempt for the "backward" and "undependable" workers who attended church or supported bourgeois parties. In that period, then, the fiercely antireligious polemics accurately reflected the rank and filers' genuine feelings, which were strong enough to frustrate the leaders' plans for winning friends among the workers. When the Party's public stance changed, that contempt remained. It can be read between the lines of Foster's reply to a letter from a priest in 1954. After formally thanking the priest for being concerned about his "spiritual welfare," Foster loftily explained why that concern was misplaced:

the dialectical materialist viewpoint fully satisfies me in meeting the everyday problems of life, as well as in confronting the perspective of eventual natural dissolution by death. . . .

It is now about sixty years since I parted company with religion. In my book, *From Bryan to Stalin*, I have described at some length how I came to break with my early religious beliefs through a boyhood reading of Paine, Lecky, Draper, Gibbon, Darwin, Spencer and others. The atheist position I developed through this reading has been greatly strengthened by my experience in life, including eventually the reading of Marx and Lenin. . . .

Religion . . . was first evolved by primitive man everywhere as the most logical explanation he could devise of the complex, mysterious and often terrifying natural phenomena with which he was surrounded, as well as to work out a plausible conception of his own and the world's existence. . . .

The advance of science (and also that of industry which accompanies science) has rendered obsolete those metaphysical and legendary conceptions upon which all religions, without exception, are based. Science has long since given irrefutable materialist explanations of all the phenomena which terrified and puzzled the simple hunters and cultivators of the soil of long ago, which caused them to improvise . . . the supernatural explanations that still provide the basis for all the major religions of today. . . . In the modern world . . . there is therefore no longer the inevitability, and in the long run, even the possibility, of a religious interpretation of man and the world.[6]

This document touches on every aspect of the Party's attitude toward religion. Knowing his correspondent was predisposed to disagree, Foster doubtless thought he had anticipated all the likely counterarguments. Since he published his reply, he probably also meant to show Jimmy Higgins how to respond in similar situations. If Foster had realized that tracing the origin of religious ideas was not the same as refuting them, he would have tried to plug that fatal gap in his reasoning. The thought obviously never entered his mind. This is especially remarkable in that his arguments were well known, even commonplace, and he knew that the priest had drawn different conclusions from them. These dreary banalities and the flippant dismissal of the need to examine and defend them expressed the authentic experience of the rank-and-file comrade who nodded in approval as he read Foster's reply. Foster's key messages were: First, a layman was fully qualified to discourse on the etiology of religion from prehistoric times onward, provided he had read a few books on the subject. Second, science and religion excluded each other. Third, since modern man knew the material causes of the phenomena that had frightened his ancestors, the persistence of religion in advanced societies must be due to deliberate efforts by the ruling class, whose rule was, however, doomed by the advance of science. Fourth, a person could shed his religion by using facts and reason, without a predisposition to interpret the evidence in accordance with his "conclusions."

Another assumption implied in Party writings on religion can be illustrated by a passage in Browder's essay "We Extend the Hand of Brotherly Cooperation to the Catholics." After explaining why an alliance would benefit both Communists and Catholics, he added: "True, Catholics as a whole turn to the doctrines and dogmas of their Church for formulation and justification of ethical and moral standards, while Communists base their standards wholly on the needs of society." In other words, Catholic (or any other) theology had nothing to do with the needs of society, and Browder evidently assumed that Catholic readers would agree. Contradictorily, he added that "in practical life, among the masses, it all comes to the same thing, justice, truth and fair dealing between man and man."[7] He did not explain how a doctrine that was false and a diversion from the real needs of society happened to sanction the same practical standards of behavior as Marxism did. In short, the Party could find that the moral code of a religion was good or bad, as tactical needs required; but it never altered its assumption of a basic philosophic opposition between "idealism" (including the religious form) and its own materialism.

Louis Budenz, a prominent Party editor who later became a Catholic and anti-Communist, recalled a conversation he had had in 1941 that relates to the last point. A leading comrade in New York told him that certain officers of the Transport Workers Union who remained Catholics after they joined the Party should not be allowed "to retain this 'peculiar dual allegiance.' " An authoritative Party committee had pointed out that, if those men left the Church, the workers would vote them out of office. Nevertheless, this Party functionary "was afraid that constant attendance at Mass and the like would make them 'uncertain in their loyalty to the Communist movement.' " If membership in a church, unlike membership in other institutions, posed a problem of divided loyalty, then a basic ingredient of Communist commitment must have been at stake. In his memoirs, Budenz says that, although a member of a religious body could join the Party, he would then encounter pressure to abandon his religion. "For anyone in a post of leadership, . . . religious affiliation is strictly forbidden unless the Political Committee says that for 'tactical purposes' he must join a religious group. But in order to do so, his basic atheism is first well established."[8]

The Party's descriptions of how the Soviet regime treated religion suggested what the nonatheist allies could expect after the American CP came to power. These documents followed the same pattern as those we have surveyed already: open hostility until the early 1930s, and ambivalence thereafter. The May 1, 1930, issue of *The Young Worker* contained a review of *The Soviet War on Religion*, a pamphlet published by Workers Library. Two months earlier, however, the same publication explained that

in the Soviet Union religion is an individual matter. One can worship any religion or creed. At the same time, the Soviet Government teaches the masses that "Religion is the opium of the people." However, when religion is used for counter-revolutionary activity, the workers deal with the priests and rabbis like with all enemies of the Workers Republic. When the workers or peasants of a certain community are tired of the church, the government turns the "buildings of superstition" into schools or workers club houses for the interests of the masses.

Five years later, Browder explained that the Soviet regime's repression of the Orthodox Church had not meant repression of religion. On the contrary, that state church had become corrupt and "unspiritual"; its destruction therefore increased religious freedom, just as disestablishment had done after the American Revolution. "In practice," said another writer in 1952, "Marxism in the socialist state and peoples' democracies actually provides more genuine freedom for religious belief, as well as for non-religious belief, than prevails anywhere else." Foster was, as usual, more candid; in 1932 he wrote:

In the U.S.S.R., as part of the general cultural revolution, religion is being liquidated. Religion, which Marx called, "the opium of the people," has been a basic part of every system of exploitation that has afflicted humanity. . . . Its glib phrases about morality, brotherly love and immortality are the covers behind which the most terrible deeds in history have been done. Religion is the sworn enemy of liberty, education, science. Such a monstrous system of dupery and exploitation is totally foreign to a Socialist society; firstly, because there is no exploited class to be demoralized by religion; secondly, because its childish tissue of superstition is impossible in a society founded upon Marxian materialism; and thirdly, because its slavish moral system is out of place, the new Communist moral code developing naturally upon the basis of the new modes of production and exchange.

But he also quoted the Soviet constitution as guaranteeing freedom of worship, and added that religion would die out as the people's culture developed. "As the factories and schools open the churches close." The regime could wait patiently for religion to wither away.[9]

But if religion was a lie and a narcotic, why should its exercise be an individual matter? In the Communist's universe nothing lay beyond the purview of the political authority, for good (after the revolution) or for evil (before it). The explanation of these inconsistencies—including the wildly self-contradictory characterizations of religious morality—could not be that socialism would abolish the conditions that fostered religion,[10] for the same argument would hold for racism and anti-Semitism. The Party blamed them too on class society, wanted them outlawed even before the revolution, and boasted that the Soviet Union had prohibited them by law. A more plausible answer would start with the recognition that the Party's tactics were shaped by the milieux in which it worked. The majority of members were students, professionals, and middle-class people whose "contacts" on the outside were mainly the same sorts of people, generally uninterested in debating religion. The comrades who mingled with workers found more receptive audiences if they argued over the cause of the depression than over the existence of God. The need to defend the Soviet Union against a possible war threat dictated the united-front tactic. But the comrades themselves had changed as well. The Party had come to consist mostly of native-born Americans, who felt no need to distance themselves from religious family heritages. By the time the Party extended the hand of friendship to any religious group willing to form alliances on secular issues, religion had ceased to arouse the passion of most comrades.

After World War II, discussions of religion declined in number. A few Party writers polemicized against it; most simply took the materialist frame of reference for granted. Within its own community, the Party now treated religion mostly as a subcategory of the larger ontological question. Religion was just the most simpleminded version of the basic philosophical antago-nist—"idealism." Unable to empathize with the experience that engendered faith in God, they assumed it was a matter of scientific proof or disproof, unaware that their atheist "conclusion" was embedded in that starting as-sumption. We shall examine this logic later. First, we should survey the foundation upon which it rested: the assumption that religion and science were mutually exclusive ways of explaining the same data.

No other tenet of Marxism more clearly marks it as a nineteenth-century ideology than "the war of science and religion." Not coincidentally, that was the one tenet that the Party shared with innumerable nonleftists who did not realize that European science had developed within the Church milieu and that belief in materialism was (at least) as much an act of faith as was belief in God. But unlike those non-Communists who merely accepted scien-tistic dogmas learned in school and from the mass media, the Party theorists incorporated "the opposition of science to religion" into a militant philosophy.

They appealed to history to prove their case. Since, they argued, the history of thought reflected the history of the material circumstances of men's lives, the class struggle had historically produced "struggles" between ma-terialism and idealism. Materialism was the philosophy of "rising" classes, although such classes had sometimes couched their criticisms of the old order in religious terms. Materialism had earlier been "mechanical," but with the progress of science and technology it had evolved into its highest, "dialec-tical,"[11] form, Marxism-Leninism. Idealism, the philosophy of ruling classes, had also evolved into ever more sophisticated versions. But notwithstanding the disclaimers by some agnostic or even atheist idealists, the *reductio ad absurdum* of their own doctrines was God. The chairman of the Los Angeles Party organization set forth one of the consequences of organized religion's supposed hostility toward science:

The church fought against the Copernican system ostensibly because, by showing that man is not the center of the universe, it lowered the importance of man, and therefore of God. It hampered the development of anatomy and physiology as "leaving no room for the soul," and retarded the emergence of modern medicine. It fought the science of evolution for tracing man's origin to lower animals as against the "Creation" theory that man was fashioned "in the image of God." It fought against the theory of evolution of society and of the family, as lowering the moral dignity of man. In reality, however, these discoveries, far from lowering man, aggrandized him and freed him from superstition.

Even those modern scientists who seemed least concerned with politics were really obeying the dictates of their capitalist masters. When capitalism was progressive, explained Foster, all its great scientists, "the Darwins, Spencers, and Huxleys," were atheists. But as it degenerated it tried "to preserve religion in order to check the rebellion of the workers. This is why Einstein ('cosmic religion'), Milliken, Eddington, and other bourgeois scientists now are trying so diligently to 'harmonize science and religion.' " "The new 'science' must provide sermon material for pastors who will proclaim to their congregations that science and religion have been 'reconciled all over again,' " wrote a science writer in *New Masses* in 1934. "Back of this retreat from reason and logic to mysticism and irrationality is the general crisis of capitalism which produced in turn a crisis in bourgeois thought." The decay of that system had undermined "the foundation of further scientific progress."[12]

The historical arguments were supplemented by two others. First, the writers distinguished between science and scientists. Even if only a minority of scientists throughout history had been atheists, they alone personified the spirit of science and reasoned consistently. (The essayists who praised the materialists and denounced the nonmaterialists among eminent modern scientists never asked whether the former had advanced science more than the latter had.) Second, they equated Marxism with science. Harry K. Wells summed up this contention succinctly: "the attack on Marxism is the attack on all science, and the attack on all science today has for its main objective the attack on Marxism. . . . The defense of materialism and science is the defense of Marxism; and the defense of Marxism is the defense of materialism and science." Another theorist drew the inescapable corollary: "the rejection of Marxian social science leads to the rejection of all science and to the study of—theology." Logically, then, an anti-Marxist scientist did not comprehend the essence of his own work. "It is . . . not accidental that honest scientists have been led by logic and integrity of thought to profess atheism."[13]

The equation of Marxism with science assured Jimmy Higgins that his belief system was not essentially negative. The Party's philosophy rang true because he really did experience the universe as godless. He felt certain that the idealists, not he, delimited reality; a universe that had a beginning and an end needed a god "before" the beginning and "after" the end. They, not he, denigrated human reason by postulating the Unknowable; but since mind was matter become conscious of itself, and since knowledge "reflected" its object, everything was in principle knowable. What they regarded as his denial of a whole realm of being and experience was really his refusal to share their illusions.

Needless to say, most Party members never gave much thought to these questions. But they were aware of them and accepted the answers that the Party taught in its publications and classes. For the reasons discussed in chapter six, it is clear that the Party's general approach to philosophic issues was grasped by many more members than were qualified to grasp the issues themselves. As a result, the labels "scientific," "unscientific," "materialist," and "idealist" automatically elicited the correct responses from Jimmy Higgins, for each evoked a host of associations inculcated over the course of years.

From the documents surveyed in chapter six we may also infer that comrades who were scientists may have had a special problem: to keep two separate compartments in their minds for the word "scientific." In the professional compartment it denoted the method of formulating a hypothesis and then testing it against all relevant evidence, especially evidence that seemed to disprove it, taking account of the arguments and data adduced by fellow scientists who disagreed with it, and, finally, considering the results tentative and subject to later challenges and discoveries. It also denoted the theories and bodies of knowledge that had survived this process. In the Party compartment, however, the word expressed an attitude that conflicted at every point with the spirit of science. There, "scientific" meant either "correct" in a fundamental sense or "materialist."[14] Beyond its denotation it conveyed a polemical connotation. Some examples will illustrate the contexts in which the word came naturally (and often) to the writers' minds.

In an article on psychiatry, one writer used "scientific" three times in two sentences, linking it with "Marxist materialism" in opposition to idealist "philosophies which are for the most part corroded by an unprincipled glossing over of major issues, and are properly called eclectic." After word arrived of the publication of the *History of the Communist Party of the Soviet Union (Bolsheviks)*, but before the Party had received the English translation, Browder recommended it to all comrades as "a scientific textbook to be studied and mastered." One theoretician used "scientific" six times and "scientifically" once, in three consecutive paragraphs, to refute non-Marxist analyses of the economic role of women under capitalism. According to another, among the reasons the ruling class wanted to fire Marxist professors was "their belief in, and ability to present, a scientific approach to history and society." An authority on the Negro question used "scientific" and "correct" interchangeably throughout a polemic against "scientifically incorrect" and "scientifically unsound" notions, counterposing his own "scientific concept," "the scientific conception," and "the truly scientific Marxist-Leninist position on the question of race," which expressed "the scientific reality," and so on. "Science," wrote Howard Selsam, "can operate in the value sphere and can determine values only if all men can and do agree that the values of human life are scientifically determinable. And the precondition for this agreement is a scientific theory of history and society. In other words, if we take a completely scientific materialist approach to human life, then science and ethics are harmonious." Bourgeois theory was faulty because "if the capitalist world used a thoroughly scientific standard it would have to abdicate." The Party's other chief philosopher announced in 1954: "For the history of philosophy the only scientific thesis is that most recently formulated by A. A. Zhdanov."[15]

But Marxism was not just scientific; it was a science. It did not just *meet* the standards by which a theory could be judged scientific; it *was* the standard. Marxism-Leninism, wrote two Soviet scholars in an essay republished in *Political Affairs*, was

the science of the laws of development of nature and society, the science of the revolution of the oppressed and exploited masses, the science of the triumph of Socialism in all countries, the science of the construction of communist society. . . . [It] *generalizes all scientific knowledge*, discovers the universal laws of all development, the most general laws of nature, society and thought, a science which elaborates questions of the world-view, of the scientific method, of the theory of knowledge, of logic.

According to Browder, "Marxism is the science of the transition to socialism," and "Marxism is the science of history as a whole." Answering those who thought that the American CP received its policies from the Soviet Union, Ben Davis proclaimed that "Marxism is a science and like all sciences, it is universal, resulting in a similarity of thought among all who adhere to it." A YCL officer boasted that his organization was "guided by the science of Marxism-Leninism," and a writer in that organization's magazine wrote that "Marxism-Leninism is a living creative science." Marxism-Leninism was "the workers' basic science," according to Foster. "The science of Marxism-Leninism," explained Wells, was "the generalized experience" of the working class, and he elsewhere referred to "materialist working class science," "Marxist ethical science," "the working class science of Marxism-Leninism," and "the science of Marxism."[16]

At the same time, the word "science" continued to designate the separate scientific disciplines. Each of them had broken away from religion and philosophy, as increasing knowledge exploded the mythical explanations of its subject matter. Each studied one "particular form of motion of matter, a form or aspect of social development, or a series of interconnected forms of motion." Each "reflected" the objective laws in its own area.[17]

The reader will notice that the ideas we have sampled form a logical circle. Marxism was judged scientific because it was materialist; but Marxism furnished the principles and methods by which a theory was judged materialist and therefore scientific. Marxism thus stood at both the starting point and the "conclusion" of the reasoning process. To break the circle, the theoreticians would have had to prove Marxism scientific by some criterion independent of its own component principles. For this purpose they invoked "practice." But how did they interpret the lessons of practice? By Marxist criteria. The circle remained closed—as securely as the circle that we noted in the discussion of religion: assuming at the outset that God's existence must be provable or disprovable in terms that implicitly excluded it, the theoreticians quite logically "concluded" that He did not exist. It is safe to assume that Jimmy Higgins, if told that the arguments were circular, would not have cared. His unshakable conviction that Marxism was true was, as I argued in chapter two, prerational. Furthermore, he regarded belief in it in moral terms, as a sign of virtue.

The latter conviction is especially evident in the published polemics against the doctrine that some things were unknowable—that is, ungraspable by reason working with sense data "reflecting" material things (Marxism did not recognize any other mode of knowing). Some of these polemics sounded more like boasts than like arguments. "Dialectical materialism, contrary to idealism," Betty Gannett explained,

asserts that mankind can achieve a positive scientific knowledge of reality.... For the Marxist, as against the idealist, agnostic, and skeptic, there is no unknowable, but only a still unknown.... Marxists ... have complete confidence in the limitless possibilities of knowledge, in the continuous process of science. That is why Marxists also have complete confidence in the inevitable victory on a world scale of dialectical materialism, the philosophic foundation of the Marxist world outlook which will arm the working class with the knowledge to lead all humanity to become master of its fate in a world at last free.

We find the same juxtaposition, of the doctrine that nothing is unknowable, with self-praise and faith in the people, in the peroration of a pamphlet criticizing American historiography: the attack upon Communists during the early 1950s

is upon man himself. Positing his loathsomeness, all else logically follows: unbridled exploitation, rampant racism, tyranny, inhumanity, slaughter.... The Communists see, as Stalin taught, that, "Confidence in the creative power of the masses ... is the peculiar feature in the activities of Lenin." The Communists hold, as Stalin wrote:

"There are no things in the world which are unknowable, but only things which are still not known, but will be disclosed and made known by the efforts of science and practice." The Communists, as Stalin said in his last speech, have been and always will be *in the struggle for the radiant future for the people*."[18]

Why must all things be knowable? Theoretically, because all things are material, and "all things material are knowable."[19] The theoretical justification for this doctrine cannot, however, explain its urgent reiteration; something closer to home was at stake. It is at this point that we approach the center of the seamless web of doctrines. Any boundary around the knowable would enclose Marxists along with non-Marxists, with no advantage to either—at least theoretically. But if everything was knowable, and the non-Marxists' philosophy and political purposes prevented them from probing to the nature of reality, the artificial boundary served their interests. The doctrine that everything was knowable therefore implied the potential omniscience (and future omnipotence) of the Marxists who alone possessed the key to universal knowledge. "All things are knowable" meant "all things are knowable to *Marxist-Leninists*." This is the deeper meaning of the conflation of science with ontology that we have observed in the documents. It depicted the universe as analogous to Soviet society, in which nothing whatever lay beyond the authority of the government.

So necessary was this claim to omnicompetence that it was worth the risk of logical circularity.[20] Very seldom do the documents hint that ultimate axioms cannot be proven. Far more commonly we find the theoreticians claiming that Marxism had been proven true and that it had proven its own tenets true. Occasionally they attempted logical demonstration, but more often they simply stated the "facts." Pavlov's work, wrote Wells, "finally and conclusively and scientifically *proves* the materialist contention. After Pavlov there can be no question any longer, in my opinion, of the absolute truth of materialism. It is now a *scientific fact* as well as a *philosophic principle*." It is hard to see how the more sophisticated Jimmy Higginses could have accepted this extreme formulation. The flat declarations that were more common were also easier to accept, for he could assume that the more technical works of Marxism contained the proofs. Such declarations often took the form of offhand remarks—for example: "truth, which Marxism has shown to be a reflection of reality. . . . " Others appealed to authority:

"The Marxian doctrine is omnipotent," wrote Lenin, "because it is true." A disarmingly simple statement. And yet it embraces ages of philosophic contention and social struggle. Of what other doctrine can it be said, not that it is brilliant or original or streaked with valid insights, but that it is *true*? True not only today, but for the whole of human history—true because it is derived from and corresponds to the actual process of social evolution.[21]

Still others employed repetition. One such document happened to be one of the few that conceded (citing Lenin) that ultimate concepts cannot be defined; perhaps this accounts for the almost incantatory repetition, that

matter is objective and absolute. . . . The forms of the existence of matter—space and time—are also objective and absolute. The existence of material bodies, the motion of matter, occur in space and time independently of any "transcendental" forces and are absolute and objective. . . . The motion of matter . . . [is] absolute and objective. Space and time are therefore absolute and objective. . . . Dialectical materialism rejects the subjectivity of space and time and asserts their objectivity and absoluteness. . . . The motion of matter is absolute and objective.

And so on, on the same and the following pages.[22] And still other documents employed such verbal tricks as "it is well known" and "as everyone knows."[23]

A more subtle method of validating the Party's theory was question-begging. For example, Selsam's reference to "the luxury of holding to a realm of value or essence over and above the concrete world of fact" begged the question whether that realm was indeed nonfactual. (If it was not, then *dis*belief in it was the luxury.) That luxury, he continued, "must give way to a concrete scientific approach to value problems in the closest relation to the actual desirable objectives of human social life." Selsam did not, apparently, realize that he was assuming what he thought he was proving, for not everyone defined "desirable" as he did. Or consider the same philosopher's approval of various thinkers' attempts "to free ethics from supernatural origins and sanctions and to root it in the nature of man and the world at large." He did not, evidently, realize that proponents of supernaturally oriented ethics argued that *their* ethics was "rooted" in the nature of man and the world. More important, he did not notice that his conclusions were implied in his premises.[24]

Such instances of unconscious question-begging form parts of a larger pattern, which we may label "prohibition of certain questions." Selsam deplored philosophers' preoccupation with "worn-out and hackneyed problems such as 'free will,' the ontological argument, the reality or unreality of evil, and whether or not we can know that other human beings exist"—demonstrating that if one wishes to prohibit certain question, it is helpful to misstate their meaning.

Instead . . . of asking such questions as: In virtue of what is this or that good? or: What is the basis of moral judgments? they [certain idealist philosophers] asked the questions: How is it that man can have any notion of a good (as if he would *naturally* not be expected to)? and: What is it in man's nature that causes or enables him to act in accordance with what he believes to be good (as if, of course, there were some peculiar divorce between the good and what men normally seek)?

Why *not* ask questions about what everybody finds natural, so as to find out what "natural" means? Wasn't that what science, including the Marxist version of it, did? Moreover, Selsam's parenthetical questions were themselves loaded with unexamined assumptions (e.g., among all the objects of men's seeking, which are "normal"?). The questions he prohibited were, in fact, prior to those he wanted to ask, for without answers to the former, the latter must be answered tautologically or aprioristically. The "philosophical" grounds for prohibition of certain questions rationalized the moral-psychological basis, which we observed earlier, of the writers' linking of correct theory with devotion to the people and faith in the Party. Ernst and Loth observed the same phenomenon in their informants' recollections: the Communists "welcome the great amount of study and indoctrination that goes with initiation into the party. This course of study is stern and absolute, even to the point where novices"—and, I would add, old members—"have been afraid to ask questions for fear of being suspected of deviation—the word which Communists have adopted as a synonym for heresy."[25] This is true, but if fear had been the only hindrance, the Party, as a voluntary organization, could not have functioned. The prohibited questions were thought ridiculous because the real questions had already been answered to the members' satisfaction.

If, as I believe, the theoreticians themselves did not notice the fallacies in their reasoning, Jimmy Higgins certainly did not. If we notice the questions he never thought to ask, including the prohibited ones that he did not want to ask, we can learn something about the lineaments of the "reality" he perceived. Comrade Jimmy accepted the doctrines because his perception of reality corresponded to the premises and assumptions embedded in the writings. To that extent he was not lying or mistaken when he felt he had assented freely. The authoritarian structure of the Party, and the slightly menacing pronouncements concerning what he must believe, were helpful hints to keep him on the straight path and help his weaker comrades to resist the enemy's propaganda. It is in this light that we should read, for example, this declaration by Browder:

Our Party claims to give political guidance directly to its members, in *all* fields of work. . . . Our theory is *the* understanding of the laws that govern history in its development, the laws of social change. . . . It is in moments of crisis, of great changes, of historic turns, when there is revealed especially the utter inadequacy and harmfulness of *all* anti-Marxist theory. Our theory, as the science of social development, like all science universal in its validity, is *alone* able to provide an understanding of moments of change, to identify the forces involved and the laws of movement of these forces, to pass over from explanation of past changes to foreseeing of future changes—and thereby to direct and shape these changes and the destiny of humanity that is involved. Our theory . . . is *the* science of social development, it is *the* generalization of *all* past history, and forecasts future history.[26] (Emphases added.)

The prohibition of certain questions had greater significance in the area of the Party's philosophy than in the area of its politics and economics. When reading discourses on the latter topics, the rank and filer could assume that the basics had already been settled. If Marxism-Leninism constituted an integrated theory, a seamless web of doctrines, then answers to the derivative questions had grown out of answers to the fundamental ones. In philosophy, however, the prohibition could not be regarded as a time saver, shortcut, or dismissal of unnecessary complications; it was, rather, part of the philosophy itself.[27] The questions that must not be asked were false questions, because they admitted the possible existence of a Supernature or the legitimacy of non-Marxist philosophies. Here was the most basic tautology, the most crucial taboo, the most complete circularity of all—all rolled into one. For when Comrade Jimmy insisted that only those things dreamed of in his philosophy comprised all of reality, he had to turn his own theories back upon themselves to "prove" the basic ones among them true. If he must perceive and interpret all reality in the light of Marxism, then nothing could prove the truth of Marxism. Nothing but faith. Yet Comrade Jimmy did not suspect that faith lay at the foundation of his own convictions. He did not realize that one cannot prove a doctrine by means of principles contained in the doctrine. By expanding material reality to the status of All That Is, he contracted All That Is to the compass of his own experience and shaped it in accordance with his need for intellectual control of reality. As Eric Voegelin has put it: "In order to appear the unlimited master of being, man must so delimit being that limitations are no longer evident."[28] For some comrades, the wish and the result were probably reversed: never having experienced an intimation of anything beyond Nature, they could reasonably have rested content with agnosticism—except that nothing in their experience then restrained them from succumbing to the temptation, rationalized by materialist theory and devotion to Humanity, to aspire to unlimited mastery of being.

In each previous revolution, said Marxism-Leninism, the new ruling class had believed its own philosophy expressed truths applicable to all men at all times, rather than just its own class interests; the socialist revolution was the first in which this universal claim was not a delusion. Since the Party was destined to lead the revolution that would abolish classes, its "science" belonged ultimately to all humanity. Marxism was destined to overcome not just the latest forms of idealism but idealism per se. The inauguration of socialism would abolish the material conditions that produced false consciousness. Jimmy Higgins knew that this put him in a uniquely privileged position: alone among revolutionary groups throughout history, the Party and its members understood their historic role and destiny. For the first time, self-understanding and understanding of external reality became one.

NOTES

1. The basic text was Stalin's "Dialectical and Historical Materialism," a section of the *History of the Communist Party of the Soviet Union (Bolsheviks)* (New York: IP,

1939), esp. pp. 111–12. See, e.g., N[emmy] Sparks, "Marxism and Science," *PA* 26 (December, 1948): 1123–24; George Kursanov, "Space and Time—Forms of the Existence of Matter," third in a four-part series reprinted from *Pod Znamieniem Marxizma (Under the Banner of Marxism)*, *COM* 20 (June, 1941): 568.

2. See cartoon in issue of March 14, 1925, p. 2, and articles in issues of May 16 and 23, 1925. Page 4 of the April 25, 1925, issue has four articles on religion. Excellent illustrations of this preoccupation can be found in the issues throughout 1930. In tone and rhetoric, these documents resembled those of the Industrial Workers of the World during its heyday before World War I. An editorial in the April 6, 1931, issue, "Easter Eggs for Hungry Workers," for example, could have appeared in a Wobbly paper twenty years earlier. See also antireligious articles and cartoons in *NM* throughout 1934, and documents quoted in Ralph Lord Roy, *Communism and the Churches* (New York: Harcourt, Brace, 1960), pp. 33, 35.

3. Earl Browder, sixth article in series "What Is Communism?" *NM*, June 11, 1935, p. 18; Gil Green, "We're Not Lost," *CL* 2 (July, 1936): 5. The *YW* unblushingly adopted the new line. See, e.g., Mac Weiss, "Building the YCL as a Step to Unity," *YW*, January 14, 1936, p. 5; Earl Browder, quoted in Forrest S. Adams, review of Browder's *What Is Communism?*, *YW*, March 10, 1936, p. 10; "A False Prophet," *YW*, October 1, 1935, p. 6. According to William A. Nolan, *Communism versus the Negro* (Chicago: Henry Regnery, 1951), p. 129, the *Daily Worker* devoted an entire page during Christmas 1936 to showing "the similarity between communism and primitive Christianity." Comrades especially interested in the unchanging truth about religion read a pamphlet in the Little Lenin Library: V. I. Lenin, *Religion* (New York: IP, 1933).

4. John Hutchinson, "Has the Church Failed?" *CL* 2 (March, 1937): 7, 28; letter, *CL* 2 (Summer, 1937): 2. The March issue, not coincidentally, contained "An Open Letter to American Liberals by a Group of Distinguished Professors and Writers," excoriating critics of the Moscow Trials and arguing that the "alignment of liberals with enemies of the Soviet Union . . . can only result in confusion and the distortion of true liberalism." (Some of the signers were Party members.) Pro-Communist propaganda by religious people did, however, help to recruit a few people to the Party. What an English ex-Communist wrote about his countrymen applies to Americans: a book by a pro-Soviet Quaker had lulled his doubts "about the Marxist's militant atheism. It provided a bridge by means of which the man with some religious belief could cross with a clear conscience into the camp of unbelief." He added that the books and lectures by Hewlett Johnson, dean of Canterbury, were having the same effect on a later generation of potential Communists. See Douglas Hyde, *I Believed* (New York: G. P. Putnam's Sons, 1950), pp. 23–24.

5. Earl Browder, *Communism and Culture* (New York: Workers Library, 1941), p. 38. See also Michael Gold, *Change the World!* (New York: IP, 1936), pp. 220–23. The animus previously directed at all believers was now focused on religious institutions that played reactionary roles in secular life, especially the Catholic Church. One particularly vehement diatribe is V. J. Jerome, "The Vatican's War on Peace," *PA* 25 (April, 1946): 310–26. The claim that Marxism was "applied Christianity" produced some hilarious contradictions. In William Z. Foster, *The Negro People in American History* (New York: IP, 1954), the chapter "Religion and Slavery" dutifully opens with Marx's dictum that religion is the opiate of the people, and Lenin's that religion teaches the oppressed to be resigned and hope for reward in heaven, and

then devotes two paragraphs to showing that these were the messages taught to the slaves. Then, without explanation or transition, Foster discourses on how the slaves used the Bible to justify their claim to equality and as an antidote to apathy. Later, in his discussion of the abolitionists, he says, "The preachers among them cited Christian ethics and mustered religious texts to counter the pro-slavery Bible quotations of the Southerners" (pp. 160–61, 203). In other words, Foster's wish to claim the slaves' struggles as part of the Party's heritage was too strong to let logic stand in its way.

6. "S. D.," "To the Study and Application of the United Front Policy," *PO* 5 (November–December, 1932): 17; Foster, "Reply to a Priest's Letter," *PA* 33 (October, 1954): 45–46. See also William Z. Foster, *The Twilight of World Capitalism* (New York: IP, 1949), Chap. 7, "The Decline of Religion."

7. Earl Browder, *The Democratic Front* (New York: Workers Library, 1936), pp. 53–54.

8. Louis Budenz, *This Is My Story* (New York: McGraw-Hill, 1947), pp. 173–74, 362–63. So far as rank and filers' religious beliefs are concerned, the American CP differed from the Italian. See Gabriel A. Almond and others, *The Appeals of Communism* (Princeton, N.J.: Princeton University Press, 1954), pp. 311–13. Furthermore, the descriptions of the attitudes of the American CP's rank and file do not apply to those clergymen who signed the Party's petitions and public declarations and sat on the boards of front organizations. Some of them became Party members. (Budenz, on his pp. 329 and 334, mentions his recruitment of one of them.) They did not become ordinary rank and filers, attending branch meetings and Party classes, distributing leaflets, etc.

9. "Defend the Soviet Union!" *YW* 3 (March, 1934): 4; Browder, *Communism and Culture*, pp. 35–36; Milton Howard, "The Holy War on Reason," *MM* 5 (July, 1952): 11; William Z. Foster, *Toward Soviet America* (New York: Coward-McCann, 1932), pp. 113–14.

10. This argument (which originated with Marx) was, however, used; see, e.g., Howard, "Holy War on Reason," p. 11.

11. I shall omit discussion of the "dialectical" half of "dialectical materialism," because among rank-and-file members the word was little more than a label. They rarely bothered to work out the intricacies of the doctrine, and the official writings that focused on that half of the philosophy were, even by Party standards, muddy and strained, suggesting puzzlement among the theorists. Its most useful function was as an epithet ("Comrade, you're being mechanistic" or " . . . metaphysical," rather than "dialectical") or to evade problems ("this seems self-contradictory but really isn't; that's dialectics"). Dialectics was, of course, taught in Jefferson School and Party classes. One illustration was used by all the teachers, to teach the dialectical principle of "quantity into quality": the change of H_2O from a gas to a liquid and then to a solid. Between 32°F. and 212°F., additional units of heat did not change the form of the water, but at some point the accumulation of quantitative changes caused a sudden leap to a qualitatively new form. I recall having an uneasy feeling about this, especially after I had heard it several times in different classes. Why was the same example used over and over, if the principle applied to all things (a few other examples were sometimes used, but not enough to dispel the uneasiness)? Also, what did the dialectical terminology add to our knowledge of the chemistry of H_2O? I blamed my doubts on my ignorance of science, and I assume that most of my comrades thought

the same way. (I do not know how those who were science majors felt about this.) I now see that the teachers did not know much more about this principle than I did and that the purpose of the instruction was not so much to explain a basic aspect of reality as to support the claim of Marxism to scientific status. What is true in the theory is not unique to Marxism, and what is unique to Marxism is of no help to scientists. It is highly doubtful that anyone ever converted to Marxism because of these principles of explanation. More likely, people who had been converted for other reasons then welcomed the "scientific" principles as confirmations endowing their philosophy with the prestige of science. It is hard to think otherwise of real scientists, such as Dirk Struik and Frédéric Joliot-Curie, for the applicability of these principles—the other two being "contradiction" and "the negation of the negation"—to scientific research becomes apparent only after the fact. They are too general and vague to guide the research. A Marxist would contend that the scientists who adequately explained phenomena without recourse to dialectics were not fully aware of what they were seeing, for example, in the transformations of H_2O. But that means either that the tenets of dialectics were unnecessary to their understanding of the phenomena or that those tenets were principles of a philosophy, not of a science. Finally, it should be noticed that the Party ideologists were using dialectics to have their cake and eat it too: they invoked the authority of "bourgeois" science to legitimize Marxism, but they also invoked the authority of dialectics to criticize "bourgeois" science.

12. Sparks, "Marxism and Science," p. 1115; Foster, *Toward Soviet America*, p. 114; David Ramsey, "The Slithy Electron," *NM*, September 18, 1934, p. 19; David Ramsey, book review, *NM*, September 25, 1934, p. 26. See also Foster, *Twilight*, p. 82; William Z. Foster, *History of the Communist Party of the United States* (New York: IP, 1952), p. 535; Foster, *Outline Political History of the Americas* (New York: IP, 1951), p. 489; Milton Howard, "Materialism and Psychoanalysis," *MM* 5 (November, 1952): 19, 20. Foster's dismissal of Einstein had the authority of Soviet scientists; see, e.g., Kursanov, "Space and Time," pp. 574–75.

13. Harry K. Wells, *Pragmatism: The Philosophy of Imperialism* (New York: IP, 1954), pp. 162, 163; Morris U. Schappes, "Problems of Jewish Culture," *MM* 3 (March, 1950): 31 (Schappes was polemicizing against Jewish intellectuals who, having turned against Marxism, were tending toward the study of theology, but his statement clearly was intended to have wider application); Marcel Cachin, *Science and Religion* (New York: IP, 1946), p. 16.

14. *The Handbook of Philosophy*, edited and adapted by Howard Selsam from the *Short Philosophic Dictionary*, by M. Rosenthal and P. Yudin, translated from the Russian (New York: IP, 1949), gives a Marxist-Leninist interpretation of the nature, history, and future of science but defines the word conventionally. For a far more interesting definition and discussion of the nature of science, see M. Kammari and F. Konstantinoff, "Science and Superstructure," *PA* 32 (February, 1953): 53–55. The use of "scientific" in ordinary Party writings was less self-conscious and therefore more revealing for present purposes.

15. Harry Martel, "Some Aspects of Materialism and Consciousness," *Benjamin Rush Bulletin*, No. 2 (May, 1949): 5 (see also the four uses of "scientific" on p. 9); Earl Browder, *Social and National Security* (New York: Workers Library, 1938), pp. 25, 27; A. Landy, "Two Questions on the Status of Women under Capitalism," *COM* 20 (September, 1941): 828–29; Howard Selsam (here identified as "Director of The

Jefferson School of Social Science"), "Should Communists Teach in Our Colleges?" *NF* 6 (June, 1953): 7; Harry Haywood, "Further on Race, Nation and the Concept 'Negro,' " *PA* 31 (October, 1952): passim, esp. 48, 52–53; Howard Selsam, *Socialism and Ethics* (New York: IP, 1943), pp. 106–7; Wells, *Pragmatism*, p. 104. Kammari and Konstantinoff, in "Science and Superstructure," pp. 58–59, say, "Marxism for the first time raised philosophy, sociology, historiography, jurisprudence, Socialism to the level of a science." See also many other documents that can be found by random leafing.

16. Kammari and Konstantinoff, "Science and Superstructure," pp. 55, 53; Earl Browder, *Teheran and America: Perspectives and Tasks* (New York: Workers Library, 1944), p. 44; Browder, "The Study of Lenin's Teachings," *PA* 34 (January, 1945): 9; Ben Davis, "Foster, Fighter for Correct Theory," *PA* 35 (April, 1956): 43; Henry Winston, "Organizational Problems of the Young Communist League," *CL* 2 (Spring, 1941): 39; Frank Cestare, "War Service through the Young Communist League," *CL* 3 (Summer, 1942): 7; William Z. Foster, "The Party Crisis and the Way Out, Part II," *PA* 37 (January, 1958): 63; Wells, *Pragmatism*, pp. 135, 157, 166, 187, 11.

17. Kammari and Konstantinoff, "Science and Superstructure," pp. 54, 53, 58.

18. Betty Gannett, book review, *PA* 26 (May, 1947): 449, 453; Herbert Aptheker, *Laureates of Imperialism: Big Business Re-Writes American History* (New York: Masses & Mainstream, 1954), p. 93. See also Martel, "Some Aspects of Materialism and Consciousness," p. 7; and note the tone in which Stalin presents the same arguments, in *History of the CPSU(B)*, p. 113.

19. Martel, "Some Aspects," p. 7. See also Kammari and Konstantinoff, "Science and Superstructure," p. 53.

20. For a comment, see Massimo Salvadori, *The Rise of Modern Communism*, rev. ed. (New York: Holt, Rinehart and Winston, 1965), pp. 53–54.

21. Harry K. Wells, " 'Philosophy in Revolution,' " *PA* 36 (July, 1957): 35; Philip Carter, "Pitfalls of Pragmatic Logic," *COM* 18 (February, 1939): 164; A. B. Magil, "Scientist of Socialism," *NM*, January 22, 1946, p. 9. For comments on this passage from Lenin, see Alain Besançon, *The Rise of the Gulag: Intellectual Origins of Leninism* (New York: Continuum, 1981), pp. 5, 209–10.

22. Kursanov, "Space and Time," p. 570. It is worth noting that the four-part series by Kursanov appeared in a periodical that was supposed to be read by all Party members, few of whom knew anything about physics or philosophy. Internal evidence suggests that the Soviet readership for whom it was written were also nonscholars. Its technical concepts and terms therefore must have been included to impress laymen who had to take on faith its characterizations of the controversies among physicists and to awe them by its sheer incomprehensibility—except for the easily grasped reiterations about objectivity and absoluteness. Among the "bourgeois" theories it ridiculed, by the way, was that of the expanding universe, which had to be false because it conflicted with Marxist ontology (it was, as we know, demonstrated in the mid–1960s). One document that used all three methods of "proof" mentioned above is Philip M. Tilden, "Lenin's 'Materialism and Empirio-Criticism' and the Crisis in Physics Today," *PA* 32 (October, 1953): 50–60.

23. Articles reprinted from Soviet publications resorted to this trick more often than did those by Americans, perhaps because the former had less need to convince doubters. Yet the Americans did use it, and the Party publications did reprint Soviet essays. An extreme example is A. Sokolov, "Democracy," *PA* 24 (June, 1945): 518–

26: "No sane person can deny," "as all thoughtful and unbiased observers . . . admit," "Can it be denied that" (twice), "Everybody knows," "no special researches are needed to determine," "it cannot be denied that," and "Obviously." Every such phrase introduces a highly controvertible assertion. See also M. Alpatov, "On the Transition from the Ancient World to the Middle Ages," *PA* 31 (July, 1952): 58: "It is well known that," twice, both times introducing assertions that were not at all well known.

24. Howard Selsam, "To Make Philosophy Useful," *NM*, June 27, 1944, p. 17; Selsam, *Socialism and Ethics*, p. 107.

25. Selsam, "To Make Philosophy Useful," p. 17; Selsam, *Socialism and Ethics*, pp. 107–8; Morris L. Ernst and David Loth, *Report on the American Communist* (New York: Henry Holt, 1952), p. 118. The reader may wonder whether Selsam provided the missing analyses elsewhere in the 207 pages of the text of *Socialism and Ethics*. He did not. In fact, the book is full of begged questions, circular reasoning, tautological statements, and self-contradictions. Space limitation forbids the analysis it deserves.

26. Browder, *Communism and Culture*, pp. 6, 13, 14.

27. For analysis of this mode of thinking and its implications, see Eric Voegelin, *Science, Politics and Gnosticism* (South Bend, Ind.: Gateway Editions, 1968), Chap. 1.

28. Ibid., p. 55. See also Besançon, *Rise of the Gulag*, pp. 47, 49.

9

The Nature of Reality II:
Man

THE ETERNAL MOTION of eternal matter had a history. It produced ever "higher" combinations, each with its own laws. The highest so far was mind, the unique development that defined the species man. Was the human portion of nature "good"? And what, for that matter, was the reference point of "higher" and "lower" in a godless universe that had produced higher and higher combinations of matter eons before any mind existed, and in which the recently evolved human mind judged itself "highest"? The devout rank-and-file member of the Party did not ponder questions such as these, and the answers he heard and read sent him conflicting signals. The subject of this chapter differs from the others in that the Party's theories about human nature lacked even spurious coherence. The chapter will therefore show a gap in the very foundations of Jimmy Higgins's "world" and for that reason will focus on the Party writings rather than on his thinking.

PARTY LITERATURE presented Jimmy Higgins with a choice of three possible theories of human nature—that it was innately good, that it was a mere potentiality, and that it was innately evil. He had strong *reasons* for choosing the first two, but his *feelings* all converged on the third. The third, the one that the Party rejected with vehemence and indignation, was alone consistent with the true believer's feeling that reality itself was the enemy. The first two theories translated "reality" into "capitalist system" and thus made it possible to contrast the ugly present with the beautiful future, to make sin temporary and blame it on The System, and to identify the Party with the good in the common people. However adamantly the comrades insisted that their theory was scientific (that is, fact-based and objective), it rested ulti-mately on an "is"-denying "ought." This is why they looked forward to creating a wholly "new man" and, as we shall see in chapter thirteen, even reshaping the natural world.

One bit of folk wisdom that Jimmy Higgins never quoted except in scorn was "you can't change human nature." The Party's writers and classroom teachers ridiculed it often enough to train Comrade Jimmy to react correctly whenever he heard or read it. But even without that conditioning he would have recognized the saying as false and dangerous. Implying something static, unaffected by environment or practice, it was "undialectical" and "idealist." It acquitted capitalism of blame for the character flaws and neuroses that he saw all around him, and sometimes within himself. Procapitalist ideologues wanted people to believe that "you can't change human nature," to discourage them from constructing a system that would make people healthy and happy, as the Soviet Union was doing. Besides, any doctrine that denied to Comrade Jimmy (or to his surrogate, the Party) intellectual control over a crucial part of reality—and practical control after the revolution—must be wrong.[1]

Although the theoreticians knew what was wrong with the "static" theory of human nature, they were not so clear about what they should put in its place. On this question, more than on any other, the documents show chronic ambiguity and ambivalence. For one thing, did the mind have different levels of consciousness? Theoretically, no; the writers denounced all psychological theories that posited an unconscious or subconscious. They denounced theories that advocated an introspective therapy, rather than participation in the people's struggles, to cure emotional disorders.[2] Yet "the unconscious" had its uses: comrades were often criticized for not having "rooted out" their unconscious residues of bourgeois ideology. Second, the theoreticians preached Pavlovian psychology, sometimes in starkly behavioralistic terms, yet also denounced behavioralism for being "mechanistic," "reductionist," and "undialectical."[3] Third, some writers cited the changeability of the psyche to prove that there was no such thing as human nature. But on that logic nothing whatever existed. According to dialectical materialism, *everything* changed continuously but kept its identity until a qualitative change, resulting from the contradictions within the thing and the accumulation of quantitative changes, transformed it into something else. When discussing the psyche, however, the theorists were so anxious to avoid recognizing any interior, constant self that the remaining collection of surface "reflections" of exterior circumstances sometimes lacked any "glue" to hold them together and give them a collective identity. Some Party writing about psychology virtually reduced the psyche to the mere meeting place of environmental determinants.[4] Yet the writers had no such problem when they wrote about other changeable phenomena; "capitalism," for example, had changed a lot since its birth, yet remained essentially the same system. Fourth, some writers said outright that whatever the phrase "human nature" referred to was basically good; others (or the same writers) said or implied that it referred to nothing at all; yet the basic tenets of historical materialism implied that human nature was fundamentally evil. The reader familiar with Marxism will be astonished by that last generalization, and indeed the documents that denounced the theory that human nature was basically evil were shrill and unambiguous.[5] Nevertheless, the Party's theory of the origin of class divisions implied a sort of original sin.

Engels's *The Origin of the Family, Private Property and the State*, first published in 1884 and reissued by International Publishers in 1942, remained the basic text in historical sociology, supplemented by others that left its general outline intact. One was the section on historical materialism in *History of the Communist Party of the Soviet Union (Bolsheviks)*—customarily called *The History of the CPSU*—which International published in 1939. This section, credited to Stalin, began: "Five *main* types of relations of production are known to history: primitive communal, slave, feudal, capitalist and Socialist" (p. 123). Engels, Stalin, and all the other expositors of the theory presented the following general picture of the transition from the first to the second mode of production, that is, the transition to the first class-divided social order: At first, productive technique was too primitive to yield a surplus; the group could survive only if everyone worked and owned everything in common. In time, technique advanced to the point where the group produced more than it needed for sheer survival. Some could now eat without working. Victors in wars no longer killed their prisoners, but enslaved them, and the owners henceforth lived off their slaves' work. Property became privately owned because survival no longer depended on common effort and sharing.

Jimmy Higgins never realized that the Party version of the Expulsion from Eden implied a theory of human nature. It said in effect: "As soon as a community becomes able to produce a surplus, a few will use the surplus to enslave the rest." If the inability to produce a surplus above subsistence level had *forced* people to share everything, the ability to produce a surplus must have *permitted*—not forced—some to exploit others. Yet one of the most intelligent and thoughtful Party writers backed off from this dangerous conclusion: "Once the productive forces have developed sufficiently to allow for a division of labor based on the ownership of diverse means of production, and to necessitate a distinction between those who work and those who direct their work," said Charles Humboldt, "the division of society into classes becomes inevitable."[6] This argument ran in a circle, for when Humboldt dropped the "allow for" in favor of the "necessitate," the final "inevitable" became a mere restatement of that premise. He did not ask what "necessitated" the distinction between workers and nonworkers. The reader cannot help suspecting that it was made necessary solely by the demands of the historical model of Marxism-Leninism. From the standpoint of those primitives, however, the "allow for" certainly fits the situation as described. That is, some people who had the choice to work or to exploit others chose the latter course. This looks very much like innate selfishness. Why did they not choose to continue working, sharing, and prospering together? Engels, in his original statement of the theory, did not try to explain this either. (A philosophy that does not regard private ownership of the means of production as essentially exploitative does not have this problem.) True, the Marxist classics credited private ownership with fostering technological progress and the production of ever-greater surpluses of wealth, until capitalism entered the period of its "general crisis." But the first appropriators of their tribes' herds and fields were unaware of their historic role. When they (according to the theory) grabbed portions of the common possessions and sat back to supervise their slaves' work, they were not intending to set society on the road to communism-on-a-higher-level. They were choosing one of two alternatives newly opened to them, in the face of the ingrained moral code of sharing, backed by age-old tradition.[7]

This image of a selfish, cruel human nature lurks elsewhere in the Marxist-Leninist world, sometimes in unexpected places. Movie critic Richard Grenier has discovered it in Soviet animal films:

Boa constrictors swiftly wrap themselves around trapped rabbits (seen in close-up), pause, and then squeeze. The rabbit's head bulges hideously as he dies. Cuddly swamp animals swim desperately across lakes to escape a predator but are—not sometimes but always—caught and promptly eaten. A baby fox which strays from the litter is caught and eaten. Hunt, pursue, kill, eat. Kill, eat. Kill, eat. Nature is merciless in a Soviet animal movie. When I first saw a whole series of these quite extraordinary films, and reflected on their impact on a Soviet audience, I felt that their thrust was essentially Hobbesian: men, left to themselves, would be in a state of constant war with each other, like animals, and any form of government at all is preferable to anarchy. Let us say it is unlikely that a spectator would emerge from a Soviet animal film with the impression that we live in a benign universe.[8]

Whatever the intentions of the Soviet movie producers, this justification for power—the equation of the lack of rational, "scientific," control with evil— pervaded American CP writings on all subjects, in the period under study. They always gave a pejorative meaning to the word "spontaneity." The implicit message to Jimmy Higgins went: "Leave individuals to their own devices and evil will result, because a few people will inevitably oppress the many. The 'free market' is a misnomer. Except for primitive communism, with its extreme scarcity, and future communism, with its unlimited abundance, every social order is controlled by the class that controls its means of living. To build a good society, the populace as a whole must own and control everyone's means of living." Did this mean that people after the revolution could be trusted? No. According to Foster, after socialism has been established "proletarian discipline and solidarity will be quite sufficient to prevent possible idlers from taking advantage of this free regime of distribution by either refusing to work or by unsocial wasting."[9] This meant that even in the presence of abundance and the absence of bad influences, at least some people will still want to take advantage of their brothers.

The conception of human nature implied in this image of a Hobbesian universe cannot be found frankly expressed in American CP literature, and the writers certainly never knew it was there. All the more reason to ask, first, why Party members perceived reality in this way, and second, why they suppressed this perception in favor of the theory that human nature was basically good or that there was no such thing. As I suggested in chapter three, the Type I member—whose attitude toward the world dominated Party literature—felt a hostility toward proximate reality that caused him to see all external reality as hostile toward *him*. When this individual perception became embodied in a political theory, he saw himself writ large as "the working class" or "the people." The victims of the evil ruling class must be good, as he himself was. Yet their goodness, like his own, was not trust-worthy, for, as Jimmy Higgins knew from experience, it depended on correct belief. It was so easy to err that even he needed the constant instruction and discipline provided by the Party, to shield him from the enemy's influence. Moreover, individual members of the exploiting class could become good Communists, just as individual members of the oppressed classes could lynch Negroes, cross picket lines, and commit other crimes. So it seemed that fundamental human nature, whatever it was, had little connection with prac-tical reality. Yet, since evil had to be projected outward, onto the exploiting class, inner human nature had to be good. All these conflicts in feelings and ideological needs found expression in the Party's discourses on human nature.

One category of documents was mainly negative: they denounced bour-geois theories or denied that there was any such thing as human nature, without however setting forth the correct alternative. "We have," announced *New Foundations*, "the vital obligation to explode the myths that . . . despair of changing human nature, that see our society's evils as incurable." Another writer explained that "human nature is in a continual process of change. There is no static human nature, there are no static instincts, there are no static drives, there is nothing static in the development of human beings, in the development of society in general." On the contrary, wrote another, "psychological categories" such as " 'reality,' 'hostility,' 'repression,' 'adjust-ment,' 'love,' 'harmony,' 'integration,' 'effectiveness,' etc.," "are not univer-sal, good for all time and places. They mean different things to different classes. They are not applicable to all human history in the same manner, but apply differently to different societies, feudal, capitalist, socialist or communist," and to different classes within the same society. The same writer also announced that there was no such thing as the unconscious and that "the nature of the individual consciousness is nothing but the sum total of the organism's life and experience, in the form of inherited adaptations, and in the form of current activity which is socially-conditioned." (In case Jimmy Higgins might hesitate to form an opinion on such a technical subject, the author of this ten-page, recondite analysis admitted that he himself was "not a psychologist, but a political journalist." As in all other fields, the sole necessary qualification here was a solid grounding in the Marxist classics.)[10]

The positive formulations of the Party's conception of human nature did not get much guidance from Marx's oft-quoted dictum that "it is not the consciousness of men that determines their being, but, on the contrary, their social being that determines their consciousness." Of course, consciousness reacted back upon being, and people were, as Engels added, free if they "recognized necessity," but the classic formula clearly gave primacy to external determinants—not only of consciousness but of human nature as well, for the Party equated the two. But from that point on, the modern theoreticians were on their own.

When we turn to their explorations of the subject, we learn, first of all, that although human nature was a product of social being, some aspects of social being were more influential than others. "Early childhood experiences, parental influences, and so-called inter-personal relationships" were among the others; on principle they were less influential than "objective reality," which included "such factors as class position, poverty, discrimination, and type of occupation."[11] National culture was also among the others. The enormous variety of customs and values throughout history and in the modern world served as convenient disproofs of the theory that there was some constant and universal human nature.[12] But when the writers described the positive determinants of human nature they treated national cultures mostly as barriers to progress. Wherever possible they found economic and class explanations; these referred to the "base," whereas culture was "superstructural." Variations in gender roles, among and within different societies, were due to class and to different levels of the division of labor. Blacks, because they were the most oppressed group, should be most eager to join the Party once it had formulated and explained the correct line; that is, class interests would quickly and painlessly override whatever cultural patterns might influence the blacks' receptivity to the Party's message. Among all peoples, socialism would drastically change human nature in an astonishingly short time. This meant that age-old customs and culturally determined personality traits were superficial and easily shed. Wrote Foster in 1932: "Light and prosperity are being brought into the dark Russian villages. . . . The winning of the 'fundamentally anti-Socialist' middle peasants to Socialism has been practically accomplished."[13] In short, Party assertions that "human nature is changeable" had a tacit qualification: "the chief influences are economic and class, not cultural, religious, or family."

When we survey the entire corpus of those documents, however, we do not find clear answers to our initial questions, whether there was such a thing as human nature and, if there was, whether it was good or neutral (the "bad" image was, as we have seen, rejected outright—in words). If being determined consciousness, one would expect that servitude to a brutal ruling class—and all ruling classes were brutal—would have had brutalizing effects on the victims' "human natures." Indeed, one of the principal aims of the socialist revolution was to create a "new man," thus implying good riddance to the old one. As M. J. Olgin wrote in 1936, "the Soviet world has been . . . reshaping humanity, creating a new kind of humanity fundamentally different from that of capitalist countries," implying that not only the capitalists and petty bourgeoisie were being reshaped.[14] Yet elsewhere in the literature (see all the Party's historical works) the masses were generous, hardworking, hospitable, wise, honest, heroically struggling against their oppressors. In other words, they manifested personality traits impervious to external influences, or else traits formed by resistance to oppression (but where did the impulse to resist come from?). The writers apparently never noticed this contradiction, and neither did Jimmy Higgins.

Both images sometimes appeared in the same essays. Foster, for example, denounced the theories that blamed war on the nature of man. "This is all nonsense, of course. Man is by nature a gregarious and friendly animal." A few pages later, however, the reader learned that "the revolution will create . . . a new and better development of the individual. . . . Changed social conditions develop different 'human natures.' " A far more intelligent theorist wrote just as confusedly. "Only in a Communist society," said Charles Humboldt, "can the simple virtues be fulfilled by which literally billions of people have tried to live through history." Apparently, then, those values were suprahistorical and transcultural, and so was the recognition of their permanent desirability; surely this implies something permanent and innate in human nature. But two pages later, Humboldt wrote that "communism means more than the satisfaction of all individual desires. Its full flowering will be accompanied by changes in the character and quality of those desires, just as responsibility toward others becomes less a matter of external compulsion—even the compulsion of reason—and more a matter of habit. . . . Socialist society is the first to set itself the conscious task of changing human nature." Evidently, then, human nature before the revolution had been bad, or it would not need changing. But wait; in the next sentence Humboldt reverted to a fixed human nature: "Having abolished private property and the social relations which are the basis for almost all distortions of character and personality, it [socialist society] now proposes to build men and women in whom no trace of such injury will remain, and to convert egoism, no matter how enlightened, into its opposite. Then man will be truly man's creation."[15] What were those bad traits "distortions" and "injuries" of, if there was no such thing as human nature? Yet Humboldt would not have used the word "creation" if he had not had in mind something new under the sun, not seen in class society (except embryonically in the best Communists).

In addition to the generous, hospitable, indomitable poor throughout history, there was one group to whom Party writers never hesitated to impute innate good traits: blacks. Foster, for example, wrote of the American slaves' "human love of freedom" that explained why they resisted slavery although they sometimes feigned submission. "To say, as many bourgeois writers have done, that the Negroes tamely submitted to the terrible subjugation of slavery, is an outrageous distortion of reality and a burning insult to the Negro people." It was thus insulting to say that *their* being determined *their* consciousness, that slavery produced slavish personalities. In the same passage he added that the modern working class "also has its passive periods as well as those filled with activity and general progress,"[16] and so perhaps white workers too feigned accommodation when they were really feeling a human love for freedom. But where did this human love for freedom originate? How can we account for this unchanging, innate trait?

The historian Herbert Aptheker took one step toward a frank confrontation of this problem; he at least saw it as "a problem in historical dialectics":

The fact is that there is a fundamental continuity in the struggles of the oppressed and the exploited which persists and, as it were, transcends particular social forms. That is, the struggles of a Spartacus, a Wat Tyler, a Nathaniel Bacon, a Denmark Vesey, a William Sylvis, a Martin Luther King have in them a common desire to remove the burdens of oppression, to achieve some form of human dignity, which make of them a unit despite the fact that they appear in eras of ancient slavery, medieval feudalism, early colonial capitalism, modern commercial slavery, and monopoly capitalism. In these cases the programs varied, of course, as the time and conditions varied, but in them all was a common striving for something we can call freedom. I do not mean only varying levels of freedom; I mean that each of them had *in common* a desire for something that may be called freedom.[17]

The defensive "the fact is," the escape hatch "as it were," the ambiguous and repeated qualification of "freedom," and the "some form of" human dignity, which backs away from the implication of a permanent essence— all were uncharacteristic of Aptheker's style, and all hint that he knew he was skirting heresy. This essay, not coincidentally, appeared during the thaw following the Twentieth Congress, when the boundaries around permissible thinking receded a bit. But that was as far as he went; the status of this suprahistorical trait remained unexplained.

The same question arises when we observe how Party writers used the word "potentialities," as in "socialism will enable man to realize his potentialities." Most expressions of this idea omitted any qualification before that last word, suggesting that the good potentialities were more authentic than the bad.[18] But did the theoreticians mean the potentiality of the acorn to become an oak, or the potentiality of the marble block to become a statue? To the dialectical materialist, matter was not inert; all things developed according to their internal "contradictions." Yet, as we have seen, the writers forgot this basic theory when they dealt with human nature. They had to, owing to the unique nature of mind: it alone consisted of "reflections" of other entities.

The "empty receptacle" image of human nature alone makes sense of certain significant metaphors that Party writers resorted to repeatedly—significant because they likened people to things and plants. "Stalin rears the young generation like a careful, experienced gardener," said one. "The revolutionary novelist," said another, must "create, by his imagination, the typical man, the hero of our times, and in this way to become, as Stalin has phrased it, 'an engineer of the human soul.' " The Soviet Union was "the greatest laboratory of human nature the world has ever known," according to a Party scholar. It is worth noting that Communists were not alone in failing to see anything insulting to human beings in these metaphors. Sidney and Beatrice Webb, in their two-volume description of the Soviet Union, genially remark, "As Stalin has said, 'man must be grown as carefully and attentively as a gardener grows a favourite fruit tree.' " If the masses guided by the Party resembled plants, their mis-leaders were beasts—higher on the evolutionary scale but still subhuman. A YCL leader wrote that "the Hitlerite beasts" reared "a whole generation of youth" to believe "in predatory war, aggression, murder, pillage, rapine as a way of life," and later referred to the "brutish" conduct of the Hitler youth. A writer in *Clarity* called Hitler's ideology "bestial." Another called American politicians who opposed the war effort "political maggots" and added that "total war requires . . . the productive harnessing [N.B.!] of every man, woman and child in our nation's fight for survival against the fascist locusts." The editor of *Spotlight* went beyond metaphor: "Nazis are not men, but beasts."[19]

What ever happened to Foster's naturally gregarious and friendly animal and the other theoreticians' faith in man's potentialities and capacities (unmodified by "good")? If the Nazis had become subhuman by divesting themselves of those traits, then the Party's formula shrivels to a tautology: human nature remains basically good (actually or potentially) simply because people who actualize evil become subhuman. It should be noted, moreover, that this logic excludes the other theory we have found in the documents—that human nature is a neutral, empty receptacle—for, on that theory, people would not lose their humanity if the receptacle were filled with evil. So, did the Party accept the theory that there is a human nature after all?

If so, what are we to make of a statement by Mao Tse-tung (in an essay that *Political Affairs* published before the Sino-Soviet break excluded Chinese works from Party publications): "Not to have a correct political point of view is like having no soul. . . . In building a Socialist society, all need remolding, exploiters as well as the working people"?[20] If a wrong-thinking person virtually lacked a soul, he was hardly more than an animal, although, unlike animals, people had the potentiality to acquire souls. Since all good Communists accepted Lenin's doctrine that the working class, by its own experience and activities, could not acquire socialist consciousness, which must therefore be brought to it "from without,"[21] what was innate was only the empty space waiting for Marxist-Leninists to infuse the soul of correct ideas into the people.

The hatred that Type I comrades felt for wrong-thinking people found a splendid rationale in this conception of human nature. Mao's dictum was consistent with the aforementioned dread of "spontaneity," as were Stalin's well-known "cultivation" and "engineering" metaphors. To grasp the full significance of these locutions, we should contrast them with the Jewish and Christian doctrines of the equality of all men as children of God. That equality is consistent with inequality of intelligence, virtue, and every other attribute and, by the same token, cannot be lost. Mao and the others quoted above, by contrast, appear to have been willing to erase the line separating people from animals, insofar as they measured humanness in terms of a greater or lesser grasp of correct ideas. They might have replied that since mind or soul (they equated the two) constituted a qualitatively new thing in the evolutionary movement of matter, even the least enlightened human being was far more human than the wisest ape. Nevertheless, he was less human than a Marxist-Leninist, who was thus obliged to "remold" him.

Here we must recall and extend an observation made earlier, concerning the difference between the Party theoreticians' view of human nature and their view of all other entities. I noted that some writers depicted human nature as little more than the meeting place of an assortment of traits, each "reflecting" something external to the psyche. Other things could change a great deal, quantitatively, without losing their qualitative nature as what they were. A mere conglomeration of traits cannot have such cohesion. According to dialectics, the change of a thing to a new thing is due primarily to its inner contradictions; external influences can speed up or slow down the process, but not determine its general direction. Capitalism did not become more or less capitalistic according to the lesser or greater size of the public sector; it remained capitalism so long as the bourgeoisie owned the decisive means of production, and thus there could be no gradual change to socialism or any system intermediate between capitalism and socialism. But if "human nature" is reduced pretty much to a verbal convenience, saving the writer from the need to list all the disparate "reflections" of extra-mental phenomena, then the dialectical laws of contradiction and quantity-into-quality do not apply to "it." The way is thus open for the postulation of inequality greater than any conceivable to a Jew or Christian.

By now the reader may be as confused as were the writings we have sampled. So a digression is in order, to help us step back from this topic and comment on its general pattern. Because it is easy to substitute the author's own logic for that of the subjects, I have tried to restrict my inferences to those that the writings under discussion make inescapable (there are plenty of other plausible comments that I have refrained from including). In fairness to the Party writers, we should remember that they worked under constraints that most writers on human nature were free of. They had to keep an eye on what their Soviet mentors were writing on the same subjects. They also had to supply ammunition for activists to use in arguments with outsiders— liberals and members of minority groups, unions, and front organizations—

and so had to make their arguments as appealing as possible. Add the in-consistencies and lacunae in their basic theory itself, and it is no wonder that, when all the statements on this theme are read together, the result is incoherent. Jimmy Higgins did not, of course, read them all at the same time, and he had his own constraints and ambiguous feelings toward "human nature" matching those in the literature. He felt "love for the people" and contempt for them at the same time. His truth was so self-evident to him that he could not understand how intelligent people could reject it; yet all outsiders did so. He saw Soviet movies that depicted the new man under socialism, so different from people he encountered every day that it was hard to feel the love for individuals that he felt for them in masses. Of course he blamed "capitalism" for the bad things he saw men do to each other. But he had escaped the conditioning; why hadn't they? I think it reasonable to conclude that the very self-contradictions in the Party's writings on human nature, especially since he did not notice them, *strengthened* their plausibility to him, for each side touched a chord in his own divided mind.

The denial of humanity to Nazis, and to Americans who did not support the war effort, was more than a hyperbolic expression of extreme hatred. Communist Parties in power have, in fact, treated enemies as nonhumans (although Jimmy Higgins only half-believed they did). In American CP writings this rhetoric was sometimes meant literally, and this made the mere metaphorical uses more significant and ominous than they seem. The contexts as well as the entire pattern of Party ideology permit us to discern several levels of significance. On the intellectual level, the metaphors signified the Communist's superiority. If the soul consisted of correct ideas, then the Marxist-Leninist was more human than everyone else. On the ethical level, it justified the treatment of people with wrong ideas as animals—trained performers, draft animals, or jungle predators. Yet at a still deeper level this rhetoric hinted at a faint recognition of a truth: that contrary orientations toward reality manifested something far more basic than differences of opin-ion that could change in the course of debate, and that orientation toward being was the most fundamental and important fact about a person. At the same time, the comrades' own orientation toward being was delusory, hence the mutual incompatibility of the various theories we have surveyed. Insofar as the thoughtful comrade knew that when he considered this subject he was reaching toward the very core of his own being, he adopted a mode of expression pertaining to the difference between men and nonmen; but in-asmuch as his own orientation toward reality was false, he evaded the fun-damental questions at the instant he began to probe them. The result was incoherence and self-contradiction.

Paradoxically, human nature, in the Party's view, was both the highest and best product of the evolution of matter and the lowest and worst. Lowest? Not developmentally, of course, but organizationally. Its components were as weakly bonded as those of the most primitive multicelled organisms, as easily broken apart, changed, and recombined, as easily degraded into those of its evolutionary predecessor. This mass of contradictions was the price the Party unwittingly paid for a theory of human nature that combined materialism with the Party's role as the vanguard of history. Before the comrades could play that role, they had to destroy something that was in every respect the antithesis of the weakly bonded conglomeration of elements they called "human nature": the organically integrated, two-centuries-old, entity they called "the System."

NOTES

1. The "practical" topics—the "new man" in the Soviet Union and in the future Soviet America, and the ruling class's evil motives—will be discussed in later chapters. Here we shall focus on the "theoretical" topics.

2. See, e.g., Al Leonard, "Eric[h] Fromm: Escape from Reality," *NF* 4 (November, 1950): 14–16; Milton Howard, "Materialism and Psychoanalysis," *MM* 5 (November, 1952): 20, 23.

3. See, e.g., Herbert Aptheker, *History and Reality* (New York: Cameron Associates, 1955), p. 62; Albert Starr, "Psychosomatic Medicine," *MM* 6 (June, 1953): 17–20; Joseph C. Clayton, "Some Problems in the Struggle against Psychoanalysis," *PA* 33 (April, 1954): 40–52; Howard, "Materialism and Psychoanalysis," pp. 25–27. The last two essays were criticized in one brief paragraph in Ann Levine and Paul Robertson, "Partisanship and Science," *PA* 35 (October, 1956): 59–60; this article is a daring and unprecedented critique of Party scholarship on many subjects. What is most interesting about it, however, is how much it continued to take for granted, how little it really probed to the causes of the errors it criticized. Nevertheless, it was articles like this, published during the brief thaw following Khrushchev's "revelations" about Stalin at the Twentieth Congress, that soon brought on a new freeze in the name of discipline.

4. E.g., Howard, "Materialism and Psychoanalysis," p. 26.

5. E.g., Samuel Sillen, "The Irrationals," *NM*, October 29, 1940, p. 21; Herbert Aptheker, "A Liberal Dilemma," *NM*, May 14, 1946, p. 4; Aptheker, "Task Force A.D.A.," *MM* 1 (June, 1948): 29; Aptheker, "The 'New Conservatives,'" *MM* 6 (April, 1953): 24, 29, 28. One curiosity in this connection is Aptheker's explanation of the disaffection of the Hungarian rebels from the regime, in his chapter "Sources of Popular Discontent," in *The Truth about Hungary* (New York: Mainstream Publishers, 1957). One source was "the teachings of the Church: man's fall and sinfulness," and another was the age-old fatalism especially in rural areas: "Things will never change; we are meant to suffer; don't stick your neck out; why take a chance" (p. 133). How this explained the unwillingness to suffer any longer, the sticking-out of necks, the chance-taking, of enough Hungarians to force the Soviet army to intervene, Aptheker does not explain. Elsewhere in that book he admits that the people had reason to complain. In his writings on the United States, original-sin theory and the preaching of fatalism are offered as reasons for Americans' *failure* to rise up against their oppressors.

6. Charles Humboldt, "What Is Freedom?" *MM* 3 (May, 1950): 75.

7. William Z. Foster describes preclass ethics in a suggestive passage in *Toward*

Soviet America (New York: Coward-McCann, 1932), pp. 335–36: Those who say that "the destructive type of competition . . . is rooted firmly in human nature" are wrong. That theory would imply

that the rich capitalist who heartlessly casts workers out of his shops penniless and gives no thought as to their future has quite a different 'human nature' than [sic] the African Negro hunter who, with his high sense of clan solidarity, before eating his kill, calls loudly in the four directions in case perchance there may be another hungry hunter nearby. Changed social conditions develop different "human natures."

Thus, to illustrate the good nature produced by common ownership, Foster cites a member of a preclass society rather than a modern proletarian in capitalist society, whom he elsewhere describes in glowing terms. It all depended on what he was trying to prove at the moment of writing. The generous proletarian was a weapon aimed against bourgeois theorists of original sin, when Foster was defending the Party's future recruits; the primitive hunter, however, fitted a context in which Foster was forecasting Soviet America, when common ownership would return "at a higher level." But how did the "changed social conditions" at the dawn of class society "develop" a selfish human nature so different from that hunter's, when there was no ruling class to enforce the new modes of behavior? And if a new human nature did develop, how could Foster explain the common people's retention of those traits he lauds elsewhere? He does not explain.

8. Richard Grenier, "Summertime Visions," *Commentary* 74 (August, 1982): 66n.

9. Foster, *Toward Soviet America*, p. 130.

10. "Just to Learn Is Not Enough," *NF* 2 (Fall, 1948): 6; Harry Martel, "Some Aspects of Materialism and Consciousness," *Benjamin Rush Bulletin*, No. 2 (May, 1949): 12; Howard, "Materialism and Psychoanalysis," pp. 21, 24, 27. See also Harry K. Wells, *Pragmatism: Philosophy of Imperialism* (New York: IP, 1954), pp. 82, 87, 165; Joseph Wortis, in "Forum: Three Views on Psychoanalysis," *MM* 2 (November, 1949): 59; and documents quoted in Frank S. Meyer, *The Moulding of Communists* (New York: Harcourt, Brace, 1961), pp. 195–97, nn. 5, 6, 8.

11. Starr, "Psychosomatic Medicine," p. 16. See also Ellen Gold, "The Roots of Racism," *NF* 5 (Fall, 1951): 14–15.

12. See, e.g., Howard Selsam, *Socialism and Ethics* (New York: IP, 1943), Chapter 2 and passim.

13. Raymond Gardner, "The Psychology of Women under Capitalism," *Benjamin Rush Bulletin*, No. 2 (May, 1949): 15–26; William A. Nolan, *Communism versus the Negro* (Chicago: Henry Regnery Co., 1951), p. 107; Foster, *Toward Soviet America*, p. 92. (Each of these works is just one of many that could be cited on its subject.) Only toward the very end of our period did the Party's theoreticians adopt a more realistic view of national culture.

14. M. J. Olgin, "What Does Lenin Mean to Workers and Farmers of America Today?" *PO* 9 (January, 1936): 23.

15. Foster, *Toward Soviet America*, pp. 324–25, 333, 336; Humboldt, "What Is Freedom?" pp. 82, 84, 85.

16. William Z. Foster, *The Negro People in American History* (New York: IP, 1954), p. 41.

17. Herbert Aptheker, "On the Concept 'Bourgeois Democracy,' " *PA* 35 (August, 1956): 56–57.

18. E.g., Howard Selsam, "Do Ends Justify Means?" *MM* 9 (September, 1956): 4–5; Earl Browder, *Communism and Culture* (New York: Workers Library, 1941), p. 40; Earl Browder, "A Glimpse at Soviet America," *NM*, July 9, 1935, pp. 9–11; Selsam, *Socialism and Ethics*, pp. 98, 187, 198, 201; Sidney Finkelstein, "Psychoanalysis and the Arts," *NM* 4 (August, 1951): 75.

19. N. Slutsker, "Lenin, Stalin and the Communist Youth Movement," *CL* 1 (April–May, 1940): 72; Ralph Fox, *The Novel and the People* (New York: IP, 1945), p. 84; Harry Martel, book review, *NM*, December 4, 1945, p. 25; Sidney and Beatrice Webb, *Soviet Communism: A New Civilization?* 2 vols. (New York: Charles Scribner's Sons, 1936), 2: 804; Mac Weiss, "The Twentieth Anniversary of the Young Communist League," *CL* 3 (Spring, 1942): 14; Frank Cestare, "Earl Browder—Molder of Character," ibid., p. 36; Eli Jaffe, "Mobilize Youth for Victory Crop," *CL* 3 (Summer, 1942): 69, 71; Claudia Jones, "From the Editor," *SP* 2 (July, 1944): 2. In this connection we should recall the comment by Richard Grenier quoted earlier in this chapter, depicting a savage universe, and the other evidence of fear of any reality that was not dominated by reason, which meant Marxist-Leninist reason.

20. Mao Tse-tung, "On Contradictions among the People," *PA* 36 (July, 1957): 53, 51. Who would do the remolding? Mao referred to "the people" as permitting this and intending that, when he actually meant the Party, but he also said that "the people's government . . . must allow the people to take part in political activities" (p. 42). This unthinking image of the people as passive objects of government's decisions is found many times in Herbert Aptheker's *Truth about Hungary*, even in his recommendations of reforms to abolish the abuses that had caused the rebellion.

21. V. I. Lenin, *What Is To Be Done?* (New York: IP, 1929), pp. 32–33.

10

"The System" and Its Rulers

The historical process seems to have cracked into two diametrically opposed parts and everything from economic relations to psychological reactions is in a state of explosive dualism. . . . Two orders, two worlds, two cultures are engaged in a life and death struggle. . . . Not until this struggle is resolved in the harmony of a classless society can man hope to attain even a semblance of freedom. In the meanwhile, the only people *relatively* free are those in power. Under capitalism, it is the capitalists; under proletarian dictatorship, the workers and the poor peasants.[1]

IN JIMMY HIGGINS'S EYES, this dualism was the basic constant of class society, that is, of society from the beginning of recorded history. At times it was "explosive," at other times not. Every social order was a System, ruled by one class, which dominated all things political, social, economic, cultural, and ideological. Because a System got its character from the one class that held all effective power, a System could not change gradually into another. Revolution, the replacement of the ruling class by another, was needed. Piecemeal improvements could not touch its fundamental injustice or, therefore, make it evolve into socialism. So went the theory. But emotional needs too demanded the revolution: even if the comrades had believed that incremental reforms could inch the country toward socialism, they could not contemplate sharing power, for a time, with people they hated. No scores could be settled, no enemies liquidated. The Party's System-theory thus justified the Type I comrades' hatred.

But the theory also implied disapproval of hatred of individual oppressors, because that hatred shifted blame away from the System. Marx, though an expert hater, taught that capitalists sincerely believed in their own ideology and in the goodness and justice of the System they created and ruled.[2] This meant that oppression and exploitation were "objective," structural features of capitalist society, not caused by capitalists' wickedness. This theory appealed to many people—Type II comrades and non-Communists—who felt no hatred toward the System's rulers. So, when dozens of Party writers vented real hatred toward capitalists, they must have had a strong motive independent of the theory. In chapter four, we explored that motive, and later in this chapter we shall discuss how it influenced Party writers' image of the System's rulers and supporters. To lay the basis for that discussion, we must first examine the source of all evil: the System.

JIMMY HIGGINS, whether Type I or Type II, wanted other people to resent the System as fiercely as he did. He wanted them to feel the alien control over every aspect of their lives. The theory helped him to see beneath the surface multifariousness and spurious freedoms that his non-Communist acquaintances thought were real. Everywhere he looked he found the malign influence of the Enemy. He may have heard contrary arguments: that capitalists had conflicting interests and beliefs; that the constitutional checks and balances limited the power of government over the people as well as the people's power over government; that concerted action by noncapitalists often harmed the employers' interests and thus showed that capitalists' power was limited; and that many other facts showed that all aspects of American reality were not coordinated systematically under the rule of the top echelons of a single class.[3] If anyone resorted to these arguments in conversation with him, Comrade Jimmy patiently explained that one must distinguish "form" from "substance." Those facts—or rather, those he accepted as facts—merely showed the surface complexity of the System or the cleverness of its rulers. The reason counterevidence did not impress him is that "form" stood in the same relation to the underlying "substance" as facts stood in his mind to his ideology. His System-perception preceded the proofs he adduced for it. "In the clash between system and reality," writes Eric Voegelin, "reality must give way."[4]

The Party's theory appealed to Comrade Jimmy for another reason: an intellectual system as all-encompassing as its imaginary adversary, it gave him a talisman to ward off the System's power over him. When he marched in a May Day parade singing *The Internationale*, one line held a special meaning in the present context: "We have been naught—we shall be all!"[5] In other words, the rulers have been all, but they shall be nothing, even as we are now. The System, the Enemy, did more than rule external reality; Comrade Jimmy feared it had invaded his own soul and constantly threatened to reduce him to naught. For "we" read "I"—an "I" projected onto the Party, the proletariat, and the Soviet Union and thus rendered "objective."

Since Jimmy Higgins has such strong reasons for thinking in System terms, he overlooked the many logical difficulties and counterfactual assumptions in the Party's writings on the subject. There is room here to notice just a few. For example, it never occurred to him that the capitalist System was Marx's invention rather than a real thing. He had plenty of company, of course. Millions of people who do not consider themselves Marx's disciples use the concept unthinkingly, unaware that they are using a counterfactual reification that distorts their thinking on all the subjects subsumed under the System rubric. The arguments that seem so conclusive are actually tautological, for the "conclusions" lurk within the concept itself. Take the proposition that "capitalism contains the seeds of its own destruction." Since "capitalism" is a concept, not a thing, of course it does; the Marxist put the seeds there himself, as integral parts of the reified notion of the capitalist System. The "contradictions" of the capitalist System amount to the vulnerability of the concept to other concepts and facts (if the System does not exist, "it" can have no contradictions). Or, consider the Party's axiom that "bourgeois science defends the bourgeois system,"[6] which looks like an empirical observation but is really a logically entailed deduction from the prior definitions of "bourgeois," "science," "defense," and "system." The Party's definition of "science" included class partisanship; its definition of "bourgeois" included the notion of "defending bourgeois class interests"; its notion of "defense" included the bourgeois-versus-proletarian struggle in all areas including science; and all those concepts got their meanings from the System concept. When a college-student comrade found empirical correlates of that dictum, he though he had verified it empirically. In fact, he had interpreted the data in terms of the proposition itself. He could not have found disconfirming evidence even if he had looked for it, so long as he kept his definitions. Or, consider the Party's formula that, since no mode of production lasts forever, capitalism will die. That apparently sensible assertion rests on the tacit assumption that capitalism is a stage in the evolution of society. If, however, it denotes the free exchange of private property by millions of people in the marketplace and the freedom to invest the surplus, it is not a stage in social evolution but an accompaniment of freedom.

But the comrades carried the System concept even further. Everything not "I" belonged to the System. Typical assertions were: "this country is virtually the property of a small minority of big capitalists and it is being run primarily for their benefit." And:

The prevailing systems of education, morality, ethics, science, art, patriotism, religion, etc., are as definitely parts of capitalist exploitation as the stock exchange. The schools, churches, newspapers, motion pictures, radio, theatres and various other avenues of publicity and mass instruction are the organized propaganda machinery of the ruling class.

One writer used an organic metaphor:

whatever matter we are considering, in science, economics, culture, or philosophy, we cannot achieve a clear picture of it unless we discern its basic impetus, its class-structure heart which has brought it up to the moment and pumps into it the blood of its future development. . . . There are two conflicting purposes at work which are so all-embracing and utterly urgent that no person, whether poet or publisher, scientist or shop-worker, can avoid, in any action he performs, supporting either one or the other of them.[7]

Every state served the interests of the one class that owned the means of production, and therefore bourgeois democracy did not give political power to the workers. "America's limited democracy has only concealed the open dictatorship of the bourgeoisie." Since no intermediate form could exist between capitalism and socialism, the so-called welfare state was simply "an illusion and a deception." The Democratic and Republican parties were both instruments of bourgeois rule; "the so-called two-party system" did not present the people with real choices. The same was true of doctrines, individuals, and groups supposedly opposed to both the CP and reaction: "The 'third force,' " intoned Foster, "is part and parcel of the world camp of reaction and war."[8] The temporary alliances that the Party entered from time to time should be interpreted in this context. The allies were either progressives with a partial understanding of the truth and good intentions, or members of the enemy camp whom the Party could use.

The same was true the world over. Capitalism in the United States was essentially the same System as that in other countries, including fascism (which according to the Party included National Socialism). The kinship between bourgeois-democratic and fascist forms of capitalist rule produced highly significant metaphors: "Fascism, born in the womb of bourgeois democracy, is in the eyes of the capitalists a means of saving capitalism from destruction." According to Browder, "capitalist democracy is therefore the mother of fascism." Alternatively, "fascist dictatorship and bourgeois democracy are blood brothers," explained Carl Ross, a youth leader.[9]

As these metaphors suggest, reification of the System led easily to personification of the ruling class and the use of singular pronouns and verbs. For example: Fascism "is the desperate means by which capitalism in its extremity tries to save itself." "The American ruling class falsifies the past in order to help corrupt the present and betray the future." "[Alger] Hiss was framed by the ruling class of the United States." "Monopoly capital has deliberately prevented" an increase in consumers' purchasing power. "Capitalism has thoroughly understood how to exploit" ethnic divisions among the workers. "American finance capital" has "designs" against democracy and wants to "carry out its plans to smash labor and the democratic movement." In four consecutive paragraphs of one article we find that "the bourgeoisie has" done something, "it uses" ideas, "it thinks" in a certain way, "it pretends," "it wishes," and a few other personifications.[10]

The world thus consisted of forces, classes, and philosophies struggling against each other, and of individuals as their humble gun-carriers and mouthpieces. The we-versus-them mind-set reduced all the forces, classes, and philosophies to two in every historical epoch, that which was rising and that which was doomed to pass away. Lenin provided the most scientific text for either-or-ism:

Since there can be no talk of an independent ideology being developed by the masses of the workers in the process of their movement then *the only choice is*: Either bourgeois, or Socialist ideology. There is no middle course (for humanity has not created a "third" ideology, and, moreover, in a society torn by class antagonisms there can never be a non-class or above-class ideology). Hence, to belittle Socialist ideology *in any way*, to *deviate from it in the slightest degree* means strengthening bourgeois ideology.

Another text was Engels's: at critical moments in history "a people has only the choice between the two horns of a dilemma: 'either-or!' " Stalin's 1924 announcement that the world was "divided into two camps"[11] appears many times in Party writings, without attribution; most comrades did not know its source and would not have cared, for it was simple common sense. Said another writer, "All the eddies and cross currents in the contemporary river of events may be resolved into two fundamental ones flowing in opposite directions. Moving in one direction are the vast majority of people who, working for others, produce all the wealth. . . . They are progress." Moving in the other direction are the capitalists. "All other eddies and cross currents are born, receive their inspiration, from their underlying clash of opposing streams." Later, switching from a watery to a military metaphor, he said, "we must see every fact of history and political economy, every concept of philosophy, art, and science which lays bare the true character of reality, as added ammunition to the arsenal which we will bring to the side of the workers."[12]

All distinctions that depicted a spectrum instead of an explosive dualism went against the We-Them, either-or grain.[13] Consider Herbert Aptheker's criticism of a liberal who found "diversity of interests synonymous with democracy . . . , never considering for a moment that the forces producing such diversity are the forces necessitating struggle. . . . For if there were no lack [of freedom], the struggle would be unnecessary." The diversity that liberals celebrate "demonstrates the incompleteness of bourgeois democracy; it is not synonymous with democracy."[14] Since there was plenty of evidence of nonhostile disagreement, Aptheker's denial that it was possible obviously meant that it *should* not exist. In other words, people who disagreed with each other without rancor were actually carrying on the class struggle without realizing it. If they had known the true import of their differences, they would have felt a hostility corresponding to the war between the forces of good and the forces of evil. They would have felt as hostile toward their adversaries as Aptheker felt toward his, *his* animosity proved his higher awareness. In short, lack of freedom produced diversity of interests; diversity of interests was the sole cause of diversity of opinion (on important matters). If freedom existed, diversity would not. Socialism would end diversity and, therefore, struggle between both interests and opinions.

Because there were only two Systems, in thought as well as in social structure, anyone who combined elements from opposite "camps" erred. Such "eclecticism" was immoral as well as erroneous, for ethics and morality were as System-bound as economics and politics. "Eclecticism," according to a teaching aid in *The Communist*, "is the trend in philosophy that endeavors to reconcile diverse philosophic systems. The eclectic selects from various systems without scruples that which seems to him to be acceptable practically, unsuccessfully attempting to combine different elements that are directly contrary to one another." "The eclectic, being a person without principles, . . . takes a bit from one of the contending parties, and a bit from the other, mechanically sticks these bits together, and attempts to pass them off as something 'new.' " "The deception" pretended to be a "third force," but the history of philosophy showed that eclecticism had "always only served to cover up and mask reaction and counter-revolution." Another writer warned that an "apparently innocuous philosophic doctrine or scientific hypothesis or esthetic principle, . . . image or symbol or theme or mood invariably reveals on closer scrutiny a class content. The conflict of class attitudes does not always occur on the plane of consciousness."[15] It is not hard to imagine how useful "apparently innocuous" errors and unconscious deviations could be in intra-Party witchhunts, in the absence of more tangible offenses. The fear of being called an eclectic helped to keep Jimmy Higgins from examining outsiders' claims on their merits.

Actually, such claims had no merits of their own. "As between boss and worker, landlord and tenant, imperialist and fighter for national liberation, war-monger and peace-partisan, justice and truth are always on the side of the latter," wrote Herbert Aptheker. Two details of this remarkable statement are pertinent here. First, the "always" implies status ascription: Comrade Jimmy must choose his side on the basis of the contenders' places in the System, regardless of the facts. This duty discouraged inadvertent heresy, for if he allowed himself to examine opposing claims, there was no telling where he might wander. (For example, the mention of landlord and tenant recalls Bella Dodd's experience when she was expelled from the Party, less than two years before Aptheker published this article. As a lawyer, she had recently defended a poor, elderly neighbor who could "only technically . . . have been called a landlord," against suits by tenants. Dodd had become capable of seeing her client as an individual in a predicament rather than as a member of the oppressor class.) The second interesting implication in Aptheker's list of contraries is the oneness of the boss, landlord, imperialist, and war-monger, on the one hand, and of the worker, tenant, fighter for national liberation, and peace-partisan, on the other. A landlord who was a peace-partisan, or a boss who was a tenant, did not fit into the System-theory dualism.[16]

THE MOST GLARING FLAW in the Party's System-theory pertained to the System's "anarchy." The very linking of those two words—System and anarchy—ought to have struck Comrade Jimmy as problematic, but the thought never occurred to him.

The writers discoursed at length on the capitalists' foresight and planning, on their power to institute a certain type of pedagogy throughout the thousands of local school systems, on their cleverly staging mock fights between Democratic Tweedledums and Republican Tweedledees, on their coordinated action justifying the use of singular verbs and pronouns. Yet the same writers repeatedly denounced the System for its anarchy, wastefulness, and planlessness, all of which set it in sharp contrast to socialism. Mike Gold taught this lesson in an allegory, "Hell in a Drugstore." At midnight, he began, all the "60,000 items" in a drugstore went to war with each other, even though they differed in nothing but color and scent. They fought and fought till morning. Why? Because the System made them fight; it creates many kinds of mouthwash, for instance, where only one is needed. Wouldn't it be better to determine which mouthwash is best, manufacture large amounts of it, and sell it cheap? Just as the sun came up, ending the war in the drugstore, so "the Sun of Communism will soon shine on us all and bring us peace." The *Young Worker*'s version of this theme was:

The bosses . . . do not plan their production—they do not put out a given number of coats, for example, because that number of coats is needed. They produce as much as they think that they can sell, and make profits on. This character of capitalist production which is not planned is called anarchy of production.

It resulted in the production of more coats than workers could buy; and so the capitalists tried to sell them overseas. Other countries' capitalists did the same thing. The result was war. The article ended by calling for the abolition of the System that caused war.[17] Foster, among others, spelled out the alternative. In Soviet America, he explained, the whole economy would be "a great industrial machine, each cog of which fits into and works harmoniously with the rest." This would solve the problems caused by "the present maze of 206,556 separate American manufacturing concerns" plus the hundreds of thousands in retailing, wholesaling, and banking, with their "dog-eat-dog competition . . . , blindly producing and throwing their products aimlessly into the markets. Socialist industry means system, cooperation, efficiency; capitalist industry means chaos, conflict, waste."[18]

If capitalist industry meant anarchy, how could the capitalist System function as singlemindedly as the earlier-quoted documents said it did? Among all the writers only Foster, so far as I have discovered, even noticed the problem. The way he mentioned it is highly suggestive:

By its nature as a privately-owned economy, production under capitalism is carried on essentially upon a planless basis, under the slogans of free competition and free enterprise. . . . This is no contradiction of the fact that capitalist production is dominated by monopoly and is essentially monopoly state capitalism. The planfullness [*sic*] of Socialism is one of the most vital points of superiority of Socialism over capitalism.[19]

Although candidly admitting the apparent contradiction, Foster merely denied it was real, and proceeded to his next point. If he had thought it undermined his System-theory he would not have mentioned it; but he certainly would have explained why the contradiction was only apparent, if he had known how. No Party writer explained how "monopoly" could characterize a System that contained those 206,556 competing manufacturing concerns, or how a System ruled so singlemindedly would put up with so much duplication and waste. Jimmy Higgins did not notice this problem. Although in the real world the two types of assertions contradicted each other, in his world they did not. To him, practically any assertion that discredited American reality rang true, and he never subjected his own set of beliefs to skeptical scrutiny.

ONE WAY to evade the problem was to ignore the consumer. In the Party's image of the System, he hardly ever appears. The few writings that mention him—such as Mike Gold's essay on the competition among brands of mouthwash—merely chide him for distinguishing among identical products. Far from being an oversight, the omission of the consumer followed necessarily from the four chief ingredients of the System concept: power, coordination, exploitation, and either-or-ness. The capitalists' almost total *power* in the marketplace left no room for the consumer's power to determine the quantity, quality, nature, and design of a product. The bourgeoisie's *coordination*, justifying personification, precluded competition to please the consumers; indeed, Party writers often used the term "monopoly" as synonym for Big Business. The *exploitative* essence of the System fostered the belief that the capitalists deliberately lowered the workers' standard of living, to increase their own profits—even though they were thereby also reducing the consumers' purchasing power. And the *either-or* concept focused attention on the workplace and its two classes (capitalists and workers) and away from the marketplace with its competing buyers and sellers and its signals to manufacturers. According to Marxist theory, the exchange value of commodities reflects the amount of "socially necessary labor" embodied in them. The relationship of supply to demand did not determine prices but only caused them to fluctuate around that essential value.[20] If supply and demand had determined prices, the consumer's power would have undermined those four components of the System theory. The working majority of the population *in their role of consumers* would have wielded more power over the capitalist minority than the Party would concede.

When the consumer did appear in Party propaganda, the context was one more grievance against the System: its advertising of useless products and encouragement of installment buying. Yet, contradictorily, Party theoreti-cians complained that the capitalists wanted to keep the workers' purchasing power as low as possible. When the people's share of the wealth declined in the 1920s, wrote Browder, "that was the way *the capitalists had planned it*," and two pages later, "*they planned it that way*." The repetition and italics insured that Comrade Jimmy would know how important this truth was. Bruce Minton and John Stuart, in an economic history published in 1940, said, "Monopoly's resolve to keep living standards debased at all costs was as always its undoing. The buying power of the American public proved insufficient to consume the swelling flood of goods from the great factories." The contradiction thus lay not in the Party's theory but in the System. The capitalists' power was, then, limited by their need to sell their products, but Browder's statement alleged that they both wanted and had the power to keep mass purchasing power to the minimum necessary for physical survival. According to Joseph Freeman in 1936,

when big business attacks the living standard of the workers it does so not only by attacking wages but also by assaulting culture. The reason for this is obvious enough. The capitalists want the new generation of workers, who, as a result of the crisis, come into straitened circumstances as their ordinary mode of life, to regard these circumstances not as a temporary emergency but as something "normal."[21]

How the capitalists could thereby make their big profits, Freeman did not say. Theoretically, the explanation lay in the Party's zero-sum economic model: when wages went up, profits went down, and vice versa. But in practice, one might have expected the clever, far-sighted capitalists to forgo their immediate interest in lowering the workers' income for the sake of higher sales. This simple solution does not, however, appear in Party writings.

One Party author praised C. Wright Mills's *The Power Elite* for its scientific approach, for recognizing that "the rich are . . . parts of a system," and for showing "that they deserve only the hate and contempt of the masses." He lauded Mills for proving that big businessmen "do govern at many of the vital points of everyday life in America, and no powers effectively and con-sistently countervail against them." But, wanting to have it both ways, he then criticized Mills for underestimating the power of "the broad resistance" that set back McCarthyism.[22] In short, the people did have power, as workers via their unions, and as political protesters, but not as consumers.

We find the same logic in an essay by Foster: The "partial improvements in working class conditions, such as they are, . . . have been brought about primarily by the increased struggle of the workers" against the capitalists, although sometimes the latter made "concessions to the skilled workers in order to use them as a brake upon the militancy of the working class as a whole"—not, it will be noticed, in order to sell more of their products. The workers must struggle incessantly "to protect their living standards against every attack that the employers may deliver against them" (this concept of "attack" appears three more times in the article), suggesting that the capitalists were attacking their own market and the workers were struggling to enable the capitalists to make profits by selling their products.[23]

The capitalists could have their own way—within limits set by the people's struggles—because of the second component of the System concept: coordination, often expressed by the use of the synecdoche "monopoly" or "the monopolists" as synonym for big business.[24] Howard Selsam explained that a few stockholders owned the bulk of all corporate stocks and were therefore the real owners of American industry. "They control what shall be produced, what wages shall be paid, what working conditions shall exist, and even what governmental policies respecting big business shall be followed." The consumer is conspicuously absent, along with small business. "A factory," he went on, "is not built to make shoes because people want and need shoes. It is built because, people needing shoes, a profit can be made by producing them." And since more profit could be made producing luxury goods that only a few could buy, these were produced in large quantity. The crucial message here was Selsam's equation of motive with result.[25] It went without saying that the profit motive was incompatible with the mass production of reasonably priced, high-quality goods that the people needed and wanted, regardless of the capitalists' intentions. To concede this would have been to concede more power to the consumer—including the worker—than the image of the System could tolerate. The consumer, then, was the economic counterpart of the voter, who, as we saw earlier, also had no real power.

Clearly, these writers (and Jimmy Higgins) found it difficult to think of the worker in his role as consumer; the "relation to the means of production" defined the person. One reason for the rise of Marcuseism and Gramscian Marxism in the 1960s is that the postwar increase in general affluence made even some Marxists realize that consumers had enough money to enable them to choose among commodities and brands. Unwilling to conclude that buyers thereby wielded real power over capitalists, the new-model radicals switched the emphasis from economic to ideological oppression. Now the very abundance of commodities and the workers' purchasing power, which old-model radicals had assumed impossible, became means of oppression. The growing popularity of this type of radicalism was accompanied by the flourishing of "consumers' " movements, which agreed that the untrammeled free market could not operate in the interest of consumers. The consumerists' solutions were similar to the Party's in their denigration of the marketplace and their intention to overrule or bypass consumers' individual decisions. All these movements agreed with the Party that "the free market" was a misnomer.

The Party's equation of intention with result meant that only a System ruled by people who intended mass welfare, with no recompense except the people's gratitude manifested in prestige, could create the good society. That is why Foster could say, in 1958, that the capitalist countries could never " 'catch up' to the Socialist world in the fields of science, education, technology and others, where Socialism is now in the lead."[26] The consumer would find his needs satisfied only after the abolition of the unregulated marketplace in which each buyer made his own decisions—when, as Mike Gold prophesied, someone else would decide which mouthwash was best.

Several of the writers quoted above obliquely admitted, even as they denied, the lack of obvious fit between the unitary reality as they experienced it and the seemingly multifarious reality. Foster explained how the Party's theory would reconcile the two realities. "Only a Party thoroughly grounded in Marxism-Leninism-Stalinism can possibly understand this whole complicated and swiftly changing world social process and show the way to victory for the workers through its veritable jungle of crucial problems."[27] "Jungle" calls to mind both diversity and struggle. Without that guidance, outsiders assumed that diversity of opinion showed freedom rather than its incompleteness, and that the capitalist marketplace could produce its own spontaneous "order," bankrupting the maker of the worst mouthwash while allowing people to buy whichever brands they liked. Jimmy Higgins believed in the Party's System-theory because he was predisposed to perceive a sinister coherence underlying the surface multifariousness. The chief characteristic of that predisposition was totalism: total rejection of the society, a vision of a totally planned socialism in its stead, a totalistic theory to simplify complicated reality, and a Party demanding total authority over its members' lives. Perhaps the most significant implication of this mode of experiencing reality is its negative aspects: its denial that any thought, act, science, art work, social formation, or personal experience could have meaning except in relation to the total theory of which the Party was sole custodian. When Jimmy Higgins became a Party true believer, he was fleeing *from* complexity and randomness, before he fully grasped what he was fleeing *to*. Or, to put the point another way, he saw the complexity and unsystematic nature of his society, but, unlike other people, he found them intolerable and overlaid his perception of them with a theory that denied their existence. The theory projected his feeling onto objective reality; it said that complexity and randomness were surface phenomena overlying an essential System.

One who determined his choice of friends, his taste in art, and his hopes, fears, loves, and hates in terms of the struggle to overthrow a ruling power and ideology, was consumed not merely by the struggle but, far more urgently, by that power and ideology. For such a person the Enemy had invaded the mind as well as the home, school, workplace, and marketplace. It had left no hiding place where he might feel free of it. His very joy in his family, work, and recreation was defined in terms of It and Its destruction. He was quiter logical, then, to express his emancipatory hope in equally totalistic terms, for wherever the Enemy was, there must the struggle against It be waged; he must not only fight It in Its home base but also replace It with an equally ubiquitous power. That is why he could sincerely call the latter freedom: in a personal sense it did mean liberation. As to the people who thought that institutions, private life, and culture in capitalist society had a degree of autonomy, that the economic power of the capitalists, though influential and pervasive, yet left social space for autonomous behavior and personality development—they were unconscious of the chains that bound them. Comrade Jimmy thus projected his own total captivity onto all mankind and believed that his obsession was their enslavement. All the facts offered in support of the totalist theory were links in a chain of circular reasoning. A seemingly autonomous phenomenon was "really" a means of fooling people into thinking they were free. One who offered evidence against the totalist theory was proving he had been fooled by it. Thus, evidence against the theory was really evidence for it (evidence for it was, of course, also evidence for it).[28]

HATRED OF THE SYSTEM did not require hatred of its rulers, nor did hatred of the capitalist class entail System-thinking. In fact, Jimmy Higgins's discovery that some capitalists had good intentions confirmed his belief in the System's iniquity. He was happy to learn that a boss who wanted to raise his employees' wages or to spend money to make the workplace safe and comfortable would soon find himself out of business, while his heartless competitors prospered. The Party also ridiculed people who thought that the cure for the workers' problems lay in an appeal to employers' consciences; if it had, the System would have shattered into discrete parts shaped by the bosses' personalities. Furthermore, historical-materialist doctrine taught that, inasmuch as "being determines consciousness," most capitalists really did not see that their social order was exploitative and unjust. Since the theory gave Party writers a number of strong reasons not to preach hatred of individual capitalists and their supporters, the fact that they did preach hatred is all the more significant. They were, in short, expressing their feelings, not their theory. That is the only explanation that makes sense of a peculiarity in Party literature: the depiction of capitalists and their supporters as fully aware that their System was oppressive, their ideology false, their values hypocritical.[29]

A double perception of the Enemy runs like a red thread throughout Party writings. On the one hand, since only Marxism enabled a person to see reality accurately, the non-Marxist enemies must sincerely believe in their own erroneous theories and values. On the other hand, capitalists and their allies knew they were justifying oppression; this implied that they agreed with the Party on what constituted oppression and shared the insights that only Marxism made possible. On the one hand, no one could analyze events correctly unless he loved the victims of the System and had mastered Marxism-Leninism; "deviation" was easy even for devoted Communists. On the other hand, the truth was so obvious that disagreement must be hypocritical.

Perhaps it would be unfair to say that the writers wanted to have it both ways; let us say that they had to have it both ways: to condemn both the theories and the morals of the Enemy. Logically, they had the choice of condemning an enemy's theories and conceding his sincerity, or of calling him a hypocrite and saying that his understanding of reality was as Marxist as the Party's. But the Party claimed a monopoly on both truth and morality. If it depicted a sincere enemy with wrong beliefs it would not instigate the energizing emotion that it needed in its ranks. If it depicted a hypocritical enemy who knew the truth, it might undermine the claim that Marxism-Leninism provided the sole access to truth. But the second alternative, though risking the Party's monopoly on truth, brought compensating benefits. It ratified a temperamental tendency to see conspiracies everywhere. It justified a visceral hatred of an enemy who was far more hateful if he knew the truth than if he were sincerely misguided by his class interests. Lastly, it satisfied the need to believe that Party theory was so obviously true and common-sensical that the workers would quickly convert after the Party had explained it to them. Given such emotional needs, the writers probably did not consciously choose among these alternatives or even recognize them. Hints of a glimmering recognition of the difficulties appeared in only a few documents; they were rare even in the brief thaw following the Twentieth Congress. Because the need to express hatred of a hypocritical enemy lay deeper than the conscious doctrine, the writers and certainly Jimmy Higgins overlooked contradictions that might shatter their mental universe.

According to a leading theoretician, "the bourgeoisie seeks to establish . . . that the interests of the bourgeoisie and of the nation are identical. It hopes thereby to deceive the mass of the people into identifying themselves with the interests of the monopolists and to accept them as the leaders of the nation." The capitalists, then, knew that their interests were opposed to the people's. "The bosses," said another writer, "cleverly try to mislead the workers. They do not desire the workers to know the truth—that imperialist wars are caused by the present system of society—*capitalism*." [30] The bosses thus knew that imperialist wars were caused by capitalism in its last stage, imperialism—evidently having mastered Lenin's *Imperialism: The Highest Stage of Capitalism* without ever attending a Party school.

These big deceptions required several smaller ones. The most important was racism. The more conspiratorial the ruling class was, however, the more dubious was the Party's accusation of racism. True, people who would plot genocide against blacks, as the Party accused the bourgeoisie of doing, were racists in the sense that they treated blacks even more inhumanely than they treated whites. But since the purpose behind the plot had nothing to do with race, Party writers inadvertently depicted the plotters as disbelieving their own racist doctrines. That these were merely a cover for objectives irrelevant to race was explained by William Patterson, the Party's leading lawyer:

the object of this genocide, as of all genocide, is the perpetuation of economic and political power by the few through the destruction of political protest by the many. Its method is to demoralize and divide an entire nation; its end is to increase the profits and unchallenged control by a reactionary clique.... This crime of genocide is the result of a massive conspiracy, more deadly in that it is sometimes "understood" rather than expressed, a part of the mores of the ruling class often concealed by euphemism, but always directed to oppressing the Negro people. Its members are so well-drilled, so rehearsed over the generations, that they can carry out their parts automatically and with a minimum of spoken direction. They have inherited their plot and their business is but to implement it daily so that it works daily.... [A] conspiracy exists in which the Government of the United States, its Supreme Court, its Congress, its Executive branch, as well as the various state, county and municipal governments, consciously effectuate policies which result in the crime of genocide being consistently and constantly practiced against the Negro people of the United States.[31]

Liberals had their assignments, too. The "ultimate purpose" of the Americans for Democratic Action (ADA), founded in 1947, was "to prolong the life of an obsolete social order" and "to hide the decay with euphonious lies."[32] If those liberals did not believe the social order was obsolete, their statements were not lies; the ADA therefore agreed with the Party on that basic tenet.

Another category of plotters were intellectuals and artists. For example, "large segments of the working class are being duped by the bourgeoisie into the decadence and violence of beebop. For beebop is a reflection of the use of music in a class society as part of the effort of a ruling class to enforce its attitudes and mores upon society as a whole." All bourgeois "culture," in fact, was designed by the general staff for that purpose. It is "always the aim of the capitalist 'culture,' " wrote Foster, "to make intellectual slaves of the toilers." According to the Party's expert on movies, "Hollywood" deliberately falsified Mexican history in its film *Viva Zapata!* It "selects a moment of Mexican history for its lesson in the 'futility' of people's movements. The choice is not accidental. Careful, and conscious, political analysis determined the selection of the time and the place." The director "ignored the facts because his employers and the Un-American Committee had ordered him to make an anti-democratic picture." Art critics were equally hypocritical. Lionel Trilling, for one, "pretends to admire Mark Twain by turning him into a Jungian superstition monger"—which meant, of course, that he did not really admire Mark Twain.[33]

The real motives of bourgeois psychologists showed the same hypocrisy. Recent developments in psychology were "part of the trend which seeks to distract attention from the socioeconomic basis of human unhappiness and place emphasis instead on the alleged irrational or unconscious reactions of individuals." This meant that the perpetrators of that distraction agreed with the Party on the socioeconomic basis of unhappiness. As to bourgeois educators, "their aim is to befuddle the minds of the youth, to separate them from reality, from the problems of daily life—from the class struggle." The capitalists and their supporters knew their interests conflicted with "reason itself." They sought "to so corrupt taste and morality, to so obscure reason and eclipse science, as to kill the appreciation of and desire for either the preservation or the extension of that heritage."[34] Such reasoning in behalf of unreason must, of course, have been rational. Its perpetrators could not, logically, believe in their own propaganda and the rightness of their own acts.

WITH NO SENSE OF INCOHERENCE, Party writers occasionally stated just the opposite: the bourgeoisie did not, could not, know the truth. Sometimes they explained that the capitalists were cut off from the social practice that yielded truth; this meant that the ignorance was genuine. Most often, however, the writers said that the capitalists willed their own ignorance. But self-deception implies a subconscious, and the Party rejected the notion of a subconscious on "scientific" grounds. The result of the desire to have it both ways was self-contradiction.

For example, an article by the Party's two chief philosophers proclaimed that "only the Marxist dialectical materialist world outlook permits the scientific analysis of the 'laws of motion' of capitalism." This statement was orthodox Marxism. But two sentences further on, the authors began to backtrack: "Bourgeois economics, faced with a rising working class, cannot cope with the social relations of capitalism because the bourgeoisie is interested solely in cloaking its own class domination." And a bit later they took it all back: "Keynes sought to develop a theory which, while necessarily unscientific, yet has the appearance of being scientific."[35] The first sentence claimed the dialectical materialist's monopoly on understanding of capitalism; the second said that the bourgeoisie's ignorance was self-imposed, implying that it knew but decided not to know; and the third said Keynes knew he was writing lies.

Sometimes the mutually exclusive propositions appeared within the same passages. Herbert Aptheker accused certain liberal intellectuals of "*deliberate* blindness to the source of the present assault upon civil liberties" because they had "fallen *victim* to the key weapon of the assaulters," namely, anticommunism. (Emphases added.) Howard Selsam wrote that professors could hardly say "I am speaking not for the truth, objectively, but for Standard Oil, General Motors, U. S. Steel, the Chase Manhattan Bank. . . . No! . . . They dare not tell the truth. Their partisanship prevents scientific objectivity. Too often they are only the 'hired prizefighters' Marx spoke of, their incapability of following ideas wherever they lead is concealed by this pretense of the open mind."[36] If they dared not tell the truth, however, they must have known the truth. If these people were victims of the blinding weapon of anticommunism, how could their blindness have been deliberate?

"It is clear," wrote Harry K. Wells, "that the bourgeoisie cannot afford to have a science of history, for history is not on its side today. Thus the class objective of perpetual rule is founded exclusively on its own desire and will. The latter are determined by the position and character of the class." The "for" in the first sentence was, obviously, a non sequitur. Only a science of history, according to Party doctrine, could reveal that history was not on the side of the bourgeoisie. If the bourgeoisie knew this, it must already have had a science of history, and the only such science was Marxism-Leninism. The same self-contradiction appears in a Party economic history; the authors wrote that "to have diagnosed what ailed the system would have led the ruling class to conclusions that no capitalist could embrace without at the same time acknowledging the fact that capitalism was eventually doomed and that any effort to save it was of necessity a stop-gap."[37] None of these writers explained how the ignorance resulting from the bourgeoisie's class position—cut off as it was from the social practice that yielded under-standing—could coexist with the prescience here attributed to the capitalists who knew their class had no future.

THE QUOTATIONS given above could be multiplied tenfold, but they are suf-ficient to illustrate the Party writers' dilemma. On the one hand the bourgeoi-sie irrationally presided over a rational System; on the other hand it rationally presided over an irrational System. The capitalists could not afford to see reality plain, because to do so would have meant predicting their own demise as a class; yet they knew that the Party was right and saw as clearly as the Party did that the future belonged to the workers. The most important fact to be grasped as we read these documents, however, is that Jimmy Higgins never saw a contradiction in them. He lived in a mental universe in which all these statements were consistent with one another.

Starting with a rejection of reality, he gathered up all the bad things he could find to construct a complete picture. His selection produced a tightly patterned System. Data that would have revealed accident, randomness, individuality, and inconsistency he either excluded or interpreted to confirm the pattern. So highly coordinated a System could not have just happened; there must have been conscious, deliberate foresight and planning by a un-itary and incredibly intelligent directorate. Yet because he knew that the System was doomed and the Party alone possessed the science of history, the System must be irrational and its rulers blind.

In all the books and articles describing the nefarious deeds of socialists, labor leaders, reformers, conservatives, and other non- and anti-Communists (other than proletarians), the reader rarely encounters the notion that a par-ticular target might really have believed that the American social order was better than the Soviet Union's, or that the CP was not the best defender of the masses' interests, or that certain beliefs and values should be taught to schoolchildren because they were good and true rather than because they served a class's interest. The writers apparently did not know that their tight syllogisms were really enthymemes. Self-evident parts of the pattern composed from the selective perception of American reality did not need to be stated. The "conclusions" followed equally self-evidently because the reasoning was not only enthymematic but also circular. It was also, consequently, very impressive to Jimmy Higgins. How insightful his leaders were, how obvious their analyses, once put into words! And how privileged he was to have a Party and a Theory that could penetrate into the heart of reality! Both Jimmy Higgins and his enemies knew the truth, but only the Party stated it openly. His task was to teach the people the truth that they alone did not know.

NOTES

1. Joshua Kunitz, "Literary Wars in the U.S.S.R.," *NM*, June 26, 1934, p. 18.
2. Karl Marx and Frederick Engels, *The German Ideology* (New York: IP, 1939), p. 40.
3. Louis Fleischer, "Who Rules America?" *PA* 35 (July, 1956): 706–7 (among other documents), makes clear that just the richest, not the whole class, comprised the ruling directorate.
4. Eric Voegelin, *Science, Politics and Gnosticism* (Chicago: Gateway Editions, 1968), p. 45; see also entire passage on pp. 42–45.
5. How odd it is that those who identify this verse with Luke 1:52—"He hath put down the mighty from their seats, and exalted them of low degree"—assume that the "He" is an irrelevant detail!
6. M. Kammari and F. Konstantinoff, "Science and Superstrucutre," *PA* 32 (February, 1953): 62. Many other documents say the same thing, in more or less the same words.
7. William Z. Foster, *The Twilight of World Capitalism* (New York: IP, 1949), p. 48; Foster, *Toward Soviet America* (New York: Coward-McCann, 1932), pp. 313–14; Jesse Ehrlich, "Marxism, Spain, and Art," *NF* 1 (Summer, 1948): 241.
8. John Gates, "The Soviet Union in the World Today," *CL* 1 (Fall, 1940): 12; "Party Program Discussion," document "adopted by the Draft Program Committee," *PA* 37 (December, 1958): 61; William Z. Foster, *History of the Communist Party of the United States* (New York: IP, 1952), p. 211; Foster, *Outline Political History of the Americas* (New York: IP, 1951), p. 601. The last-cited item also said that the world was divided into two camps but did not credit Stalin with originating that formula; Foster's was one of innumerable documents that did this. On the general points in the text paragraph: these contentions are so numerous in Party literature that the reader can find more by random leafing.
9. "Militarization and Fascization of the Youth and Tasks of the Young Communist Leagues: Resolution of January Plenum of the Executive Committee of the Young Communist International," *YW*, March 27, 1934, p. 2A; Earl Browder, " 'Such

a War Will Surely End in the Birth of a Few More Soviet Republics,' " *YW*, April 24, 1934, p. 7; Carl Ross, "America's Youth in the Struggle against the Imperialist War," *CL* 1 (April-May, 1940): 12.

10. Foster, *Toward Soviet America*, p. 206; Herbert Aptheker, *History and Reality* (New York: Cameron Associates, 1955), pp. 200, 231; Earl Browder, *The Democratic Front* (New York: Workers Library, 1938), p. 25; Foster, *Toward Soviet America*, p. 260; Howard Johnson, *The Negro Veteran Fights for Freedom!* (New York: National Veterans Committee, Communist Party, 1947), p. 4; Charles Humboldt, "What Is Freedom?" *MM* 3 (May, 1950): 70–71 (see also p. 76). For other examples, see Henry Winston, "Negro and White Unity against War," *CL* 1 (April-May, 1940): 22, 30; Sidney Finkelstein, "Psychoanalysis and the Arts," *MM* 4 (August, 1951): 69 (opening sentence); Bruce Minton and John Stuart, *The Fat Years and the Lean* (New York: IP, 1940), p. 337 ("big business decided"), 397 ("Monopoly's resolve to keep living standards debased"), and passim; Joseph Freeman, "Issues True and False," *NM*, October 27, 1936, p. 3; William Z. Foster, "The Superiority of World Socialism over World Capitalism," *PA* 37 (May, 1958): 26 ("capitalism focuses its attention . . . on"). Anna Rochester, in *Rulers of America* (New York: IP, 1936), p. 136, acknowledges that "much of" the propaganda that divides the working class "is not personally guided by the finance capitalists themselves. But they have a strong indirect influence." Yet later (p. 150) she resorts to the conventional personification ("the capitalist class has used . . . ") that is hard to reconcile with her qualification.

One does not commit the fallacy of reification when one refers in singular terms to an organization that issues official statements or speaks with one unanimous voice (such as the CP). The CP's passion for unanimity within its own ranks and in the future Soviet America should be seen, on one level, as an expression of the same attitude toward reality as its assumption that all other groups were essentially as unitary as it was, beneath "formal" or surface variety.

11. V. I. Lenin, *What Is To Be Done?* (New York: IP, 1929), pp. 40–41; spacefiller in *PA* 27 (January, 1948): 13 (party writers most often quoted only the middle third of Lenin's text); Samuel Rosen, "Zionism and Bourgeois Nationalism," *PA* 32 (June, 1953): 43. Frederick Engels, *Dialectics of Nature* (New York: IP, 1940), p. 207; Howard Jennings, "Revisionism and American History," *PA* 25 (August, 1946): 750. Joseph Stalin, *Foundations of Leninism* (lectures delivered in April, 1924) (New York: IP, 1939), p. 82 (the nonexploitative camp includes the capitalist camp's colonies as well as the Soviet Union). Gerhart Niemeyer's term for the object of this perception is "A Polarized World." See his *Deceitful Peace* (New Rochelle, N.Y.: Arlington House, 1971), p. 50.

12. "Just to Learn Is Not Enough," *NF* 2 (Fall, 1948): 4, 6. For comments on either-or thinking, see Jules Monnerot, *Sociology and Psychology of Communism* (Boston: Beacon Press, 1953), pp. 15, 38; and Nathan Leites, *A Study of Bolshevism* (New York: Free Press, 1953), pp. 43, 384–87, 429–34.

13. Browder himself inadvertently proved this when, after the Yalta conference, he announced that the world was divided into two camps and everyone must choose between Roosevelt and Hitler; there was no third side! See Earl Browder, *America's Decisive Battle* (New York: New Century, 1945), pp. 3–5. The either-or perception, in short, shaped attitudes whatever the circumstances. Browder followed that passage with a list of those Americans who chose Hitler's side, and the list included people "who act in a way designed to achieve that same end." That is, the dichotomizing

mind first eliminates third, intermediate, or irrelevant positions a priori, and then "concludes" that of course those not on one's own side are on the other. Yet when Browder developed his theory of postwar progressive capitalism, he proved that the either-or approach to reality was not so deeply ingrained in his thinking as it was in his comrades'. The fury of the anti-Browder diatribes, after the Duclos letter arrived, can perhaps be explained in these terms. His comrades could not blame the Party's authority principle, which had induced them to suppress a basic element in their thinking and to mouth Browder's theory. They could therefore not blame themselves, either, for their loyalty. He had forced them to violate their natures.

14. Herbert Aptheker, "Task Force A.D.A.," *MM* 1 (June, 1948): 28–29.

15. "The Fundamental Distinction between Dialectics and Eclectics: Material for Study of the 'History of the Communist Party of the Soviet Union,'" *COM* 18 (November, 1939): 1080–83; Joshua Kunitz, "Divided Loyalties," *NM*, August 7, 1934, p. 20. "Eclectic" and "eclecticism" were commonplace epithets; typical uses are in Aptheker, "Task Force A.D.A.," p. 34; and Morris U. Schappes, "Myths about Anti-Semitism," *MM* 1 (October, 1948): 57.

16. Herbert Aptheker, "Epic History," *MM* 4 (March, 1951): 88 (the article includes a reference to "the weak-kneed eclecticism of a Schlesinger the Little"—i.e., Arthur M. Schlesinger, Jr.—whose denial of causation and scoffing at progress prepared the way for fascism); Bella V. Dodd, *School of Darkness* (New York: P. J. Kenedy & Sons, 1954), pp. 216–17. During World War II and even shortly after Browder's ouster, Party writers argued against either-or-ism on a few occasions, and in the mid–1950s a very few essays advocated making more complex analyses than either-or-ism allowed. From the earlier period, see, e.g., Earl Browder, *Teheran and America: Perspective and Tasks* (New York: Workers Liberary, 1944), pp. 24–28; Robert Minor, "Workers' Education and the War against Hitler," *COM* 20 (November, 1941): 975; Rob F. Hall, "Labor in the 1946 Primaries," *PA* 25 (August, 1946): 706–7. From the later period, see two criticisms of books by Harry K. Wells, who always pushed either-or-ism to an extreme: Arnold Berman, "Some Questions about *Pragmatism*," *MM* 7 (September, 1954): 61; Ralph Doyster, "The Conditioned Reflex" (review of Wells's *Ivan P. Pavlov*), *MM* 10 (March, 1957): 58.

17. Michael Gold, *Change the World!* (New York: IP, 1936), pp. 88–91; "Study Course," *YW*, July 27, 1931, p. 5. The authors did not explain who would decide which formula for mouthwash was best or how the planners would know how many coats would be needed.

18. Foster, *Toward Soviet America*, pp. 289–90.

19. Foster, "Superiority of World Socialism," p. 25.

20. Since our purpose here is not to expound the basic theory but to analyze Jimmy Higgins's mental universe, I shall merely refer the reader to the texts that members read for instruction on these matters. The principal texts were two pamphlets by Marx: *Wage-Labour and Capital* and *Value, Price and Profit* (New York: IP, 1933 and 1935 respectively).

21. Browder, *Democratic Front*, pp. 26, 28; Minton and Stuart, *The Fat Years and the Lean*, p. 397; Freeman, "Issues True and False," p. 3.

22. Fleischer, "Who Rules America?" pp. 13–15.

23. William Z. Foster, "Karl Marx and Mass Impoverishment," *PA* 35 (November, 1956): 36–39. The same contradiction is evident in Howard Selsam, *Socialism and Ethics* (New York: IP, 1943), pp. 117–19.

24. See, e.g., Albert J. Lima, "The California Primary Elections," *PA* 37 (May, 1958): 29; John Gates, "Time for a Change," *PA* 35 (November, 1956): 46–47. Gates's use of this synecdoche is especially significant because his article was a major cause of the split of the Party between the Fosterites and the more realistic Gatesites; here is one of many evidences, then, that the two factions remained in agreement on fundamentals.

25. Selsam, *Socialism and Ethics*, pp. 18–20. The same equation is found in Frank Brewster and Mark Logan, "Automation: Abundance for Whom?" *PA* 34 (November, 1955): 38.

26. Foster, "Superiority of World Socialism," p. 28.

27. William Z. Foster, "Party Education for Our Present Tasks," *PO* 11 (May, 1938): 1.

28. The New Left contained some people who seemed to feel just the opposite way. But there is an underlying kinship between Type I Party members and those New Left anarchists who embraced chaos. They too saw total power and total chaos as the only alternatives, but they rushed into the latter's arms and called it freedom. Significantly, most of them soon swung back to the order-and-power extreme.

29. In a book published after the period covered by the present work but expressing a belief prevalent in the Party throughout its lifetime, Herbert Aptheker wrote that "all exploitative ruling classes . . . are devoid of humanistic feelings; suffering means nothing to them, since their rule is posited on human travail and their wealth and power derive from its infliction." Aptheker, *The American Civil War* (New York: IP, 1961), p. 6.

30. Rosen, "Zionism and Bourgeois Nationalism," p. 43; Samuel Herman, "Religion—Weapon of Boss Class," *YW* 3 (March, 1930): 4.

31. William L. Patterson, ed., *We Charge Genocide: The Crime of Government against the Negro People, A Petition to the United Nations* (New York: Civil Rights Congress, 1951), pp. 5–7. It should be mentioned that Party writers often wrote that the "superexploitation" of Negro workers brought an extra $4 billion to the capitalists as well as the benefits of competition between black and white workers and consequent depression of whites' wages. No one explained how to reconcile this evidence of the value of keeping black workers alive with the policy of exterminating them.

32. Aptheker, "Task Force A.D.A.," p. 28.

33. James Elmer Hutchinson, "Beepop [*sic*]—A Narcotic," *NF* 3 (Fall, 1949): 37; Foster, *Toward Soviet America*, p. 109; John Howard Lawson, *Film in the Battle of Ideas* (New York: Masses & Mainstream, 1953), pp. 43, 46; Finkelstein, "Psychoanalysis and the Arts," p. 77. See also Harry Martel and Marvin Reiss, "Art and Class," *PA* 29 (September, 1950): 79, on art critics. Incidentally, much of the latter article was devoted to a criticism of Finkelstein's book *Art and Society* for being too generous toward bourgeois art. From the Party's standpoint the critics were right; having attended some lectures by Finkelstein, I recall him as unusual among Party authorities in possessing a genuine artistic sensibility and love of beauty.

34. "Editorial Comment: How Much Psychiatry Do We Need?" *Benjamin Rush Bulletin*, No. 2 (May, 1949): 3; Gil Green, "Lenin and the Principles of the Revolutionary Youth Movement," *COM* 13 (January, 1934): 73; "Science Staff," "Science and the Student," *NF* 3 (Fall, 1949): 30; Robert Fogel, "A Special Supplement: McCarthyism against Education," *NF* 6 (June 1953): p. 14 of Supplement (paginated separately from regular issue); Herbert Aptheker, "Ideas in Our Time," *PA* 37 (April,

1958): 21. On philosophers, see Harry K. Wells, *Pragmatism* (New York: IP, 1954), practically every page of which accuses the subjects of lying, plotting, conscious obfuscation—to such an extent that the Party's other chief philosopher, Howard Selsam, gently chided Wells for confusing "objective meaning and subjective intent." See Selsam, "Marxism vs. Pragmatism," *MM* 7 (May 1954): 64. Yet Selsam himself wrote the introduction to Wells's book.

35. Howard Selsam and Harry K. Wells, "The Philosophy of John Maynard Keynes," *PA* 28 (February, 1949): 82.

36. Aptheker, *History and Reality*, p. 137; Howard Selsam, "Should Communists Teach in Our Colleges?" *NF* 4 (June, 1953): 5.

37. Wells, *Pragmatism*, p. 195; Minton and Stuart, *The Fat Years and the Lean*, pp. 231–32.

11

The People

FROM PARTY LITERATURE we learn that the historical drama of the twentieth century had three main protagonists. Two of them—the ruling class and the Party—understood the script. The "unconsciousness" of the third protagonist was an essential part of its role, for a conscious working class would not have needed the Party, except as mere executor of the popular will.

The double role of the masses—as passive material for the two active forces to work upon, and as active makers of the revolution—was reflected in two mutually exclusive images of the people. On the one hand, they were active: courageous, struggling throughout history against their oppressors, wise enough to see through the capitalists' lies. On the other hand, they were passive: taking seriously the fake rivalry between the Republican and Democratic parties, swallowing the bosses' racist lies that harmed the people's own interests, and believing religious superstitions that dampened hopes for justice in this world. Both these images of the people omitted aspects of their lives that played no role in the historical drama; the script left no room for anything that did not bear on the drama's action as it moved toward its happy ending. Yet Jimmy Higgins saw no contradictions or important omissions; he did not realize that the script was fiction. Once again, then, we must look behind the words to see if they all articulated aspects of an experience of reality in which the inconsistencies either dissolved or were indispensable and therefore suppressed.

READING THE POLEMICS against enemy spokesmen who expressed contempt for the people, one might conclude that the Party held an unambiguously contrary view. Its literature is sprinkled with defenses of the people against their traducers: for example, a historian who explained history as the work of great men leading "the inert and passive masses" who were "apathetic and stupid," "sheep to be led around by the nose"; ruling classes throughout history, which had felt "contempt for the masses"; the Socialist party and unions, which expressed "contempt for the masses"; and Hollywood producers, who made movies for gullible morons and who portrayed a crowd in one movie as "at the mercy of anyone clever enough to stir its volatile feelings."[1]

The Party's own depictions of the people were not, however, as clearcut as these documents would lead the reader to expect. An economic history published in 1940 said that the Democrats won in a landslide in 1936 because the people had refused to swallow the propaganda they had read in the newspapers, three-fourths of which had endorsed Landon. Yet Party literature repeatedly deplored the voters' delusions about the phony two-party system. Foster several times mentioned the masses' "struggles against the two-party system" but in the same years deplored their habit of voting exclusively for the two capitalist parties, mainly the Democratic; in fact, in one article he made both those statements in one paragraph. Harry K. Wells noted "the revolt of the masses against religion"; they saw through "the obscurantism which it had been the function of religion to preach." Yet, as we saw in a previous chapter, Party writers had all too many occasions to say the opposite. Some expressions of respect for the masses sounded like obligatory declarations of faith. A leading theoretician intoned that "the common people are the heart and soul of democracy. . . . Lenin and Stalin . . . teach us to have faith in the masses, to identify ourselves with them, to learn from them." Echoed Aptheker: Stalin taught us to have confidence in the creative power of the masses. In another place the authority was Chu Teh, who had said, "All our forces and power come from the people. All our ways and means are created by the people. Relying on the power of the people we have defeated the enemy and overcome every difficulty. We have only one secret weapon—complete unity with the people"—a quotation that closes Aptheker's book-length apologia for the suppression of the Hungarian revolt.[2]

In contrast to these formulaic expressions of faith in the masses, the documents that reveal a less complimentary view seem to have reflected the writers' real feelings. This is especially true of the denunciations of the capitalists' duping the masses, for here the writers were focusing on the enemy's vicious intentions; they were defending the masses, and the implication that the masses were gullible was evidently unwitting.[3]

Mike Gold's version of the three-character drama concerning the capitalists, the Party, and the people took the form of a parable: A grafting politician named Booley hates pigeons and sends the police to chase them away. The pigeons then call upon kindly Lenin, who appears as a ragged, unemployed old carpenter and tells Mr. Booley to stop persecuting the pigeons. He refuses to listen, and later that day finds himself transformed into a hungry pigeon. Now he is glad that people feed the pigeons. One wonders why Gold, who must have been aware of the slang connotation of "pigeon," did not choose squirrels to symbolize the workers. Even so, it is noteworthy that only their persecutors and their savior were humans. Foster's version of the three-character drama perhaps explains why Gold's readers saw nothing odd in his symbols. He wrote that "bourgeois culture" aims chiefly to make workers "slave-like robots who will accept uncomplainingly" the conditions that the bosses see fit to impose on them; "unthinking soldiers" enthusiastically dying for their masters; and "superstitious dolts" accepting the promise of paradise instead of a decent life in the here and now. That is why, he explained, "the workers are regimented in the schools, . . . enmeshed in fascist-like sport organizations, herded into the strike-breaking Y.M.C.A., stuffed with endless rot in the newspapers and movies, jammed into religious training before they are able to think for themselves, etc." That these efforts had succeeded is evident from the ensuing passages in Foster's book, in which he explained how the American Soviet regime would eradicate all those bad influences and their effects on the people. It is evident also in his assertion that the current situation, "with the people getting their heads stuffed with capitalist ideas from every direction, largely renders our elections farcical from the democratic standpoint." Another theoretician scolded bourgeois sociologists specializing in the minority problem for avoiding its essence: "how small but powerful groups controlling our American economy can rule 140,000,000 Americans." Scores of other Party documents make it clear that the active parties to the struggle were the capitalists and the Party, competing for hegemony over the working class. John Williamson, for example, wrote that "without our contributions and activity, the masses would be left to the influence of all the currents and counter-currents of non-Marxist forces and ideologies."[4] Williamson wrote this shortly after the Party had reconstituted itself, ending the long Browder period when the Communists *had*, they believed, left the masses with no antidote to the enemy's ideology.

The masses had no antidote of their own, for, as Lenin said, socialist consciousness must be brought *to* the workers and did not arise spontaneously from their own experience and struggles. The two warring belief systems— the capitalists' and the Party's—both originated outside the working class: the capitalists' from their class interests, and the Party's from the scientific generalization, by intellectuals, of the workers' experience and the data of history. As Lenin said, there was no third ideology, which meant that none could evolve within the people's own communities. The image of the helpless proletariat was thus intrinsic to the Party's general belief system.

This perception of the people, as the only one of the three groups in the historical drama that did not produce its own worldview—that is, as the one group that received all its beliefs from either of the other two—helps to explain a number of pervasive features of Party literature. Two are especially pertinent here.

The first was the Party writers' habit of interpreting ordinary people's actions solely as reactions to the capitalists' or Party's initiatives, as though they had no life or culture apart from the class struggle. In an essay written in 1932 and republished in 1947, Foster explained that, "when suffering extreme privation they [the workers] are literally compelled to think and act, and when the pressure of the exploiter is relatively light, during good times, they take courage and move forward of their own volition." Evidently, during so-so times, they did not think or act and were cowardly. Evidently, too, they had no independent means and ends, for Foster's word "forward" meant forward toward socialism, regardless of what meaning the workers might have given the word. In a 1937 article Foster virtually said so: "The striking workers should be systematically taught the meaning and implications of the strike," which meant they did not know the meaning of their own actions. "The militant minority," wrote Foster,

. . . is the thinking and acting part of the working class, the very soul of labor. . . . It is the source of all real progress—intellectual, spiritual, and organizational—in the workers' ranks. . . . The fate of all labor organization depends directly upon the effective functioning of these militant, progressive spirits among the backward and sluggish organized masses.

In another essay he referred to "the great unconscious trade union mass." If the organized, trade-union masses were backward, sluggish, and unconscious, what would he have called the majority, who did not belong to unions? Even when the masses acted unusually militantly, indeed in defiance of a Communist Party in power, they could be depicted in this way. Herbert Aptheker's book on the Hungarian uprising portrayed the Hungarian masses mostly as victims, or as objects of propaganda, or as instruments of other people's organizational and administrative measures.[5] Still another evidence of this attitude is the absence, from the historical works by Party scholars, of any study of community, family, cultural organizations, recreation, or other topics that take seriously ordinary people's acts and thoughts in their own terms.

The second feature of Party literature resulting from the above-described image of the people was the way it assigned responsibility for bad behavior. The best illustration is the Party's response to racist acts committed by white workers and farmers. The moral aspects of the acts dictated the Party writers' "factual" findings concerning causes and responsibility.

In the late nineteenth century, wrote Foster, the white leaders of the unions grew closer to the Democratic Party and refused to admit blacks to their ranks; these actions were decisive in dividing the unions from "the Negro people's movement." Shortly before World War I, race riots "were deliberately planned, organized attacks against the Negro people by armed white thugs in the service of the planter-monopolist reaction. . . . And, tragically, poor white farmers and workers often took a hand in these dreadful enterprises." During World War I, when southern blacks migrated to the North to work in factories, "the white chauvinist attitude of the top leaders of labor led to unfortunate relations between white and Negro workers in the industrial localities." Anti-Negro bias in A. F. of L. unions "reflect[ed] the employers' policy of discriminating" against black workers. " 'Race riots' were precipitated [after the war] by the employers and their lackeys in scores of towns and cities." Coming up to the 1950s, Foster generalized: "Race hatred, injected among the toilers by the exploiters," saturates American society.

White chauvinism is a cancerous disease in American culture. . . . Large sections of the working class, constantly subjected to this flood of intellectual filth, are also more or less afflicted with it. . . . Despite the assertions of reactionaries, white chauvinism is not a natural phenomenon. It is definitely propagated by those who benefit financially from it.

The crimes against the Negro people amounted to "genocide," according to William L. Patterson, the Party's principal lawyer. "Those responsible for this crime," he wrote, "are not the humble but the so-called great, not the American people but their misleaders, not the convict but the robed judge, not the criminal but the police, not the spontaneous mob but organized terrorists licensed and approved by the state to incite to a Roman holiday."[6] Thus, to absolve the masses of responsibility, the Party called the acts by the instigators "criminal"; those of the duped white workers and farmers were merely "unfortunate" and "tragic." Foster, a close student of the labor movement, must have known that the A. F. of L. under Samuel Gompers was a loose federation; the top leaders could not impose antiracist policies on the Jim Crow unions. But Foster had to assert the contrary, so as to equate leadership with responsibility.

The problem with this defense of the people, however, is that, if they were so easily influenced from the one side, they should under proper circumstances be as easily influenced from the other.[7] This casts doubt on the depth of their expected conversion to the Party's truth. And if they were not responsible for their misdeeds, how could they be responsible for their good deeds?

In fact, the Party usually claimed credit for "progressive" trends among the populace. Note, for example, the logic of this passage of Foster's:

The Communists played a decisive part in the great strikes and organizing drives that established the C.I.O. . . . The new unions certainly did not learn their militant organizing spirit, intensified political activity, internationalism, more enlightened Negro policy, shop steward system, rank-and-file democracy, anti-racketeer fight, mass picketing, union singing, sit-down strikes, slow-down strikes, and sound fighting policies from the old-line trade union leaders who officially headed the historic movement.

The Communists did play an important part in establishing the Congress of Industrial Organizations (CIO), but the significant aspect of Foster's logic is that it ruled out any initiative by the rank and file or by leaders produced from the ranks and formulating their own policies. Either the old-line leaders or the Communists must have been responsible; Foster assumed that by excluding the one explanation he proved the other.[8]

This was not just pride; it was dictated by the Party's self-image. Marxism-Leninism, as was shown in an earlier chapter, was the working class's own science, the articulation of its own role and destiny. It was "the philosophy of the liberation of the masses by themselves." Sometimes this identification of the proletariat with the Party was deliberate; sometimes it seems inadvertent. Ignoring Lenin's dictum about the inability of the workers to develop socialist consciousness from their own experience, and Engels's, that socialism, having become a science, must be studied as any science is studied, Wells wrote:

Dialectical and historical materialism is the scientific world view and method of the proletariat and the Communist Party. . . . It is a philosophy created by the entire class. . . . It creates its philosophy out of the wisdom of head and hand passed from generation to generation . . . throughout centuries of struggle against poverty and exploitation, against oppression and war. . . . Out of such experience does the working class create its view of life, it mode of thought, its philosophy.

Since only a small minority knew the working class's own philosophy and had to teach it to the majority, Wells's last sentence must mean that the working class created its philosophy *through* the Party, which therefore "represented" it not numerically, but in essence. This was, incidentally, true even in a country in which the working class had ruled for seventeen years:

in most cases a mood of refractoriness in a Soviet worker can be traced to an inadequate understanding of some specific Party policy or measure. . . . A worker who is chronically disgruntled is diagnosed as "backward." Everything is done to "raise his cultural level," to "educate" him; for the Bolsheviks are firm in their conviction that a worker who realizes his own interests cannot possibly be opposed to a workers' dictatorship whatever its mistakes and occasional failings. . . . The same is true of the poor peasant. He may . . . be intransigent in his opposition to collectivization, for he doesn't understand it. When he grasps the idea, when it is patiently demonstrated to him, not by force but by suasion, that he and his would be the beneficiaries of the change, he is intransigently for it.[9]

Disagreement was, then, "diagnosed" and cured, for there was no question of the truth of the policies. Refractoriness, especially in a Soviet worker or peasant who had more opportunities than his American counterpart to see the truth demonstrated, must be pathological.

Most often, however, the writers' habit of equating the working class with its most "advanced" section seems to have been automatic. Two typical passages can illustrate the usual style. One appeared in Foster's discussion of workers in the late nineteenth century:

In these decades *the* toilers of factory and farm militantly resisted this stepped-up capitalist exploitation and oppression. . . . *The* workers' main fight was along trade union lines. . . . *The* workers were not yet fully caught in the trap of the two-party system, and *they* organized many local labor parties and independent political movements. (Emphases added.)

The second illustrative passage is by Mike Gold: "What makes the revolutionary working class superior to the capitalist class is intellect. The workers have a superior philosophy of life. They understand the meaning of these wars, depressions and famines. . . . [They] have a new proud confidence in life, and know they will make a new world," and so on. That is why a leading theoretician could say that fear of communism was really just exaggerated fear of democracy and that "the writings of Lenin and Stalin are the twentieth century's greatest textbooks on democracy."[10]

Since the lion and sheep images of the people were obviously more than mere propaganda messages, we should ask why the writers chose them in particular contexts. One conclusion leaps from the pages of the literature: that the availability of both images enabled the Party to be right, whatever happened. For example, on page 80 of *History and Reality*, Aptheker mentioned the "irrationality" of a white worker's supporting Jim Crow, "because he is infected by the dominant ideas of racist society, whose ruling class created and maintains that racism as both useful and profitable to itself." On page 83, however, he declared (answering David Riesman) that of course the people believe there is a ruling class. They "believe it because they see it and know it, despite the contrary teachings of the ruling class itself. They believe it because it is true." But was not the denial of this fact another of the "dominant ideas" of the society? Why did the people see through one lie and not the other? Both formulas—"the workers think thus because it is true," and "the workers think thus because they are infected by ruling-class ideas"—were a priori tools waiting in the ideological tool-kit to be used whenever needed. Another example of a priori imputation of causation appears in an editorial in *New Foundations*: "The working class in every capitalist country has historically been, and is today, the leading progressive force because, as Karl Marx declared over 100 years ago, it 'has nothing to lose but (its) chains.' " If that logic had been valid, few of the documents quoted earlier throughout this chapter would make sense. It says that "because" Party theory assigned the working class a certain historic role, "therefore" individual workers' beliefs that deviated from that role were exceptions— even if numerically dominant—caused by ruling-class ideological infection. The class, not individuals, took precedence in Party thinking. "The working class . . . [is] not . . . a static, hopeless, mass, but . . . a class that is moving as a whole, with specific sections moving in the vanguard," wrote one leader (who assumed it must be one or the other). Added another, "the working class, upon which the Communist Party bases itself, is the bulwark and most consistent champion of democracy, the nation and social progress." A final example of a priori imputation of thought patterns to the masses appears in Aptheker's comments on historians who had interpreted the American Revolution as a minority movement, and the secessionists of 1861 as the majority of southern whites. "Thus, a progressive, democratic movement is held to represent the will of a minority, while a reactionary, anti-democratic movement is said to represent the will of a majority!" Whether or not the historical facts support Aptheker's interpretations of the two events is a separate question; what is significant is the exclamation point, which implies that these theories are false a priori.[11] Thus, every good revolution *must* have had majority support and every bad revolution *must* have been the work of a minority. The relevance of this assumption to various twentieth-century revolutions may not have been accidental.

One way to dispose of the problem of mass support for reaction was to exclude recalcitrant workers and peasants from the category of the people. According to Mao Tse-tung in a speech in 1957:

The term "the people" has different meanings in different countries, and in different historical periods in each country. Take . . . [China] for example. During the Japanese aggression, all those classes, strata and social groups that opposed Japanese aggression belonged to the category of the people, while the Japanese imperialists, Chinese traitors and the pro-Japanese elements belonged to the category of enemies of the people. . . . At this stage of building socialism, all classes, strata and social groups that approve, support and work for the cause of Socialist construction belong to the category of the people, while those social forces and groups that resist the Socialist revolution, and are hostile to and try to wreck Socialist construction, are enemies of the people.

He regarded the individuals who had recently rebelled against the Hungarian regime as not belonging to the Hungarian people. The people by definition never wanted to abolish socialism. This thesis helps explain Mao's statement later in the same speech that "because conditions in Tibet are not ripe, democratic reforms have not yet been carried out there." In other words, the majority of Tibetans were not yet "the people."[12]

Perhaps some such distinction between the theoretical people and the actual people (whom Foster had referred to as sluggish masses) was in Aptheker's mind when, reviewing a book by Foster, he rhapsodized over Foster's "pride in and love for the masses of toiling and producing men and women. He details their struggles and dreams, their bravery and determination. He conveys in this volume the incalculable strength which the working people possess, their endurance and their indestructibility." The distinction is also the only way to make sense of the statement, by the editors of *New Masses*, that the reactionaries, not the people, won the election of 1946. The editorial then quoted Senator Claude Pepper (D., Fla.)—indicating that not only Communists differentiated between the people and the majority—saying he "spoke for millions when he said: 'We serve notice on the anti-democratic forces of America that they have won a battle but not a war.' "[13]

But the distinction between the lion and the sheep images of the people was not, strictly speaking, between theory and fact, for the sluggish mass and unconscious workers were no more real than were the heroic proletarians of Party poster art. Both were invented to explain the Party's successes and failures and to support its predictions. Neither reflected reality, because neither took cognizance of flesh-and-blood workers and of the fact that they lived partly without reference to either their employers or the self-designated vanguard. This is the answer to the question how Party members could hold those contradictory images of the people in their minds with no sense of inconsistency. When Jimmy Higgins looked at real workers, he saw them solely in terms of their roles in the revolution, as participants and opponents. Even if a worker engaged strenuously in activity in behalf of goals that the Party did not recognize, Jimmy Higgins saw him as inert; activity by definition was activity toward the Party's goals. If a worker disagreed with or voted against a Party program, he could not be doing so for autonomous reasons; he had to be reflecting the ideological hegemony of the enemy class.

THAT WAS NOT ALL that Comrade Jimmy saw when he looked at a flesh-and-blood member of the masses. He also saw elements of his own mind, and by seeing them in other people he could avoid recognizing them in himself. Nathan Leites has noted how important it was to the Party to demarcate clearly the space between itself and everyone else: "the Party is an island in the midst of the masses," and "the raging ocean tends to submerge the island, which defends itself, first, by ascertaining its boundaries."[14] The noble proletarian and the deluded slave began their existence within the personality of Jimmy Higgins, who felt alien within his own society and feared its influence over him. The Party's vanguard role combined the two elements, of separateness from and contact with the people, and it transformed a psychological conflict into agitational and leadership problems that could be dealt with openly.

But to deal with a psychological problem as though it were a problem of the relation of theory to practice is to guarantee an unsatisfactory solution. For, of all the Party's tenets, those concerning the people were the most vulnerable to disproof in the course of Jimmy Higgins's daily experience. During the late 1940s, many student comrades left college to "go into industry," to effect the unity of intellectuals (who knew the theory) and the workers (who would put the theory into practice).[15] The "colonizers," as they sometimes called themselves, expected their shopmates to welcome them gratefully and admire them for their insights and moral purity. More articulate than their fellow workers, some did become shop stewards. A few even remained in the union movement. For most, however, the experience taught disturbing lessons: their shopmates were no nobler than anyone else and showed more interest in sports and movies than in politics. Besides, the work was boring. Most of these students soon drifted back to school. Working-class comrades (many of whom I knew in "industrial" branches, which I belonged to for a few years) were more able to tolerate the conditions of factory work, and they did not romanticize the workers. The heroic prole-tarian, hungry for the message, they relegated to the history books, the Soviet Union, and the future United States. It was the Communist intellectuals—and ex-workers who became full-time Party functionaries, such as Foster—who tended to romanticize living American workers.

The Party members, and not just intellectuals, should have asked the obvious question: "Why didn't ruling-class ideological conditioning 'take' in my case?" The scholars who generalize about the ordinary Party member should also try to explain his exceptionalness. (The usual, and usually im-plicit, off-the-cuff explanation is his greater sensitivity to injustice.) The party's own documents touching on this question are not very helpful; in fact, they are among the primary sources that need explaining.

Several of them attempted to answer a related question: how does the worker learn the truth? The typical formula appears in a 1940 speech by a YCL leader: "These are times in which the masses learn rapidly from their own experience." In Foster's version, "The great masses of the workers learn, not primarily from Marxist books or propaganda, but from the daily con-ditions of their lives." A working-class Jimmy Higgins, reading such state-ments, may not have consciously reflected, "that's not how *I* learned the truth," but in some corner of his mind he must have suspected so, for *his* daily experiences had not differed from those of the still-unenlightened masses. Communist and ex-Communist memoirists usually credit outrage at poverty and injustice for their conversion. But none of them explains why the same experience had not taught the majority. What was it that the workers learned from experience, according to those documents that said that they did learn? (I refer to the statements that ring true, not those odes such as Wells's quoted on page 206 above.) Not Marxism; that was a science that generalized from all human history and scholarship. Not the need for so-cialism; Lenin said that it must be introduced to the workers "from without" their own experience, by the Party. Evidently, all they could learn from their own experience was the intolerability of their lives. Their horizons seemed incorrigibly narrow; according to Browder, when the majority of Americans decide to establish socialism, most of that majority "will not understand or consciously accept the Marxian philosophy, but will be moved by immediate needs which will be expressed in their minds in religious, ethical, or philosophical-idealist forms of thought." Far from being a de-plorable limitation, this motivation may have gratified Party members, for it had the double benefit of insuring the distinction between them and the masses and of guaranteeing the Party its vanguard role. This supposition finds support in Richard Wright's reflection when he tried "to grasp why Communists hated intellectuals":

there existed in the Western world an element that baffled the Communist Party: the prevalence of self-achieved literacy. Even a Negro, entrapped by ignorance and exploitation—as I had been—could, if he had the will and love for it, learn to read and understand the world in which he lived. And it was these people that the Communists could not understand.[16]

Perhaps they did understand, but feared; people who, like Wright, learned without Party guidance threatened to deprive Comrade Jimmy of his mission.

Comrade Jimmy's need for his role as vanguard gives a special meaning to the Party dictum: *"Teach the masses and learn from the masses."*[17] Learn what? We have already eliminated everything but how the masses experienced their sufferings, and which agitational and propaganda tactics would prove most fruitful. Party members tried hard to mingle with the masses, but the effort went against the grain. Why else would a writer in *The Young Worker* feel the need to tell his comrades that

as *"vanguards of the toiling masses" we must learn to mingle and fraternize with them, not* BELOW *or* ABOVE *but on the same level with them.* LET US NOT, IN PURSUIT OF OUR AIMS, FORGET THAT OUR BELOVED LEADER, LENIN, ADVO-CATED ALSO THE PURSUIT OF HAPPINESS. WE ARE YOUTH AND AS YOUTH MUST PARTICIPATE IN AND ENJOY THE THINGS OF YOUTH. WE MUST NOT LOSE THE JOY AND TASTE OF LIVING.

Addressing young people who were not yet part of the vanguard, the same periodical said, "This newspaper is published by an organization, the Young Communist League. The members . . . are young fellows and girls like your-self, young people who work for a living, or who are looking for work, or go to school." When *Champion of Youth* replaced *The Young Worker*, it im-mediately took up the burden of portraying Communist youth as just folks. We shall, it explained, analyze our society and show the solution to our problems. "But don't for a moment think that it's all work and no fun. We're young and naturally have young interests. We hope our pages will be well-humored, sunny and spicy; written in the unmistakable idiom of America—with the tang of the earth and the sea, the mines and the factories, the campus and the cornfield."[18]

The Party members and "the masses" were, in fact, interested in different things, and one gets the impression that the former sometimes felt that a person who knew the truth could not feel much interest in trivial matters such as bowling, movies, or the other topics that took up so much of the attention of workers and nonradical students. The affectation of folksiness to enable the comrades to mingle with the masses was meant to be temporary; its ultimate goal was to induce the masses to stop being interested in all those

pursuits that held no attraction for the comrades. Selsam explained the scientific justification for this feeling: we have only recently become able to
determine

what men ought to want in terms of what they actually need within the possibility
of scientific determination. . . . There are cultural needs . . . that can be empirically
arrived at, and that may run against opposed desires under certain conditions. . . .
What people need is one thing and what the dominant economic class would like
them to desire is something different.[19]

To return to the question asked at the beginning of this section—how
Party members accounted for their having escaped the society-wide conditioning: they did not try, and the documents sampled above help to explain
why.

IT IS TIME to bring to the surface a submerged theme in the preceding discussion, concerning the comrades' feelings—in contradistinction to their theories—about the masses of ordinary people. Party historians who copied the
heroic masses from theory and ignored the complex lives, cultures, problems,
and activities of actual people were not really celebrating but contemning
them. When Foster described "the" workers in terms that applied only to
the most "advanced" minority, he was writing real workers out of the history
books. Party writers who refused to blame noncapitalists who committed
crimes were thereby dehumanizing them. The odes of love for the masses
should not obscure this inescapable undercurrent that runs through Party
literature from the earliest years to the present. Floyd Dell, a contributing
editor of *New Masses* till his resignation in 1929, went further; according to
Daniel Aaron, Dell had begun "to feel that the pervasive radical satire . . .
revealed 'hatred for the human race, mistaken as a hatred for the bourgeoisie.' "[20]

An essay by Mike Gold illustrates this animus perfectly because it expressed something quite different from what Gold intended. In his essay
"Indian Massacre," Gold attacked older anthropologists who had justified
"imperialism's" massacres of Indians because they were "savages." Savagery,
he said, once meant a lower stage of culture. But modern anthropologists
have shown that

it means only that a nation is living, not at any inferior, but at a younger stage of
culture. You do not say that a child is inferior to a man. He is merely younger than
an adult. All humanity once passed through this youthful stage of culture, and sections
of it, like the Africans or Polynesians, or our own red Indians, have[,] for historic
reasons, lingered there.

If the Indians had not been decimated by whites but had been allowed to
progress, they would have caught up. Imperialism

hides the fact . . . that for thousands of years the Africans had a well-rounded culture of their own—a great body of traditional poetry and science, a system of law, the finest sculpture, pottery, iron-work and other traditional arts.

For a century the white American robbers managed to hide the fact that our own Indians had a culture, too. But devoted scientists have searched out the story, and now we know a great deal about the poetry, music, dancing, philosophy and science of the American Indian.

The Mayan calendar stone in Yucatan (which state is thought to be the cradle of the Indian culture) was a stone recording the high state of Indian astronomy. They could foretell eclipses, and the revolution of the planets. They had gone into the higher mathematics, and who knows what else?

All this was destroyed by the whites. No wonder many of them today are beginning to find their way to Communism.

Gold seemed unable to make up his mind; children do not invent philosophy, higher mathematics, and astronomy. But since he wanted to depict "the" Indians as victims of whites—and never of other Indians—it did not matter whether they were cultural children or highly civilized. Even more revealing is Gold's homogenizing of all Indians on the one side and all whites on the other. That the Central American societies were class-divided, that the Mayan state could not have been the "cradle" of, say, Iroquois culture, that Indians fought Indians more often than they fought whites and did so before and after the European invasions, and so on—Gold might have learned even in the 1930s, when he wrote this essay, if he had studied the literature rather than picking through it for ammunition. What this passage shows, then, are Gold's feelings about whites, feelings undisciplined by theory.[21]

Type I rejecters of reality start close to home, and some then work their way outward to include their ethnic or religious community, then their class, then their country, then their race, and finally the human species. At every step, a rationalization in the guise of theory waits and beckons them to stop there. So we have seen in recent years a few Jews stopping at the point where they become propagandists for the PLO. Farther along the road, some whites have discovered that the whole white race is a "cancer." Even farther along are those "environmentalists" who portray the human species as a spoiler of Nature. The CP's theory beckoned the reality-loather early on the journey, telling him to focus his loathing on one small minority in every capitalist country. But Gold was a creative writer with license to embody his feeling in symbols, and in this case he forgot his doctrine and wrote from the heart, which took him much farther along the road than Marxist-Leninist orthodoxy allowed. He conjured up an image of "Indians"—or rather, two incompatible images, unless the Indian "children" were also scientific prodigies—merely as a counterimage to that of an undifferentiated category which he loathed: the white race, the destroying race, Gold's race. Foster, too, in an outline of what a Marxist history of the North American Indians should say, forgot the class divisions among the whites. He referred to "*the* greedy and on-pushing settlers," "oppression by *the* whites," "war provocations by *the* whites," "the genocide policies of *the* white colonists," and "*the* colonists [who] fought to exterminate the Indians" (emphases added).[22]

Inadvertent slips such as Gold's and Foster's support a conjecture that the dual lion-sheep image of the people reflected a conflict between the Type I comrade's genuine attitude and the Party theory that both suppressed and rationalized it. Other belief systems that reject simple populism and plebiscitarian democracy do not get tangled up in the contradictions we have noticed in the Party's writings. Not the sheep, but the lion image caused the problems. We have surveyed the ways in which the writers tried to solve them: they defined reactionaries out of the people category; they used a sort of "virtual representation" theory of the relation of the Party to the proletariat; they postulated different levels of consciousness. All these inventions had one thing in common: they all abstracted admirable traits from real human beings. When Party historians writing about "the slaves" and "the workers" described only the rebellious slaves and the militant workers, it was not the people selected to represent the whole group whom they were admiring, but the rebelliousness, militancy, and consciousness. This separation of the traits from the people is consistent with the Party's imputing value to people, including Party members, according to their social functions and levels of understanding and not to their sheer humanness.[23]

This general attitude evokes a comment on a current controversy among social theorists. Some of them say that the primary struggle in the modern world is between The Party of Liberty and The Party of Equality.[24] Perhaps so, but although the CP certainly did not belong to the former (notwithstanding its professions of concern with freedom), I hesitate to include it in the latter. The word equality was not one of the Party writers' favorites. We find it occasionally in discourses on racism, but in the negative sense of the opposite of anti-Negro discrimination. It must be remembered that to Jimmy Higgins, Marxism-Leninism was a science, to master which required study and (he observed as he tried to teach his neighbors and fellow workers) a certain aptitude. Socialist society would be guided scientifically by the foremost masters of the science of Marxism-Leninism. Science was, of course, "undemocratic." It remained for the next generation of radical students to demand that professors engage in no scientific research that their students did not participate in. In the period we are concerned with, student comrades would have laughed at that idea—as they would have laughed at the idea of rank-and-file Party members' contributing to the advance of the Party's science. Jimmy Higgins knew that there was no equality between the master of that science and the ordinary worker, even in the Soviet Union. If it be suggested that the CP belonged in The Party of Equality because the vision of equality, with or without that word, informed Party ideology, I would still hesitate to concur. True, the writers repeatedly forecast the future communist society in terms of people's freely pursuing their own interests, without economic worries to restrict their choices. That vision, however, depicted not equality but justice. The Party's writings on every subject other than liberty prove that it did not really value liberty. But it did show a monumental grievance against the world for being unfair, for not allocating rewards and penalties according to desert. The Soviet Union appealed to Jimmy Higgins not because people there were equal, but because it was just.

NOTES

1. Herbert Aptheker, *History and Reality* (New York: Cameron Associates, 1955), pp. 21, 61, 243; Aptheker, "Communism and Chaos," *MM* 1 (September, 1948): 25; William Z. Foster, *Toward Soviet America* (New York: Coward-McCann, 1932), p. 143; John Howard Lawson, *Film in the Battle of Ideas* (New York: Masses & Mainstream, 1953), pp. 35, 37. Cf. the admission by Aptheker during the post–Twentieth Congress self-critical period: "We have ... tended to follow bourgeois historians in ascribing too much of a passive, or follow-the-leader role to the masses in bourgeois revolutions. We have been prone to accept a reading of history which sees the 'enlightened' and the educated and the propertied as maneuvering the masses." Herbert Aptheker, "On the Concept 'Bourgeois-Democracy,' " *PA* 35 (August, 1956): 54. Not long afterward, Aptheker depicted the Hungarian masses in the passive way he here criticized.

2. Bruce Minton and John Stuart, *The Fat Years and the Lean* (New York: IP, 1940), pp. 276–77; William Z. Foster, "The Struggle for a Mass Labor Policy," *PA* 38 (May, 1959): 2; Harry K. Wells, *Pragmatism* (New York: IP, 1954), p. 20; A. Landy, "The 'Foreign Agent' Fraud and the Battle for Democracy," *COM* 19 (February, 1940): 131; Herbert Aptheker, *Laureates of Imperialism* (New York: Masses & Mainstream, 1954), p. 93; Aptheker, *The Truth about Hungary* (New York: Mainstream Publishers, 1957), p. 256.

3. In this respect the Party was not unique: all conspiracy theories of social reality imply a passive populace. An incident in a U.S. history seminar in the early 1970s can illustrate this in two ways at once. My students had read excerpts from *The International Jew*, a book composed of articles that had been published in Henry Ford's *Dearborn Independent* in 1920. The articles quoted from and commented on the notorious forgery "The Protocols of the Elders of Zion," which purport to present the plan of world Jewry to rule the world, and which Ford believed authentic. Among the comments are: "the Protocols ... give a clue to the modern maze.... They constitute an education in the way the masses are turned about like sheep by influences which they do not understand." (See David Brion Davis, ed., *The Fear of Conspiracy* [Ithaca, N.Y.: Cornell University Press, 1971], pp. 230–31.) My students expressed horror at the fantastic invention and the anti-Semitism, but when I directed their attention to the depiction of ordinary people, their minds went blank; they had all overlooked this aspect of the document. Their great difficulty in seeing the point was due to the fact that their own, radical, ideology shared this element of "The Protocols' " (and Ford's) ideology, differing mostly over the specific content of it and the personnel of the conspiring group. What one takes for granted is usually invisible even when it is before one's eyes.

4. Michael Gold, *Change the World!* (New York: IP, 1936), pp. 27–31; Foster,

Toward Soviet America, p. 314 and passim; Foster, *The Twilight of World Capitalism* (New York: IP, 1949), p. 55; Morris U. Schappes, "Myths about Anti-Semitism," *MM* 2 (October, 1948): 50 (see also rest of article); John Williamson, "The Reconstitution of the Communist Party," *PA* 24 (September, 1945): 802. Foster criticized the Socialist party's policy of neutrality toward the unions for "allowing [N.B.!] the workers to be influenced by the bourgeoisie." See William Z. Foster, *History of the Communist Party of the United States* (New York: IP, 1952), p. 99. See also ibid., pp. 550–51; M. J. Olgin, *Trotskyism* (New York: Workers Library, 1935), p. 68; Alex Bittelman and V. J. Jerome, "Leninism Is the Only Marxism of the Imperialist Era," *COM* 13 (November, 1934): 1125.

5. William Z. Foster, *American Trade Unionism* (New York: IP, 1947), pp. 64, 237, 66, 67, 78; Aptheker, *Truth about Hungary*, passim. See also "We Must Learn from the American Revolution," *YW*, July 1, 1928, p. 3, in which two opposite statements appear. First: "The capitalists, exploiters and reactionaries" claim the heritage of the struggle for freedom and independence, "and yet this barefaced swindle is still swallowed by millions of American workers and young workers"; and second: "These traditions [of the American Revolution] belong to the American proletariat, the revolutionaries of today!" The second statement is theory; the first, "fact." As to the assimilation of ordinary people's interests and behavior in all spheres of life into the Party's class-political model, see an exposé of the true significance of the World Series—to distract the workers from their problems—in Walter Burke, "Shows That Workers Really Lost Out in World Series; Class Angle of the Great American Game," *YW* 7 (October, 1928): 4. In later years the *Daily Worker*, trying to appeal to a broader readership, ran a well-informed sports column that treated baseball as a legitimate interest; the only political angle then was the demand for the end of the color bar and, later, the preference for the integrated teams over those that still had no black players. On the general point in the text, see Alain Besançon, *The Rise of the Gulag: Intellectual Origins of Leninism* (New York: Continuum, 1981), p. 232.

6. William Z. Foster, *The Negro People in American History* (New York: IP, 1954), pp. 344, 420, 438; Foster, *History of the CP*, pp. 225, 70; Foster, *Negro People*, p. 544; William L. Patterson, ed., *We Charge Genocide* (New York: Civil Rights Congress, 1951), editor's introductory remarks, p. 5. See also, among many other documents: Wells, *Pragmatism*, p. 59; Carl Ross, "Booby Trap for Youth," *SP* 2 (January 1944): 26; "Destroy White Chauvinism," *NF* 2 (Summer 1949): 211–12.

7. Yet here too "life itself" failed to obey theory. A *Pravda* editorial in 1953, quoted in Joshua A. Gilboa, *The Black Years of Soviet Jewry, 1939–1953* (Boston: Little, Brown, 1971), p. 296, complained that, in addition to the foreign imperialist enemies that the Soviet regime had to contend with, "we still have one more enemy—the gullibility of our own people"—this after thirty-six years of Party control of the schools and communications media.

8. Foster, *History of the CP*, p. 346.

9. Aptheker, *History and Reality*, p. 71; Wells, *Pragmatism*, p. 209; Joshua Kunitz, "Literary Wars in the U.S.S.R.," *NM*, June 26, 1934, p. 18. For perceptive comments on the relationship between vanguard and masses, see Philip Selznick, *The Organizational Weapon* (New York: Free Press, 1960), pp. 9–10, 74, 81–82, 86.

10. Foster, *Negro People*, p. 376; Gold, *Change the World!*, pp. 146–47; A. Landy, "Marxism Is Democracy," *NM*, April 13, 1943, pp. 17–18. For other equations of the masses with the Party, see, e.g., Alex Bittelman, "For Leninism—For a Soviet

America," *COM* 14 (January, 1935): 7; V. J. Jerome, "Communism for Americans: A Review of Earl Browder's *What is Communism?*," *COM* 15 (March, 1936): 270 (in "this book . . . a class is speaking—the working class, through its political leader, the Party"); M. Kammari and F. Konstantinoff, "Science and Superstructure," *PA* 32 (February, 1953): 65; William Z. Foster, "On the Party Situation," *PA* 35 (October, 1956): 23. A particularly revealing document is George Blake and Herbert Aptheker, " 'Flesh and Bone of the Working Class . . . '—On Foster's 'History of the Communist Party,' " *PA* 31 (September, 1952), on p. 52 of which we learn that the Party's founding "represented a great step forward by the working class . . . , evidencing its growing maturity, its awakening to recognition of its class position." The Party "springs" out of the working class and "is indispensable in the day-to-day struggles" to emancipate itself. Yet in the very next passage, the authors say that the Party from the outset "strove to extend its ties with the working masses and to win their confidence and establish its political leadership in the course of daily struggles"—with no indication that they saw any inconsistency between the two passages.

11. "Wake Up Students!" *NF* 3 (Fall, 1949): 7–8; Gus Hall, "The Importance of Communist Cadres," *PA* 31 (January, 1952): 46; Williamson, "Reconstitution of the Communist Party," p. 803; Herbert Aptheker, "Was the American Revolution a Majority Movement?" *PA* 35 (July, 1956): 1 (note also his p. 2, which ridicules historians who depict the masses during the Revolution as "gullible" and "hood-winked" and as "pawn-like masses being manipulated by their betters").

12. Mao Tse-tung, "On Contradictions among the People," speech delivered in February, 1957, and reprinted in *PA* 36 (July, 1957): 36, 37, 41, 54. See also A. Sokolov, "Democracy" (reprinted from a Moscow publication), *PA* 24 (June, 1945): 522 ("A democrat is one who . . . looks ahead"), 523–25.

13. Herbert Aptheker, "Epic History," *MM* 4 (March, 1951): 90; The Editors, " 'We Serve Notice—They Won a Battle, But Not a War,' " *NM*, November 19, 1946, p. 3. It should not be assumed that such passages were written only for propaganda purposes. To the ideological mind, glaring contradictions between tenets, and between tenets and facts, could be invisible. John Gates recalled that during the Wallace campaign of 1948 the Party leaders "convinced [them]selves that the rank-and-file of labor would revolt against its officialdom." (See John Gates, *The Story of an American Communist* [New York: Thomas Nelson & Sons, 1958], p. 116.) If they could believe that, they could believe any of their statements quoted in this chapter. Another illustration may be found in Howard Fast, *The Naked God* (New York: Frederick A. Praeger, 1957), p. 176.

14. Nathan Leites, *A Study of Bolshevism* (New York: Free Press, 1953), p. 291. See the present study's chapter three and the sources cited there, for discussion of this theme in another context.

15. See, e.g., "Wake Up Students!" p. 10. The unity of theory and practice was a basic Party tenet that supposedly pertained to all aspects of the Party's work, in which practice corrected theory and theory guided practice. The repeated proofs of the *disunity* of the Party's theory and practice came from all areas of its work and predictions, but the inability to understand the meaning of the proletariat's noncon-version, despite the theory's predictions, is the most conclusive evidence that the comrades' faith had psychological sources, for the facts here were firsthand.

16. Gil Green, "Youth Reject Roosevelt Program," *CL* 1 (April-May, 1940): 2; Foster, *Twilight of World Capitalism*, p. 62; Earl Browder, *Communism and Culture*

(New York: Workers Library, 1941), p. 39; Richard Wright, in Richard Crossman, ed., *The God That Failed* (1950; New York: Bantam Books, 1965), p. 139. See also John Gates, "The Soviet Union in the World Today," *CL* 1 (Fall, 1940): 11: "Life itself is the great teacher. Events are cutting through the fog of capitalist deception. The great significance of the actions and policies of the Soviet Union are beginning to be understood by the masses of the people."

17. I. Kastrow, "Don't Stifle Initiative!" *PO* 10 (June, 1937): 31. Blake and Aptheker, on p. 52 of " 'Flesh and Bone of the Working Class,' " say that this is "a basic tenet of Party work," that is, "to cement our ties with the masses, to learn from, be of, and teach and lead" them.

18. Myra Archer, "Just among Us Girls," *YW*, December 3, 1935, p. 9; "The Way to Life, Liberty, Happiness," *YW*, April 30, 1935, p. 5; "Introducing," *CH*, [1] (June, 1936): 2. See also Hal Draper, "The Student Movement of the Thirties: A Political History," in Rita James Simon, ed., *As We Saw the Thirties* (Urbana: University of Illinois Press, 1967), pp. 180–81. The youth periodicals in the 1940s eschewed blatant affectation of folksiness. *Spotlight* featured articles on sports, science, and movies that made the point more subtly. It is probably not coincidental that the worst offender was *The Young Worker*, which was the most abstrusely, esoterically theoretical of all the youth journals and therefore had to try hardest to reach out to potential converts while at the same time feeling most uncomfortable as it did so.

19. Howard Selsam, *Socialism and Ethics* (New York: IP, 1943), pp. 120–21. For an authoritative analysis of the correct balance between closeness to and separateness from the masses, and of what and how the masses learn, see *Strategy and Tactics of the Proletarian Revolution* (New York: IP, 1936), pp. 48–50 and passim.

20. Daniel Aaron, *Writers on the Left* (New York: Avon Books, 1961), p. 234.

21. Gold, *Change the World!*, pp. 253–56. It may be contended that Gold deviated from his pattern insofar as he loved his own little platoon, the Jews of the East Side, as he showed in his book *Jews without Money* (first published in 1930). That love was, however, ambiguous at best. See, for example, his remark that his mother "observed all the minute, irritating details of the Jewish orthodoxy, a ritual that affects one's most trivial acts, and complicates life like a bad neurosis" (Avon edition, 1965, p. 129).

22. William Z. Foster, "On a Marxist History of the North American Indians," *PA* 31 (May, 1952): 55–56, 58–59. As in the case of Aptheker's theories about the American Revolution and Civil War, the accuracy of Foster's facts is a separate question from the consistency of these characterizations with the Party's theory of class-divided white society and its perception of the white victim-masses. Foster says that a "Marxist history of the North American Indians must be fundamentally an analysis of the Indian peoples' reactions to the ever-increasing flood of European colonists"; this recalls the observation made earlier in this chapter, concerning Party writers' perceptions of oppressed peoples as having no lives outside their relations with their oppressors. For other comments on this essay, see chapter six, above.

23. This is why they could paste subhuman labels on evil people. See, e.g., Herbert Aptheker, "An Intensified Racist Offensive," *PA* 54 (July, 1975): 57: the leaders of the antibusing movement in Boston are "lice," and Ku Klux Klan members are "vermin." I cite this more recent document to support the point that the lessons the

Party did *not* learn from its troubles after the Twentieth Congress indicate which elements in its worldview were basic. For comments on the theme of this section, see Besançon, *Rise of the Gulag*, p. 231.

24. I am here continuing the comment begun in chapter one n. 6, above.

12

The Soviet Union as the
American Future

IMAGINE A CONVERSATION among some American Communists in 1958. Browder's name comes up; the comrades respond with loathing. Later, someone mentions Stalin; the response this time is . . . embarrassment. Why the difference? The answer, I think, lies in their image of the Soviet Union. They could not hate the greatest mass murderer in history as they hated the Kansas-born bureaucrat, without giving up their image of the country "Where Dreams Come True," the country that a Canadian CP leader visited and then described under the title "Journey into the Future."[1]

When Khrushchev discredited Stalin, Party leaders rushed to announce that tyranny and "the cult of the individual" were foreign to socialism. One might logically expect that the Party's writers then felt free to denounce Stalin's crimes loudly and in detail. They could thus prove—to themselves as well as to others—their humanitarianism, honesty, and devotion to "true" socialism. But the logical response would have created new difficulties, which they could not confront. During the thaw following the Twentieth Congress, however, some rank-and-file members did ponder certain questions, in private conversations among themselves. For instance, since the Soviet political system was infinitely more democratic than any other, why had it not prevented Stalinism? (The obvious, related question, Why had nothing remotely resembling Stalin's regime ever existed in the United States?, was too heretical even to think of.) How could Stalin's regime be squared with the Marxist tenet that powerful individuals were produced by historical forces, which they might slow down or speed up but never reverse? (The Party blamed Hitler's monstrousness on the "system" of capitalism in crisis.) Was "the role of the individual in history" much greater than Marxism-Leninism allowed, or was the Soviet system in some sense responsible for Stalin?

By the time the thaw ended, about 1958, the questioners had not found real answers, and most had departed. The minority who remained in the Party had accepted mere rationalizations and evasions, for no matter how troubling the questions were, they could not disturb these members' utopian image of the Soviet Union.[2] The very scale of the crimes "revealed" by Khrushchev prevented them from taking the way out of the dilemma offered by the dissociation of Stalinism from Soviet socialism. They simply ignored most of the evidence.

What permitted the comrades to evade the facts after as well as before the Twentieth Congress was their aprioristic conception of socialism. For example, Foster wrote in 1951 that "there can be no imperialism in the U.S.S.R., because, with the country completely in the hands of the toiling population, no capitalists can exist there."[3] The circle of this thought was so hermetically sealed that empirical facts could not enter: the Soviet Union is socialist; socialism puts power completely in the hands of the toilers; therefore, the Soviet Union is ruled by the toilers; the toilers have no interest in imperialism; therefore, the Soviet Union cannot be imperialistic. A reader who did not share Foster's tacit postulates would have noticed the circular reasoning. Jimmy Higgins, however, shared those postulates; they were among the first truths he learned after joining the Party. Statements such as Foster's therefore struck him as cogently reasoned and obviously convincing to any sensible person. This style of thinking about the Soviet Union will be explored below.

THE SOVIET UNION "now forecasts the general outlines of the new social order that the world is approaching," wrote William Z. Foster in *Toward Soviet America*. Intermingled throughout that book are three themes: denunciation of American society, idyllic descriptions of the Soviet Union, and forecasts of postrevolutionary America. Published in 1932, the book caused embarrassment after the rightward turn a few years later. Certain locutions and minor statements had become injudicious, but its essential vision remained orthodox, and the volume remains a marvelous source of what true believers continued to dream throughout the Party's lifetime. It also provides insights into the mentality of the Party members who could not imagine how any sensible person could think differently from the way they did. Here is a passage that Foster assumed would whet any American's appetite for socialism:

The press, the motion picture, the radio, the theatre, will be taken over by the government. They will be cleansed of their present trash of sex, crime, sensationalism and general babbitry, and developed into institutions of real education and art; into purveyors of the interesting, dramatic, and amusing in life. The press will, through workers' correspondents on the Russian lines, become the actual voice of the people, not simply the forum of professional writers. . . . A national Department of Health will be set up, with the necessary local and State sub-divisions. . . . The people will be taught to live correctly. They will be given mass instruction in diet, physical culture, etc. . . . Only a few years ago many of the forgoing proposals would have seemed fantastic, merely utopian dreams. But now we can see them growing into actuality in the Soviet Union. In making the cultural revolution in the United States, the workers and farmers, facing the same general problems as the Russians, will solve them along similar lines.[4]

Foster assumed, then, that the reader looked forward to all those changes (and many others not quoted above). To journey into the future and to the place where dreams came true, one had to book only one flight—to the Soviet Union.

Jimmy Higgins made the trip through the writings of his Party spokesmen. Since their theories originated in hatred of the American social order, they naturally blamed all the difficulties that the Soviet Union encountered on vestiges of the prerevolutionary mentality and on the plots of foreign capitalists. The Soviet people would overcome these problems quickly once their industry had laid the material foundation for military strength and for urban and rural prosperity. The Soviet Union would be able to defend itself and to count on the support of millions of workers abroad, who would know of its achievements. Domestic progress would eliminate the enormous differences in wealth and culture inherited from the old regime. The whole country was eagerly participating in this project under the guidance of the workers' and farmers' own party.

Browder explained in 1939 that millions of illiterate peasants were flocking into the factories and had to be trained in new skills and habits. That was why per capita productivity was lower in the Soviet Union than in the most advanced capitalist countries. Once trained, however, the work force would quickly become more productive, and if the American and Soviet economies performed in the next decade as they had in the previous one, "then before that time is over the Soviet economy will have surpassed our country." The news would quickly spread throughout the world.

It is, therefore, . . . a matter of decades at most, until the superior merits of the socialist system in the Soviet Union will have proved itself by producing a land so overwhelmingly rich, prosperous, and culturally advanced, above all the rest of the world, that the peoples of all lands will inevitably be compelled by the simple dictates of common sense, to adopt the same principles as the Soviet Union, or resign themselves to permanent backwardness and decay.

Ten years later, Foster announced that "not only has socialism been built in the Soviet Union, but it is expected that within fifteen or twenty years communism will be fully introduced." Two years after that, Alexander Bittelman observed that "the Soviet Union . . . is now moving to communism, the highest stage of socialism."[5]

Communism was a society without a state or money, in which everyone worked according to his abilities and took what he needed from the general store of goods. What the Soviet Union had was not communism but socialism. The workers and peasants needed the state to defend their revolution against enemies at home and abroad, and they could not dispense with money before capitalist traits such as greed had disappeared. They had to create not just a new economy but also a "new man." This seems to have caused a theoretical difficulty: how could the Party writers find such glorious achievements to publicize unless the "new man" had already come into being? How could they proclaim socialism as infinitely more democratic than the freest capitalist country, unless the overwhelming majority of Soviet citizens already manifested the sense of collective interest that must replace individualism? They solved the problem by exaggerating the plots, internal and foreign, that forced the Soviet Union to retain a strong state and large police force even after the mass appearance of the "new man." Indeed, it was the "new man" who demanded severe measures against the enemies of socialism.

The "old man" could not have been very tenacious, for, as Olgin pointed out in 1931, those Soviet citizens who had been children in 1917 were already showing "the contours of the new man," who "is a combination of manual and intellectual worker. The difference between hand work and brain work is being more and more obliterated." According to Browder,

the Soviet Union has given us a few glimpses into the profound revolution in human nature that is brought about by the operation of this new motive in human activity [socialist emulation, the honor of serving society]. Socialism is not only a revolution in economic life. It makes an entirely new human race. It takes this man who has been brutalized and degraded through the ages by the violence and oppression of class societies, frees him from this woeful heritage, carries over from the past only the achievements of the human mind and not its crimes and stupidities and remakes man, molding him in the heat of socialist labor into the new social being.[6]

Still another consequence, said Foster in 1953, was "the high quality of the political leaders produced by the Soviet system, by Marxism-Leninism. Lenin and Stalin were no accidents; they were the natural results of the workings of the whole philosophy of Socialism."[7] Foster's formulation was ambiguous. His first sentence equates the Soviet system with Marxism-Leninism. Yet Lenin and Stalin were too old to have been products of the Soviet system, and Lenin was obviously not the product of Leninism. Evidently "the natural results of the workings of the whole philosophy of Socialism" were the *roles* they played; only a socialist system would recognize their genius. Three years after Foster wrote those words, Stalin's role did become an "accident," definitely not a natural result of the Soviet system. In one respect, however, de-Stalinization changed nothing: the leading role of the Party.

The workers' and farmers' state had room for only one party. How stupid the victorious workers would be, exclaimed Foster, if, having abolished capitalism so as to "liquidate all classes," they permitted counterrevolutionary parties to continue trying to sabotage the new regime and reestablish the system of robbing workers and hindering progress! "No organization in the whole history of mankind has had such a magnificent record of sacrifice and achievement as the Communist Party of the Soviet Union, and none is more beloved by its people." It consists of the best members of other organizations—"trade unions, peasant, youth, and others—chosen by the Party with the recommendations of their co-workers," explained the editors of *New Foundations* in 1949; "the Party has always emphasized the necessity of the democratic participation of all the people in making political decisions. The Party is recognized and welcomed as the leader and the most vigilant fighter for the peoples' needs and desires."[8]

This close relationship between the people and their vanguard was evident in all areas of life. A high official in the American CP explained that Soviet science belonged to all the people, who therefore had the right to judge scientists' contributions to the good of society. Naturally, their vanguard party had

a vital interest in such matters, and so has the Soviet Government, since they involve the all-important question of how the nation's funds and energies shall be best utilized in the economic interests of the people. The genetics controversy is therefore not an academic discussion for the edification of a handful of the elite, but a matter of enormous practical importance to all Soviet citizens.[9]

Similar statements concerning art, music, literature, physics, history, and all other pursuits and fields of scholarship appeared in Party writings. All such discourses started from the tacit premise that individually chosen projects, activities, standards, and objectives were antisocial, wasteful, and likely to result in error. Hence the need for organization, planning, and guidance. Hence the leading role of a single party. The writers emphasized over and over again that *the Soviet people* insisted on this role and elevated their own best members to leadership.

Thus, no sooner had news of Stalin's death reached these shores than Foster wrote that the new leader, Georgi Malenkov, was

a Marxist-Leninist of a high order—anything else is unthinkable for a man holding his high position in the great Communist Party of the U.S.S.R., which possesses many hundreds of thousands, actually millions, of students of the science of Socialism. . . . His superb Marxist-Leninist training and his high natural ability, will make him a giant compared to the petty politicians currently heading the capitalist states of the world.[10]

American Communists knew little of Malenkov, and Foster almost admitted as much when he deduced the new leader's excellence from the unthinkability of the alternative. The general Stalin-worship that we sampled in chapter five probably originated in the same kind of deductive thinking. (That it was intensified by other factors is obvious.) The train of thought went as follows:

hatred of American reality produced the "dream come true" of "the future" embodied in the Soviet Union; the need for an all-explaining "science" made it self-evident that the-future-as-present (the Soviet Union) guided itself by that science; the Soviet leaders therefore had to be both beloved by the people and their best scientists. The identification of the leader with the people precluded authoritarianism; the Party leadership was really the people's self-leadership, focusing their energies as a magnifying glass focuses light rays so as to achieve results that the rays cannot achieve when scattered.

In short, all the glorious achievements of the Soviet Union were due to the blazing enthusiasm of the people, who followed their leaders voluntarily because they themselves had produced their leaders. The results should inspire American workers, whose own creative genius would be set free after they had broken their capitalist chains. That was why the Soviet Union was America's future. And that was why the American CP had to publicize every accomplishment and every evidence of happiness in the Soviet Union.

PARTY LITERATURE, accordingly, dwelt at length on the Soviet Union's industry and its people's initiatives in furthering industrial development; on its prospering agriculture; on its young people's happiness and future prospects; and on its progress in various social and cultural spheres.

The nature and volume of industrial production in the Soviet Union were determined by the people's needs, according to Foster:

Socialism abolishes the chaos and anarchy of capitalist production and social organization; it does away with the dog-eat-dog competition of capitalist industry, breeder of industrial crises and war. It sets up instead a planned system of economy in harmony with the national and international character of modern industry and social relationships. Only under Socialism, with its great nationalized industries and collectivized agriculture, is such a scientific planned economy possible and inevitable. . . . The Five-Year Plan . . . figures out the number of workers required for production and plans their mobilization. It determines the total wage funds, including those for the cultural needs of the workers, for social insurance, etc.

As a result, the Soviet Union was the only country without crises or unemployment and in which the people's standard of living constantly rose. "No one who works lives in poverty." These results came from rational organization, not from overwork. Michael Gold contrasted the "inhuman tempo" of work on the conveyor belt in "Henry Ford's Inferno" with the more leisurely pace in Soviet factories. There, workers were given a five-minute break each hour to smoke and relax, and a paid annual vacation of a month. Doctors and social workers were on hand to make sure no one overworked, and the system insured workers "against all the contingencies of life."[11]

Not surprisingly, the Soviet workers responded with enthusiasm. Thousands, independently of each other, volunteered to exceed their production quotas. Alexei Stakhanov was merely one of those heroes of socialist labor, although this spontaneous movement bore his name. In 1935 the editors of *New Masses* revealed how this young miner had recently demonstrated that with the automatic hammer he had, with two helpers, increased production from the usual seven tons in a six-hour shift to 310 tons.

Since then another miner in the Don Basin has increased . . . the output to four hundred and five tons and he declared before a meeting of 1,500 cheering miners who waited for him outside the mine that 405 tons was just a beginning and that his immediate objective was 500 tons! . . . Stakhanovism has . . . fired the imagination, moral fervor and even, it seems, the aesthetic sense of the masses. Stakhanovism has become synonymous with daring, vigor, efficiency, precision, neatness, cleanliness, punctuality, devotion. To speak of it, as press dispatches have within the past week, as a "speedup" is ignorant and malicious twaddle.[12]

Because socialist emulation and higher productivity did not cause unemployment in the Soviet Union, technological innovation was proceeding rapidly. Mines without miners and "machines that read blueprints" were "some of the wonders of Soviet science." As a result, "the greatest news story of all history . . . is the story of the epoch-making successes of the new socialist economy."[13]

Soviet farming showed equally spectacular progress. It will be recalled that Browder explained Soviet industry's slow start by the influx of untrained peasants into the factories. This apparently did not prevent the peasants who remained on the farms from welcoming the collectivization of agriculture and using the new farm machinery with skill and enthusiasm. "The extreme modernity of Soviet industrial equipment" made Stakhanovism possible in agriculture as well as in factories and mines. "The primitive techniques of Tsarist days were replaced by modern mechanized farming on the most advanced level. . . . Agriculture was developed on a planned, rational basis, unlike capitalist agriculture where anarchic production, based only on the prospects of fast profits, is the universal rule." Because capitalist farming caused endemic rural poverty, American farmers "are increasingly eager to understand how the Soviet Union is solving the problem of agriculture through collectivization."[14] CP writers obliged, by publishing many informative accounts filled with statistics, which rank-and-file Party members used when talking to outsiders.

Anti-Soviet propagandists lied when they wrote that the authorities had forced unwilling peasants into the collectives, murdered thousands of peasants, and caused the worst manmade famine in history. The Hearst newspapers spread tales of starvation during the early 1930s, to boost sales and whip up hate toward the Soviet Union.[15] The truth was that "the preponderant majority of the peasantry streamed into the collective farms and defeated the furious organized resistance of the capitalist elements in the village—the kulaks." The Party's philosopher Howard Selsam said that the great privation that many people experienced, though "tragic," was a small price to pay for a future without famines. Future generations would acknowledge their debt to the collectivization that enabled the Soviet Union to grow food in abundance to satisfy "its civilian and military needs and made possible the 'scorched earth' policy and the vast guerrilla warfare against the Nazi invaders." M. J. Olgin's version of the anti-kulak campaign was less defensive:

The collectivization of the individual households meant the elimination of the kulak. He had to join, if he was at all admitted, and that meant to be shorn of all privileges. If he was a pernicious element his property was confiscated and he was sent to a distant collective farm. There remained no room for an exploiter in a collectivized village.

According to Betty Gannett, some officials had wanted to hurry up the rural revolution, but "under the sure leadership of Stalin, the principle of the voluntary character of the collective farm movement was firmly defended against those who would impose collectivization by coercion and force." She recalled that Stalin, in a 1930 article, had "castigated those who stood in the way of winning the peasantry for collectivization through persuasion, by convincing them of the superiority of large-scale production."[16]

As a result of collectivization, "Soviet agriculture was transformed into the most advanced agriculture of the entire world," wrote Gannett, and it is today (1953) "the most mechanized in the world, having at its disposal the most up-to-date machinery and scientific methods of farm cultivation. Grain production . . . has been solved once and for all." In 1940 another writer cited statistics to show that farm productivity had increased significantly since the pre-collective-farm days and added that such a tremendous rise in farm productivity was impossible under capitalism.[17]

Wishful thinking, rationalized by Party theory, is apparent in some of these quotations. The "fact" that, under capitalism, industry and agriculture could never match the achievements of the Soviet Union was true a priori, deduced from the theory. And wishful thinking produced the assertions that the Soviet Union's plans for the future were practically *faits accomplis*; theory said that failure was unthinkable. For example, a Party leader boasted—as though describing an achievement—that Soviet scientists in cooperation with the farmers had made possible

the epochal Fifteen-Year Plan which has been launched since the end of the war, whose vast scope is indicated by the recent announcement of the use of atomic energy to level mountains for the purpose of reversing the direction of two large Siberian rivers and converting an area greater in size than France from arid desert to fertile, productive land. Through such projects drought will be banished, the climate of large regions will be radically improved, and large, stable, crops will be assured in the years to come. Such are the unprecedented goals toward which Soviet science is moving.

Even that was not all. Soviet agrobiologists had the further "task of creating new, more productive forms of useful plants and animals, forms able to take the fullest advantage of the best possible conditions of development." They had already transformed "winter wheat into rye, a plant belonging to a different genus."[18]

Socialist man was becoming, and Communist man would be, the master of nature. Guided by the science of Marxism-Leninism, which accurately reflected the structure of reality, he would remold the entire world—geological, biological, psychological, and social—nearer to his heart's desire. His heart's desire itself reflected the laws governing all reality, for the new man's hopes and feelings also conformed to those laws now that he had sloughed off his age-old class conditioning.

THAT TRANSFORMATION of consciousness, which had already begun in Jimmy Higgins, had, of course, proceeded further in Soviet youth. They enjoyed economic security, productive labor, excellent free education and health care, recreation facilities, and long vacations. They could look forward to even better lives in the future, when they would participate fully in the building of communism. Party writers in the United States elaborated these themes throughout our period, especially during the Great Depression when, they reiterated, American youth had nothing to look forward to under capitalism.

The youth periodicals specialized in these messages aimed at young people. During the 1930s they often published matching articles: for example, "Starvation Hearing Shows Child Hunger/Same Conditions Exist All Over the United States among Workers' Children," next to "Children in U.S.S.R. Happiest in the World/Receive Good Food, Live in Most Modern Homes; Never Know Hunger or Want." Or (with matching photographs): "Negro child laborers picking peppers in Louisiana" next to "Young farm workers in the Soviet Union. Note the happy smile on the girl's face. She works, yet gets a chance to get an education, too. In the Soviet Union the young workers work 6 hours a day."[19]

Especially before the war, descriptions of Soviet youth's leisure-time activities often took the form of photographs and drawings, with appropriate captions. In 1932 a photo of "Soviet Young Workers on Their Vacation" showed one playing the balalaika; the caption said:

This photo was taken in a summer camp to which the Soviet working youth go on their annual paid vacation. Their carefree holiday spirit is a result of the fact that they know there is no fear of unemployment, hunger and boss terror under the dictatorship of the proletariat in the Soviet Union. In place of paid vacations, young workers in the United States get unemployment, wage cuts and a misery comparable to a living death as the crisis gets worse every month.

In 1935 a picture of five laughing young people in bathing suits was captioned: "Young Soviet workers troop to the beaches these days, building health and strength in the Workers Republic. Here is a group of young Leningrad workers, healthy and happy, relaxing from the building of Socialism." In the same year, a photograph purported to show that young Soviet workers were "horse-racing fans"; "40,000 worker-spectators recently rooted for their favorite nags at the All-Union Trotting Derby. The Derby, 'sport of kings,' is only enjoyed by socially elite millionaires and the better class of bootleggers in the U.S." Two years later, a set of four photographs showed sunbathers on a beach, young men playing rugby, couples dancing the fox-trot, and four young people with tennis rackets on their way to the courts. The caption with the last picture is " 'Whoopee, now for a fast set of tennis,' exclaims this foursome of agricultural workers vacationing in Yalta."[20] These documents, which pictured the nonworking life of Soviet youth as similar to that of rich young Americans, clearly aimed at inciting the readers' resentment of class distinctions in their own country.

A SIMILAR COMMENT applies to the Party's messages to American adults: the descriptions of Soviet life emphasized those "facts" best calculated to make the readers notice and resent the ugliness around them.

To the lonely person, it said, "under socialism the individual no longer has to make his way against a world of strangers. . . . Individuality is respected precisely through the community of interests of all men; the collective alone insures the actual, legal and moral existence of the individual." The present tense in that statement had a double meaning: the author was explaining both the essence of socialism and the Soviet Union as it then was. To the New York City commuter, Michael Gold described the magnificent Moscow subway, with its frequent trains, palatial stations, and courteous riders. When the Soviet workers entered the newly opened subway, they saw more than a train: "That express rushing out of the darkness of the tunnel was a locomotive of the future. An express of Socialism." To architects, Gold offered merited appreciation and vaster opportunities. Soviet architects were implementing a plan that in ten years would make Moscow the finest city on earth, "a magnificent garden city for free and equal humanity." To the American afraid of being robbed or assaulted (and perhaps to another reader who might end up in prison), Foster said:

the Soviet Union . . . is fast becoming a crimeless country. . . . Capitalism blames crime upon the individual, instead of upon the bad social conditions which produce it. . . . Socialist criminology . . . attacks the bad social conditions. . . . In the new Russian prisons . . . the prisoners have the right to marry and to live with their families; they are taught useful trades and are paid full union wages for their work; there are no guards or walls or bars; the discipline is organized entirely by the prisoners themselves. The prisoners are also allowed freely to visit their friends in other towns.

The lengths of the terms to be served are determined by the prisoners' committees, on the basis of the fitness of the given prisoners to resume their places in society. The whole terminology of crime, criminal, prison, etc., has been abandoned in such institutions. Upon release, a prisoner is not only able to make his own way in society but is welcomed.

To the neurotic or relative of a neurotic came the assurance that mental illness in the Soviet Union had already markedly decreased, owing to the "profound qualitative change in the social environment." To anyone who was unhappy, for any reason, Foster said:

Socialist man and woman are happy beings. . . . More than in any other country, the U.S.S.R. is the land of song, music, and laughter. All revolutionary peoples display a similar mass happiness. . . . Socialist men and women also possess new and more powerful incentives to work and live and enjoy. . . . Socialist woman and man are in harmony with their environment. . . . The Soviet people, for all their hardships, are a far happier and better balanced people mentally than those of the United States.

Added Olgin: the Soviet Union "shows all the oppressed and exploited what their life could be if the incubus of capitalist exploitation were removed."[21]

THIS CHAPTER began with an imaginary conversation among Party members in 1958, two years after they had been forced to admit that many of the bourgeois press's lies about the Soviet Union had been true and that many of the Party press's truths had been lies. Even in the Party's brief time scale for cultural and psychological change, 1958 was too soon for the admitted effects of Stalinism to have disappeared from industry, agriculture, health service, medicine, culture, and social patterns. Yet in that year, a top Party theoretician published a glowing survey of Soviet life, containing many statistics and other facts that pertained to conditions prevailing during Stalin's lifetime.[22] What is most remarkable about that essay—and others like it—is the total absence of the ghost of Stalin. The implication is that *his regime had had no effect whatever on the conditions described.*

What then had Stalinism meant? A true believer might have answered in either of two ways: "Despite Stalin's crimes, he did put the Soviet people on a forced march toward communism. It would have been better to go more slowly, but the Soviet Union *is* farther along than it would be if it had had a less severe regime." Or: "Socialism is inherently so democratic, progressive, and dynamic that even Stalin's crimes and errors could not push it off the track of history." Both those answers evade the questions posed near the beginning of this chapter. And they do not explain why comrades felt embarrassment when Stalin was mentioned. In fact, anyone who really believed either of those answers might willingly have read descriptions of the Stalinist[23] horrors and denounced the terror as vehemently as anyone else. Yet ex-Communists have said that few members have ever read the exposés.

Obviously, then, one last question remains to be asked: did the evidence, false or true, produce the comrades' image of the Soviet Union? or did their image of the Soviet Union originate in something else and make any and all evidence, false or true, mere propaganda material for the benefit of outsiders? The second alternative alone fits the facts.

But, it will be asked, was this true of that majority of Party members, including most true believers, who did take empirical evidence seriously enough to leave the Party after the Stalin "revelations"? In large part, yes. Before that shock, they had admitted only those "facts" that rationalized their feelings. But the sleep of the dreamer was rarely so deep as to exclude the real world altogether. Jimmy Higgins did live part of his life in the waking world, and, unlike those who stayed in the Party after 1958, he kept some wee part of his mind independent of the Party. That was why the leaders had to direct most of their propaganda at their own members, constantly reinforcing ideological conviction and repairing the mental wall separating Jimmy Higgins from the real world. Although it took the bulldozer of Khrushchev's speech and the uprisings in Eastern Europe to crash through the wall, those events proved that the wall could be breached—but only by facts of much greater significance than any or all of those that could have refuted the pseudofacts that we have sampled.[24]

The reason it took a bulldozer to enable facts to shatter ideological self-delusion was that the self-delusion had had nothing to do with facts. It arose out of revulsion against nearby reality—but reality as perceived, not as it was. Although Jimmy Higgins thought he was modeling the American future on the Soviet present, he was actually modeling the Soviet present on the American future. That is, he dreamed of a future utopia in which everything he saw, and thought he saw, around him had been turned upside down and inside out. And to prove that this sweeping revolution was no pipedream he had to believe that it had already happened somewhere else. (To someone living in the realm of wishful thinking, reversing the courses of rivers and creating a new man are as commonsensical as the invention of machines that read blueprints.) So, to summarize what we find if we look beneath Jimmy Higgins's conscious beliefs, we should reverse the two elements of this chapter's title; it will then the "the American future as the Soviet Union."

NOTES

1. Jessica Smith, "Where Dreams Come True," *CH* 1 (June, 1936); Tim Buck, "Journey into the Future," *PA* 33 (November, 1954). An example of the selective hatred I refer to was evoked by the suicide of Howard Rushmore in 1958. Rushmore had been a YCL and Party activist in his youth, had written for the Party and YCL press, and had organized, traveled, and lectured—and been beaten up—for the movement. Later he turned against the Party. According to the *New York Times*, April 1, 1958, he shot his estranged wife and then himself. In the April issue of *PA*, Herbert

Aptheker referred to the "degenerate who belatedly ended his own miserable life after adding the crime of murder to his long record." Rushmore killed two people, including himself; Stalin killed millions. To my knowledge, Aptheker has never written about Stalin in such vitriolic terms.

2. The Soviet satellites were depicted in the same way. See, e.g., a three-article series on Poland, by John Stuart, in *NM*, December 30, 1947, and January 6 and 13, 1948. The titles summarize the approach: "The Secret of Poland's Success," "Poland: New Land, New People," "Poland: How the United Front Works."

3. William Z. Foster, *Outline Political History of the Americas* (New York: IP, 1951), p. 607.

4. William Z. Foster, *Toward Soviet America* (New York: Coward-McCann, 1932), pp. 268, 317–18.

5. Earl Browder, "The Progress of Soviet Economy," *National Issues* 1 (April, 1939): 19, 21; William Z. Foster, *The Twilight of World Capitalism* (New York: IP, 1949), p. 132; Alexander Bittelman, "Where Is the 'Monthly Review' Going?" *PA* 30 (May, 1951): 40.

6. M. J. Olgin, "A Generation That Did Not Know Capitalism," *YW*, October 19, 1931, p. 5; Earl Browder, "A Glimpse at Soviet America," *NM*, July 9, 1935, p. 9.

7. William Z. Foster, "Malenkov at the Helm," *PA* 32 (April, 1953): 20.

8. Foster, *Toward Soviet America*, p. 140; Foster, *Twilight*, p. 104; The Editors, "Bulwark for Peace," *NF* 2 (Spring, 1949): 148.

9. Hyman Lumer, "The Achievements of Marxism-Leninism in the Field of Genetics," *PA* 29 (July, 1950): 51.

10. Foster, "Malenkov at the Helm," p. 21.

11. William Z. Foster, "The 'Managed Economy' of the U.S. (Pt. I)," *PA* 35 (July, 1956): 22; Foster, *Toward Soviet America*, pp. 72–74; Gil Green, "We're Not Lost," *CH* 2 (July, 1936): 5; "Earl Browder Answers Questions," *NM*, March 28, 1939, p. 8; Michael Gold, *Change the World!* (New York: IP, 1936), p. 198. Throughout his essay, entitled "Henry Ford's Inferno," Gold contrasted American and Soviet conditions, switching back and forth between the two types of factories. Like all the other writers, he assumed that the American conditions were permanent features of the capitalist "system."

12. "Stakhanovism" (editorial), *NM*, November 12, 1935, p. 3. See also "Along Came Stakhanov," *NM*, December 24, 1935, pp. 18–21; William Auer, "Soviet Culture in the Fight against Fascism," *COM* 20 (November, 1941): 993; "Irene," "Stakhanovism," *PO* 9 (February, 1936): 27–29; *Earl Browder on the Soviet Union* (New York: Workers Library, 1942), p. 36.

13. Arnold Goldman, "Red Magic," *SP* 2 (June, 1944): 26–27; *Browder on the Soviet Union*, p. 22. See also Frank Brewster and Mark Logan, "Automation: Abundance for Whom?" *PA* 34 (November, 1955): 31–42; Betty Gannett, "Towards a Society of Abundance," *PA* 32 (November, 1953): esp. 31–33.

14. Auer, "Soviet Culture," p. 993; Lumer, "Achievements of Marxism-Leninism in the Field of Genetics," p. 42; Anna Rochester, *Rulers of America* (New York: IP, 1936), p. 239.

15. "Hearst—Liar, Forger!" *YW*, February 26, 1935, p. 8; "Eat Your Words, Mr. Hearst!" *YW*, March 12, 1935, p. 8; and occasional articles later in that year, denouncing others who had reported on starvation and fear, and quoting visitors who

saw plenty of food and healthy peasants. It seems that Hearst had indeed misused photographs, as charged; for a convenient summary, see Eugene Lyons, *The Red Decade* (1941; New Rochelle, N.Y.: Arlington House, 1970), p. 118. In contrast, see Fred Beal, *Proletarian Journey: New England, Gastonia, Moscow* (New York: Hillman-Curl, 1937), Chap. 22, "Famine." Beal went to the Soviet Union as a true believer and returned disillusioned, and as a result he is not mentioned in Foster's history of the Party or Haywood's account of the Gastonia strike, in which he played an important role.

16. Betty Gannett, "Stalin: Architect of Socialism," *PA* 32 (April, 1953): 60 (for the first and last quotations in my text); Howard Selsam, *Socialism and Ethics* (New York: IP, 1943), p. 211; M. J. Olgin, "The Soviets on the Threshold of the Twentieth Year," *COM* 15 (November, 1936): 1017. The difference between Selsam's and Olgin's statements recalls the difference between Types I and II discussed in chapter three above. Olgin (Type I, the hater) took the brutality in stride because he felt no sympathy for the kulaks and therefore had nothing to excuse; Selsam (Type II, sincere lover of humanity) seems to have worried about the suffering and therefore had to justify it as historically necessary in order to end suffering once and for all. But neither Type I or Type II could accept sheer objectless sadism; hence the denials of the existence of the Gulag and of the facts about the anti-kulak campaign. As to Selsam's rationalizations: no one excused what the Nazis did on the theory that you can't make an omelet without breaking eggs; the observer's notion of what the ends were made all the difference, especially if the observer had such faith in the predictability of the consequences of social engineering as to be sure that the result would *be* an omelet.

17. Betty Gannett, "Towards a Society of Abundance," pp. 25, 26; Gannett, "Stalin: Architect of Socialism," p. 60; C. G. Lande, "Dynamic Changes in the Population of the Soviet Union," *COM* 19 (November, 1940): 1033.

18. Lumer (who had a Ph.D. in biology), "Achievements of Marxism-Leninism in the Field of Genetics," pp. 43–44. Joseph Gordon, "The Epic Advance of Soviet Agriculture," *PA* 30 (November, 1951): 22, also mentions the reversal of rivers and "the remaking of climate."

19. *YW*, May 23, 1932, p. 3, and November 27, 1930, p. 3. Virtually every issue of that periodical contained similar material.

20. *YW*, April 18, 1932, p. 3; "Summer in the Soviets," *YW*, July 16, 1935, p. 5; *YW*, August 20, 1935, p. 1; *CH* 3 (November, 1937): 22–23. It should not be inferred that this sort of thing typified all the contents of the youth periodicals. The *YW* in particular ran interminable, jargon-filled discourses on abstruse problems of theory, strategy and tactics, and organization. The later youth periodicals went to the opposite extreme and strove to be popular.

21. Charles Humboldt, "What Is Freedom?" *MM* 3 (May, 1950): 83, 84; Gold, *Change the World!*, pp. 133–35, 151 (see also Sidney Finkelstein, "Soviet Culture: A Reply to Slander," *MM* 3 [January, 1950]: 51–55, 57–62); Foster, *Toward Soviet America*, pp. 321–33 (see also Lester Cohen, "A Prison in Russia: Soviet Penal Colony: 2300 Prisoners, 3 Guards," *NM*, February 12, 1935, pp. 9–14); Albert Starr, "Psychosomatic Medicine," *NM* 6 (June, 1953): 19; Foster, *Twilight*, pp. 151–55; M. J. Olgin, "What Does Lenin Mean to Workers and Farmers of America Today?" *PO* 9 (January, 1936): 24.

To victims of racial, religious, and ethnic discrimination, the writers sent similar messages. See, e.g., *Browder on the Soviet Union*, p. 42; Joseph Clark, "Jewish Youth and the War," *CL* 1 (Summer, 1940): 27–36; Samuel Rosen, "Zionism and Bourgeois Nationalism," *PA* 32 (June, 1953): 45; Gold, *Change the World!*, pp. 56–58, 255; Selsam, *Socialism and Ethics*, p. 185; Harry Haywood, *Negro Liberation* (New York: IP, 1948), pp. 160–61; Foster, *Outline Political History*, pp. 40–41; Morris U. Schappes, "Problems of Jewish Culture," *MM* 3 (March, 1950): 27–29. One proof of the absence of anti-Semitism in socialist countries was the large number of Jews among the defendants in the Prague trial of 1953! They were leading members of Czech society, and what capitalist country had proportionally so many Jews in its ruling circles? An example of this ingenious argument is in A. B. Magil, "Wall Street, Zionism and Anti-Semitism," *MM* 6 (March, 1953): 14–15, 16. A particularly interesting document is Joshua Kunitz, "Jews in the Soviet Union," *NM*, August 28, 1934, pp. 19–21. After explaining how the Soviet regime was fostering Jewish culture, including schools that used Yiddish as the language of instruction, and that no religion was prohibited, he added: "It is quite true that the Hebrew language is prohibited by the Bolsheviks. But who in the U.S.S.R., except philologists, would now care to study this thoroughly obsolete tongue of the ancient Hebrews[?] The Jewish masses never knew Hebrew. They knew as much Hebrew as the average Catholic worker or peasant knows Latin." He did not explain why it was necessary to prohibit a language that only philologists were interested in studying.

22. Herbert Aptheker, "Americans View the Soviet Union (Part II)," *PA* 37 (December, 1958): 40–53.

23. This focus on Stalin's regime is required by the context; it should not be misinterpreted as denying the Soviet regime's tyranny before and since Stalin.

24. To deal with all the aspects of Soviet society described by means of pseudofacts, this chapter would have to be at least three times as long as it is. Among those I have not dealt with are women's status, health care, foreign policy, religious freedom, education, labor unions, elections for public office, and civil liberties. Also pertinent in a more complete survey would be depictions of the Eastern European satellites. The material presented here, however, should enable the reader to guess what the Party writers said on those subjects.

13

Soviet America and the Science
of Prophecy

THE TWO HALVES of the concept "the Soviet Union as the American future" were not quite synonymous: postrevolutionary America would surpass its model. On the eve of its socialist revolution the United States would have a far more advanced economy and society than the Russian Empire had in 1917, and it would benefit from recent technological progress. Another difference between the two countries was that the Party prophets themselves, or at worst their children, would lead the new regime. They would have been more than human if they had not (probably unconsciously) shaped their predictions by their dreams of how they themselves would wield power. Guided by an omnicompetent science, with the masses' enthusiastic support, unconstrained by political checks and balances, Party leaders could do anything they wished. Thus, when they contrasted the future with the present, they revealed their perceptions and evaluations of the present more fully than when they wrote only about the present. Their predictions of the postrevolutionary future were literally daydreams: "If I had the power to shatter this sorry scheme of things to bits and shape it nearer to my heart's desire, here's what I would do. . . ."

The predictions fall into two categories: first, assertions that the near future would bring more poverty to workers and farmers, worse oppression to minorities, and narrower restrictions of the civil liberties of the masses; and second, descriptions of how things would be after the revolution. The first category dwelt on those incidents and statistics that supported their predictions; those facts that did not, they ignored, reinterpreted, or explained away. The carefully selected "facts" constituted the essence of the social order. In the second category, the predictions of postrevolutionary America, the writers indulged their fancies even more freely than they could when writing about the Soviet Union; there were no facts to explain away, no need to hedge their bets.

Both types of predictions, and the way the writers handled the data to support them, rested on the three firm convictions mentioned in chapter two:

that socialism was good, that it was inevitable, and that the Soviet Union was the model socialist society. The single thought comprising these three elements shaped Jimmy Higgins's attitude toward the future. If the sub-rational ground of the predictions is not understood, the reader is likely to be puzzled by the contradiction between the tone of certainty and the flimsy evidence coupled with faulty logic. To Comrade Jimmy the evidence and logic seemed more than adequate. He could be perceptive in criticizing pre-dictions that were based on other philosophies, thus showing that he was aware of the pitfalls of prophecy: first, that one who extrapolated from the known to the unknown assumed that past trends would continue, and second, that the prophets' forecasts might rest on incomplete or wrong facts. When it came to his own predictions, however, he did not display this critical attitude, and the reason was his absolute faith in those three propositions—or rather, that single thought expressed in three ways—discussed in chapter two.

IF THE MASSES thought they had anything to lose but their chains, they would not be tempted by the postrevolutionary prophecies. Therefore, the writers must first prove that this sorry scheme of things would become worse and eventually intolerable. But this was more than just propaganda. The com-rades' own certainty that everything would get worse is the best evidence that feelings underlay and determined their belief in their "scientific" theory. Consider the implications of the opposite expectation. Any admission that the workers' living standards might rise, or that discrimination against mi-norities might diminish, or that radicals might propagandize freely on cam-puses, and so on, would have collided fatally with the true believers' revulsion against the American social order. Marx's prediction of ever-deepening im-poverishment of the masses[1] assured Party members that their expectations came not from their own feelings but from scientific generalization grounded on empirical data. Even without Marx's authority, they would have invented the theory themselves, for everything else depended on it. This is why they held onto immiseration theory for generations after everyone willing to face facts had abandoned it. As early as 1898, the German Marxist Eduard Bern-stein realized that the working class was not sinking into destitution. Once he and some other socialists dropped immiseration theory, others found they had to drop another and yet another Marxist tenet. By the late 1950s, during the greatest surge of prosperity reaching the largest proportion of the pop-ulation in history, even some Party members were beginning to question the theory, and several leaders were inventing new ways of construing it. Amer-ican workers' affluence, they explained, was temporary and limited to the most skilled, and it depended on the poverty of underdeveloped countries and the "superexploitation" of Negroes. This was not what Marx had meant, but it was the best they could come up with. Eventually, most radicals who needed to rationalize their hatred of American society abandoned immiseration theory altogether and discovered that the mass poverty caused by "the capitalist system" was spiritual. Enter Herbert Marcuse and the New Left. The Left's shift from a material to a spiritual emphasis is among the principal causes of the CP's demise.

Yet as late as 1952, here is Foster explaining why the American workers would soon turn to socialism: nowhere else, he said, are workers "so heavily exploited, for all their alleged 'high wages,' as they are in this country." This is what Marx called relative impoverishment; it inevitably causes overproduction, depressions, mass unemployment, poverty, and, in time, the breakdown of the capitalist System. This relative impoverishment brings absolute impoverishment, and capitalist Europe's mass destitution shows what is in store for workers here, unless they block "Wall Street's war-fascism plans" and move toward socialism.[2] In short, the tendency was inexorable, built into the System itself. Therefore, during each period of economic distress, Party writers predicted that conditions would never improve, and during each boom they predicted a worse crash than that of 1929. Except for that difference, the forecasts never changed.[3]

Even before Khrushchev's speech in 1956 freed Party members to question received doctrine, some of them had grown tired of these perennial predictions. One leading member had the temerity to deplore "the tendency to believe that each economic downturn constituted the onset of a crisis of the 1929 type."[4] But her comrades did not abandon their pessimism—actually optimism, from the Party's standpoint. The need for it overrode logic and consistency, as Foster proved when he argued in 1957 that the main cause of the Party's huge loss of members and morale was "the corroding effects of the long-continued upward swing of American imperialism"—which he had previously proved was impossible. World War II and postwar rebuilding, he added, had caused "an unprecedented industrial boom, and with relatively steady employment. Besides, the bourgeoisie has been compelled to improve economic conditions for large sections of the working class, wage increases were won fairly easily, etc. This situation has created powerful 'prosperity illusions' among the workers." In short, he both admitted the prosperity and called it an illusion; he admitted that the wage increases had come fairly easily and at the same time said that the bosses had been compelled to grant them. Those Party members who thought that the prosperity was real were "revisionists," whose influence he blamed on "the low theoretical level in the Party."[5] Jimmy Higgins, reading this article, understood that he must see through the surface prosperity and recognize the false flush of health on the face of a terminally ill patient. He accepted Foster's reasoning for the same reason as Foster did: he did not want the patient to recover.

"WITH THE EMERGENCE OF MONOPOLY CAPITAL," wrote a high Party official, "technological improvements, always limited by the degree to which they offer prospects of immediate profits, become still further suppressed to protect the huge vested interests of the trusts." When I was in the Party, comrades illustrated this suppression of technology by citing the patents for reusable matches and permanent light bulbs allegedly locked away in the vaults of the match and bulb manufacturers. These small-scale proofs of the iniquity of the profit system carried infinitely more weight than all the evidence of the opposite sort combined. When a new invention did come to market, the comrades forgot the match and the light bulb and predicted technological unemployment. The same doubtless applies to the improvements in the incandescent bulb, the phonograph record, and gasoline (the last, by mixing it with alcohol), all of which, a writer in a youth periodical in 1936 predicted, the capitalists would never permit on the market.[6]

For example, one writer prophesied that the mechanical cotton picker would spell "starvation for the masses now chained to cotton." Thousands of farm laborers and sharecroppers would lose their jobs and land, "huddle together in the rural areas of the South, pools of humanity stranded by capitalism," or drift into the southern cities and intensify the social and racial problems caused by the contradictions of capitalism. Another writer forecast that the invention of nylon would put hosiery workers out of their jobs. Nylon would hurt the American cotton-growing industry and bring disaster to Japan, which depended on silk exports. The writings on this theme never hinted that the new inventions might lower prices and thus expand the market, or that new jobs might replace the old. On the contrary, automation and new inventions would lead to depression, for "the ratio of effective demand relative to total production capacity is decreasing, and must, therefore, at a certain point give rise to relative overproduction and crisis." Contrariwise, "capitalism . . . can no longer step up production if it is to survive. Its direction is towards greater and greater scarcity. . . . Capitalism has entered a period of the relative stagnation of technology." "There is no more profit in discovery and invention. . . . In the period of capitalist decline," said *New Masses'* science writer in 1934, "there are no more prospects of inventions that would lead to the emergence of new industries and a new period of prosperity." If Jimmy Higgins felt perplexed by these mutually refuting statements, Foster assured him that the contradictions were those of capitalism.[7]

Having demonstrated the decay of the capitalist economy, the Party next had to prove that the political system was about to break apart. Predictions to this effect appeared throughout the Party's lifetime. The results of each election showed that the two-party system was cracking, a labor-based third party was about to form, and the CP would soon grow enormously in size and influence.[8]

The Party's repeated failure to induce the workers and their "natural allies" to leave the Democratic and Republican parties did not alter its determination to try again, or its certainty that the next try would succeed. In February, 1948, Foster wrote that "the Wallace movement . . . is the first stage of a far-reaching political realignment, the beginning of the formation of a great new national democratic coalition." The next month Herbert Aptheker italicized his prophecy that "*this third party movement is a permanent one.*" It signified, said another comrade four months before the election, "the beginning . . . of the historic breakaway from the classic two-party system of capitalist class rule in the U.S." Foster, writing four years after the Wallace fiasco, remained certain that the Party's tactic had been correct. Since its theoreticians had taken account of all the "objective" elements in the situation in terms of their theory, the only remaining variable had been the comrades' handling of their tactical problems in the course of their day-to-day work among nonbelievers. So Foster blamed the comrades. In the future, however, they would live up to their responsibilities, as objective conditions forced the masses more and more to turn to the Party for guidance. "The near future," he wrote, will show faster development of the American working class, which will make more advanced demands upon the ruling class; the workers will build a mass political party with a labor base, and the unions will acquire progressive leaders. Socialist thinking will spread, and a mass Communist Party will appear. All these changes are inevitable. "They will arrive upon the political scene . . . far sooner than the power-drunk capitalist ruling class now even dreams." And the CP will play a leading role; that is "in the very nature of things."[9]

The philosopher Harry K. Wells, writing during the Party's death throes, envisioned an even more glorious prospect: "We have a future of not a hundred-thousand member Party, but hundreds of thousands and millions. . . . The crucial struggles against imperialist war and for peace and against depression and for a land and a world of plenty, a socialist United States, and a socialist planet, are, historically speaking, immediately before us."[10] And why not? If the facts had warranted Foster's miscellaneous predictions and Aptheker's belief that the Progressive Party movement was permanent, then they entailed Wells's prediction of a multimillion-member Party.

Why did the comrades feel so sure of these prophecies, when all the visible facts pointed in the opposite direction? The answer may lie in the Party's theory that the "objective" conditions for socialism had existed in the United States for several generations and that only the "subjective" condition—the conversion of most workers and large numbers of their allies—remained to be fulfilled. A handful of Bolsheviks had led the revolution in a country much less "ripe" than the United States. (It is important to realize that every American comrade believed that the Russian masses had followed the Bolsheviks because they wanted what the Bolsheviks subsequently did, not because of the Party's promise to bring them peace, bread, and land.) But the more they blamed the subjective conditions, the more scope they gave to tradition, ideology, and the effects of bourgeois "concessions"; and in so doing they contradicted their belief in an almost one-to-one relationship between the material consequences of the general crisis of capitalism, on the one hand, and the masses' awakening, on the other. The more important the subjective factors were, the less determinate the future became and the less the comrades felt in control of the present and the future. Those Party writers who most strongly emphasized control over natural and social phenomena (the bourgeoisie's control now and the Party's control after the revolution) were also those who prophesied most confidently. The need to feel in control may, then, help us explain the fantastic yet confident predictions such as Wells's.

We shall take up this question of control again later, after we have examined it in another context: the prophecies about Soviet America. First we must survey the way the Party writers saw the circumstances that would lead straight to the revolution.

One reason for their optimism was the supposed *worldwide* crisis of capitalism. As that System weakened elsewhere, American capitalism would inexorably be pulled downward to its grave. This international perspective accounts for such forecasts as that by Foster in 1932, in a book on Soviet *America*, that "the proletarian revolution advances irresistibly in Germany. It is in the vain hope of defeating it that the employers are building up Fascism through the Social Fascists, the Bruening government and the Hitler movement." The international perspective also explains why Browder announced, three months before Germany violated the Nazi-Soviet Pact, that the popular notion that Hitler would attack the Soviet Union "comes to wreck upon the rock of a simple fact: . . . Hitler and the German High Command know it is less costly for them to fight all the rest of the world put together than to fight the Soviet Union. And not all Roosevelt's billions [of dollars spent to help the Allies] can change that hard fact, disagreeable as it may be for the bourgeoisie of all lands." The international character of capitalism assured Foster early in 1948 that "all the gold and bayonets of Wall Street cannot make stricken West-European capitalism strong and healthy again. Actually, the far more badly war-devastated nations of Central and Eastern Europe," that is, the Soviet Union's new satellites, "which have had little or no American 'help,' are recovering much more rapidly than the great 'aided' countries of Western Europe."[11]

Turning back to the American sector of world capitalism, we discover that "Truman's War Mobilization Program" in 1951 evoked predictions just like those that the Party made before June 22, 1941: "The conversion to a 'total' war economy will be presaged and accompanied by an increase in the material misery of the masses," especially for blacks, warned James E. Jackson. The Fair Deal programs will be scrapped, discrimination in education will increase, the railroads will intensify segregation of blacks in substandard cars, and new housing and hospital construction will stop.[12] Jackson here hinted at a theme common in Party writings though never expressed directly: its low estimate of the masses' ability to learn. Jackson's wishful thinking implied that nothing but unprecedented suffering and oppression could teach them. Party members, however, felt conditions to be intolerable already; that was why they had joined the Party. Yet if only a great increase in suffering could fulfill the "subjective" condition for the coming of the revolution, what was left of the Party's theory, repeated decade after decade, that its own agitation and propaganda, helping the workers to learn from their own experience, would suffice, inasmuch as the objective conditions had been intolerable all along? The worse the conditions had to be to rouse the masses, the more contemptible the masses were (although no Party member ever said so). That was why the Party had to keep predicting, and believing, that objective conditions would get worse and worse. But in each decade the Party felt certain that the people's deplorable patience would soon end; a nationwide upheaval impended in the not-too-distant future.

How far in the future? The answers varied. In 1952 Aptheker felt sure that it would take "the vast majority of the American people a great deal less time than" twenty-five years to see that the Communists were right. Browder, writing in 1941, foresaw that "this generation of the masses of America are going to bring our America to the flowering of socialism." Mike Gold, in his book *Change the World!* (1936), described the celebration of the sixty-seventh birthday of Art Young, the cartoonist, and hoped to see Young at age 107—that is, in 1973—"in a Soviet America" telling children stories about the "dark ages" of long-gone capitalism. In another essay in the same book, a similar setting occurs within thirty years of the time he was writing.[13]

The nature of the revolutionary event itself was not so certain. Sometimes the comrades foresaw civil war. No ruling class had ever given up its power without armed struggle, they said; and occasionally they quoted Marx's dictum: "Force is the midwife of every old society pregnant with a new one."[14] During the war they more often predicted an orderly vote by the majority of the electorate. After Browder's ouster, violence again became likely. When the Party leaders became defendants under the Smith Act a few years later, however, and in later years too, the writers explained that if violence occurred, it would be committed by the capitalists defying the expressed will of the people, whose counterviolence would be purely defensive.[15] This topic, which concerned a brief episode of little interest to the comrades, did not play a role in their daydreams of the future.[16]

More important was what the revolutionary authorities would do upon taking power. Foster described the new regime in great detail, and there is no reason to believe that his comrades ever disagreed with what he foresaw, except for a few minor predictions and the Russian terms he used, which later became unfashionable. He began this part of *Toward Soviet America* by saying that "our task is not to work out all the details of an American Soviet system, as that would exceed the scope of this book, but to trace out, upon the basis of actual experience to date, the general structure and workings of such a regime."[17] He then described the immediately postrevolutionary regime as though every feature of it existed in his mind's eye.

Soviets will be organized before the revolution; afterward, they will seize industrial plants and establish factory committees to run them. All of society will be organized into soviets; representation will be based on occupation, not location.

Citizenship is restricted to those who do useful work, capitalists, landlords, clericals [read: clergymen, monks, and nuns] and other non-producers being disfranchised. . . . The national Soviet government, with its capital in Chicago or some other great industrial center, will consist of a Soviet Congress, made up of local delegates and meeting annually, or as often as need be, to work out the general policies of the government. Between its meetings the government will be carried on by a broad Central Executive Committee, meeting every few months. This C.E.C. will elect a small Presidium and a Council of Commissars, made up of the heads of the various government departments, who will carry on the day-to-day work.

Courts will be "class-courts. . . . The mildness or severity of the repressive measures used by the workers to liquidate . . . [the capitalist class] politically will depend directly upon the character of the latter's resistance." This resistance will necessitate "the organized armed might of the workers, soldiers, local militia, etc. In the early stages of the revolution, even before the seizure of power, the workers will organize the Red Guard. Later on this loosely constructed body becomes developed into a firmly-knit, well-disciplined Red Army." Leading all these bodies will be the Party.

Under the dictatorship [of the proletariat] all the capitalist parties—Republican, Democratic, Progressive, Socialist, etc.—will be liquidated, the Communist party functioning alone as the Party of the toiling masses. Likewise, will be dissolved all other organizations that are political props of the bourgeois rule, including chambers of commerce, employers' associations, rotary clubs, American Legion, Y.M.C.A., and such fraternal orders as the Masons, Odd Fellows, Elks, Knights of Columbus, etc.[18]

All factories will reopen, Foster continued. This statement was only one of several that imply that the revolution would come before the Great Depression had ended, or that that depression would continue for an indefinite period. An official Party statement made the same assumption:

The first acts of such a revolutionary workers' government would be to open up the warehouses and distribute among all the working people the enormous unused surplus stores of food and clothing. . . . Such a government would immediately provide an endless flow of commodities to replace the stores thus used up by opening up all the factories, mills and mines, and giving every person a job at constantly increasing wages.

In Foster's version: production will resume at once,

to relieve the impoverished workers and farmers. The great stores of necessities, now piled up and unsaleable [*sic*], will be released to the masses. The unemployed will be fed, housed and given work. Pending any delay in putting the industries into full operation, the unemployed will be paid social insurance on the basis of full wages.

The Soviet government will comply with all "the immediate demands that the workers are now demanding of capitalism." There will be a vast new housing program. The government will take possession of all buildings. The cars and yachts of the rich will go to the workers' organizations. Slum housing will be razed and new homes built. Farmers' debts will be canceled and farm rent abolished. Poor farmers will receive land, seed, fertilizer, machinery, and instruction. On this question of farm policy, the Party document quoted above agreed with Foster: the government will "secure the farmers the possession of their land ... [,] make it possible for the farming population to unite their forces in a cooperative Socialist agriculture, and thus bring to the farming population all of the advantages of modern civilization," and thereby vastly increase farm productivity. Foster conceded that private property would probably survive

in small farms, in petty industry and in trade. But this will be only temporary. With the consolidation and growth of Socialism and the general spread of well-being all the land will eventually and without serious difficulty be nationalized, and all industry will be concentrated into the Socialist Soviet economy.[19]

Industry and mass consumption, he went on, will expand enormously, owing to planning, the elimination of useless occupations and middlemen, government bureaucrats, "clericals," advertising men, lawyers, traveling salesmen, and so forth. Each type of industry and economic function will be consolidated under a single authority, all "headed by a body analogous to the Supreme Economic Council of the U.S.S.R." The whole will constitute "a great industrial machine, each cog of which fits into and works harmoniously with the rest." Unions will take over educational, social, and health functions. "The revolutionary unions of the Trade Union Unity League [a Party front that existed between 1929 and 1935] are the nucleus of the eventual great labor organizations of Soviet America. Whatever remnants of the present A. F. of L. may exist at the time of the revolution will be merged into the series of industrial unions based on all-inclusive factory committees."[20]

"The establishment of an American Soviet government will mark the birth of real democracy in the United States." Enough has been quoted so far to raise the question of what "real democracy" meant to Foster. Although, as we saw above, he would allow small farmers to own land for a time, sixteen pages later he implied just the opposite: private property has "no more place on Soviet farms than in the factories. An immediate and fundamental problem to confront the American Soviet government, therefore, will be to carry through the Socialist collectivization of the land. This, for the poor and middle farmers, will be done upon a voluntary basis."[21] The word "voluntary" did not fit easily into Foster's thinking, and it had a special meaning in this passage. Many things he wrote show that he did not envision millions of people freely debating alternatives, making up their minds, and then accepting the majority's wishes. Rather, the prediction that the poor farmers would voluntarily join collective farms meant merely that Foster's science enabled him to predict what the people would think and want immediately after taking power—for otherwise they would not have made the revolution— as surely as he could predict what the Party would do. Freedom, "the recognition of necessity" (according to Party theory), meant freedom to choose right. A wrong choice was by definition unfree—that is, involuntary—and unscientific, hence unworthy of respect. The masses would support the revolution when and because they had learned to follow the Party. Only in that sense would the farmers' choice to collectivize be "voluntary."

ALL THE ABOVE was merely prelude—not even prelude, but the tuning-up of the orchestra that would later play the great symphony of socialism in America. Discordant notes had to be corrected, uncooperative players fired, the various instrumental groups taught to play in perfect coordination to the beat of the conductor's baton. And, as Foster proved by writing *Toward Soviet America*, the score would exist long before the players arrived on stage.

There is a crucial difference between the forecasts of the immediately postrevolutionary period and those of the more distant future. The former told the reader what the Party would do to the enemy, how it would organize the masses, and what institutions it would set up. The latter described the permanent changes that would result from those merely preparatory actions. These forecasts described the time that Engels called the realm of freedom.[22] But that was also the time when the Party would have untrammeled power to translate its most extravagant daydreams into real life. In these two, not-quite-consistent perspectives lies the significance of the more imaginative prophecies.

Foster gave his readers a glimpse of the world destined to emerge from the transitional state:

The proletarian revolution is the most profound of all revolutions in history. . . . The overthrow of capitalism and the development of Communism will bring about the immediate or eventual solution of many great social problems. Some of these originate in capitalism, and others have plagued the human race for scores of centuries. Among them are war, religious superstition, prostitution, famine, pestilence, crime, poverty, alcoholism, unemployment, illiteracy, race and national chauvinism, the suppression of women, and every form of slavery and exploitation of one class by another. Already in the Soviet Union, with the revolution still in its initial stages, the forces are distinctly to be seen at work that will eventually liquidate these handicaps to the happiness and progress of the human race. But, of course, only a system of developed world Communism can fully uproot and destroy all these evils.

The system, said Foster, would "develop a culture based upon science and the welfare of the people as a whole, in place of the capitalist-inspired drivel, superstition, and intellectual obscurantism of today."[23] (The last two terms were Party jargon for religion and non-Marxist philosophy.)

On the level of belief, the basic evil to be extirpated was religion. "For after seventy centuries of religious discipline, including twenty centuries of Christian teaching, man is still a wolf to his fellow man! . . . Where religions have failed, science comes forward to achieve a human civilization worthy of the name," said a French Communist whose pamphlet *Science and Religion* was published in English in 1946. Foster agreed: "Not Christianity but Communism will bring peace on earth." It will also bring benefits to scientists, added J. B. S. Haldane, British biologist and Communist. To professionals who wanted to know what their position would be after the revolution, he said, "if you are good at your job you would have more power and more responsibility than you have now." In the Soviet Union, scientists "are very important people." According to the American CP's official program, socialism would "utilize to the fullest the immense scientific and technical know-how of the American people, including atomic energy." An American scientist foresaw "a condition in which both natural and social forces are brought under full control. This condition is desirable since it will allow every human being to satisfy his needs rationally and harmoniously."[24]

How would the American socialist regime use this control? In 1946, a writer in *New Masses* portrayed science as bursting with possibilities that the revolution would set free:

Today we face a period of invention and expansion that makes the last century look like the Pleistocene Age. Except that the bourgeoisie is regressive; so we are not going forward, except in the bomb department.

Spokesmen for the cartels and trusts tell us that we are fifty, seventy-five, maybe a hundred years away from commercial application of atomic energy. Which as far as they are concerned means never. But if they used the same amount of concentration for the peaceful uses of atomic energy as they do for war, then, brother, what wouldn't be possible? We could have leisure, culture, a life-span in which the hundred-year-old geezer would be a commonplace, and he wouldn't be a geezer. Some scientists have speculated that if enough atom bombs were exploded at a certain height above the polar ice cap, all the ice would melt, the climate of the world would be affected, and we could live a life of unwintered ease. I do not have the exact statistics, but something like the atomic equivalent of an average lump of coal could heat twenty blocks of apartment houses for two or is it three years, or provide enough fuel to power all the transatlantic boats for an unbelievable length of time. . . . Industrially backward countries like India and China would not have to stumble through the coal and iron age to become self-sufficient. In a few years, all countries of the world would enjoy a wealth that would make the present affluence of the United States look like the contents of a bindle-stiff's bundle. . . . Socialism, like food to a hungry man, becomes something to think about, because only when the means of production get to be owned in common will we have the full flourishing of the atomic age.

By now, of course, even enthusiasts of that writer's type know that the melting of the polar ice cap would bring not a life of unwintered ease but death to the billions who live in coastal lowlands. Early in this century Socialist Party prophets foresaw the draining of all wetlands, unaware of the ecological disasters that would ensue. The appropriate comment on these projects concerns not just the prophets' ignorance but the untrammeled power that their *political programs* would give them to impose their daydreams on their human as well as nonhuman materials. We may recall Foster's statement that the details of the American socialist society were beyond the scope of his book. He did not say that they were beyond the scope of his ability to predict. In fact, he considered himself qualified to decide on measures as sweeping, *and as irreversible in their effects*, as those that the *New Masses* writer imagined. "Under socialism, society will literally remodel the planet to suit its own needs and with a boldness of plan impossible to disorganized, anarchistic, self-seeking capitalism. Many examples of this elementary [N.B.!] trend of socialism are already beginning to shape up in the U.S.S.R."[25]

Another sign that the Party leaders had all the knowledge they needed was Foster's advocacy of a project that Nazi Germany but not the Soviet Union had undertaken—eugenics. Since Foster never advocated anything that he thought the Soviet Party would frown on, he doubtless believed that this pet project of his lay in the Soviet Union's future, too. (I call it a pet project because he proposed it repeatedly.) On this point most of Foster's comrades unquestionably disagreed with him, especially after World War II, although his enormous prestige saved him from open criticism.[26] Both Foster's eugenicism and other comrades' anti-eugenicism were, however, consistent with basic tenets that they all shared. Foster's age helps explain this part of his vision of the future. Born in 1881, he never outgrew certain attitudes and beliefs that were common in the late nineteenth and early twentieth centuries. Rudolph J. Vecoli has pointed out that many reformers in the Progressive Era "were convinced of the efficacy of eugenic remedies for certain social problems" and that sterilization laws, "the ultimate weapon in the arsenal of the eugenists," were passed in those states in which Progressives enjoyed the most political power. Wisconsin Socialists were split on the question; some called eugenics a pseudoscience, but "of the five Social Democrats in the legislature, four voted in favor of the sterilization bill." Eugenicists and Progressives shared a faith in "science" as means to "humanitarian ends," a "collectivist" outlook, and a belief that "*laissez faire* would result in disaster and that the interests of the individual must be subordinate to the welfare of society. Both were willing to restrict personal liberty in behalf of the corporate good, and both turned to the State as the instrument of reform."[27] This was exactly Foster's reasoning.

Foster, writing in 1949, thought "the biggest of all tasks" in this area was "to improve the human species itself in an evolutionary sense. . . . Capitalism is actually degenerating our species by its reckless violation of the laws of natural selection." War and factory exploitation killed the best young men and stunted the growth of workers.

Socialism will reverse these harmful effects of capitalism upon the welfare of our species and will start the latter upon an upward course of development. . . . To what extent a part will be played by eugenics, by controlling the endocrine glands, and especially by the creation of favorable environmental factors, as Lysenko maintains, or by a combination of all three of these methods, I am neither a biologist nor a geneticist to pass an opinion on. The vital matter of the evolution of mankind is not one that can any longer be left to chance, especially as capitalist society is now having such a negative effect on the development of the species. The law of natural selection, which built the marvelous complexities of plant and animal species, no longer can work spontaneously. Now the evolution of the human species must be done artificially, by the conscious action of man himself.

"Chance," of course, meant the free decisions of men and women; therefore, "the conscious action of man himself" two sentences later had to mean the conscious action of only some men. The date of the above passage is significant: 1949 was more than a decade after the Party had repudiated Foster's *Toward Soviet America*, which contained a passage expressing the same thoughts, though more briefly.[28]

All the comrades wanted a new human race, but most of them assumed that environmental changes would suffice to produce it. Human nature, like science and technology, had merely to be freed from capitalist impediments. Browder put the theory this way in 1935: "The class structure of society is designed to prevent the superior abilities and intelligence existing among the masses of the exploited from finding their normal expression, development, and resulting influence upon the course of social development. A socialist society will release all these unequal abilities from *class restrictions*, allowing them free development, entirely upon the basis of merit." Browder's environmental determinism was unquestionably sincere; it is not so certain that he really believed in innately unequal abilities. In that article, the third in a series explaining communism, he was speaking to outsiders, one of whom had asked how the Party reconciled innate inequality with its vision of a classless society. In his tenth article Browder said that the Soviet Union had already given the world a glimpse of "the entirely new human race" that socialism creates. Freeing man from his woeful heritage of oppression, it "remakes man, molding him in the heat of socialist labor into the new social being."[29]

Another Party writer who described the new man of the future in ideological and psychological terms was the philosopher Howard Selsam. He prophesied that "individual men and women will naturally through their understanding of themselves and society perform the labor they are best fitted for." They will want to do what they ought to do. Thomas More, he explained, had correctly foreseen the character traits of communist man, but the productive forces in the sixteenth century were too primitive to allow his Utopia to come true. Unlike More, he added, Marx and Engels did not make a blueprint; they presented "communism as the inevitable consequence of a socialist order and as the precondition for the further development of a man's mastery over himself and external nature." It is true that Moses, Jesus, Confucius, Aristotle, Epicurus, Spinoza, Thomas Aquinas, and More all taught man to lead a rational life, control his passions, develop his capacities, and life a peaceful and harmonious life. But all of them were, "naturally, limited by their place and time." Only now has their "vision of a rational order of society" become materially and scientifically possible, and inevitable.[30] It is Communism. Selsam's reference to the limitations of those eight teachers obliges us to interpret very narrowly his professed inability to draw up a blueprint. He doubtless expected future thinkers to look back upon *him* as limited by *his* place and time. But he and his comrades who, unlike Foster, did not draw up blueprints already knew everything important about Communism—not the timing or the details but its essential characteristics. For the historical epoch that produced all the moral teachers from Moses to the latest bourgeois philosophers constituted one historical unit defined by class division. As *The Communist Manifesto* said: "The history of all hitherto existing society"—after the first class division, that is—"is the history of class struggles." The transition to Communism would inaugurate truly human history; for the first time all reality would become subject to the scientific control of man. It was already *intellectually* controllable by Marxist-Leninists.

THE PROMISE of intellectual control of reality, here and now, constituted the basic appeal of Marxism-Leninism and its embodiment, the highly disciplined Communist Party. No matter how many predictions turned out wrong, nothing could weaken the comrades' certainty that a master of their science could foretell the future. Obviously, then, they felt more certain of that tenet than of all the predictions combined—except for the coming of Communism, which was actually the same belief. Even when the comrades' special universe shattered into fragments, in mid–1956, one of them blamed all the wrong predictions on the comrades' having "departed from Marxist method."[31] Previously, a member must not doubt the prophecies, because they had been based on Marxism; now, every member must denounce the errors, because they had *not* been based on Marxism. The comrades therefore had to accept the blame; they had either misperceived the facts (although only a Marxist could perceive the facts accurately) or misapplied the science.

Marxism, wrote Herbert Aptheker, "passes the ultimate test of science— accuracy of prediction, and significance for the future." The chairman of the Party in Los Angeles county used almost the same words: "Marxism possesses the supreme objective criterion of every true science, that is: the power of prediction."[32] Both writers referred to Marxism, not Marxists. In this way, the science of Marxism would remain true even if every prediction made in its name were wrong. But as chapter five showed, the Party's institutional and power needs required that the predictions made by the topmost authorities never be wrong; moreover, those men proved that Marxism used correctly did make a person infallible. Here is how an author in *Pravda*, whose essay appeared in *The Communist* in 1940, tied all these threads together and presented Stalin as a model for Jimmy Higgins to emulate:

Fundamental to science is the task of predicting the future on the basis of the study of the past and present. Such prediction is a necessary condition for action that will change the world. . . . The theory of Marxism-Leninism is invincible because it makes possible the penetration into the very depths of the historical process, and the perception of the laws of its development *to the very end*. . . . Comrade Stalin studies historical events all-sidedly, taking into account all inter-connections and media, and penetrating into the deepest reasons for these events. He always examines a subject in terms of its development, knowing how to study any phenomenon *in embryo*, seeing the direction and manner of its growth. To Comrade Stalin belongs the remarkable statement: that in order to guide, it is necessary to foresee. The most complicated intertwining of historical events, the most ramified net of social phenomena unfold vividly under the rays of the Stalinist analysis.[33] (Italics added.)

The reason the science of Marxism possesses this power is that it is grounded solidly on reality, which is wholly material and lawful. Reason obeys the same laws. Therefore, "science and reason are the only sources of human knowledge and . . . there are no problems which they will not some day be able to solve!"[34] So a master of the "Marxist scientific method" need not "proceed by guess work, by trial and error, by improvisation; one can proceed by prediction, planning and projecting." Pragmatists, who advocated the trial-and-error method, therefore incurred the wrath of Party theorists. Reviewing Browder's *Communism in the United States*, Robert Minor applauded a passage denouncing Sidney Hook, the pragmatist philosopher and socialist, and then quoted Browder's alternative:

"you cannot control the future if your approach to the future is that it is impossible to know what is the truth until after the future has become the past. Those who are going to control the future must know what is the truth before the event, before it happens, and by knowing it, determine what is going to happen and see that it does happen."[35]

Wishful thinking could hardly have found better expression, for as Jules Monnerot justly observes, "a mission can only be proved after the event," and therefore the affirmation of the proletariat's mission is an act of faith.[36] What has to be explained is the need for the faith. I suggest the answer lies in the believer's feeling that he lived in a world dominated by menacing powers and forces beyond his control. He needed to understand, "unmask," and destroy them. The only way he could do this and be sure that he would never again lose his grip would be to substitute his own (the Party's, the proletariat's) control for that of the present powers—in short, to "change the world" to externalize his daydream as he had externalized his nightmare.

Intellectual control came first, and this explains all the inevitabilities that filled the Party's literature. Belief in inevitable outcomes is really belief in the infallibility of the theory that predicts them. Some examples (italics added): "A correct analysis of the development of capitalism . . . *inevitably* leads to the conclusion that capitalism must be abolished, and that the proletariat *must inevitably* be victorious." And: "*It is, after all, known* that the future of nations lies in the creation of Socialism. . . . That in the end both great and small nations will go over to Socialism *there can be no doubt*, because that is historically *inevitable*." And: "Marxism is the scientific world-view of the working class, of the most revolutionary class in history, *destined* to abolish capitalism and all exploitation of man by man, and to erect the communist society." And: "Marxists . . . have complete confidence in the *inevitable* victory on a world scale of dialectical materialism, the philosophic foundation of the Marxist world outlook which will arm the working class with the knowledge to lead all humanity to become master of its fate in a world at last free."[37] The authors (and Jimmy Higgins) did not realize that all those statements were tautological. But that is the nature of wishful thinking: when a person confuses his wishes with objective reality, he believes that his deductions from his own definitions are inductions from empirical evidence. In short, the true believer believed in infallible Marxism because he wanted Communism to come, and he believed Communism inevitable because he wanted to possess the infallible science that predicted it. These two beliefs were really one belief—and one wish.

But doesn't this control-of-reality theme contradict the orthodox Marxist vision of an anarchic future, the expectation that the state would "wither away" and the government of men would give way to the administration of things? I do not think so. All Party writers professed to believe in these prophecies, but some probably did so only because Engels had made them.[38] Some of these authors, when writing on other subjects, imply a wholly different preference. They all agreed on the need for strong Party leadership of the entire society during the *socialist* (that is, early) stage, but for some, strong rule seemed to hold an attraction quite apart from the end it ostensibly served.

The dates of the documents help us decide which writings expressed genuine conviction. Prophecies of a future characterized by spontaneity and individuation appear only during the popular-front period in the 1930s and again during the late 1940s and 1950s, when the Party was desperately trying to appear civil-libertarian. For example. Browder in 1935 ridiculed the "bogey-man" picture of Soviet America as a regimented society. The revolution, on the contrary, will end the poverty that has imposed uniformity and will permit "the full unfolding . . . of individuality raised to the nth power." Twenty-one years later we learn that the civil liberties of antisocialists will not be curtailed. Although a "socialist society is necessarily led by the vanguard party of the working class, the party of Marxism-Leninism," this does not necessarily mean "one-party rule" or the "non-existence of dissenting or opposition parties." The latter will be free to operate provided they do not try "to overthrow the government by force and violence." Those other parties and groups will have access to "the mass media." "There will be no 'administrative imposition' of cultural standards in a socialist America." Another writer, in 1950, looking even farther ahead, predicted that after socialism has succeeded in "changing human nature," it will no longer need the state or laws, "and men may someday find it strange that we should ever have needed edicts to govern our conduct."[39]

That last statement, of course, alters the ostensible meaning of the others. Individuality was permissible only after human nature had been deliberately engineered to insure that the freedom would take forms approved by Marxists now. The author of the foregoing denial that the government would direct culture by administrative measures also wrote, in the same passage, that the media "will be subject, we think, to the decisions of public bodies expressing the will of the vast majority of the people." He did not mention minority rights. Furthermore, since "of course, cultures reflect their social bases, there will develop socialist standards out of the people's needs and not out of any 'administrative imposition.' . . . Under Socialism the people will seek and require higher standards than are permitted today." For example, "racist propaganda should be outlawed now; there is no need to wait for a Socialist America for that. This would no more challenge the First Amendment than do libel laws." One wonders how dissenting parties would fare, inasmuch as they would certainly advocate policies that "the vast majority of the people," speaking through their vanguard party, would consider unworthy of First Amendment protection. If the people are to demand higher standards of culture, they will surely demand higher standards of politics and social policy; what then of the assurance that dissenters would remain unmolested even if they restricted their activity to talk? If my own recollections of rank-and-file thinking during the mid–1950s apply to most Party members, few took these professions of concern for civil liberties seriously; the members knew that the official statements were meant to mollify liberals (many of whom also drew the line between racist propaganda, which could be outlawed, and other speech).

These statements were, in any event, atypical. But perhaps the most uncharacteristic assertion that ever issued from a Communist leader's pen was Browder's, that "Communists unconditionally approve of" Jefferson's belief that government was "a necessary evil at best."[40] "Necessary evil" was a dangerous phrase for admirers of the Soviet Union to use, and Party writers did not use it or anything like it in periods when they could openly express their real attitude toward power.

American entrance into the war gave them that opportunity. Now we find repeated calls for a coercive authority that went far beyond the needs of the war effort. The YCL's magazine, for example, called for "total mobilization and . . . the productive harnessing of every man, woman and child," for "a centralized war economy under administrative control," for the mobilizing of "all the workers, the labor movement, the youth generally for the legislative and political fight for a planned centralized war economy under administrative control," for an atmosphere "in which . . . no worker will resent the speed-up of the job or feel that it is against his interests," for "the establishment of a *centralized economic administration* . . . with full power as to the allocation of men and materials, as advocated by Earl Browder," and so on, repeating the phrase "centralized war economy" over and over.[41] The Party knew all about centralized government, total mobilization, planning, administrative control (which meant beyond the control of Congress and therefore of the voters), and the "harnessing" of citizens. It thus felt qualified to offer its advice to an administration that seemed to think a somewhat less total policy could do the job. It is hard to escape the inference that the job at hand was not all that the writers had in mind. *All their justifications for these measures applied to their own postrevolutionary government*—as well as to the Soviet Union in peacetime. If speedup served the workers' interest in 1942–1943 (to enable the United States to save the Soviet Union), it would serve their interest after the revolution; and exactly the same is true of every other policy advocated in the above quotations.

The basic difference between the prerevolutionary, peacetime American government and the postrevolutionary socialist government consisted in the classes of which they were the dictatorships. The early New Deal's lesser enhancements of federal authority had evoked cries of "Fascist!" from the Party, because the government was the dictatorship of the bourgeoisie. After the revolution, the working class and its allies would rule. "Communism," explained Browder, "will and can be nothing but what the majority of the people make of it, and if we cannot trust the people then all talk of human liberty has become so much hypocrisy."[42] Yet since the government would be the dictatorship of the proletariat, its uses were predictable (within broad limits). So Comrade Jimmy had a fair idea of what the majority, guided by their Marxist-Leninist vanguard party, would do with their freedom. Browder promised him that the society and the individual would be "unified." An editorial in *New Foundations* spelled out what this meant: "Under socialism, all human activity is consciously and collectively directed towards the goal of plenty for all. In such a society, our aspirations of [sic] security, peace, freedom will . . . be realized through the collective activity of all the people." After the state has withered away, said Foster, "proletarian discipline and solidarity" will suffice to keep people in line. "A Communist world will be a unified, organized world." Indeed, "democratic" in such documents seems to have meant "correct" and "involving the masses." For example, Foster, after calling for a long series of draconian edicts during the war, including "the cleansing from the radio of such defeatist types as" H. V. Kaltenborn and Boake Carter (radio commentators) and Norman Thomas, "the complete suppression of the fascist press and the public condemnation of the defeatist Hearst, Patterson, McCormick, and Scripps-Howard newspapers," "a careful and thoroughgoing check-up of saboteurs in industry," and "the creation of a broad network of local committees to organize the people for war work," added that these measures "need not, however, be anti-democratic in their effects." This odd meaning of "democratic" appears as well in his assertion that "the Soviet political system rests upon broad, democratic mass organizations of the people, formed for every conceivable purpose: economic, political, military, cultural, etc." Forecasts of Soviet America can be inferred from his descriptions of the Soviet Union's " 'comradely courts' in the factories, which give praise or blame to competent or neglectful workers," and of the Soviet trade unions, which "operate on a scale and with an authority quite unknown in any other country."[43]

To SUM UP: "free" and "democratic" did not conflict with "controlled," "unified," and "predictable." The state must not wither away until the rulers of Soviet America had created the new man—a human being as much their artifact as were the technological inventions and reshaped landscape. Until then, they must wield absolute control; in effect, they would still be wielding control after the state had withered away, and the new man would behave as they had programmed him to do—or, in Foster's atypical version, as he had been eugenically bred to do.

It is not too farfetched to surmise that the true believers' quarrel with the world was, at bottom, not only that it was unjust but also that it was not of their own making. If they pushed it, it did not yield but pushed back. The appeal of the Soviet Union lay not merely in its justice, prosperity, freedom, and democracy, but also in its being an artifact of the Marxist-Leninist mind blessed with total freedom to bring external reality into conformity with its wishes. Reality was no longer something "out there," running along its own track and *therefore* hostile toward oneself. It was under control, predictable. It held no surprises in store, to force one to stay on the alert and apprehensive.

What a feeling of power and freedom one could gain if one knew that one *could* reverse the rivers, level mountains, transform wheat into rye! Comrade Jimmy quarreled with reality not because the rivers ran the wrong way or because the polar ice caps should not exist, but because the world of nature had resulted from mindless cause-effect sequences. They must be infused with his own consciousness, producing a humanized "nature" wholly subject to the will of the dialectical materialist. The same observation applies to society. Many of the Party writers who raged at submission to oppression, whether it was present or not, seem to have been enraged at submission per se, at people's acceptance of reality as it was, at their lack of the urge to take control over every aspect of their lives by calling into question custom and tradition.[44] In short, the daydream could not tolerate a world it had not created.[45] If this explanation is true, it suggests how we may reconcile the two images of the Communist future: of total control and of stateless freedom. The specific characteristics of the world after it had been remolded nearer to the hearts' desire of the dreamers carried far less weight than the fact that they had molded it. Their hearts' desire had become the external reality; inner and outer realities now mirrored each other, manifesting that "unified" state yearned for in some of the quotations above. The revolution must come, so that nothing could bar their total freedom to create their Eden.[46] In the meantime, the Party sheltered these comrades from the unrenovated world. The Party's intellectual control (its omnicompetent theory) and systematized style of living (its discipline) buffered its members from the randomness and unpredictability of the world outside.

NOTES

1. Karl Marx, *Capital* 1 (New York: IP, 1947, identical to the 1889 edition): 660–61; Marx and Engels, *The Communist Manifesto* (New York: IP, 1932), p. 21.

2. William Z. Foster, *History of the Communist Party of the United States* (New York: IP, 1952), pp. 545–47. See also Alexander Bittelman, "Where Is the 'Monthly Review' Going?" *PA* 30 (May, 1951): 39; Albert Prago, "Sweezy's Theory of Capitalist Development," section entitled "The General Law of Accumulation and the Tendency to Absolute Impoverishment," *NF* 1 (Spring, 1948): 119–22 (a polemic against a book by Paul Sweezy, one of *Monthly Review's* editors); Hyman Lumer, "Strachey's 'Contemporary Capitalism,' " *PA* 35 (November, 1956): 25–30; William Z. Foster, "Karl Marx and Mass Impoverishment," ibid., pp. 33–42.

3. See, e.g., "Review of the Month," *COM* 9 (July, 1930): 580; C. Smith, "The Growing Political Significance of Organizational Work in the Present Situation," *COM* 11 (March, 1932): 240–41; "The Present Situation and the Tasks of the Communist Party of the U.S.A.: Resolution of the Eighth National Convention . . . ," *COM* 13 (May, 1934): 453–54; Bruce Minton and John Stuart, *The Fat Years and the Lean* (New York: IP, 1940), p. 184; Alexander Bittelman, "How Shall We Fight for Full Employment?" *PA* 25 (January, 1946): 57–58; Ralph J. Peters, "Depression Is a Horrid Word," *NM*, December 10, 1946, pp. 3–6; William Z. Foster, *The Twilight of World Capitalism* (New York: IP, 1949), pp. 33, 64; Alexander Bittelman, "Wall Street's War Preparations and the People's Living Standards," *PA* 29 (October, 1950): 58; National Committee, CPUSA, "The American Way to Jobs, Peace, Democracy (Draft Program of the Communist Party)," *PA* 33 (April, 1954): 4. Terminology,

however, did change. In the mid–1930s the postrevolutionary United States stopped being called Soviet America, Soviet U.S., the United States of Soviet America, etc., all of which names appear commonly up to that time.

4. Celeste Strack, "Concerning 'Method in Political Economy,' " *PA* 35 (September, 1956): 41. She was here quoting her own article, published under the pseudonym Mary Norris, in the June, 1955, issue, and she later criticized that article and three others of hers for not going far enough.

5. See William Z. Foster, "The Party Crisis and the Way Out: Part I," *PA* 36 (December, 1957): 55–58. Yet the Party always called for the measures that bred those illusions (because it professed to be concerned above all with the welfare of the workers and also because the workers would learn only in the course of struggle for their immediate demands). The Party's "immediate demands" added up to extreme welfare-statism: taxing away most profits, government spending for job creation (never adding where the investment capital would come from), socialized medicine, public housing, and so on. A particularly interesting document in this connection is "Why the Boom Will Bust" by the English Marxist Emile Burns, in *NM*, October 22, 1946. To avert economic catastrophe, which he said impended, he prescribed the measures that the British government later enacted (including nationalization, government planning of production and capital allocation, public housing, and heavy taxation of profits) that eventually brought the country to near-stagnation and bankruptcy, and that in other countries caused runaway inflation and huge deficits.

6. "Science, Ltd.," *CH* 1 (August, 1936): 4.

7. Hyman Lumer, "The Achievements of Marxist-Leninism in the Field of Genetics," *PA* 29 (July, 1950): 33; editors' introduction to Harold M. Ware, "A Revolution in Cotton: The Mechanical Picker Opens Up an Era of Greater Struggle," *NM*, October 5, 1935, p. 11; Stefan Rader, "Nylon: Mr. du Pont Turns Silkworm," *NM*, April 30, 1940, p. 13; Frank Brewster and Mark Logan, "Automation: Abundance for Whom?" *PA* 34 (November, 1955): 32, 34; David Ramsey, "Press-a-Button Counter-Revolution," *NM*, September 11, 1934, pp. 11; David Ramsey, "The Slithy Electron," *NM*, September 18, 1934, p. 20; Foster, *Twilight*, pp. 44–45.

8. E.g., Bill Gebert, "Organize Rallies for an Anti-Capitalist Labor Party!" *PO* 8 (June, 1935): [1]; Earl Browder, *The Democratic Front* (New York: Workers Library, 1938), p. 15; Minton and Stuart, *The Fat Years and the Lean*, pp. 376–77.

9. William Z. Foster, "Organized Labor and the Marshall Plan," *PA* 27 (February, 1948): 109; Herbert Aptheker, "The Face of the Lesser Evil," *MM* 1 (March, 1948): 35–36; Theodore Bassett, "The New People's Party and the Negro People," *PA* 27 (July, 1948): 605; Foster, *History of the CP*, pp. 472, 549. See also William Z. Foster, *American Trade Unionism* (New York: IP, 1947), p. 358 (this essay was dated 1946); Foster, *Twilight*, p. 165. According to Al Richmond, *A Long View from the Left* (New York: Delta, 1972), p. 293, even after the election, Eugene Dennis compared Wallace's vote "with the showing of the new-born Republican party in 1856," implying "that in 1956 the Progressive party would be contesting for power."

10. Harry K. Wells, letter to editor, *PA* 37 (February, 1958): 59.

11. William Z. Foster, *Toward Soviet America* (New York: Coward-McCann, 1932), pp. 57–58 (after Hitler came to power, the Party blamed the social-fascists—that is, the socialists—even though its own predictions had taken full account of their "reactionary" role); "Speech of Earl Browder," in *The Path of Browder and Foster* (New

York: Workers Library, 1941), pp. 17–18; Foster, "Organized Labor and the Marshall Plan," pp. 100–1. See also Foster, *Twilight*, p. 12.

12. Jim Jackson, "The Effect of the War Economy on the South," *PA* 30 (February, 1951): 106–7, 114.

13. Herbert Aptheker, *History and Reality* (New York: Cameron Associates, 1955), p. 245; Earl Browder, *Communism and Culture* (New York: Workers Library, 1941), p. 24; Michael Gold, *Change the World!* (New York: IP, 1936), pp. 92–93, 144–45.

14. Marx, *Capital* 1: 776. One quotation of this passage appears as late as 1956: Harry Martel, "On Marx and 'Force,' " *PA* 35 (July, 1956): 61. Martel, gently criticizing the misleading context in which Foster had recently used the quotation, feared that readers might infer that violence as well as force would be necessary. In fact, according to Martel, violence might not be necessary, and Marx had left open the possibility of nonviolent—though forceful—revolution.

15. E.g., Ben Davis, "Foster: Fighter for Correct Theory," *PA* 35 (April, 1956): 42–43.

16. It was, however, of extreme importance to some far-left comrades. In his autobiography, one of them, Harry Haywood, repeatedly cites the "peaceful transition" line as proof of the Party's abandonment of Marxism-Leninism, a crime of which he accuses the Soviet Union, too. Needless to say, Haywood was expelled, although he had been a leading theoretician on the Negro question. See his *Black Bolshevik* (Chicago: Liberator Press, 1978), pp. 569, 599, 608, 612, 676 n.2. Haywood's position is pertinent here because it shows that in the community of the far Left the CP occupied a "moderate" position, having to keep an eye on both flanks. It had to work out lines that were "correct" and yet would not cause the Party to become another of the tiny sects on the radical fringe.

17. Foster, *Toward Soviet America*, p. 269. See also Earl Browder, "A Glimpse at Soviet America," *NM*, July 9, 1935, p. 9, one of many proofs that the Soviet America daydream should not be considered peculiar to Foster.

18. Foster, *Toward Soviet America*, pp. 271–76. Mike Gold also put the capital in Chicago: see his *Change the World!*, p. 227. The Progressive party to which Foster refers was Robert LaFollette's, which had rejected alliance with the CP. Though LaFollette had died in 1925, Foster expected that it or similar parties would remain in the political arena before the revolution.

19. Foster, *Toward Soviet America*, pp. 279–81; "What Will Soviet U.S. Do for the Toiling Masses?: From the Manifesto of 8th Convention of C.P.," *YW*, April 24, 1934, p. 7.

20. Ibid.; Foster, *Toward Soviet America*, pp. 284–93.

21. Ibid., pp. 276, 296–97.

22. Frederick Engels, *Anti-Dühring* (New York: IP, 1939), p. 310.

23. Foster, *Toward Soviet America*, pp. 338–39; Foster, *History of the CP*, p. 567.

24. Marcel Cachin, *Science and Religion* (New York: IP, 1946), p. 31; Foster, *Toward Soviet America*, p. 326; J. B. S. Haldane, "The Party for Professionals," *NM*, March 12, 1946, p. 12; CP program quoted in Brewster and Logan, "Automation," p. 35; Dirk J. Struik, "Public and Private Morals," *MM* 1 (December, 1948): 59.

25. "J. F.," item in "Just a Minute" column, *NM*, December 10, 1946, p. 2; Foster, *Twilight*, p. 149. See chapter thirteen for references to Soviet projects. The capitalist System's perversion of science to war and profits, and its turning away from materialism, were responsible also for the failure to conduct research into "problems of

health, agronomy, cosmology and oceanography," and to find cures for polio and cancer—according to "The N. F. Science Staff," in "Science and the Student," *NF* 3 (Fall, 1949): 27. All these deplorable conditions would be reversed after the revolution, and only then.

26. On Soviet eugenicism, see Igor Shafarevich, *The Socialist Phenomenon* (New York: Harper & Row, 1980), pp. 246–47; the context is the 1920s, when eugenicism was popular in the United States, too (see next note). It is interesting to note that in his article "Sterilization, Experimentation and Imperialism," *PA* 53 (January, 1974): 37–48, Herbert Aptheker contends that the first two items in the title are integrally linked with the third. He traces the history of the link to the mid-nineteenth century and notes the reactionary views of various people who believed in hereditarianism. See also Aptheker, "Racism and Human Experimentation," *PA* 53 (February, 1974): 46–59. Even more significant, because written during the same period as that in which Foster was expressing his theory, is Morris U. Schappes, "Myths about Anti-Semitism," *MM* 1 (October, 1948): 55, where Schappes expresses surprise at discovering that Henry Pratt Fairchild, long active in progressive causes and a perennial signer of Party front petitions, was an Anglo-Saxon supremacist. Fairchild had been an immigration-restrictionist and eugenicist when these positions were considered compatible with progressivism. The noteworthy point here was the compulsion of Aptheker and Schappes to link all evil (as it was defined at the moment) with the enemy's System. For opinions more common than Foster's in the Party, see e.g., William Vila, "Malthusianism: The Threat against Our Right to Be Born" (against sterilization of the unfit; the article does not mention abortion or birth control), *NF* 6 (June, 1953): 8–10, 27; and especially Lumer, "Achievements of Marxism-Leninism in the Field of Genetics," p. 42 (a screed against reactionary perverters of Darwinism who think they can solve social problems by eugenically breeding fitter people).

27. Rudolph J. Vecoli, "Sterilization: A Progressive Measure?" *Wisconsin Magazine of History* 43 (Spring, 1960): 191, 200–202. See also Michael R. Marrus, "The Theory and Practice of Anti-Semitism," *Commentary* 74 (August, 1982): 39: "eugenics was so common a notion in social-scientific circles before the advent of Hitler that it is difficult to find people *not* attracted to it."

28. Foster, *Twilight*, pp. 150–51; Foster, *Toward Soviet America*, p. 341. See also Foster, *Outline Political History of the Americas* (New York: IP, 1951), p. 605.

29. Earl Browder, third and tenth articles in series "What is Communism?" *NM*, May 21, 1935, p. 20, and July 9, 1935, p. 9.

30. Howard Selsam, *Socialism and Ethics* (New York: IP, 1943), pp. 207–8.

31. Arnold Berman, "On Method in Political Economy," *PA* 35 (June, 1956): 46.

32. Herbert Aptheker, "Marx and Engels on the Civil War," *NM*, July 30, 1946, reprinted in Aptheker's *Toward Negro Freedom* (New York: New Century, 1956), p. 85; N. Sparks, "Marxism and Science," *PA* 26 (December, 1948): 1127. See also John Williamson, "A Program for Developing Communist Cadres," *PA* 24 (April, 1945): 359.

33. N. Mitin, "The Power of Stalinist Prediction," *COM* 19 (February, 1940): 141–42. On p. 146 Mitin proves his point by citing Stalin's 1929 prediction that Soviet agriculture would surpass American and Canadian agriculture in three years. Sure enough, he says, it has come true; now the Soviet Union is first in the absolute size of grain crops and in per capita production of those crops. See also Moissaye J.

Olgin, "Revolution in the Making," *NM*, February 8, 1938, pp. 20, 22, for a statement that "many of the writings and speeches of Lenin and Stalin are prophetic," etc.

34. Cachin, *Science and Religion*, p. 26. For cogent comments on this shrinking of reality to the capacities of the Marxist's mind, see Frank S. Meyer, *The Moulding of Communists* (New York: Harcourt, Brace, 1961), pp. 53, 71; and Jules Monnerot, *Sociology and Psychology of Communism* (Boston: Beacon Press, 1953), p. 185.

35. V. J. Jerome, reply to letter to editor, *COM* 17 (April, 1938): 382; Robert Minor, "Somebody is 'Distressed'—But Not Karl Marx (A Review of Earl Browder's 'Communism in the United States')," *COM* 14 (September, 1935): 846.

36. Monnerot, *Sociology and Psychology of Communism*, p. 134. See also Robert Nisbet, "The Function of the Vision of the Future in Radical Movements," in *Radical Visions of the Future*, Vol. 2 of *Radicalism in the Contemporary Age*, ed. Seweryn Bialer and Sophia Sluzar (Boulder, Colo.: Westview Press, 1977), p. 20.

37. "Dialectical and Historical Materialism," *CL* 1 (April-May, 1940): 96; Georgi Dimitrov, "The Communists and the Fatherland Front," *PA* 25 (August, 1946): 701, 702; M. Kammari and F. Konstantinoff, "Science and Superstructure," *PA* 32 (February, 1953): 60 (see also rest of article); Betty Gannett, book review, *PA* 26 (May, 1947): 453. Cf. the documents cited in chapter seven, n. 2, which said that the working class would not inevitably follow the Party. The discrepancy is, I think, due to the different purposes of the two kinds of statements—to put the blame for failures on Jimmy Higgins, in the one case, and to assert the infallibility of the vision, in the other. The latter was certainly more authentic.

38. Engels, *Anti-Dühring*, p. 307.

39. Browder, "Glimpse at Soviet America," p. 9; "Civil Liberties under Socialism," *PA* 35 (April, 1956): 37–39 (the article was signed *"Political Affairs"*); Charles Humboldt, "What Is Freedom?" *MM* 3 (May, 1950): 85.

40. Browder, *Democratic Front*, pp. 90, 93.

41. Eli Jaffe, "Mobilize Youth for Victory Crop," *CL* 3 (Summer, 1942): 7; and three articles in *CL* 3 (Winter, 1942–43): Frank Cestare, "Charting the Next Steps in Building the Young Communist League," pp. 18, 21, 22; Mary Southard, "The Nation Needs Southern Youth in the War Efforts," p. 79; Harold Schachter, "Farm Youth Fights for Victory," p. 83. James West, "Keep 'Em Floating," in the same issue, pp. 59–61, also advocates speed-up. See also Foster, *American Trade Unionism*, pp. 289–316.

42. Browder, *Communism and Culture*, p. 45. See also text accompanying photographs in *YW*, November 5, 1935, p. 7.

43. Browder, *Communism and Culture*, p. 14; "Just to Learn Is Not Enough," *NF* 1 (Fall, 1948): 5; Foster, *Toward Soviet America*, pp. 129–30, 326; Foster, *American Trade Unionism*, pp. 305–7, 319, 329. The Communist world will be "unified" in culture and language too, according to Stalin; see Nathan Leites, *A Study of Bolshevism* (New York: Free Press, 1953), p. 438.

44. This stopped short of the New Left's complete rejection, however; Party members tended to be conventional in attire, family life, and personal habits. Partly this was due to ingrained habit, but it was also deliberate: I recall that comrades about to go picketing were advised to dress respectably so as not to antagonize potentially sympathetic passers-by or divert attention from the object of the picket line.

45. I think the Cambodian holocaust should be interpreted partly in these terms.

Cambodia had fed itself, exported surplus food, and lived peacefully, enjoying an ancient culture, before the Khmer Rouge took power. The latter killed almost all literate people and millions of others, caused mass starvation, broke up families and made people live in barracks, and deliberately set about to destroy all tradition and history. Communists say they wish to destroy injustice and therefore must create a new society. This is true of Type II Communists, but Type I, who wield the power after the revolution, want to create a new society and therefore must find the present one unjust. Any society differing from the blueprint is unacceptable by definition. And if the world-changers are to be justified in changing everything, they must assert that the old forms had been imposed on the people. No matter that most of the people must be terrorized or otherwise coerced in order for "the people" to get their new, democratic society. The Khmer Rouge do not, of course, typify Communists. But they do reveal the possibilities of the world-changing mind once freed from the political and traditional-cultural-ethical constraints to work its will. Type II radicals, described in chapter three, welcome the freedom from the political constraints, but not from all the traditional-cultural-ethical ones. In Cambodia they were among the victims.

46. For a brilliant commentary on this mentality, see David Levy, "Reality, Utopia, and Tradition," *Modern Age* 20 (Spring, 1976): 153–63.

PART 3
Conclusion

14

Genus and Differentia

THE FINAL PAGES of this book glance at a phenomenon much larger than the Party, but including it. I shall repeatedly recall passages in the earlier chapters, so as to point out the similarities and differences between the Party and other groups on the Left.

IN THE PRECEDING CHAPTERS, I have used three different metaphors to generalize about the Party true believers: they lived in a "special universe"; they comprised one of several "species" within an ideological "genus"; and they occupied a "stopping place" on the "road" away from the real world. The astronomical metaphor suggests how hard it is for people who experience reality so differently to communicate—a difficulty that, incidentally, is bound to be encountered by a book about the subject. The biological metaphor argues that, since the Party was not *sui generis*, its attitudes were and are shared, to one degree or another, by groups both before the Party was born and since its demise. The linear metaphor allows for greater and lesser distances from the real world. It would take another book to do justice to the thesis expressed in these three ways, so I shall quote from other authors and urge the reader to explore the arguments and supporting data in the works excerpted and the others cited.

In Reinhold Niebuhr's opinion, "the Russian-Communist pretensions of innocency and the monstrous evils which are generated from them, are the fruit of a variant of the liberal dogma." He contends that "all typical moderns, Marxist or non-Marxist," share the

hope . . . that man may be delivered from his ambiguous position of being both creature and creator of the historical process and become unequivocally the master of his own destiny. The Marxist dream is distinguished from the liberal dream by a sharper and more precise definition of the elite which is to act as surrogate for mankind, by more specific schemes for endowing this elite with actual political power; by its fanatic certainty that it knows the end toward which history must move; and by its consequent readiness to sacrifice every value of life for the achievement of this end. The liberal culture has been informed by similar hopes since the eighteenth century. It has been as impatient as Marxism with the seeming limitations of human wisdom in discerning the total pattern of destiny in which human actions take place, and the failure of human power to bring the total pattern under the dominion of the human will.

According to John T. Marcus, totalitarianism is

the belated price of the burdening of historicity with the weight of salvation. The totalitarian pathology of modern civilization is a result of the historicizing of our values, and the development of a redemptive secular historicity, that had grown during the last centuries. Demonic historicism took root because there existed a contradiction inherent within our historical ideals, which had sought to achieve secular transcendence and immortality within historical time. When this historical faith came to face the contradiction between its secular utopian goal and the redemptory task of literally immortalizing the alter ego, it underwent a tragic collapse. The consequence of this failure was the demonic intensity of modern totalitarian movements.

Gerhart Niemeyer sees "a certain generic kinship" among Communism, Nazism, and "ideas prevalent in leading intellectual circles" in the West:

They all partake in a basic mood of discontent with life and the world which expresses itself in a total critique of all of present-day society, i.e., of every vestige of order and authority known to the present generation. There is the vision of a totally different life, a life free from shortcomings, from evil, from restrictions of all kinds, and all of it realized through some kind of social engineering. There is finally an ethic that is cast in terms of a social cause, in the sense that being or doing good means being against someone or something, and fighting for a certain institutional rearrangement which in turn is considered the culmination of history, the epitome of progress.

The elite and the ethic that Niebuhr and Niemeyer refer to, Ward E. Y. Elliott calls "the Guardian Elite" and "the Guardian Ethic." Whether Elliott would agree with the two-realities thesis, I do not know, but in the following passage he describes an attitude toward society that comes out of the general philosophic outlook summarized by Niebuhr, Marcus, and Niemeyer (Elliott's past tense is required by his context and does not mean the phenomenon he describes no longer exists): the Guardian Ethic was

the bureaucratic, elitist ideology of action-minded intellectuals in the modern age, most of whom thought they were beyond ideology.... The Guardians shared a mixture of idealism and absolutism such as we normally associate with adolescents: they were impatient of the past, sick of ambiguity and diversity, steeped in the ancient and honorable philosophic longing for unity and rationality, and chafing to pound the real world into a rationality consonant with that of the symbolic world.... The distinctive and disturbing characteristic of the 1960's was the degree to which the Guardians were not only left to themselves but encouraged to impose their theories on society. . . . The curious ideal of democracy without consent, so popular among intellectuals of the 1960's, and among politicians and judges sensitive to intellectual vogues, had overtones of colonial administration. The Guardians, like their namesakes in the Indian Civil Service during the heyday of the British Raj, meant business about bettering the lot of the public, and they could not afford to tolerate the natives' attachment to their outmoded ideas and institutions.[1]

These four quotations cannot be reconciled with Ignazio Silone's prediction that "the final struggle will be between the Communists and the ex-Communists." True, ex-Communists often understand better than others what the struggle is "all about."[2] But after leaving the Party, Silone remained prosocialist, that is, on the "left"[3] side of what I believe will be the "final" battle line. We should not be misled by the mutual hostility of various groups on the Left; after all, no two groups hate each other as lethally as do Communists and Trotskyists, yet everyone (except them) recognizes their ideological kinship. Many "democratic socialists" who have tirelessly publicized the facts about the Gulag nevertheless fit the descriptions written by the four authors quoted above. To illustrate this fact, I offer a statement in the same collection of essays, *The God That Failed*, that contains Silone's remark: Stephen Spender says (p. 245): "perhaps violence, concentration camps, the perversion of the sciences and the arts are justified if these methods result eventually in making the classless society. This is . . . an argument of such weight that if it were true it would make objections to a Communism which could really create a just international society, trivial." Spender, who had no illusions about Soviet reality, complained only that the means to achieving its goal had not yet been discovered; if it had, then all those atrocities might have been worthwhile. (It was perhaps such exhibitions of pride cloaked by logic that inspired the ancient, flat prohibitions expressed in the Thou Shalt Nots.) Another ex-Communist, Howard Fast, continued to define socialism as "brotherhood, love, reason, work with dignity," which could make our country become "like a garden," and so on, and continued to hate what he saw as the American System. But as Eugene Lyons pointed out in his reply, everyone is for those Good Things, and he exclaimed: "What a nightmare world he [Fast] must be living in!"[4] For the connection between the traditional ideals and a perception of the hateful American System was not "out there" but in Fast's mind.

Eleanor Roosevelt, who lived in the real world, inadvertently illustrated the difficulty of communicating across the boundary between the two worlds, when she described her encounter with a delegation from the American Youth Congress: "I told [them] . . . that if any of them were communists I would quite understand, for I felt they had grown up at a time of such difficulty as to explain their being attracted to almost any ideas that promised them better conditions." When her husband spoke with some of them and "told them some truths which, though they might be unpalatable, he thought it wise for them to hear," they did not respond as hoped. "The young people were in no mood for warnings, however kindly meant, and they booed the president. Although I could see how the young people felt on this occasion, I was indignant at their bad manners and lack of respect for the office of President of the United States."[5] No, she did *not* see how they felt. She lived in a world in which good will could yield compromises and in which closer acquaintance could lessen disagreements, and she thought they did too. In short, although she lived in the real world, she did not understand that it included people who did not. They saw themselves as the destined destroyers of a doomed System, booing its leader, and they would have laughed at the notion that, once in power, they might share it with the enemy. How could oppressors and their victims share power?

In the present generation the symptoms of this "disorder of the soul" (as Eric Voegelin calls it) include the attitude toward world affairs that puts quotation marks around "free world" or prefaces the phrase with "so-called." It says, "if someone is anti-American he can't be all bad" and "if a regime or ruling party has 'People's' or 'Socialist' or 'Democratic' in its name, it is on the side of history and its 'abuses' are excusable." In domestic affairs, one symptom is the equation of whole categories of the population—women, blacks, Hispanic-Americans, workers—with small elites, and the belief that people who disagree with those "spokespersons' " means oppose their professed ends (which is only sometimes true). For example, those who oppose the nuclear freeze want war; those who oppose forced busing and quotas must be racists—for the ideological mind equates error with evil motives. Another tenet is that the free-market economic system and the profit motive are immoral. Still another sign is the rejection of transgenerational experience, called "tradition," in favor of theories deduced from some grand paradigm of human nature and society—theories about pedagogy, child rearing, penology, gender roles, economic relationships, political-party structure, city planning, and everything else.

All those symptoms and tenets, and others, had their counterparts in the Party's ideology. The details have changed over time (for example, the Party favored nuclear energy and the current second-reality inhabitants oppose it; the Party favored economic growth, which is now in disfavor among many of the Guardians). Transient issues in the public eye suggest how the basic animus against reality will express itself. The Party, and the other far-left sects that disagreed with it on secondary doctrines, differed significantly from the larger genus mainly in their organizational discipline, checkup on performance of tasks, and criticism and self-criticism. If we set aside these species traits, which concerned organization, not ideology, and if we observe the attitudes that remained constant while particular issues came and went, the generic kinship becomes clearer.

Not all supporters of present-day movements of the Left believe in the entire array of tenets or share the attitudes that signal rejection of reality, any more than all Party members believed in the entire Party ideology or shared those attitudes. For the inhabitant of the spurious universe, however, all the tenets and attitudes fit together to form an integrated worldview, and he deduces "empirical" facts from his perception of "reality." Since the elements all fit together, they are less vulnerable to the lessons of experience than are the beliefs of people who judge issues one by one. When a program produces unintended consequences, ideologues rarely reconsider their theory but rather blame insufficient funding, or opponents' resistance, or something else that allows them to keep their faith in their ideology and its future validation.

That faith had had nothing to do with facts to begin with. To the person I described in chapter two who looked forward to socialism because a trades-man cheated him or a teenager mugged him or a neighbor was a religious hypocrite (the list of possible grievances is endless), one might respond: "Why do you assume that a change in the political and economic systems would have any effect on these things?" To the pamphleteer quoted in chapter thirteen, who said that after centuries of religious preaching, "man is still a wolf to his fellow man," one might respond: "Why do you blame Judaism and Christianity for not keeping promises they never made?" And so on, down the entire list of tenets (and the perception of System that included them all)—all of which prejudged the pertinent facts so as to yield the "con-clusions." Why did Jones become a Communist and Smith become a religious believer, other things being equal? Obviously, when Jones looked to a secular and radical philosophy for the answer to his questions, he was already half converted, since he already assumed the first thing that that philosophy told him: its view of the world contained the answers. If you are ill and you go to a witch doctor, you already half believe in witch doctors, even though you will learn the particulars of his intellectual system only after you have gone to him.

If the very perception of reality is involved, we must concede that most true believers really think they mean what they say. I say "think they mean" be-cause, like Jimmy Higgins before them, they delude themselves. Consider, for example, the motive all such ideologues emphasize: compassion. One day in about 1948, my comrades and I were assigned the task of helping a certain tenement family that had been evicted for nonpayment of rent. The furniture was piled on the sidewalk, and we carried it back inside. Then we went home and never gave another thought to that family, to ask if they needed help or money. We thought our motive was compassion, but it actually was the pas-sion for "justice" that, as I have argued, masked a colossal grievance against the world. If the claim of compassion had been genuine, then comrades would have donated money to help victims of earthquakes, hurricanes, and other dis-asters that even they could not blame on the System. But Party members did not respond to such appeals; the backward masses do. Yet neither did the comrades doubt the genuineness of their motives. That means that the logic of the special universe does not necessarily parallel the psycho-logic of its inhabitants.[6] Or, to use a different metaphor, the person who sets out on the road that ends in nihilism and totalitarianism is rarely a nihilist or totalitarian. The passages from Niebuhr, Marcus, Niemeyer, and Elliott quoted above describe the road, but not the milestone that any individual traveler has reached. Yet each traveler makes it easier for others to reach that point—and proceed farther.

Even the Party helped the other travelers, although it seemed to hinder them for a time. The whole Left received a setback at the end of World War II when millions of Americans learned the truth about the Soviet Union, which had represented the ideal of the entire Left (except Trotskyists). But in the long run the Party's demise removed a heavy load that the travelers along the road had had to carry. By the mid–1960s other radicals were free to mourn the victims of the Gulag, because China had supposedly killed no one during its Cultural Revolution. The Soviet Union's oppression of national minorities had become a propaganda asset to people who admired the "Third World" for expelling the white imperialists. Later, the "right" of air controllers to strike received legitimation from a comparison with the struggle of Poland's Solidarity against wholly different conditions. Enemies of family and sexual morality have proudly declared their abhorrence of the Soviet Union's and Cuba's "puritanism."

Most helpful of all was the discrediting of the Party's myth of the proletariat. This myth and the Party had benefited from the Great Depression and the wartime alliance with the socialist state where the workers supposedly ruled. Rather than recruiting many intellectuals to the Left, however, the depression and the war had merely legitimated their beliefs. The discrediting of the Soviet Union after the war, and especially after the uprisings of East European workers against regimes that they obviously did not rule, prepared the way for a much wider spread of radical ideologies among middle-class intellectuals, for those events removed the main obstacle: the delusory equation of radicalism with the proletariat. This is why the term "fellow traveler" is somewhat misleading. It suggests that the Party was the dominant partner in a symbiotic relationship. But as even John Gates admitted, the Party "never mastered the art of persuading very large numbers of Americans, deceptively or otherwise."[7] The Party needed the progressives more than they needed it, and *its* members were the fellow travelers of the larger collection of left movements, an extreme sect that made the others look moderate.

The picture of reality purveyed by ideologues of the spurious universe would not be plausible to so many people if it did not incorporate a moral message rarely found elsewhere in our time. That message can be summarized thus: "Here is a picture of reality that will permit you to satisfy your desire to transcend your immediate circumstances and selfish interests, your yearning to be of service. It is the philosophy of a movement that, by placing hard demands on you, will give your life meaning; a philosophy that rejects moral relativism and insists that *good* and *bad* are not empty words; a philosophy that gives your every act, feeling, and thought a cosmic significance." What mere facts can stand against such a message? What traditional institutions say these things with conviction?

The Party's proletarian myth, and its strict discipline and doctrinal rigidity, were dispensable baggage piled on top of the above essential messages. The Party's demise facilitated the spread of the New Left's and Gramscian Marxists' frank contempt for the Hard Hats and assigned a correspondingly larger role in the future to the Guardians.[8] In place of the myth of the proletariat as the carrier of all progressive values and as ruler after the revolution, we now have the myth of categories—women, blacks, Hispanics, homosexuals, consumers, inhabitants of the "environment"—all of whom will find their problems solved when the new system puts all those people-parts back together again. Yet, disparate as these Causes are, the zealots in each of them support the others. The transiently popular grievances are still all blamed on the System, the "rational" surrogate of reality itself. That is, the passage from the real world to the spurious one now is effected first by the shattering of the person into separate shards, each with its special grievance, and then by the recombining of the shards into a new whole on the other side of the boundary line separating the two universes—the line that the ideologues symbolize by the Revolution.[9]

Peter Berger tells of a student who was wearing four buttons when she came to see him. Having forgotten his glasses, Berger could read only the button that said ERA. But he "guessed the other three—one was U.S. out of El Salvador, one was pro-abortion, and the fourth was anti-nuclear." The student belligerently confirmed his hunch.[10] In the 1950s the array of buttons sent other messages, and in the 1990s they will send still others. But the basic animus will have remained the same. The Party died partly because its policy pendulum swung on a single plane and between too-limited policy poles. It legitimated just one way of expressing the animus against reality, the "disorder of the soul."

BECAUSE THE MENTALITY depicted by Niebuhr, Marcus, Niemeyer, and Elliott is grounded in an egocentric perception of reality, I wrote in chapter two that defection from the Party had consisted chiefly in the lessening of the need to wear distorting lenses. The road that a true believer took out of the Party, now that he could see more clearly, started deep within his mind. Some individuals had, unbeknownst to themselves, kept a corner of their minds independent of the Party's worldview, a private plot of soil in which a seed of reality could grow. The sign that this corner existed could have been something quite trivial: for example, a love for Wagner's music or nonobjective painting, or a fascination with the Middle Ages aside from any doctrinal relevance; or something important, such as a loyalty to a non-Party tradition, not wholly subordinate to the comrade's identity as a Communist (for example, some Jewish members' attitudes toward Israel). In either case, it was something that the Party condemned but that the person stubbornly (and privately) refused to give up.[11] Other comrades merely lost their need for externally imposed discipline but not their worldview or, in some cases, their zeal, and now found the Party atmosphere constricting.

The vast majority of Jimmy Higginses who left the Party found ready-made a line of stopping places along the road back to, and then within, reality; most of those few who traveled the entire route sojourned for years at each of them. Early on the road, Jim (ex-comrade) arrived at a place called "democratic socialism"; its message was: "The Soviet and Chinese system is contrary to the democratic essence of socialism. True socialism will keep public ownership of the means of production but guarantee political freedom for dissenters." If he traveled further along he came to a place called "liberalism"; its message was: "All the socialist regimes pervert the early Marx's vision of liberation and the end of alienation, a vision best embodied in a 'mixed economy' such as Sweden's, or Britain's under a Labour government, or the American welfare state if expanded beyond its present limits." If Jim proceeded even further, he reached a place call "conservatism"; its message was: "Socialism is the logical working-out of the welfare state; Soviet tyranny is the logical working-out of socialism; and all these phenomena are implicit in the secular view of man (even if sometimes preached by clergymen)."

If Jim reached this point and looked around, he saw he had few traveling companions. Most of his fellow defectors stayed at the two earlier stopping places. True, many (not all) of his fellow defectors whom he had passed along the way had stopped deducing their beliefs on all subjects from a grand paradigm. Like him, they had abandoned ideology and reentered the real world. But he had gone farther and begun to reflect upon the entire experience. It began to dawn on him that he had done more than reach a new milestone. He probably spent some time orienting himself in his new location and finding his way among all the new ideas that he kept stumbling on. This process took many years (even a sudden conversion, which is rare, is just the conscious mid-point of a protracted inner process). A time came when he wanted to tell his acquaintances who remained in the Party what he had learned. But they now avoided him, and a few of his new non-Communist friends thought as his ex-comrades did in certain basic ways. He tried and tried, but could not communicate with them about the really important questions. Then perhaps he remembered how he, when a true believer, would have "heard" the things he now wanted to say. He realized that he would not have heard at all, so that, even if he could get those friends and ex-comrades to read and listen, the words would not mean to them what they meant to him. Now he understood why: he had crossed a chasm into a different reality.

NOTES

1. Reinhold Niebuhr, *The Irony of American History* (New York: Charles Scribner's Sons, 1952), pp. 19, 66–67 (see also pp. 3–11, 13–15, 19–23); John T. Marcus, *Heaven, Hell, and History* (New York: Macmillan, 1967), p. 268; Gerhart Niemeyer, *Deceitful Peace: A New Look at the Soviet Threat* (New Rochelle, N.Y.: Arlington House, 1971), pp. 163–64 (see also pp. 164–69); Ward E. Y. Elliott, *The Rise of Guardian Democracy: The Supreme Court's Role in Voting Rights Disputes, 1845–1969* (Cambridge, Mass.: Harvard University Press, 1974), p. 2, 258, 311 n. 73. For a sample of the literature, approaching the thesis from different angles, see: Frank S. Meyer, "The New Conservatives," in David Brudnoy, ed., *The Conservative Alternative* (Minneapolis: Winston Press, 1973), p. 32; George F. Will, "Welfare State: An Incompetent Leviathan," ibid., pp. 123–26; William F. Buckley, Jr., *Up from Liberalism* (n.p.: Honor Book, 1965), p. 141 and passim; Jules Monnerot, *Sociology and Psychology of Communism* (Boston: Beacon Press, 1953), p. 272; Peter Viereck, *Shame and Glory of the Intellectuals: Babbit Jr. vs. the Rediscovery of Values* (1953; New York: Capricorn Books, 1965), pp. 195, 197, 272; Eliseo Vivas, *The Moral Life and the Ethical Life* (Chicago: University of Chicago Press, 1950), passim, esp. Chap. 8 (this chapter is omitted from the Regnery-Gateway paperback edition published in 1963); Gerhart Niemeyer, *Between Nothingness and Paradise* (Baton Rouge: Louisiana State University Press, 1971), passim; Eric Voegelin, *The New Science of Politics* (Chicago: University of Chicago Press, 1952), pp. 125, 131, 135–36, 175–78, and passim; Eric Voegelin, *Science, Politics and Gnosticism* (Chicago: Henry Regnery, 1968), pp. 86–88; C. S. Lewis, *The Abolition of Man* (1974; New York: Macmillan, 1965), Chap. 3; Aaron Wildavsky, *The Revolt against the Masses and Other Essays on Politics and Public Policy* (New York: Basic Books, 1971), Chap. 1.

The references to secularism in the text quotations should not—and I believe the authors did not mean them to—exclude "progressive" religious people, the sorts who were called Social Gospelers and Christian Socialists around the turn of the century and are now called liberation theologians, and include the Catholic priests in the Sandinista junta in Nicaragua and the Protestant ministers who lead the World Council of Churches. Their claims notwithstanding, they have recruited God to their Causes rather than recruited themselves to His.

2. Ignazio Silone, essay in Richard Crossman, ed., *The God That Failed* (1950; New York: Bantam Books, 1965), p. 101; Arthur Koestler's remark quoted by Crossman, ibid., pp. 1–2.

3. I put "left" in quotation marks because the left-right terminology is not quite satisfactory. In the course of this book I do occasionally use the term "leftist" because a better label has not yet won wide acceptance. For an argument against this terminology, see Tibor Szamuely, "The Meaning of 'Left' and 'Right,' " in Brudnoy, ed., *Conservative Alternative*, pp. 41–48.

4. Exchange between Howard Fast and Eugene Lyons in *New Leader*, July 30, 1956, pp. 16–17, 19.

5. Eleanor Roosevelt, *This I Remember* (New York: Harper & Brothers, 1949), pp. 200–201.

6. This is why I dissent from Robert Nisbet's contention, as quoted approvingly by Arnold Beichman, that to concede the sincerity and idealism of campus rioters is to set "this violence into a perspective which serves both logically and psychologically to justify and encourage it." (Arnold Beichman, *Nine Lies about America* [New York: Library Press, 1972], p. 193.) Logically, no. Psychologically, yes, only if one ignores millennia of religious teaching and experience. First, one would then imply that if the vandals' intentions had been good, their acts might have been justified. Second, many of the rioters knew their motives were (consciously) good; and ex–true believers who recall their former mindsets know that adversaries misinterpret the phenomenon. Third, the assumption that everyone sees reality the same way and judges issues in the same moral terms is vulnerable to the arguments I offered in chapter two. In other words, I think that when Nisbet infers the rioters' motives from their immoral acts, with the intention of defending the objectivity of values, he is actually relativizing values.

Another comment: the left ideologue differs from both the "good German" who "didn't know" what was going on next door, and the true-believing Nazi who knew and approved. The true believer of the Left, unlike the good German, is an active supporter of an ideology, and, unlike the Nazi zealot, thinks he is working for peace, justice, and brotherhood. Of course there are hypocrites in these movements. I recall a conversation with two students in the mid–1970s during which one of them argued eloquently in behalf of the New Left. He left to go to a class, whereupon his friend confided to me that that idealistic radical had told *him* that he had joined "to meet girls." That type of supporter would have run away if called upon to sacrifice for the Cause. But what about the millions who have tithed themselves for their Causes and made other sacrifices (which, as I argued earlier, they did not consider sacrifices) and the thousands of others who have accepted far worse? I said earlier that the better the people recruited to the Cause, the worse the horror; I therefore believe it is Nisbet's argument that lets the vandals off lightly.

7. John Gates, *The Story of an American Communist* (New York: Thomas Nelson & Sons, 1958), p. 5.

8. Gramsci's theory of ideological hegemony may be on its way to oblivion, too, however. Its basic contention, that the masses are dominated by the ideological spokesmen of the ruling class, requires a special effort of the imagination in the face of the fact that it is businessmen who want to trade with and lend money to Communist regimes, and longshoremen and other workers who have objected. As to the "spokesmen" of the capitalist class (which class, say the Gramscians, controls the intellectual life of the country)—the journalists, teachers, scholars, clergymen, artists, and entertainers—most of them are obviously far to the left of the masses who supposedly languish under the former's ideological hegemony. On clergymen, see The IEA/Roper Center, "Theology Faculty Survey," *This World*, No. 2 (Summer, 1982): 27–75, and comments thereon, pp. 78–108. On journalists, see the findings and generalizations in Edith Efron, *The News Twisters* (Los Angeles: Nash Publishing, 1971), which remain valid. On liberal-arts faculties, see Everett Carll Ladd and Seymour Martin Lipset, *The Divided Academy: Professors and Politics* (New York: Norton, 1975), and the recenter polls in various issues of *Public Opinion*.

9. Reasons for this fragmenting of the personality into pieces corresponding to

the various movements' Causes can be explored in studies of the weakening of community bonds. Good places to start are Robert A. Nisbet, *The Social Bond* (New York: Alfred A. Knopf, 1970); Nisbet, *Twilight of Authority* (New York: Oxford University Press, 1975); and William Kornhauser, *The Politics of Mass Society* (New York: Free Press, 1959), Chap. 10. The egoistic preoccupation of post-CP types of radicals is one of the main themes of Edward E. Ericson, Jr., *Radicals in the University* (Stanford, Calif.: Hoover Institution Press, 1975).

10. Peter L. Berger, in Steven D. Munson, ed., *Our Country and Our Culture* (New York: Orwell Press, 1983), p. 58.

11. The fascination with the Middle Ages is mentioned in Douglas Hyde, *I Believed* (New York: G. P. Putnam's Sons, 1950), repeatedly (see pp. 188, 197, 230, 232, 255), to the point where he does not have to tell the reader that it was a lifeline to the real world, which he had to disguise as past history. The love for officially disapproved-of composers and painters, and other secret heresies that varied from individual to individual, I recall from my own Party years. The latent clash between some Jewish comrades' Party and traditional loyalties became manifest after the close of the period covered by this book—to the point of an open break between the Party and its two Jewish-interest periodicals, *Freiheit* and *Jewish Life*. After the Six-Day War, Party writings about Israel became so virulent as virtually to present Jewish members with a choice between self-hate and a break with the Party, although that was not the way the leaders saw the issue. For an easily accessible overview of some of the facts and documents, see Arnold Forster and Benjamin R. Epstein, *The New Anti-Semitism* (New York: McGraw-Hill, 1974), Chap. 8 (which includes the New Left).

Recommended Reading

Aaron, Daniel. *Writers on the Left*. New York: Harcourt, Brace & World, 1961.

Besançon, Alain. *The Rise of the Gulag: Intellectual Origins of Leninism*. New York: Continuum, 1981.

Conquest, Robert. "The Role of the Intellectual in International Misunderstanding." *Encounter* 51 (August, 1978): 29–42.

Crossman, Richard, ed. *The God That Failed*. New York: Harper & Row, 1950.

Ernst, Morris L., and David Loth. *Report on the American Communist*. New York: Henry Holt & Company, 1952.

Feuer, Lewis S. *Marx and the Intellectuals*. Garden City, N.Y.: Doubleday Anchor, 1969.

―――. *Ideology and the Ideologists*. New York: Harper & Row, 1975.

Gitlow, Benjamin. *The Whole of Their Lives*. New York: Charles Scribner's Sons, 1948.

Gornick, Vivian. *The Romance of American Communism*. New York: Basic Books, 1978.

Hollander, Paul. *Political Pilgrims: Travels of Western Intellectuals to the Soviet Union, China, and Cuba*. New York: Oxford University Press, 1981.

Hook, Sidney. *Reason, Social Myths, and Democracy*. New York: John Day, 1940.

Howe, Irving, and Lewis Coser. *The American Communist Party: A Critical History*. Boston: Beacon Press, 1957.

Hunt, R. N. Carew. *A Guide to Communist Jargon*. New York: Macmillan Company, 1957.

Jaffe, Philip. *The Rise and Fall of American Communism*. New York: Horizon Press, 1975.

Johnson, Paul. *Enemies of Society*. New York: Atheneum, 1977.

Klehr, Harvey. *Communist Cadre: The Social Basis of the American Communist Party Elite*. Stanford, Calif.: Hoover Institution Press, 1978.

―――. *The Heyday of American Communism: The Depression Decade*. New York: Basic Books, 1984.

Leites, Nathan. *A Study of Bolshevism*. New York: Free Press, 1953.

Meyer, Frank S. *The Moulding of Communists: The Training of the Communist Cadre*. New York: Harcourt, Brace & Company, 1961.

Monnerot, Jules. *Sociology and Psychology of Communism*, trans. Jane Degras and Richard Rees. Boston: Beacon Press, 1953.

Nisbet, Robert. "The Function of the Vision of the Future in Radical Movements,"
     in *Radical Visions of the Future*, Vol. 2 of *Radicalism in the Contemporary Age*, ed.
     Seweryn Bialer and Sophia Sluzar. Boulder, Colo.: Westview Press, 1977.
O'Neill, William L. *A Better World. The Great Schism: Stalinism and the American
     Intellectuals*. New York: Simon & Schuster, 1982.
Selznick, Philip. *The Organizational Weapon: A Study of Bolshevik Strategy and Tactics*.
     New York: McGraw-Hill, 1952.
Shafarevich, Igor. *The Socialist Phenomenon*, trans. William Tjalsma. New York: Har-
     per & Row, 1980.
Talmon, J. L. *Political Messianism: The Romantic Phase*. London: Secker & Warburg,
     1960.
Voegelin, Eric. *The New Science of Politics*. Chicago: University of Chicago Press, 1952.
     Especially Chapter 6.
———. "On Debate and Existence." *Intercollegiate Review* 3 (1967): 143–52.

Index

American Youth for Democracy
(AYD), 10, 20 n.15
Aptheker, Herbert, 106, 109; on controversy, 183; as historian, 113, 114, 120–21 n.18; on the Hungarian revolt, 52, 85, 176 n.5, 204; on liberals, 193; on Marxism as science, 251; on Michael Oakeshott, 115; on Sidney Hook, 62–63; on sources of workers' beliefs, 207; on Stalin, 87, 202; on the struggle for freedom throughout history, 172; on why reactionaries hate Communists, 95

Beal, Fred, 98 n.2
Bedacht, Max, 128
Bentley, Elizabeth, 43
Berger, Peter, 271
Bernal, J. D., 108
Bernstein, Eduard, 238
Bittelman, Alexander, 81, 127, 135, 223
Browder, Earl, 15, 16, 110, 129; on the capitalists, 187; on cooperation with Catholics, 148; on the CP as heir of American traditions, 95, 125; on the CP as Stalinist, 17; on the CP as vanguard of the masses, 92; denies directions from Moscow, 86; describes ideal Bolshevik, 127, 131–32, 133; on the historic responsibility of the CP, 130; on Marxism as guide out of chaos, 97, 157; on Marxism as

science, 153; as object of adulation, 83; as object of hatred, 66–67, 221; predicts Hitler will not attack the Soviet Union, 242; on religion in the Soviet Union, 149; on religious people in the CP, 146; as revisionist, 25, 53, 54, 88; on the socialist "new man," 224, 249–50; on united front with religious masses, 145–46
Budenz, Louis, 11, 148

Cambodia, genocide in, 38 n.6, 60, 260–61 n.45
Camus, Albert, 3, 6
Capitalism: "anarchy of," 184–86; CP predictions about, 108, 189, 239–40; "general crisis of," 111, 240, 242; as "system," 7, 26, 27, 31, 62, 108, chap. 10, 242
Chu Teh, 202
Clarity, 52–53, 146
Clausewitz, Carl von, 84
Communist International (Comintern), 85, 86
Communist parties of Western Europe, 40 n.14, 159 n.4, 160 n.8
Communist Party of the United States (CP, CPUS, CPUSA): abhorrence of "spontaneity," 115, 168; on American history, 108, 110–111, 216 n.5; on anti-Communist intellectuals and artists, 192–93; on anti-Communist liberals, 192; as "army," 84; on blacks, 17 n.1, 95, 127–28, 171–72, 242;

concept of democracy, 207, 208, 214, 246, 253–55; concept of ideal Bolshevik, 130–34; on controversy, 66–68, 183–84; criticism and self-criticism, 33, 134–38; depictions of the U.S., 61, 67, 74 n.3, 181–82, 204–5, 239–40; "either-or" style of thinking, 179, 181–84, 196 n.13, 197 n.16; environmental determinism, 166, 249; functions of theory in, 37, 39 n.11, 47, 68, 106, 108; history of, 7, 15–17, 25, 52, 270, 271; image of capitalists, 190–92, 239; image of the consumer, 186–87; image of the Soviet Union, 206, chap. 12; on Indian history, 112, 212–13, 218 n.22; jargon, 12, 20 n.19, 71, 91, 123; Jewish members of, 100 n.20, 272, 275 n.11; "linking-up" principle, 33, 108, 110, 113; literature about, 8, 9; on "the masses," 35, 84, 126–27, 170–72, 177 n.7, chap. 11, 224, 243; on non-Party scholars, 105, 106, 107–8, 112, 119 n.10; organizational structure, 35, 89, 124, 128–29; predictions by, 125, 171, 222–23, chap. 13; on professionals and intellectuals in the Party, 105–6, 111–12; on psychology, 166, 169; relation of ends and means in, 34–36; relationship with the Soviet CP, 84, 86–88, 132; on religion, 11, 66, 145–51, 159–60 n.5, 247; on scholarship, 107, 108, 109, 113–14, 116–17, 120 n.15; self-image, 92–97, 105, 133, 205–6, 217 n.10; on Stalin (see Stalin, Joseph); as surrogate community and family, 74, 89–91; "tasks" concept, 123–30; theory of the unity of theory and practice, 20–21 n.22, 35, 121–22 n.26, 217 n.15; on Trotskyists, 46–47, 60, 63–66, 72, 74; types of members, 8, 16; use of "dialectics" as evasion, 160–61 n.11, 172; on World War II, 48. See also Jimmy Higgins

Communist Political Association, 15

Davis, Benjamin, Jr., 84
Dell, Floyd, 212

Dennis, Eugene, 85, 87, 99 n.17
Dewey, John, 50–51, 69, 111
Dimitroff, Georgi, 69, 125
Dodd, Bella V., 30, 43, 69, 73, 74, 184; her analysis of her disillusionment, 32, 59–60, 74 n.1, 79, 98 n.2
Dreiser, Theodore, 82
Du Bois, W. E. B., 109, 119 n.10
Duclos, Jacques, letter on Browderism, 15, 30, 53, 87
Dyson, Lowell, Red Harvest, 5

Elliott, Ward E. Y., 266–67
Engels, Frederick, 80, 81, 98 n.5, 105, 109; as authority on anthropology, 114; as authority on history, 167, 183; characterizations of communism, 246, 252; definition of freedom, 170. See also Marx, Karl, and Frederick Engels
Ernst, Morris L., and David Loth, Report on the American Communist, 41, 157
Eugenicism, 248–49, 259 n.26

Fascism, CP definition of, 69
"Fascist" as CP epithet, 68–69
Fast, Howard, 35–36, 43, 85, 267
Faulkner, William, 136, 137
Field, Frederick Vanderbilt, 124
Finkelstein, Sidney, 198 n.33
Flynn, Elizabeth Gurley, 82
Foner, Philip, 106, 107, 109, 113, 118 n.7
Foster, William Z., 13, 16, 54, 80, 106; on American history, 115; on bourgeois philosophy, 111; on capitalist anarchy, 185–86; on the CP as vanguard of the masses, 94, 96, 204; on cultural oppression of workers under capitalism, 192, 202–3; describes capitalists, 62; describes Soviet America, 185, 222–23, 224–25, 243–46; describes the Soviet Union, 223, 230–31; on eugenics, 248–49; forecasts of communism, 246–47, 255; on human nature, 171: image of the masses, 203–4, 210; on Indians as victims of

white settlers, 214, 218 n.22; on Marxism as science, 153; on the need to improve Party work, 129; on the "new man" under socialism, 170; as object of adulation, 208; as polymath, 82–83, 109, 110–112; predicts revolution in Germany, 242; predicts revolution in the U.S., 239; on religion, 147–48, 247; says capitalism corrupts science, 111; says Marxism-Leninism produces healthy personalities, 92; says socialism necessarily produces great leaders, 224; says worldwide capitalism is breaking down, 48; states the CP's basic principles, 25–26

Freeman, Joseph, 187

Gannett, Betty, 48–49, 228
Gates, John, 25–26, 50, 66–67, 91, 217 n.13, 270
Gilboa, Yehoshua A., *The Black Years of Soviet Jewry, 1939–1953*, 71
Gold, Michael, 73, 218 n.21; on capitalist "anarchy," 185; describes Soviet Union, 89–90, 230; images of the Indians, 212–13; images of the masses, 202, 207, 214; predicts Soviet America, 243
Gornick, Vivian, *The Romance of American Communism*, 28, 36, 56 n.11, 72
Gramsci, Antonio, and Gramscian theory, 188, 271, 274 n.8
Grenier, Richard, 168
Gulag Archipelago, The (Solzhenitsyn), 38 n.6, 55–56 n.5

Haldane, J. B. S., 108, 121 n.20, 247
Hall, Gus, 21 n.24
Hanford, Ben, 2
Hathaway, Clarence, 123
Haywood, Harry, 55 n.4, 109, 119 n.10, 258 n.16
Healey, Dorothy, 84
Hearst, William Randolph, 71, 233–34 n.15
Heidegger, Martin, 111
Herberg, Will, 29, 37

Higgins, Jimmy. *See* Jimmy Higgins
History of the Communist Party of the Soviet Union (Bolsheviks), 86–87, 100 n.21, 152, 167
Hollander, Paul, *Political Pilgrims*, 31
Hook, Sidney, 62–63, 66, 75 n.5, 115, 141 n.26, 251
Horner, Charles, 26
House Committee on Un-American Activities, 100 n.18
Howe, Irving, and Lewis Coser, *The American Communist Party: A Critical History*, 47, 68, 73
Humboldt, Charles, 87, 167, 171
Hungary, rebellion in, 49, 52, 85, 176 n.5
Hyde, Douglas, 30, 36, 53

"Immiseration" theory, 238–39
Isserman, Maurice, 54, 57 n.20, 57 n.21

Jackson, James E., 242–43
James, William, 111
Jerome, V. J., 11, 73, 112–13
Jewish Life, 113
Jimmy Higgins: attitudes toward outsiders, 34, 45, 53–54, 268; basic assumptions, 7, 25; defection from the CP, 29–30, 271–72; differences from other rank-and-file members, 8, 11, 39 n.10; idealism, 27–33, 270; image of the Soviet Union, 26, 27, 30–31, 36, 37, 46, 180; image of the United States, 26, 27, 31, 36, 46, 62, 189; as inhabitant of a "special universe" or "second reality," 1–2, 3–5, 6–7, 18 n.7, 26–27, 29–31, 36–37, 157, 268–70; relationship to Party authority, 8, 13, 34–35, 36, 79–80, 82, 86, 90–91, 108, 124, 128, 129, 130; self-image, 73, 125, 147, 268. *See also* Communist Party of the United States
Jonestown (Guyana), 44, 45

Kempton, Murray, 16
Keynes, John Maynard, 193
Khrushchev, Nikita, "secret speech" to

the Twentieth Party Congress (1956), 7, 16, 31, 49, 84, 87, 221, 232
Kierkegaard, Søren, 111
Klehr, Harvey, *Communist Cadre*, 5
Koestler, Arthur, 29, 32, 35, 37, 71–72, 115
Kroner, Jack, 136–38
Kunitz, Joshua, 88–89

Labor Youth League (LYL), 10, 20 n.16
Lawson, John Howard, 109, 114
Leff, Gordon, *The Tyranny of Concepts*, 18 n.1
Leites, Nathan, *A Study of Bolshevism*, 9, 40 n.12, 209
Lenin, V. I., 73, 80, 81, 105, 107, 109, 203
Lewis, C. S., 5, 6, 29
Lyons, Eugene, 267

Mainstream, 85
Malenkov, Georgi M., 98 n.10, 225
Mandel, William, 87
Mano, D. Keith, 38 n.6
Mao Tse-tung, 173–74, 208
Marcus, John T., 266
Marcuse, Herbert, 188, 239
Marx, Karl, 3, 80, 81, 98 n.5, 109, 124, 169–70, 243. *See also* Marx, Karl, and Frederick Engels
Marx, Karl, and Frederick Engels: *The Communist Manifesto*, 207, 250; *The German Ideology*, 179
Marxism-Leninism: as antidote to perplexity, 103 n.42, 189; environmental determinism, 169–72; epistemology, 154–56; as guide to action, 49, 57 n.14; as justification for power, 37, 51–52, 252–55; as omnicompetent, 73, 93, 108–9, 112, 155–56, 162 n.22; as sacred scripture, 87, 92, 100 n.21; as science, 32, 72, 86, 105, 108, 152–54, 193, 206, 214, 251; as source of confidence, 48–51, 92, 154, 250, 251–52; theory of the conflict of science with religion, 151; theory of dialectical materialism, 166; theory of his-

tory, 167–68; theory of the struggle between materialism and idealism, 150–51

Masses & Mainstream, 87–88
Meyer, Frank S., *The Moulding of Communists*, 9, 29, 37, 56 n.11, 59, 79, 89
Mills, C. Wright, *The Power Elite*, 187
Minor, Robert, 82, 84, 251
Minton, Bruce, and John Stuart, *The Fat Years and the Lean*, 187
Mitford, Jessica, 12, 53
Monnerot, Jules, *Sociology and Psychology of Communism*, 9, 36, 55 n.3, 132, 252
Morgan, Lewis Henry, 114
Morgan, Thomas J., 44–45

National Issues, 52
New Foundations, 87, 169, 207, 254–55
New Left, 10, 198 n.28, 239, 260 n.44, 271
New Masses, 53, 66, 247–48
Niebuhr, Reinhold, 265–66
Niemeyer, Gerhart: *Between Nothingness and Paradise*, 2, 3, 4, 5, 6, 7, 26, 37; *Deceitful Peace*, 2, 266
Nisbet, Robert, 102 n.42, 274 n.6
North, Joseph, 82, 94
Novak, Michael, 3–4, 18 n.6, 37

Oakeshott, Michael, 115
Olgin, M. J., 52, 69, 74, 80, 170, 224, 228, 231; *Trotskyism: Counter-Revolution in Disguise*, 46–47, 51, 64–66

Party Organizer, 107, 127
Patterson, William, 192, 205
Pavlov, Ivan, 155
Pepper, Claude, 208
Perlo, Victor, 113
Political Affairs, 11

Radicals, non-Communist, 45, chap. 14
Roche, John, 36
Rochester, Anna, 113
Roosevelt, Eleanor, 267–68
Roosevelt, Franklin D., 15, 52–53
Rubinstein, Annette T., 108
Rushmore, Howard, 232–33 n.1

Sartre, Jean-Paul, 111
Science & Society, 113
Selsam, Howard, 84, 98 n.5, 106, 153, 156–57, 188, 212, 250
Selznick, Philip, *The Organizational Weapon*, 2, 9, 46, 70
Seventh Congress of the Communist Party of the Soviet Union, 15
Sillen, Samuel, 106
Silone, Ignazio, 47, 267
Solzhenitsyn, Aleksandr, 38 n.6, 55–56 n.5
Sontag, Susan, 38 n.6
Soviet Union, in CPUS thinking: agricultural policy of, 227–28, 234 n.16; culture and science in, 230–31; "new man" in, 224; organization of industry in, 226; peacefulness of, 222; predictions about, 228–29, 259 n.33; role of CP in, 224–26; technological progress of, 223, 227; young people in, 229–30
Spender, Stephen, 267
Spotlight, 218 n.18
Stakhanovism, 227
Stalin, Joseph, 7, 11, 49, 132, 172–74, 202, 221–22, 225, 228; CP worship of, 80–83, 86–87, 89, 98 n.5, 98 n.7; as polymath, 105, 109, 111, 119–20 n.13, 167, 251
Stern, Bernhard J., 108

Thompson, Robert, 67, 91
Trade Union Unity League, 245
Trilling, Lionel, 192
Trotsky, Leon, 80
Tucker, Robert C., *Philosophy and Myth in Karl Marx*, 18 n.1
Twentieth Congress of the Communist Party of the Soviet Union, 7, 16, 25, 84, 221–22

Van Doren, Carl, 110
Vecoli, Rudolph J., 248–49
Voegelin, Eric, 4–5, 6, 7, 26, 37, 100 n.21, 158, 268

Wallace, Henry, 217 n.13
Webb, Sidney and Beatrice, 173
Wechsler, James, 50
Wells, Harry K., 50–51, 106, 202, 206
Williamson, John, 128–29, 203
Worker, Daily or *Sunday*, 11
Wright, Richard, 211

Young Communist International (YCI), 85
Young Communist League (YCL), 10, 211
Young Worker, The, 19–20 n.15, 50, 53, 66, 69, 145, 149, 218 n.18

ABOUT THE AUTHOR

AILEEN S. KRADITOR is Professor Emerita of History at Boston University. She is the author of *The Ideas of the Woman Suffrage Movement, 1890–1920*; *Means and Ends in American Abolitionism, 1834–1850*; and *The Radical Persuasion, 1890–1917*; as well as the editor of *Up from the Pedestal: Documents in the History of American Feminism*.